The European Challenge

The European Challenge

Geography and development in the European Community

edited by

Mark Blacksell and Allan M. Williams

OXFORD UNIVERSITY PRESS

1994

Oxford University Press, Walton Street, OX2 6DP
Oxford New York Toronto
Delhi Bombay Calcutta Madras Karachi
Kuala Lumpur Singapore Hong Kong Tokyo
Nairobi Dar es Salaam Cape Town
Melbourne Auckland Madrid
and associated companies in
Berlin Ibadan

Oxford is a trade mark of Oxford University Press

Published in the United States
by Oxford University Press Inc., New York

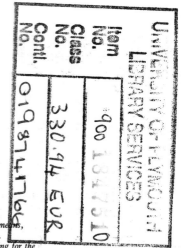

British Library Cataloguing in Publication Data
Data available

Library of Congress Cataloging in Publication Data
The European challenge: geography and development in the European
community / edited by Mark Blacksell and Allan M. Williams.
Includes bibliographical references and index.
1. European Economic Community countries—Economic conditions—
—Regional disparities. 2. European Economic Community countries—
—Economic policy. 3. Natural resources—European Economic Community
countries—Management. I. Blacksell, Mark, 1942–
II. Williams, Allan M.
HC241.2.E818 1994   330.94——dc20   93–37550
ISBN 0–19–874176–6 (cloth)
ISBN 0–19–874177–4 (paperback)

10 9 8 7 6 5 4 3 2 1

Typeset by J&L Composition Ltd, Filey, North Yorkshire
Printed in Great Britain
on acid-free paper by
Biddles Ltd, Guildford & Kings Lynn

Preface

In many ways, the publication of this book epitomizes the achievement of the ERASMUS Programme over the first five years of its existence, and it seems particularly fitting, that at such an important moment in the history of the European Community, the contribution being made by the Community's largest and most wide-ranging educational programme should be given tangible recognition of this kind. The fourteen co-authors came together in close collaboration through an ERASMUS Inter-University Co-operation Programme linking the eight academic departments to which they belong. The present textbook has grown out of the successful joint-teaching programme developed in this context.

This Inter-University Co-operation Programme in *Development, Political Integration and Environmental Management in the European Community*, was launched in 1989. It currently involves universities in seven Community countries and (since October 1992) one from the European Free Trade Association. Students attend courses relating to the programme theme at both their home and host institutions, and write a dissertation in the language of the host country. The complementary teaching-staff mobility project within the programme brings a direct European dimension to the studies of a wide range of students within the institutions concerned, including those not planning a period abroad. The project as a whole works towards the future development of the European Community, not only by the study of Community problems which demand supra-national solutions, but also—as is always true in successful ERASMUS programmes—by producing culturally and academically adaptable graduates prepared for a working life spanning national boundaries.

The importance of international educational programmes for the future of the Community was perhaps not sufficiently recognized in the pioneering years of the Common Market. However, a reference to co-operation in vocational training was made in the Treaty of Rome, and this has provided the legal basis for Community activity in the higher educational field. In the years following the Treaty of Rome, the full importance of education and training gradually came to be recognized, through the work being conducted in other areas of Community affairs, especially in the mutual recognition of certain professional qualifications and in scientific research, where the beginnings of a policy aimed at identifying education and training as the key link between scientific and technological progress and industrial innovation began to emerge. The first major articulation of this development was a Resolution in February 1978, containing the first Community-level Action Programme in the field of education, which included the inception of visit schemes designed to enhance awareness of various sectors of education systems in the member states, and a number of important pilot actions in the area of higher education—in particular the scheme of Joint Study Programmes. These Joint Study Programmes were the direct precursors of ERASMUS, which was launched in 1987, joining COMETT (operational from 1988 in promoting international links between university and industry). ERASMUS has been followed by other important educational programmes, including LINGUA (promoting the teaching of the languages of the Community) and TEMPUS (facilitating educational aid to Eastern Europe at university level).

The Treaty on European Union (Maastricht Treaty) reflects such developments in making more extensive reference to educational concerns than did the Treaty of Rome. Alongside vocational education, it provides specifically for Community action to support co-operative activities of various kinds between educational establishments in different member states, and for the development of the European dimension in education. This indicates a growing awareness of the value of broadly-based Community educational activities, which go beyond the narrowly vocational and prepare young people for life as citizens of the Community.

GÉRARD DRUESNE

The ERASMUS Bureau, Brussels
November 1992

Contents

List of Contributors

Dr Mark Blacksell

Department of Geographical Sciences, University of Plymouth, Drake Circus, Plymouth, PL4 8AA, UK (formerly, University of Exeter).

Professor J.-Paul Charrié

Institut de Géographie et Études Régionales, Université Michel Montaigne, Bordeaux III, Domaine Universitaire, 33405 Talence Cédex, France.

Dr Manuel Corbera

Departamento de Geografia, Urbanismo y Ordenación del Territorio, Universidad de Cantabria, Avienda de los Castros S/N, 39005 Santander, Spain.

Dr Dietrich Denecke

Geographisches Institut der Universität Göttingen, Goldschmidtstraße 5, 37077 Göttingen, Germany.

Dr James Killen

Department of Geography, Trinity College, Dublin 2, Ireland.

Professor Russell King

Department of Geography, University of Sussex, Falmer, Brighton, BNI 9QN (formerly at Trinity College, Dublin).

Professor Pierre Laborde

Centre d'Études des Espaces Urbains, Université de Michel Montaigne, Bordeaux III, Domaine Universitaire, 33405 Talence Cédex, France.

Professor Lila Leontidou

Department of Geography and Regional Planning, National Technical University, Zographou Campus, Athens 157 73, Greece.

Professor Solange Montagné-Villette

Département de Géographie, Université de Poitiers, 95 avenue du Recteur Pineau, 86022 Poitiers Cédex, France.

Professor Cosimo Palagiano

Istituto di Geografia, Università degli Studi di Roma, Facoltà di Lettere e Filosofia, 00185 Roma, Città Universitaria, Italy.

Michael B. Quigley

Department of Geography, Trinity College, Dublin 2, Ireland.

Dr Gareth Shaw

Department of Geography, University of Exeter, Amory Building, Rennes Drive, Exeter, EX4 4RJ, UK.

Professor Austin Smyth

Department of Civil Engineering and Transport, University of Ulster at Jordanstown, Newtownabbey, Co. Antrim, BT37 0QB, Northern Ireland, UK.

Dr Allan M. Williams

Department of Geography, University of Exeter, Amory Building, Rennes Drive, Exeter EX4 4RJ, UK.

List of Figures

NB   The data predate the reunification of Germany and relate only to the
former West Germany

List of Tables

PART I

Summaries

Le Challenge européen: Géographie et développement dans la Communauté Européenne

La création de la Communauté européenne est l'événement le plus important de la seconde moitié du xxème siècle à avoir marqué la géographie économique, politique et sociale européenne. De sa création, au début des années cinquante, ratifiée par le Traité de Paris (1952) et la naissance de la Communauté européenne du Charbon et de L'Acier (CECA), en passant par les deux Traités de Rome (1958), fondateurs de la Communauté économique européenne (CEE) et de l'Euratom, jusqu'à l'Acte unique européen (1986) ouvrant la voie au Marché unique de 1993 et jusqu'au coeur des négociations tortueuses et tendues du Traité de Maastricht, visant à l'union monétaire, la Communauté européenne est devenue une entité politique de plus en plus complexe, au point que sa domination peut maintenant influencer et orienter l'avenir des douze états européens.

Cette complexité institutionnelle croissante va de pair avec l'augmentation du nombre des états membres. Pendant plus d'une vingtaine d'années, de 1952 à 1973. on n'en comptait que six: l'Allemagne, la Belgique, la France, l'Italie, le Luxembourg et les Pays Bas, pays industrialisés, tous au cœur d'une Europe occidentale économiquement reconstruite après les deux guerres mondiales dévastatrices de la première moitié du xxème siècle. La Communauté s'agrandit en 1973, avec l'arrivée de trois nouveaux membres, le Danemark, l'Irlande et le Royaume-Uni. Tous trois appartenant au Nord de l'Europe, ils ont des liens économiques étroits aussi bien entre eux qu'avec les états fondateurs. Leur arrivée transforme la CEE. Les problèmes des régions associés aux problèmes de périphérie deviennent inévitablement de plus en plus aigus. La cohésion géographique de la Communauté qui est à l'origine de sa force est brisée par deux états insulaires dont l'un, le Royaume-Uni, compte pour plus de 20 pour cent de la population totale de la Communauté. Les années 1980 voient l'arrivée de nouvaux adhérens: la Grèce en 1981, suivie par l'Espagne et du Portugal en 1986. Une fois encore, l'effet cumulatif de cet agrandissement vers les pays méditerranéens change radicalement la nature de la CEE. Les trois nouveaux membres ne gravitent pas autant autour du noyau industriel de l'Europe occidentale, tant au niveau géographique qu'au niveau économique. L'agriculture traditionnelle marque encore le paysage rural, et aucun de ces pays ne fait vraiment partie du courant de l'économie industrielle urbaine. Pourtant ces pays offrent une main-d'œuvre peu coûteuse et souvent prête à immigrer.

Dans les années 1990, un nouveau déplacement géographique s'opère. L'unification de l'Allemagne voit l'accession, par absorption, d'un membre de l'Europe de l'Est. L'ancienne RDA ajoute en effet une dimension entièrement nouvelle à la carte économique régionale. Comment intégrer des régions dont l'économie industrielle s'est développée dans le cadre d'un système de planification centralisée, et manifestement en faillite aujourd'hui? L'Allemagne unifiée sera probablement acceptée sans que cela change fondamentalement la structure de la CEE, mais si d'autres états de l'Europe orientale—Pologne, Hongrie, états tchèque et slovaque issus de l'ancienne Tchécoslovaquie, Slovénie, Croatie, et autres états éventuellement sortis des ruines de la Yougoslavie—se joignent à elle, alors toute la logique politique et économique de la Communauté devra changer.

Les bouleversements politiques dans l'Europe de l'Est ne sont pas les seules causes de changement. Un certain nombre d'états européens de l'Ouest qui, pour une raison ou pour une autre, ne se sentaient pas capables au départ de joindre la CEE doivent maintenant attendre pour obtenir leur admission. En 1991, l'Association européenne de libre-échange (AELE), comprenant l'Autriche, la Finlande, l'Islande, le Liechtenstein, la Norvège, la Suède, et la Suisse, a signé, avec la Communauté Européenne, un accord dans le but de créer l'Espace économique européen (EEE), étendant ainsi la zone de libre-échange à toute l'Europe occidentale. Mais, l'Autriche, la Suède et la Finlande, ont fait un pas de plus et ont posé leur candidature pour devenir membres à part entière de la Communauté; il est probable que d'autres états de l'EEE feront de même.

Enfin, dans un avenir plus lointain, d'autres états sont impatients de devenir membres. La Turquie, Malte et Chypre—vont essayer de rejoindre l'Europe d'ici une trentaine d'années. Plusieurs républiques, notamment celles de la partie occidentale de l'ex-URSS, commencent également à montrer un vif intérêt. Quel que soit le résultat de toutes ces demandes, il est certain que la CEE devra continuer à adapter ses réponses aux impératifs économiques et sociaux d'une géographie politique en pleine transformation.

L'organisation du livre

Cet ouvrage, écrit par des géographes de sept pays de la Communauté européenne, tente d'évaluer l'impact que la CEE a eu sur le paysage socio-économique des états membres. 'Le développement de la CEE: sa significa-tion spatiale' (Chap. 1) de Mark Blacksell et Allan M. Williams (Exeter, Royaume-Uni) propose une introduction sur le sujet. Précisant la voie dans laquelle la CEE a guidé le développement économique, ils expliquent comment les politiques régionales ont été modifiées afin de répondre à l'aménagement de nombre de pays, et quels ont été les changements continuels des termes de l'échange tant à l'intérieur de l'Europe qu'avec le reste du monde.

Quand la CEE n'était composée que de six pays situés au cœur de l'Europe occidentale industrialisée, la politique régionale en tant que telle était reduite. L'objectif global de la Communauté était alors de promouvoir le développement économique par le libre-échange, la concurrence, sans planification centralisée ni politique d'aménagement. En pratique, des dispositions spéciales devaient cependant être prises, tant régionalement, en faveur de l'économie du Mezzogiorno dans le sud de l'Italie, que sectoriellement, pour soutenir l'exploitation agricole familiale. La croissance économique générale des années 1950 et 1960 en Europe renforça le sentiment d'un progrès économique et politique.

Cette confiance fut ébranlée par le premier agrandissement de la CEE en 1973. Similaires aux versements accordés aux zones rurales dans le cadre de la politique agricole commune (PAC), des aides structurelles furent de plus en plus réclamées pour résoudre les difficultés des vieilles régions industrielles, par le Royaume-Uni d'abord, puis d'une façon générale par l'ensemble des membres de la Communauté. En 1975, le Fonds européen de développement régional (FEDER) fut créé afin d'encourager et aider l'investissement régional. Bien que faibles au départ (3 pour cent du budget de la CEE), les moyens financiers disponibles augmentent considérablement. Mais le plus important fut de reconnaître que l'existence du FEDER suppose que les tenants du marché, seuls, ne pourront jamais réduire de façon satisfaisante les disparités régionales.

L'accession de la Grèce, de l'Espagne et du Portugal, au début des années 1980, renforce l'urgence d'une politique régionale, car elle relève l'inadéquation des politiques sectorielles. Ces trois pays souffrent de multiples difficultés que l'on ne retrouve que dans quelques isolats géographiques de la Communauté. Pour les résoudre, il est nécessaire de fournir une aide à plus grande échelle et de l'intégrer au développement économique d'ensemble. La réponse de la CEE a été double. Tout d'abord, un effort particulier a été fourni pour accroître le montant total des aides régionales utilisables et pour en accorder davantage aux pays méditerranéens. Ensuite, la structure du PIM a été modifiée pour apporter une meilleure coordination et cohérence en ce qui concerne l'utilisation des aides régionales.

L'Acte unique européen a donné une nouvelle impulsion à la politique régionale de la Communauté. Son engagement fondamental pour amener au Marché unique en 1993 nécessitait une approche nouvelle de la part de tous les états membres, et pas seulement ceux de la Méditérannée, dans le but d'éviter des disparités régionales inacceptables. En 1989, le FEDER, le FSE, et le FEOGA de la PAC fusionnent en un fonds unique visant cinq objectifs politiques (en fait six, 5a et 5b sont tout à fait distincts). Ses desseins et ses objectifs sont maintenant en place et le processus et de remplacement des anciens Fonds par un système unique est maintenant largement entamé.

Il existe également une autre facette importante de cette réforme. Auparavant, la commission de la Communauté ne pouvait travailler que par l'intermédiaire des gouvernements nationaux, gonflant les programmes déjà existants grâce à des aides supplémentaires. Avec le nouveau schéma, 9 pour cent environ des fonds régionaux utilisables seront directement affectés par la Communauté, évitant ainsi d'ajouter une aide à des programmes nationaux déjà en cours. STAR, VALOREN, RESIDER et RENAVAL, concernant respectivement l'énergie, la sidérurgie, la construction navale, et la coopération régionale, sont quelques initiatives. C'est un premier pas vers une véritable intégration et l'approche d'un développement régional communautaire.

Le phénomène urbain

Près de 80 pour cent de la population de la CEE est citadine. Les changements affectant le milieu urbain depuis que la Communauté existe concernent donc le plus grand nombre de ses citoyens. Pierre Laborde (Bordeaux III, France) dans 'L'Evolution spatiale des villes d'Europe occidentale 1950–1990' (Chap. 2) observe les effets géographiques de la rapide croissance de la population urbaine dans la CEE jusqu'au milieu des années 1970. La ville, qui avait tendance à se replier sur elle-même, maintenant explose vers l'extérieur. Ceci modifie non seulement les zones urbaines déjà existantes, mais crée également une périphérie nouvellement urbanisée, toujours en essor, en dépit du fort relentissement de la croissance de la population.

Les points de vue sur l'urbanisation se sont modifié au cours de la seconde moitié du xxème siècle. Dans les années cinquante et soixante, la rénovation était à la mode, connue sous le nom de 'rénovation bulldozer' en France, de 'bruxellisation' en Belgique, et de 'rénovation-substitution' en Espagne. Comme les noyaux historiques de ces mêmes villes, qui avaient échappé aux bombardements de la guerre, commençaient à disparaître, il y eut, et particulièrement en France, une réaction contre ces solutions drastiques. La restauration et la réhabilitation des constructions existantes devinrent le nouveau dogme. Mais en fait, il s'avère qu'aucune de ces différentes solutions ne répond aux problèmes posés par l'ancienneté des centres urbains et leur rigidité chronique face aux mutations démographiques et économiques.

La conséquence la plus visible de cette croissance rapide de la population est l'expansion des banlieues autour des villes principales, grandes ou moyennes. Le besoin, au départ résidentiel, trouva réponse dans le système pavillonnaire, grand consommateur d'espace. Les immeubles furent invariablement construits en pleine nature, sur des terres agricoles, contribuant à la perte de sites ruraux. Peu à peu, les activités commerciales, les industries et les services se déplacèrent progressivement vers la périphérie des villes, là aussi largement dominée par les constructions pavillonnaires.

Plus récemment l'extension des espaces urbanisés a été le résultat non pas de la croissance de la population mais de changements sociaux, technologiques et politiques. Le nombre de ménages a fortement augmenté, mais leur taille s'est réduite sous l'influence de facteurs tels que le divorce et l'accroissement de l'espérance de vie. La large diffusion de l'automobile signifie que la population peut choisir de vivre en banlieue sans pour autant craindre des pertes d'emploi. D'autre part, les politiques d'aménagement basées sur le principe de la dé concentration ont encouragé les tendances gouvernementales à aller vers une suburbanisation toujours plus importante. Les politiques de la CEE n'ont eu qu'un effet marginal sur ces changements. Les programmes régionaux avaient pour but de réduire le nombre de zones industrielles. L'application de normes plus rigoureuses en ce qui concerne l'environnement a été encouragée dans les nouveaux secteurs de développement, mais il serait difficile de voir là une quelconque politique urbaine.

Le résultat net de tous ces changements structuraux a été de produire un modèle d'occupation du sol très disparate en ville, reflétant et accentuant les différences de valeur foncière entre le centre et la périphérie. En France, les autorités municipales ont commencé à prendre davantage en compte ces mutations, mais les différences de structure politique font qu'il est difficile de généraliser et d'appliquer cette tendance à l'ensemble de la CEE.

Les problèmes de généralisation de la nature du changement et de l'aménagement des espaces urbains sont clairement illustrés par Lila Leontidou (Université nationale des techniques, Athènes) dans 'Les villes méditerranéennes: tendances divergentes dans l'Europe unie' (Chap. 3). La ville a longtemps joué un role culturel fondamental dans l'Europe Méditérranéen, c'est d'ailleurs toujours le cas en cette fin de xxème siècle. Bien que les disparités technologiques soient beaucoup moins marquées qu'en Europe du Nord, on assiste pourtant à des évolutions similaires dans les régions du sud.

Le centre a toujours été, et reste, un espace avant tout résidentiel à Naples, Athènes et Barcelone, tandis que les secteurs ouvriers se développent en périphérie. La ségrégation sociale et économique, si typique en France, en Allemagne et au Royaume Uni, est beaucoup moins évidente dans les pays méditerranéens.

Inévitablement, l'impact de la CEE sur le développement n'a pu être que minime. Parmi les pays industriels, seule l'Italie fut un membre fondateur, tandis que la Grèce, l'Espagne, et le Portugal n'ont rejoint la Communauté que dans les années 1980. Ce n'est cependant qu'un aspect de l'explication. En outre, beaucoup de politiques communautaires sont formulées de telle façon qu'elles sont inadéquates pour les villes méditerranéennes. Les indicateurs de pauvreté, par exemple, basés sur le nombre de sans-abri, sont peu significatifs quand les pauvres vivent dans les logements précaires autoconstruits et des bidons-villes.

Ceci souligne le simple fait que les politiques globales, même à l'intérieur d'un groupe d'états aussi homogène que l'est apparemment la CEE, ne peuvent réaliser leurs objectifs qu'en étant extrêmement attentifs aux conditions locales.

Les changements structuraux

La création de la CEE a bouleversé le contexte économique et social européen et introduit de profonds changements structuraux dans de nombreux domaines, aussi bien grâce à des politiques incitatives qu'à des adaptations involontaires. J.-P. Charrié (Bordeaux III, France) dans 'Le modèle industriel: la construction européenne face à la mondialisation de l'économie' (Chap. 4) brosse un tableau détaillé des principaux changements des pays qui furent le berceau de la Révolution industrielle au XIXème siècle. En effet, si la CEE est toujours une puissance industrielle de rang mondial, les fondements de sa suprématie sont désormais remis en cause par une concurrence internationale exacerbée.

La plupart des changements se sont produits il y a plus de quarante ans. La CEE, riche en charbon et en minerai de fer, disposait dans les années 1950 d'une importante capacité de production dans divers secteurs—fonte, acier, chimie. Ce potentiel a permis les premiers succès de la CECA. Dans un continent meurtri par cinq années de guerre, le Traité de Paris posa les bases d'une forte croissance interrompue par la crise pétrolière de 1973. La Communauté a dû depuis rationaliser ses méthodes de production, faire face au déclin des industries de base (clés de son succès initial), tout en s'adaptant à la croissance des industries de haute-technologie.

Les changements apparaissent au moment de la montée en puissance de nouveaux producteurs de biens manufacturés. La menace japonaise reste certainement la plus redoutable: son industrie concurrence directement les marchés traditionnels de la CEE, notamment ceux de l'Amérique du Nord, tandis que ses investissements dans la Communauté même lui permettent de pénétrer le marché intérieur. Ajoutons à cela la concurrence des nouveaux pays industrialisés, plus particulièrement de la Corée du Sud, qui diversifient leur production à partir de l'industrie de l'habillement et du textile.

Tous ces bouleversements ont des effets cumulatifs sur le cœur industriel de l'Europe. Les vieilles régions, qui supportent un nombre croissant de handicaps, déclinent et demandent des aides d'urgence pour se reconvertir, alors que les grandes agglomérations, dans une situation économique plus favorable, préservent jalousement leurs privilèges.

La Commission, et d'autres institutions dont les pouvoirs furent durant de nombreuses années limités à des interventions isolées dans les régions en déclin et dans les secteurs en difficulté, commencent à jouer un rôle de plus en plus important en matière industrielle. La CEE aiguillonne désormais l'industrie: distribution d'aides spécifiques, coordination des efforts de recherche et des politiques de restructuration régionale. De plus, l'achèvement du Marché unique aura d'importantes répercussions sur la production industrielle de la Communauté.

Enfin, les transports ont longtemps été considérés, aussi bien par les gouvernements que par la Communauté, comme un des facteurs de la dynamique industrielle, même s'ils n'ont pas bénéficié du niveau d'intégration auquel on pouvait s'attendre. James Killen (Trinity College, Dublin, Irlande) et Austin Smyth (Ulster, Royaume-Uni) dans 'La politique des transports de la CEE' (Chap. 5), montrent comment l'absence de cette politique a influencé la totalité de l'île irlandaise.

Les gouvernements nationaux ont toujours contrôlé les réseaux de transports et leur fonctionnement. En premier lieu, ils sont les principaux régulateurs de la circulation fixant, par exemple, les limitations de vitesse ou les conditions d'obtention des différents permis. En Europe, ils interviennent aussi directement sur le fonctionnement du réseau ferroviaire, parfois même sur le frêt routier, ce qui leur permet de contrôler la concurrence. En second lieu, en veillant à leur bonne utilisation, ils essayent d'influencer l'importance et la nature des investissements d'infrastructure par rapport aux autres secteurs économiques.

Avant la signature du Traité de Rome, chaque état poursuivait une politique de transport plus ou moins autonome. Si, théoriquement, la coopération était de règle après la conférence des Ministres des Transports de 1953, peu de choses furent réalisées au niveau européen, à l'exception du réseau ferroviaire Trans Europe Express (TEE). Malgré une référence explicite dans le Traité de Rome à une politique commune des transports, les réalisations furent minces en raison des programmes entrepris dans chaque Etat. Ce chapitre éclaire la manière dont les accords conclus pour les différents secteurs—route, réseau ferroviaire, mer, et air—ont permis à l'Irlande de s'intégrer à un réseau de transport dont elle était écartée géographiquement.

En dépit d'inévitables divergences nationales et régionales, le réseau de transport européen est dans son ensemble un atout ayant largement contribué à la cohésion de la CEE. Il a notamment facilité la mobilité de la main-d'œuvre, favorisant ainsi le succès économique de la Communauté. Russell King (Trinity College, Dublin, Irlande) dans 'Les migrations et le marché du travail dans le CEE: une solution pour le développement régional' (Chap. 6) examine le rôle des migrations internationales dans les changements économiques et sociaux de la géographie de la CEE depuis la fin des années 1950. La croissance de l'Europe industrielle et post-industrielle des années 1960 et 1970 doit en effet beaucoup aux travailleurs immigrés. Même si leur nombre a diminué après le premier choc pétrolier de 1973–1974, les regroupements familiaux et les nouvelles vagues d'immigrations de la fin des années 1980 portent le nombre d'immigrés en Europe à environ vingt millions, dont la majorité est originaire de la Communauté européenne.

Après une période durant laquelle les migrations internationales ne constituaient qu'une préoccupation secondaire, un débat récent les a remis à l'ordre du jour. Les flux de travailleurs immigrés commencés dans certains pays (Allemagne, Pays Bas) avant 1985, s'intensifient à la fin des années 1980 et explosent en 1989 avec la chute du socialisme. Cet événement stupéfiant montre combien il faut être prudent en matière de pronostics: peu d'experts, en 1988, pouvaient imaginer ces mouvements de masse, même si l'arrivée de quelques immigrés de la République Démocratique Allemande et de Hongrie déclencha le processus de migration.

D'autres problèmes ont assombri l'horizon des pays démocratiques européens. Actuellement, des millions de personnes se déplacent modifiant ainsi les caractéristiques du monde et notamment celle de l'Europe. Le nombre de réfugiés et de demandeurs d'asile arrivant en Europe a tant augmenté, durant les années 1980, qu'une répartition équitable au niveau national et communautaire est devenue nécessaire, en relation avec les Accords de Shwengen, conclus afin d'obtenir la disparition des contrôles aux frontières intra-communautaires.

Un des autres problèmes lié aux migrations internationales est le travail clandestin dont parle Solange Montagné-Villette (Poitiers, France) dans 'Mobilité et clandestinité dans l'espace communautaire' (Chap. 7). Le travail clandestin ou illégal n'est pas une nouveauté! Apparu au début du siècle avec le développement des structures administratives et de protection sociale dans les pays riches, il constitue aujourd'hui dans certains pays une tradition, voire une culture. En revanche, le récent travail clandestin dans la CEE en tant que telle présente des caractéristiques originales encore peu étudiées. La mobilité croissante de la main-d'œuvre, des entreprises et des activités, génère de nouvelles formes de gestion de la main-d'œuvre illégale dont les modalités sont étroitement liées au contexte et à l'environnement économico-juridique de la CEE. Travail clandestin de certains ressortissants pauvres de la CEE dans d'autres états membres, délocalisation et/ou sous-traitance d'activités industrielles non-déclarées dans les pays de l'Europe méditer-ranéenne, travail illégal des immigrés extra-communautaires, etc., constituent quelques unes des nouvelles formes de main-d'œuvre illégale dont on a saisi tardivement l'importance. Certains états membres par exemple, et notamment le Royaume-Uni, acceptent mal le contrôle des conditions de travail et la législation sociale, les considérant incompatibles avec le libéralisme auquel ils aspirent.

Les adaptations du monde rural

La politique agricole commune, la PAC, fut durant les trente dernières années un gouffre dévorant plus de 90 pour cent du budget de la Communauté, et qui en absorbe plus de 60 pour cent aujourd'hui encore. Ses modalités, bien connues par ailleurs, ne sont pas le sujet de cet ouvrage, mais toute étude sérieuse sur la Communauté se doit d'envisager le problème agricole. Les dépenses excessives de l'agriculture communautaire commencent à s'atténuer, et ceci risque d'avoir, à long terme, de graves répercussions sur le monde rural. Dietrich Denecke (Göttingen, Allemagne) dans 'Reconversion et désertion des terres' (Chap. 8) analyse les conséquences des changements de la PAC sur l'environnement et, plus particulièrement, sur les paysages ruraux d'Allemagne où coexistent encore le paysage traditionnel et l'agriculture moderne. Jusqu'à présent, l'insuffisance des productions agricoles et de réserves ont entraîné une intensification de l'utilisation des terres.

La surproduction récente a poussé à l'émergence des cultures alternatives et extensives, des programmes d'élevage mais aussi à l'abandon des fermes et des terres. Les politiques qui ont conduit à ces changements dominent aujourd'hui l'agriculture. Au même moment, le nombre d'exploitations se réduit et la production animale et végétale s'intensifie, avec tous les effets négatifs que cela comporte pour l'environnement. La concomitance de ces deux options bouleverse le délicat équilibre écologique jusqu'ici préservé par les méthodes traditionnelles. De ce fait, évaluer l'envergure des réalisa-tions acceptables d'un point de vue écologique, en matière d'agriculture, visant à la conservation du paysage, est devenu un élément crucial pour le développement de la Communauté. Ceci comprend d'ailleurs d'importantes ramifications dans le processus d'acceptation des révisions de la PAC. En dépit d'une amorce d'évolution, la PAC, qui récuse désormais le système des subventions trop coûteuses, reste la pierre angulaire de la politique communautaire.

Manuel Corbera (Cantabrique, Espagne) dans 'La PAC et le développement de l'agriculture: problèmes, perspectives' (Chap. 9), réévalue la PAC dans la perspective de l'Espagne, pays agricole, n'ayant rejoint la Communauté qu'en 1986. La Communauté est la première puissance agricole du monde: le premier producteur de lait, de beurre, de fromage, de vin, de sucre et de viande de bœuf; le second producteur de blé et d'orge. Elle s'auto-suffit pour toutes les denrées produites en milieu tempéré, à l'exception des fruits, du maïs et de la viande ovine.

Cette situation enviable résulte, en partie, des conditions naturelles favorables et de la complémentarité des climats atlantique, continental et méditerranéen. Les techniques employées expliquent aussi ce succès: agriculture intensive, systèmes adaptés aux conditions naturelles, efficacité des structures ainsi que haut niveau de mécanisation, favorisant le maintien d'une grande productivité.

Quoi qu'il en soit, le succès de l'agriculture européenne est aussi dû à la PAC, qui a stimulé la production industrielle durant toute une génération. On ne doit pas oublier que sans cette politique aucun des états membres ne serait aujourd'hui leader mondial dans son domaine. En dépit de nombreux problèmes et d'un besoin urgent de réformes, la PAC a été et continue d'être une réussite.

Ce succès quantitatif ne peut cependant masquer la crise de certaines régions rurales. Les besoins en terres, et surtout en terres marginales, qui ne sont plus aussi importants qu'avant, nécessitent la recherche d'alternatives, à la fois pour le sol et pour les paysans qui le cultivent. La jachère et la protection des paysages y répondent, mais remettent en question la production de masse sur laquelle repose une communauté stable et socialement unie. La meilleure solution semble être l'aménagement touristique des zones rurales, plus particulièrement dans les régions côtières et montagneuses de l'Europe.

Allan M. Williams et Gareth Shaw (Exeter, Royaume-Uni), dans 'Tourisme: opportunités, compétitions et contradictions européennes' (Chap. 10), étudient ce phénomène. Depuis l'émergence du tourisme de masse dans les années 1960, le tourisme peut être considéré comme un élément essentiel de la construction économico-sociale de la Communauté. Employant plus d'un vingtième de la population active, il représente une part non-négligeable du

PIB et du commerce international intra et extra-communautaire. Il est aussi un instrument de changement social, véhiculant valeurs et styles de vie différents, et offrant un des rares moyens d'échange entre peuples et cultures, au sein de la communauté. On s'interroge souvent sur l'existence ou non d'une culture européenne et on peut se demander si le tourisme peut y contribuer. En fait, celui-ci, en tant que phénomène migratoire, constitue le premier pas vers la libération à l'échelle du Marché unique. Son importance dans la Communauté se résume à ceci: 64 pour cent du tourisme international a lieu en Europe et, pour la plus grande part, à l'intérieur de la CEE. Plus que dans n'importe quelle autre région du monde, le tourisme est ici essentiel à la production et à la consommation dans les milieux urbains et ruraux.

L'environnement

En dépit de l'inquiétude croissante de la population au sujet de la dégradation des paysages et de l'épuisement des ressources depuis les années 1960 et 1970, l'environnement en tant que tel était complètement ignoré par les Traités de Paris et de Rome. La Commission pouvait donc difficilement apporter une solution à ces problèmes. Malgré cette prise de conscience, il semble irréaliste de traiter cette question dans un cadre purement national. En raison de l'augmentation du nombre de pays—passé de six à douze entre 1958 et 1986—et d'un développement économique de plus en plus différencié en terme de croissance et de modèle, la CEE ne constituait pas une unité spatiale naturelle pour résoudre la multitude de cas complexes et variés relevant de l'aménagement et de l'environnement. Pour le grand public, l'attrait principal de la CEE, en tant que gestionnaire de l'environnement, provient de sa fonction supra-nationale. Elle souligne en effet l'apparente universalité d'un grand nombre de questions à propos de la protection de l'environnement.

Mark Blacksell (Exeter, Royaume-Uni), dans 'Politiques environnementales, ressources et possibilités d'aménagement' (Chap. 11) observe le chemin tortueux emprunté pour parvenir à une politique environnementale qui prend aujourd'hui une place importante dans la CEE. Il est désormais évident que les meilleures solutions aux problèmes de l'environnement, tels que le contrôle de la pollution de l'air et de l'eau et la pratique de l'aménagement du territoire varient fortement suivant les états de la CEE, tandis que le consensus politique pour parvenir à des solutions est difficile à mettre en œuvre. Les sociétés les plus riches se laissent plus facilement persuader que les avantages à long terme d'une politique de l'environnement sont supérieurs aux avantages économiques à court terme. De fortes différences demeurent donc entre les états industrialisés du cœur de la CEE et ceux de la périphérie, notamment des pays méditerranéens. Les pays insulaires, tels que l'Irlande et le Royaume-Uni, qui disposent de cours d'eau mineurs semblent moins concernés par leur utilisation pour l'évacuation des eaux usées que les états continentaux, comme la France et l'Allemagne, traversés par des voies d'eau majeures et internationales. De la même manière, la pollution de l'air, poussée vers un autre territoire par les vents dominants, est perçue différemment par le pollueur et le pollué. Les états de la partie occidentale de l'Europe acceptent généralement des taux de pollution atmosphérique considérés comme préjudiciables à l'environnement dans les pays plus à l'est. Grâce aux études scientifiques et à une meilleure connaissance des effets à long terme, cette attitude est cependant de moins en moins admise.

Durant ces quarante années d'existence, la CEE a dû harmoniser dans les limites imposées par la Traité, les positions différentes des états membres, de plus en plus nombreux, et s'adapter à une prise de conscience accrue des citoyens confirmée par les débats au Parlement européen depuis 1979. Initialement, on estimait que la politique de l'environnement était directement liée à l'économie et qu'elle ne devait pas entraver la libre concurrence. Mais après la Conférence des Nations Unies sur l'environnement humain en 1972, ces deux domaines, économie et environnement, sont devenus distincts. Une suite de programmes pour l'environnement a conduit à l'introduction de cette préoccupation dans l'Acte Unique Européen.

Depuis l'entrée en vigueur de l'Acte Unique, la CEE assure un role de plus en plus déterminant dans la formulation et l'application d'une politique environnementale. Pour comprendre cette évolution, on peut relever quatre changements importants. Premièrement, on est passé de l'intention à l'incorporation des actions dans la législation nationale de chaque état membre. Deuxièmement, cinq programmes concernant l'environnement, plus de 180 directives et autres types de mesures législatives montrent l'ampleur des dispositions prises. Troisièmement, on note un élargissement du champ d'intervention—jusqu'alors surtout lié à la PAC—bien au-delà de ce qui était prévu dans la politique de l'environnement. Enfin, la mise en œuvre, le contrôle et le renforcement des actions ont une connotation plus politique.

Manifestement, l'efficacité de ces politiques dans le domaine de l'environnement ne peut être jugée que par l'impact territorial de celles-ci. Michael Quigley (Trinity College, Dublin, Irlande) dans 'Les effets de la politique de la CEE sur les paysages ruraux et l'environnement en Irlande' (Chap. 12), dresse une évaluation détaillée du cas irlandais, terre où le paysage rural est prédominant, et l'agriculture, plus particulièrement l'élevage, est l'activité principale. Certes, l'agriculture irlandaise avait progressé et s'était modernisée avant l'accession de l'Irlande à la CEE en 1973, mais le rythme et l'ampleur du changement depuis lors sont étroitement liés à la politique de Bruxelles. L'usage de la terre et la qualité de l'environnement sont ainsi affectés de trois manières différentes. La politique agricole, tout d'abord, influence largement l'utilisation des sols, et cela dans tous les domaines. Ensuite, les mesures structurelles, pas forcément agricoles, fournissent des subventions pour différents programmes opérationnels qui, dans le cadre de l'aide communautaire, transforment les paysages ruraux. Parallèlement, la politique de la CEE et sa législation tentent d'atténuer les effets négatifs des autres interventions, ou encouragent la préservation de l'environnement.

Pour l'Irlande, la PAC a une influence déterminante, non seulement en terme de développement économique mais aussi en raison des transformations qu'elle entraîne sur l'environnement. L'organisation des marchés ainsi que la fixation des prix d'intervention, de même qu'une série de mesures de restructuration visant à aider les exploitations agricoles des régions défavorisées par les conditions naturelles, ont un réel impact sur le développement agricole.

L'ancienne politique agricole, par des aides financières proportionelles au volume de production, a entraîné la surproduction et l'accumulation de stocks, mais a aussi provoqué une dégradation de l'environnement. L'impact des sommes versées dans le cadre du FEOGA est également visible dans le secteur agro-alimentaire. En réponse à ces incitations de la CEE, le nombre de moutons a augmenté de manière considérable au cours des dernières années et on assiste aussi à des phénomènes de surpâturage et d'érosion. Les économies d'échelle ont accru la spécialisation régionale de certaines exploitations, particulièrement dans l'élevage porcin et gallinacé. Malheureusement, les dommages causés sur l'environnement sont réels, dus à une accumulation d'importantes quantités de lisiers qui polluent ensuite les rivières. Un autre aspect de cette intensification est lié à l'utilisation croissante des engrais et au remplacement du foin par l'ensilage avec les mêmes conséquences sur l'eau. Parallèlement, les fonds déboursés par le FEOGA à l'intention des régions agricoles marginales afin de les rendre plus productives risquent d'avoir des effets négatifs sur certains environnements fragiles. L'ensemble des mesures et le Plan de drainage, visant à stimuler le développement agricole dans l'ouest de l'Irlande, sont des exemples des aides fournies par la Communauté, qui ont eu des conséquences déplorables sur l'environnement.

La forêt irlandaise s'étend fortement et a pour objectif de doubler sa superficie et de passer ainsi de 15 000 à 30 000 ha. Cette augmentation, sans précédent, est guidée, et financée par la CEE dans le cadre de son programme opérationnel forestier. La plus grande acidité des eaux de surface, la dégradation des zones de pêche naturelle, la destruction de l'écosystème dans les terres basses marécageuses, et l'altération des paysages sauvages d'une grande beauté constituent quelques unes des conséquences de ce développement en Irlande.

Depuis le milieu des années 1980, cette politique d'intensification agricole a commencé à changer, en partie pour rééquilibrer la production par rapport à la demande, mais aussi en raison des effets nuisibles sur l'environnement. Ceci s'affirme par des mesures radicales comme le double rôle des fermiers, à la fois producteurs de biens de consommation et gestionnaires des paysages. L'environnement tire évidemment grand profit de ces nouvelles orientations. En même temps, le renforcement de la politique communautaire dans ce domaine, par des mesures telles que la Directive sur l'évaluation de l'impact sur l'environnement et la Directive sur l'habitat, pourra certainement accélérer l'évolution. Mais, en Irlande, une des plus grandes menaces pour l'environnement vient du Fonds Européen de Développement Régional, dont les moyens se sont accrus et on peut se demander si la politique de protection de l'environnement est fondée.

L'environnement intervient également dans le secteur de la santé dans les pays de la CEE. Cosimo Palagiano (La Sapienza, Rome, Italie) dans 'Environnement, santé et soins médicaux: comparaisons européennes et étude de cas italien' (Chap. 13), examine dans quelle mesure les Communauté a pu influencer ce domaine. C'est une analyse souvent négligée dans le cadre de la CEE, même si des solutions communautaires ont été apportées par l'intermédiaire des politiques en matière d'environnement, de la Charte sociale dans le Traité de Maastricht et des politiques d'extensification agricole.

Ce chapitre présente des orientations. Il établit d'abord un panorama des conditions de santé dans la CEE à l'aide de multiples indicateurs de l'état de santé et des services. Cette analyse se poursuit en mesurant les différences d'espérance de vie et montre en quoi les maladies ont une incidence sur elle, même si les populations sont relativement homogènes du fait des niveaux de vie atteints. Les variations des conditions de santé selon les pays sont également illustrées. Le choix de l'Italie comme champ d'étude s'impose en raison de la persistence de forts déséquilibres régionaux, et parce que peu d'études en langue anglaise ont été menées sur ce thème, en comparaison avec ce qui existe sur les pays septentrionaux. Enfin sont soulignées l'importance et l'actualité des questions de santé dans la CEE.

En conclusion Allan M. Williams et Mark Blacksell (Exeter, Royaume-Uni), dans 'Mutations territoriales et nouvelles priorités: la CEE au tournant du XXIème siècle (Chap. 14), imaginent comment la CEE pourrait évoluer à l'aube du nouveau siècle. Ils donnent aussi une idée de l'impact que des changements de la politique de la Communauté pourraient avoir si le développement économique et environnemental étaient conciliés.

Entwicklung die Europäische Herausforderung— Geographie und der Europäischen Gemeinschaft (EG)

Die Gründung der Europäischen Gemeinschaft war das bedeutendste Ereignis für die wirtschaftlichen, politischen und sozialen Verhältnisse Westeuropas in der zweiten Hälfte des 20. Jahrhunderts. Von ihren Anfängen in den frühen fünfziger Jahren, d.h. mit der Gründung der Europäischen Gemeinschaft für Kohle und Stahl (EGKS oder Montanunion) 1952, über die Verträge von Rom von 1958, die die Europäische Wirtschaftsgemeinschaft (EWG) sowie Euratom ins Leben riefen, und die Einheitliche Europäische Akte (EEA) von 1986, mit der der Weg zum Gemeinsamen Binnenmarkt geebnet wurde, bis hin zu den Vereinbarungen von Maastricht, hat sich die EG zu einer immer komplexeren Einheit entwickelt und nimmt heute maßgeblich Einfluß auf die Gestaltung der Zukunft der zwölf Mitgliedstaaten.

Parallel zur wachsenden institutionellen Komplexität der Gemeinschaft hat eine ständige Erhöhung ihrer Mitgliederzahl stattgefunden. Zwischen 1952 und 1973 bestand die EG aus den Staaten Belgien, Frankreich, der Bundesrepublik Deutschland, Italien, Luxemburg sowie den Niederlanden, d.h. den Industriestaaten im Zentrum Westeuropas, die sich nach den zwei Weltkriegen, die die erste Hälfte des 20. Jahrhunderts beherrschten, wirtschaftlich erholten. Mit der ersten Erweiterung 1973 wurden drei weitere Staaten aufgenommen, nämlich Dänemark, die Republik Irland sowie Großbritannien. Alle drei sind sowohl untereinander wie auch mit den Gründerstaaten eng verbunden. Ihre Integration veränderte die Situation der Gemeinschaft, regionale Probleme sowie das Spannungsverhältnis zwischen Zentrum und Peripherie gewannen an Bedeutung. Der geographische Zusammenhang der Gemeinschaft, zu Beginn eine Hauptquelle der Stärke, wurde aufgegeben mit dem Beitritt zweier Inselstaaten, von denen einer, nämlich Großbritannien, allein 20 Prozent der Bevölkerung der gesamten Gemeinschaft ausmacht.

In den achtziger Jahren traten weitere Staaten der EG bei, 1981 Griechenland, sowie Spanien und Portugal im Jahre 1986. Auch diese Erweiterung der Gemeinschaft um die mediterranen Länder änderte wiederum die wirtschaftlich-räumliche Struktur derselben in bedeutsamer Weise.

Alle drei neuen Mitgliedstaaten waren weniger verbunden mit dem industriellen Zentrum Westeuropas sowohl in Bezug auf ihre geographische wie auch ökonomische Situation. Traditionelle bäuerliche wie auch feudale Landwirtschaft waren noch immer vorherrschend, und keiner der Staaten war in vollem Maße Teil der allgemeinen europäischen urban-industriellen Wirtschaftsweise. Vielmehr dienten sie in dieser Zeit vornehmlich als Quelle billiger Arbeitskräfte ('Gastarbeiter').

In den neunziger Jahren nun verschiebt sich wiederum der Schwerpunkt des Strukturwandels in der EG. Die deutsche Einheit bedeutete die Integration eines ehemals sozialistischen Staates, der DDR. Hiermit wurde eine ganz neue Dimension eröffnet. Wie sollte es möglich sein, Mitglieder zu integrieren, deren Wirtschaft nach dem nun offensichtlich fehlgeschlagenen System der Planwirtschaft organisiert war? Das vereinte Deutschland wird sich wahrscheinlich ohne grundsätzliche strukturelle Veränderung in die EG einfügen. Wenn jedoch andere osteuropäische Staaten beitreten—Polen, Ungarn, die Tschechei und die Slowakei sowie Slowenien, Kroatien und welche anderen Staaten auch immer aus dem zerfallenden Jugoslawien entstehen mögen— dann wird sich die gesamte wirtschaftliche und politische Strategie und Logik der Gemeinschaft ändern müssen.

Der politische Aufbruch der Staaten Osteuropas ist allerdings nicht der einzige Anstoß zu gravierenden Veränderungen. Eine ganze Reihe von Staaten Westeuropas, die bisher der EG nicht beigetreten waren, werden jetzt vorstellig und beantragen ihre Aufnahme in die Gemeinschaft. 1991 unterzeichnete die Europäische Freihandelsgemeinschaft (European Free Trade Association, EFTA), mit den Mitgliedstaaten Österreich, Finnland, Island, Liechtenstein, Norwegen, Schweden und der Schweiz, eine Vereinbarung mit der EG, um einen Europäischen Wirtschaftsraum (European Economic Area, EEA) zu schaffen. Damit ist die Freihandelszone auf das gesamte westliche Europa ausgedehnt worden. Österreich, Schweden und die Schweiz sind weitergegangen und haben sich um die Vollmitgliedschaft in der EG beworben, und es ist wahrscheinlich, daß andere EFTA-Staaten sehr bald folgen werden. Die Türkei, Malta und Zypern haben über nahezu 30 Jahre versucht, Mitglieder zu werden, und nun beginnen auch viele der Republiken im westlichen Teil der ehemaligen Sowjetunion aktives Interesse zu zeigen. Wie auch immer der Ausgang dieser Bemühungen sein wird, es ist sicher, daß die EG sich immer wieder wird anpassen müssen, reagierend auf die wirtschaftlichen und sozialen Anforderungen der sich wandelnden politisch-geographischen Verhältnisse.

Zur Konzeption dieses Bandes

In diesem Buch haben sich Geographen aus sieben EG-Ländern das Ziel gesetzt, den Einfluß zu interpretieren, den die EG-Politik auf die sozioökonomische Landschaft ihrer Mitgliedstaaten ausgeübt hat.

In der Einleitung diskutieren Mark Blacksell und Allan Williams (Exeter, England) die Entwicklung der Europäischen Gemeinschaft und ihre räumliche Bedeutung (Kap. 1). Sie versuchen die Sichtweise zu erklären, von der die EG sich hat leiten lassen, sowohl in ihrer ökonomischen Entwicklung als auch in der Art und Weise, in der sich ihre regionale Politik verändert hat, als Reaktion auf die beständige Zunahme an Mitgliedern wie auch auf die laufenden Verschiebungen der Handelsbeziehungen innerhalb Europas und weltweit.

Als die EG noch eine Gemeinschaft von nur sechs Staaten war, räumlich begrenzt auf die Länder im Zentrum des industrialisierten Westeuropa, war eine regionale Politik als solche nur wenig sichtbar. Der ganze Zweck der Gemeinschaft war, die wirtschaftliche Entwicklung durch einen freien Markt zu fördern.

Wenn auch in der Praxis besondere Vorkehrungen getroffen werden mußten—regional, um zum Beispiel die Wirtschaft des Mezzogiorno in Süditalien zu unterstützen und sektoral, um die Landwirtschaft in der Form von Familienbetrieben zu erhalten—so bestätigte der allgemeine wirtschaftliche Erfolg der fünfziger und sechziger Jahre in Westeuropa doch insgesamt den Glauben an das Allheilmittel wirtschaftlichen und politischen Fortschrittes. Diese Überzeugung wurde 1973 durch die erste Erweiterung der EG erschüttert. Die unausweichlichen Probleme angesichts rückläufiger Entwicklungen in älteren Industrieregionen in Großbritannien und in zunehmendem Maße auch an anderen Orten der Gemeinschaft führten zu steigenden Forderungen gegenüber Strukturfonds, um den Schwierigkeiten begegnen zu können, denen diese städtischen Regionen ausgesetzt waren. Diese Fonds waren denen ähnlich, die theoretisch im Rahmen der gemeinsamen Agrarpolitik (Common Agricultural Policy, CAP) für ländliche Gebiete verfügbar waren. So wurde 1975 der Europäische Regionale Entwicklungsfond (European Regional Development Fond, ERDF) ins Leben gerufen, dessen ausdrückliches Ziel darin bestand, nationale Regionalhilfen und Investitionsprogramme zu ergänzen.

Wenn auch die verfügbaren Mittel anfangs gering waren, nur drei Prozent des EG-Haushaltes wurden darauf verwendet, so wurden sie im Laufe der Zeit ständig aufgestockt. Von noch größerer Bedeutung war jedoch die Erkenntnis, der der ERDF Rechnung trug, daß Marktkräfte allein nie in zufriedenstellendem Maße den regionalen Disparitäten begegnen können.

Die Angliederung von Griechenland, Spanien und Portugal an die Gemeinschaft in den frühen achtziger Jahren verstärkte weiterhin die Notwendigkeit einer regional ausgerichteten Politik und offenbarte damit gleichzeitig die Unzulänglichkeit sektoraler Strategien. Alle drei Länder leiden unter komplexen Problemen, die in diesem Ausmaß anderswo in der Gemeinschaft nur in begrenzten Bereichen anzutreffen sind. Bei einer Betrachtung ihrer Probleme unter regionalen Gesichtspunkten ist Hilfe in einem größeren Ausmaße als bisher erforderlich und muß, um überhaupt einen Sinn zu haben, Teil einer integrierten Strategie gesamtwirtschaftlicher Entwicklung sein. Die Reaktion der EG war einerseits die Bemühung um die Erhöhung des Gesamtbetrages verfügbarer regionaler Hilfen, wobei den mediterranen Ländern gleichzeitig ein größerer Anteil zukommen sollte. Zudem ist ein integriertes Rahmenprogramm für den mediterranen Raum erstellt worden mit dem Zweck, regionale Hilfe besser koordinieren zu können.

Der Neuorientierung der regionalen Politik der Gemeinschaft ist weiterer Aufwind durch die Einheitliche Europäische Akte (EEA) gegeben worden. Der Kernpunkt derselben, nämlich den Binnenmarkt bis zum Jahre 1993 zu vollenden, machte einen grundsätzlich neuen Ansatz notwendig und zwar unter Einschluß aller zwölf Mitgliedstaaten und nicht nur derer der mediterranen Peripherie, wenn unerwünschte regionale Disparitäten vermieden werden sollten. 1989 sind die drei existierenden Fonds zusammengelegt worden, um fünf (bzw. sechs, da die Punkte 5a und 5b sehr spezifisch sind) politische Zielsetzungen zu erreichen.

Es gibt noch einen weiteren interessanten Aspekt der Reform des Strukturfonds. Bisher konnte die EG-Kommission nur über die nationalen Regierungen agieren, indem sie zusätzliche Hilfe für bereits festgelegte nationale Programme zur Verfügung stellte. Mit der neuen Regelung wird ein Teil, etwa neun Prozent, des Regionalfonds verfügbar sein für Initiativen der Gemeinschaft selbst durch Programme wie STAR, VALOREN, RESIDER und RENAVAL, die sich auf Energie, Eisen und Stahl sowie die Schiffsbauindustrie beziehen.

Die urbanen Verhältnisse

Nahezu 80 Prozent der Bevölkerung der EG lebt in Städten oder Großstädten, und so sind die Veränderungen, die sich seit der Bildung der Gemeinschaft im urbanen Bereich vollzogen haben, für den größten Teil der Bevölkerung der EG-Staaten von unmittelbarer Bedeutung.

Pierre Laborde (Bordeaux III, Frankreich) behandelt im zweiten Kapitel die geographischen Auswirkungen des schnellen Wachstums der städtischen Bevölkerung in den EG-Staaten bis Mitte der siebziger Jahre. Diese Bevölkerungszunahme hat dazu geführt, daß die Städte nicht mehr festgefügt und nach innen orientiert sind, sondern vielmehr ins Umland expandieren. So werden dabei nicht nur die vorhandenen städtischen Gebiete verändert, sondern es entsteht zudem eine verstädterte Peripherie, die sich noch immer ausweitet, obwohl sich das Bevölkerungswachstum selbst deutlich verlangsamt hat.

Konzepte der Stadterneuerung haben sich im Laufe des 20. Jahrhunderts verändert. In den fünfziger und sechziger Jahren war die Flächensanierung *en vogue*, in Frankreich oft als 'Bulldozer Sanierung' in Belgien als 'Brüsselisation' und in Spanien als 'Ersatzerneuerung' bezeichnet. Als jedoch die historischen Kerne gerade solcher Städte, die von Kriegszerstörungen nicht betroffen waren, zu schwinden begannen, entwickelte sich, besonders in Frankreich, Widerstand gegen derart drastische Lösungen. Erhalt und Renovierung der vorhandenen Bausubstanz wurden zum neuen Leitsatz.

Leztlich hat es jedoch keines der verschiedenen Konzepte zur Innenstadtsanierung vermocht, mit den Problemen fertig zu werden, die sich aus dem Altern der Bausubstanz sowie aus mangelnder Flexibilität hinsichtlich demographischer wie auch wirtschaftlicher Veränderungen ergaben.

Die am deutlichsten sichbare Auswirkung des rapiden Bevölkerungswachstums im Siedlungsbild ist die Expansion der Vorstädte, von denen fast alle größeren Städte umgeben sind. Diese war zunächst vornehmlich auf die Wohnfunktion ausgerichtet, zumeist in Form von viel Raum beanspruchenden Einfamilienhäusern. Aber auch Hochhäuser, die gebaut wurden, wie z.B. die 'grands ensembles' in Frankreich, trugen durch ihre Lage im Grünen zum Verlust von Agrarland bei. Nach und nach etablierten sich dann auch Einrichtungen des Handels, der Industrie sowie des Dienstleistungsbereiches in diesen Randgebieten, oft auch diese untergebracht in Flachbauten.

In jüngster Zeit wird die städtische Expansion nicht so sehr durch Bevölkerungswachstum verursacht, sondern vielmehr durch soziale, politische wie auch technologische Veränderungen. Die Zahl der Haushalte ist drastisch angestiegen, zugleich sind diese jedoch auch kleiner geworden, bedingt durch höhere Scheidungsraten, höhere Lebenserwartung und ähnliche Faktoren. Größere Mobilität der Menschen durch den allgemein verbreiteten Besitz eines Autos hat dazu geführt, daß Menschen sich in Vorstädten niederlassen können, ohne ihren Arbeitsplatz in der Nähe haben zu müssen. Darüber hinaus hat die Politik der Dezentralisierung die Regierungen in ihrem Trend zu weiterer Suburbanisierung bestärkt. Die Politik der EG hingegen hat nur marginale Auswirkungen auf diese Veränderungen gehabt. Die Regionalpolitik war ausgerichtet auf die Entwicklung altindustrieller Räume. In die Stadterneuerung ist zugleich in verstärktem Maße der Umweltschutz integriert worden. Es wäre jedoch kaum zutreffend, diese Maßnahmen als eine gezielte Stadtentwicklungspolitik anzusehen. Das wesentliche Ergebnis all diesen Strukturwandels ist ein stärker differenziertes Landnutzungsmuster im städtischen Bereich, das sich mehr oder weniger auch in der Differenzierung der Bodenpreise vom Stadtkern bis zur Peripherie widerspiegelt. In Frankreich haben die kommunalen Verwaltungen nun den Versuch unternommen, diese räumlich wirksamen Veränderungen aktiver zu steuern. Unterschiede in den politischen Strukturen erlauben es jedoch kaum, Entwicklungen dieser Art EG-weit zu generalisieren.

Probleme einer Verallgemeinerung der Handhabung von Stadterneuerung und Flächennutzung werden klar veranschaulicht in dem Beitrag von Lila Leontidou (Nationale Technische Universität Athen, Griechenland): 'Mediterrane Städte—divergente Entwicklungen in einem vereinten Europa' (Kap. 3).

Den Städten im mediterranen Europa kam seit langer Zeit und kommt auch heute noch eine zentrale kulturelle Rolle zu. Die Innenstädte—ob in Neapel, Athen oder Barcelona—dienten schon immer (und dienen auch heute noch) als Wohngebiete für gehobene Schichten, während Arbeiterviertel in Randbezirken zu finden sind. Die soziale und wirtschaftliche Differenzierung und Trennung, die so typisch für die Städte in Frankreich, Deutschland und Großbritannien ist, ist in diesen Ländern viel weniger ausgeprägt. Wie zu erwarten, ist der Einfluß der EG auf die Entwicklung dieser Städte bisher nur gering gewesen. Von den mediterranen Ländern ist nur Italien Gründungsmitglied der Gemeinschaft, Griechenland, Spanien und Portugal traten erst in den achtziger Jahren bei. Dies ist jedoch nur ein Teil der Erklärung. Ein weiterer ist, daß viele der dominierenden EG-Strategien bezüglich städtischer Regionen so ausgerichtet sind, daß sie für mediterrane Städte kaum relevant sind. So sind beispielsweise Indikatoren für Armut, die auf den Grad der Obdachlosigkeit bezogen sind, kaum brauchbar, wenn die Armen zwar eine 'Wohnung' haben, diese jedoch in einer behelfsmäßigen, selbst zusammengebauten Hütte in Slumgebieten besteht.

Dies illustriert die simple Tatsache, daß globale Strategien auch innerhalb einer Gruppe von Staaten, die so homogen erscheint wie die EG, kaum ihr Ziel erreichen, wenn sie nicht sehr fein auf regionale Bedingungen abgestimmt sind.

Strukturelle Veränderungen

Die Gründung der EG hat die ökonomischen wie auch die sozialen Zusammenhänge Westeuropas verändert und tiefgreifende strukturelle Wandlungen auf vielen Gebieten in Gang gebracht, sowohl durch gezielte Maßnahmen wie auch durch indirekte Anpassungen. Jean-Paul Charrié (Bordeaux III, Frankreich) zeichnet in seinem Beitrag 'Die Standorte der Industrie: Europäisierung im Gegensatz zu weltweiter Organisation' (Kap. 4) ein detailliertes Bild von den grundlegenden Veränderungen, die sich jetzt in einer Gruppe von Ländern vollziehen, von denen die größten die Wiege der industriellen Revolution im 19. Jahrhundert darstellten. Die EG ist noch immer eine wesentliche industrielle Macht in der Welt, aber die Basis ihrer führenden Position hat sich unausweichlich verändern müssen angesichts des Ausmaßes an Konkurrenz, das noch nie stärker war als jetzt. Viele der Veränderungen in den weltweiten industriellen Verhältnissen haben sich in den 40 Jahren seit der Gründung der Gemeinschaft vollzogen.

Die Länder der EG sind reich sowohl an Kohle als auch an Eisenerz und verfügen über bedeutende Produktionskapazitäten in vielen Schlüsselbereichen, wie etwa Eisen- und Stahlproduktion, Schiffbau und chemische Industrie. Die Industrie der EG stellt ein Potential dar, das seine Geburtsstunde in den fünfziger Jahren erlebte, und es ist kein Zufall, daß die ersten Erfolge auf die Montanunion zurückgehen. In einem Kontinent, der lange Zeit von Konflikten geschüttelt war, legte der Frieden von Paris die Grundlagen für eine Periode rechtlich gesicherten wirtschaftlichen Wachstums, das nur durch die Ölkrise 1973 unterbrochen wurde. Die Gemeinschaft mußte ihre industriellen Produktionsmethoden zuschneiden auf die wachsende Bedeutung des Öls sowie auch auf den steilen Anstieg seines Preises. Ebenso mußte sie sich anpassen an den Niedergang der Rohstoffindustrien, die der Schlüssel zum anfänglichen Erfolg waren, wie auch an die gleichzeitige Ausdehnung des High-Tech-Sektors.

Diese Veränderungen vollzogen sich angesichts der wachsenden Konkurrenz der erst in jüngster Zeit industrialisierten Länder. Die wirtschaftliche Bedrohung durch Japan ist am offensichtlichsten und auch am stärksten, da die Produkte dieses Landes direkt auf den traditionellen überseeischen Märkten der EG konkurrieren, besonders in Nordamerika. Gleichzeitig investieren japanische Unternehmer direkt in den EG-Ländern und versuchen so, die Bestimmungen zur Begrenzung japanischer Importe nach Europa zu umgehen. Hinzu kommt, daß ein wachsendes Interesse von den jüngst industrialisierten asiatischen Staaten, besonders von Südkorea, gezeigt wird. Diese waren zunächst auf den Markt der Textilproduktion eingestiegen, dehnen jedoch jetzt sehr schnell ihr Produktionsangebot aus.

All diese Veränderungen haben ihre Auswirkungen auf die industriellen Zentren Europas. Die traditionellen Industrieregionen leiden unter wachsenden Schwierigkeiten und sind teilweise im Rückgang begriffen. Es bedarf dringender Maßnahmen, um ihnen Möglichkeiten der Anpassung zu geben. Die wichtigen städtischen Zentren hingegen befinden sich in einer besseren Lage und sind aufs äußerste bemüht, sich diese Position zu erhalten.

Die Kommission wie auch die anderen EG-Institutionen waren über viele Jahre hinweg recht eingeschränkt in dem, was sie an Hilfsmaßnahmen, meist Maßnahmen zur Stärkung rückläufiger Wirtschaftsregionen, einzelner Wirtschaftssektoren oder problematischer Produktionsbetriebe, durchzuführen vermochten.

Jetzt jedoch beginnen sie zunehmend, eine führende Rolle in der Industriepolitik zu spielen. Die EG ist eine wichtige Kraft in der sich entwickelnden industriellen Landschaft. Sie stellt gezielte Hilfe für ausgewählte Wirtschaftssektoren bereit, koordiniert Forschungsbemühungen und übernimmt die Führung in einer neu belebten Regionalpolitik. Die Vollendung des Binnenmarktes wird darüber hinaus auch bedeutende Rückwirkungen auf das ganz allgemeine Industriepotential der Gemeinschaft haben.

Der Verkehr ist von Regierungen stets als einer der Schlüssel zur Steuerung der Dynamik industrieller Gesellschaften betrachtet worden. Auch die EG hat dieser Tatsache schon immer Aufmerksamkeit geschenkt, auch dann, wenn sie diesen Bereich auf der Ebene der Gemeinschaft nicht mit dem Nachdruck verfolgt hat, den man erwartet hätte.

James Killen (Trinity College, Dublin, Republik Irland) und Austin Smith (Ulster, United Kingdom) betrachten die Verkehrspolitik der EG im allgemeinen, unter besonderer Berücksichtigung Irlands als einer peripheren Region und im besonderen die Art und Weise, wie diese Politik—oder auch ihr Fehlen—die Wirtschaftsentwicklung der irischen Insel insgesamt berührt hat.

Die nationalen Regierungen haben traditionsgemäß auf zweierlei Weise versucht, die Verkehrssysteme wie auch den Verkehr selbst in ihren Ländern zu beeinflussen. Auf der einen Seite hat die EG übergeordnet den Verkehr strukturiert, indem sie zum Beispiel Geschwindigkeitsbegrenzungen festgesetzt und auch Richtlinien, nach denen Berechtigungen verschiedenster Art erteilt werden sollen, herausgegeben hat. In Westeuropa hat die EG schon eine direkte Rolle übernommen bezüglich des Angebots des Eisenbahnverkehrs wie auch in einigen Fällen des Bus- und Frachtverkehrs auf der Straße. Dies gibt der EG die Möglichkeit, sehr direkt den Grad der Konkurrenz unter den verschiedenen Verkehrsarten zu kontrollieren.

Zum anderen haben die Regierungen versucht, Grad und Art der Investitionen auf dem Gebiet der Verkehrsinfrastruktur zu beeinflussen, besonders im Hinblick auf die Größenordnung des investierten Kapitals im Vergleich zu anderen Wirtschaftssektoren und auf die Zielsetzungenen, für die das Geld konkret eingesetzt wird.

Vor der Unterzeichnung der Römischen Verträge war die Verkehrspolitik mehr oder weniger von jedem Staat, unabhängig von den Nachbarstaaten, selbst betrieben worden. Theoretisch war zwar eine Zusammenarbeit auf europäischer Ebene im Rahmen der 1953 eingerichteten Europäischen Konferenz der Verkehrsminister durchaus möglich, aber abgesehen von dem Eisenbahnnetz für den Trans European Express (TEE) wurde wenig Substantielles erreicht. In den Römischen Verträgen ist ein ausdrückliches Übereinkommen enthalten, das besagt, daß eine gemeinsame Verkehrspolitik anzustreben sei. Die Tatsache jedoch, daß jeder Staat schon seine nationale Verkehrspolitik entwickelt hatte, erschwerte EG-weite Vereinbarungen.

Das vornehmliche Ziel des Beitrags über Verkehr in der EG ist es zu zeigen, wie die verhältnismäßig wenigen Vereinbarungen auf den unterschiedlichen Gebieten (Straßen-, Eisenbahn-, See- und Luftverkehr) der wirtschaftlichen Entwicklung Irlands als einem Mitgliedstaat der Gemeinschaft, gelegen an der Peripherie aller großen und zentralen Verkehrsnetze, geholfen haben.

Trotz unabdingbarer nationaler und regionaler Varianten verfügt die EG insgesamt doch über ein beneidenswertes Verkehrsnetz, das wirksam zum Zusammenhalt der Gemeinschaft beigetragen hat. Es ermöglichte und ermöglicht auch die Mobilität von Arbeitskräften, die einen wesentlichen Beitrag zum wirtschaftlichen Erfolg Westeuropas geleistet hat.

Russell King (Trinity College, Dublin, Republik Irland) behandelt in seinem Beitrag 'Migration und der einheitliche Arbeitsmarkt, ein Beitrag zur regionalen Entwicklung' (Kap. 6) den Einfluß internationaler Wanderungsbewegungen seit den späten fünfziger Jahren auf die sich wandelnden wirtschaftlichen und sozialen geographischen Verhältnisse der EG-länder. Arbeitsmigranten waren ein wesentliches Element der Wachstumsprozesse der industriellen sowie postindustriellen Wirtschaft während der sechziger und siebziger Jahre. Die Zahl der eigentlichen Arbeitsmigranten war nach der ersten Ölkrise von 1973/4 rückläufig, der Nachzug von Familienmitgliedern hielt jedoch an. Ein Anstieg der Zahl der Migranten in den EG-Ländern war während der achtziger und zu Beginn der neunziger Jahre zu verzeichnen, und die Gesamtzahl der in Westeuropa lebenden Migranten, der größte Teil in der EG wohnhaft, wird heute auf etwa 20 Millionen geschätzt.

Nachdem die internationalen Wanderungsbewegungen während der späten siebziger und frühen achtziger Jahre als politischer Faktor vernachlässigt worden waren, hat in jüngster Zeit die Einwanderungsfrage in ganz Westeuropa erneut Aufmerksamkeit erregt. Die Zahl der Arbeitsmigranten hat während der achtziger Jahre wieder verstärkt zugenommen, in einigen

Ländern (Niederlande, Bundesrepublik Deutschland) schon seit 1985. Der wirklich bedeutsame Auslöser jedoch zu einer neuen Massenwanderung war der Zusammenbruch der sozialistischen Staaten Osteuropas und der Sowjetunion. Die unvorhergesehenen Ereignisse der letzten drei Jahre machen deutlich, daß Vorsicht geboten ist bei Vorhersagen internationaler Wanderungsentwicklungen. Nur wenige haben 1988 die dramatischen Ereignisse voraussagen können, die sich in Osteuropa zugetragen haben, auch wenn die Zuwanderung von Flüchtlingen aus der DDR noch vor deren Zusammenbruch eine vorausweisende Initialzündung war, die den Prozess der Veränderung in Gang setzte.

Zudem sind noch andere Faktoren für die Migration nach Westeuropa von Bedeutung. In der ganzen Welt sind Millionen von Menschen unterwegs, ihre Wanderungen verändern die Welt und auch Europa. So ist die Zahl von Flüchtlingen und Asylbewerbern in Westeuropa während der achtziger Jahre stark angewachsen. Dieser Problematik muß nun sehr klar ins Auge gesehen werden, auf EG-Ebene wie auch auf der Ebene der jeweiligen nationalen Politik. Zu nennen ist in diesem Zusammenhang das Schengener Abkommen, das Regelungen für die Aufhebung der Grenzkontrollen zwischen einigen EG-Staaten (bei gleichzeitiger Verstärkung der Außengrenzen) beinhaltet.

Ein besonderes Problem, das mit internationalen Wanderungen verbunden ist, innerhalb wie auch außerhalb der EG, ist die illegale Lohnarbeit, ein Vorgang, der sehr anschaulich von Solange Montagné-Villette (Poitièrs, Frankreich) in ihrem Beitrag 'Wanderungen, inoffizielle und illegale Lohnarbeit' (Kap. 7) beschrieben wird. Daß Menschen inoffiziell und meist illegal arbeiten, ist in den Ländern der EG keine Neuheit. Dies begann bereits in den frühen Jahren unseres Jahrhunderts, als neue Verwaltungsstrukturen in allen entwickelten Industriestaaten eingerichtet wurden und stieg ständig an im Zusammenhang mit dem enger werdenden Netz an Sozialversicherungssystemen. Heute ist eine solche illegale Arbeit in einigen Ländern Teil einer gut fundierten Tradition, sie wird von vielen als ein Teil nationaler Kultur angesehen. Im Gegensatz dazu weist illegale Arbeit auf der Ebene einer Staatengemeinschaft wie der EG traditionelle Erscheinungen auf, die bisher wenig Beachtung gefunden haben, nicht zuletzt deshalb, weil die Ausweitung dieses Phänomens recht neu ist. Die größere Mobilität von Arbeitskräften sowie das Wachstum von Industrie und Handel haben völlig neue illegale Beschäftigungspraktiken hervorgerufen, deren Formen eng mit den politischen, wirtschaftlichen und rechtlichen Strukturen der EG zusammenhängen. Die Zahl der Arbeiter, die aus ärmeren EG-Ländern kommend Beschäftigung in anderen Mitgliedstaaten suchen, Umsiedlung und/oder Unterverträge ungesetzlicher industrieller Aktivitäten in den mediterranen Ländern sowie illegale Beschäftigung von Nicht-EG-Bürgern eben dort sind Belege für die zunehmende Ausbreitung illegaler Beschäftigungspraktiken. Soweit es die EG betrifft, ist das Auftreten von Arbeitsmigranten nur sehr langsam als Problem erfaßt worden. Es besteht eine bemerkenswerte Unkenntnis und Nachlässigkeit einiger Mitgliedstaaten, besonders Großbritanniens, bezüglich der Erkenntnis, daß die Kontrolle von Arbeitsverhältnissen und auch andere Aspekte sozialer Kontrollen eng verknüpft sind mit dem freien Markt, den alle anstreben und dem sich alle verpflichtet fühlen.

Anpassung des ländlichen Raumes

Eine politische Maßnahme, nämlich die sogenannte Community Agricultural Policy (CAP), hat die EG über nahezu 30 Jahre hinweg dominiert, was sich auch im Budget widerspiegelt; zeitweilig wurden 90 Prozent des EG-Haushalts hierauf verwendet und auch heute sind es noch 60 Prozent. Dieser Sachbereich ist wohl bekannt und nicht Gegenstand dieses Buches. Jedes ernsthafte Studium der EG muß jedoch einen wesentlichen Teil der Landwirtschaft widmen. Die übermäßige Betonung der Landwirtschaft beginnt allerdings nun zu schwinden, dies wird jedoch ernsthafte und weitreichende Rückwirkungen auf die ländliche Wirtschaft wie auch auf die Landschaft haben. Dietrich Denecke (Göttingen, Deutschland) analysiert in seinem Beitrag 'Landnutzungswandel, Abwanderung und Stillegungsprogramme' (Kap. 8) das Ziel einer Landschaftspflege in Europa, besonders bezogen auf Deutschland, sowie die Konsequenzen dieses bevorstehenden Wandels hin zu einer Agrarpolitik zugunsten von Landschaft und Umwelt. Beispiele werden herangezogen aus den besonders sensiblen Agrarlandschaften Deutschlands, wo traditionelle bäuerliche und moderne technisierte Landwirtschaft noch nebeneinander bestehen.

Bis weit in unser Jahrhundert hinein hat der Mangel an Nahrungsmitteln bedeutet, daß Agrarland so intensiv wie möglich genutzt wurde. In den letzten 20 Jahren hat sich jedoch ein radikaler Wandel abgezeichnet. Überproduktion hat zum Anbau alternativer Feldfrüchte, zur Einführung von Extensivierung, zu Grünland- und Stillegungsprogrammen und nicht zuletzt zur Aufgabe von Betrieben und agrarem Nutzland geführt. Diese Veränderungen und die wirtschaftspolitischen Maßnahmen, die sie hervorriefen, beherrschen jetzt auf breiter Ebene die Agrarwirtschaft in Westeuropa. Gleichzeitig wird einerseits die Zahl der Betriebe reduziert und andererseits Viehhaltung und Feldbau zunehmend intensiviert, was umweltschädliche Nebeneffekte mit sich bringt. Beide Vorgänge tragen dazu bei, das empfindliche ökologische Gleichgewicht in der Agrarlandschaft zu stören, dessen Erhalt durch traditionelle landwirtschaftliche Methoden fast ein festgeschriebenes Bekenntnis der EG geworden ist. Das Ziel, eine von ökologischen Gesichtspunkten her akzeptable Landwirtschaft anzustreben, die auch das Ziel der Landschaftserhaltung fördern würde, ist somit zu einem entscheidenden Problembereich für die weitere Entwicklung agrarpolitischer Maßnahmen der Gemeinschaft geworden, was zudem mit wesentlichen weiteren Verzweigungen im gesamten Prozeß einer revidierten Agrarpolikit der Gemeinschaft verbunden ist.

Auch wenn sich die Agrarpolitik im Rahmen der CAP nun zu wandeln beginnt und die Strategie der Subvention agrarischer Produktion (offensichtlich ohne Rücksicht auf die Kosten oder die unmittelbare Notwendigkeit) zunehmend in Frage gestellt wird, so ist sie dennoch bis heute ein Eckpfeiler dcr EG-Politik geblieben.

Manuel Corbera (Cantabria, Spanien) schätzt die CAP aus spanischer Perspektive neu ein in seinem Beitrag 'Die gemeinsame Agrarpolitik und die Entwicklung der Landwirtschaft: Probleme und Perspektiven' (Kap. 9). Spanien, erst vor wenigen Jahren (1986) der EG beigetreten, ist ein Land, das über eine weit gefächerte agrarische Produktion verfügt. Die Gemeinschaft insgesamt steht an erster Stelle, was die weltweite agrarische Produktion betrifft, sie ist der führende Produzent für Milch, Butter, Käse, Wein, Zucker und Rindfleisch und nimmt den zweiten Platz ein in der Produktion von Weizen und Gerste. Die EG ist autark bezüglich aller alltäglichen Nahrungsmittel, mit Ausnahme von frischen Früchten, Mais sowie Schaf- und Ziegenfleisch.

Diese bevorzugte Situation liegt zum Teil in extrem günstigen natürlichen Bedingungen begründet sowie in den sich im agrarischen Produktionsprozess ergänzenden atlantischen, kontinentalen und mediterranen Klimaverhältnissen. Die angewandten Anbau- und Produktionsmethoden sind ebenfalls von entscheidender Bedeutung: intensive Bodennutzung, Anbausysteme, die gut an die natürlichen Bedingungen angepaßt sind, effiziente Betriebseinrichtungen sowie ein hoher Mechanisierungsstandard ermöglichen gesicherte hohe Erträge.

Der wirtschaftliche Erfolg der EG geht jedoch wesentlich auf den Erfolg der CAP zurück, die die Entwicklung der Industrie für eine ganze Generation angeregt und unterstützt hat. Ohne diese CAP wäre keiner der Mitgliedstaaten allein weltführend, und nur in diesem Lichte kann eine Beurteilung der Einzelstaaten vorgenommen werden. So ist sicherlich trotz vieler Probleme und der klaren Notwendigkeit weiterer Reformen die Agrarpolitik der EG heute wie auch in Zukunft ein Erfolg.

Dieser Erfolg der Agrarpolitik in Bezug auf die Nahrungsmittelproduktion kann jedoch nicht die Krise verdecken, in der viele ländlichen Regionen stecken. Es ist kein Bedarf mehr vorhanden für so viel Land, besonders für marginales Land, und es müssen Alternativen gefunden werden sowohl für das Land selbst als auch für die Menschen, die dieses Land einst traditionell bewirtschaftet haben. Das Land aus der Produktion zu nehmen und die Landschaft pflegerisch zu gestalten ist eine Alternative, die weiter oben diskutiert worden ist. Dies wirft jedoch die Frage nach der wirtschaftlichen wie finanziellen Belastung auf, die den sonst stabilen und sozial zusammen-haltenden Gemeinden aufgebürdet werden. Die offensichtlichste Alternative ist es, auf die steigende Möglichkeit der touristischen Nutzung ländlicher Gebiete zu setzen, besonders in den Berg- und Küstengebieten Europas.

Allan Williams und Gareth Shaw (Exeter, England) untersuchen in ihrem Beitrag 'Tourismus—Möglichkeiten, Herausforderungen und Widersprüche in der EG' (Kap. 10) das komplexe Phänomen des Tourismus in den Ländern der Gemeinschaft. Seit dem Beginn des Massentourismus in den sechziger Jahren kann der Tourismus als ein wesentlicher Leitfaden in der wirtschaftlichen und sozialen Struktur der EG angesehen werden, er ist von führender ökonomischer Bedeutung. Von 20 Beschäftigten sind mehr als einer in diesem Bereich tätig. Der Tourismus ist auch ein Instrument sozialen Wandels, da er den Austausch von Werten und Lebensweisen fördert und einen der wenigen Kanäle für Austausch in großem Stil zwischen Menschen und Kulturen innerhalb der EG bietet. Es wäre eine zu erörternde Frage, ob es eine europäische kulturelle Identität gibt und wenn dem so ist, in welcher Weise der Tourismus dazu beigetragen hat und beiträgt.

So steht der Tourismus im Mittelpunkt grenzüberschreitender Bewegungen innerhalb der EG, er steht an vorderster Stelle auf dem Wege der Öffnung hin zu einem einheitlichen Markt. Diese überragende Bedeutung des Fremden-verkehrs für die Europäische Gemeinschaft mag durch folgendes verdeutlicht werden: 64 Prozent des internationalen Tourismus spielen sich innerhalb Europas ab, und die EG hat den größten Anteil an diesem Markt. Mehr als in allen anderen Regionen der Welt ist der Tourismus in den EG-Ländern von grundlegender Bedeutung für Produktion und Konsum im städtischen wie auch im ländlichen Bereich.

Auswirkungen auf die Umwelt

Die Umwelt fand keinerlei Beachtung in den Verträgen von Paris und Rom, und diese Tatsache erschwerte eine direkte Beteiligung der EG an relevanten Beschlüssen trotz zunehmender öffentlicher Aufmerksamkeit und Beunruhigung über Umweltschäden und Verbrauch von Ressourcen während der sechziger und siebziger Jahre. Hinzu kam die Einsicht, daß es unrealistisch ist, Umweltprobleme im nationalen Rahmen zu lösen. Selbst der EG-Raum, zwischen 1958 und 1986 von sechs auf zwölf Länder angewachsen und zunehmend eine räumliche Differenzierung darstellend, ist in keiner Weise eine natürliche räumliche Einheit, für die sich generelle Lösungen entwickeln ließen und lassen. Vielmehr sind die Probleme des Umgangs mit der Umwelt und den Ressourcen immer komplexer geworden.

Der Hauptvorzug, den die öffentliche Meinung der EG als Träger einer Umweltpolitik zuschrieb, war wohl ihre multinationale Struktur, durch die der offensichtlichen Universalität der den Umweltschutz betreffenden Fragen Rechnung getragen werden konnte. Mark Blacksell (Exeter, England) beschäftigt sich in seinem Beitrag 'Umweltpolitik und Ressourcen-Management' (Kap. 11) mit dem recht dornigen Weg, der zur Verwirklichung einer weiten Skala umweltpolitischer Maßnahmen führte, die jetzt einen zunehmend wichtigen Teil der EG-Politik ausmachen. Es ist heute deutlich, daß die besten Lösungen für viele brennende Umweltprobleme, wie etwa Luft- und Wasserverschmutzung oder auch Müllbeseitigung, in den einzelnen EG-Ländern merkliche Unterschiede aufweisen. Ein EG-weiter politischer Konsens darüber, wie diese Probleme zu lösen sind, hat sich als nur schwer erreichbar erwiesen. Wirtschaftlich stärkere Länder lassen sich leichter von Vorteilen langfristiger Umweltverbesserung im Gegensatz zu kurzfristigen wirtschaftlichen Gewinnen überzeugen, und so ist es zu harten Auseinandersetzungen zwischen den führenden Industrienationen im Zentrum der EG und einigen erst jüngst in die EG aufgenommenen Mitgliedstaaten der nördlichen wie auch der mediterranen Peripherie gekommen.

In ähnlicher Weise tendieren Inselstaaten, auf deren Territorium kurze, schnellfließende Flüsse anzutreffen sind (Irland, Großbritannien), zu geringerer Besorgnis über die Nutzung dieser Gewässer als Abwasserkanäle als etwa die kontinentalen Länder (Frankreich, Deutschland u.a.), die von größeren, internationalen Wasserwegen durchquert werden. Gleichermaßen wird auch die Luftverschmutzung, die leicht von vorherrschenden Winden auch über nationale Grenzen hinweggetragen werden und sich auf dem Gebiet anderer Staaten niederschlagen kann, von Verursachern und Betroffenen sehr unterschiedlich beurteilt. Im allgemeinen sind die Staaten am westlichen Rand der EG bereit, Emissionswerte zu akzeptieren, die von ihren östlichen Nachbarn als bedrohlich angesehen werden. Eine solche Selbstzufriedenheit wird jedoch sehr schnell angreifbar, sobald geringe Effekte langfristiger Luftverschmutzung besser nachgewiesen werden können.

In den vier Jahrzehnten ihres Bestehens hat die EG eine schwierige Gradwanderung machen müssen zwischen den ihr auferlegten Beschränkungen, den konfliktgeladenen Verhaltensweisen einer wachsenden Zahl von Mitgliedern und einer zunehmend unabhängigen europäischen

Meinung, unterstützt und angestachelt seit 1979 durch das Europäische
Parlament.

Anfänglich waren die Eingriffe der EG in Bereiche der Umweltpolitik
ausdrücklich verbunden mit wirtschaftlichen Belangen und Maßnahmen, die
jede Beeinträchtigung freier Konkurrenz vermeiden sollten. Nach 1972
jedoch, mit der Einberufung der UN-Konferenz zur humanen Umwelt,
wurden die Eingriffe in wachsendem Maße bestimmter und, als solche
erkennbar, auch gezielter. Eine Serie von Umweltaktionsprogrammen gipfelte
dann darin, daß die Umwelt in der Einheitlichen Europäischen Akte zu
einem Zuständigkeitsbereich der EG erklärt wurde. Seit dem Inkrafttreten
dieser Vereinbarungen hat die EG eine weit dominantere und positivere
Stellung in der Abfassung wie auch in der Durchsetzung einer Umweltpolitik
erlangt. Um den Wandel hier besser verstehen zu können, müssen vier
entscheidende Punkte verdeutlicht werden:

1. die Bedeutung der Akte und ihre Verflechtung mit der nationalen
   Gesetzgebung der einzelnen Mitgliedstaaten;
2. das Feld von Umweltbelangen, das in vier Umweltaktionsprogrammen
   und mehr als 180 Direktiven und anders gearteten gesetzlichen
   Verbindlichkeiten angesprochen wird;
3. Gebiete aktiver Umweltpolitik, vornehmlich verknüpft mit der gemeinsamen Agrarpolitik, die außerhalb der Grenzen der eigentlichen Umweltpolitik entstanden sind;
4. die politischen Fragen einer Umsetzung der Verordnungen, ihre
   Kontrolle und Implementierung.

Natürlich kann die Effektivität dieser Umweltpolitik in vollem Maße nur
nach ihren realen Auswirkungen beurteilt werden. So gibt Michael Quigley
(Trinity College, Dublin, Republik Irland) in seinem Beitrag 'Die Auswirkungen der EG-Politik auf die Agrarlandschaft und Umwelt in Irland'
(Kap. 12) eine eingehende Einschätzung einiger EG-Maßnahmen in Bezug
auf Irland, einem Land, dessen Landschaftsbild weitgehend ländlich geprägt
ist und in dem die Agrarwirtschaft, besonders die Viehwirtschaft, der
dominierende Wirtschaftszweig ist. Die irische Landwirtschaft wurde bereits
vor Irlands EG-Beitritt im Jahre 1973 erweitert und modernisiert, Tempo
und Richtung des Wandels waren dann jedoch zunehmend mit politischen
Gegensätzen verbunden, die von Brüssel kamen. Agrarische Landnutzung
und Umweltqualität werden durch drei getrennte Bereiche der europäischen
Politik beeinflußt: am deutlichsten durch die CAP, die alle Gebiete der
Agrarwirtschaft betrifft, des weiteren durch Strukturprogramme, die, auch
wenn sie grundsätzlich nicht agrarisch ausgerichtet sind, Mittel für eine

Vielzahl von Leitprogrammen im Rahmen einer EG-Förderung bereitstellen, die sich auf den ländlichen Raum auswirken. Den dritten Bereich stellen Umweltpolitik und -gesetzgebung dar, entweder in Form einer Kontrolle negativer Nebeneffekte anderer politischer Maßnahmen oder im positiven Sinne in der Erhaltung verschiedener Bereiche der Umwelt.

Für Irland ist die gemeinschaftliche Agrarpolitik mit all ihren Verzweigungen ein besonders wichtiger Bestimmungsfaktor, nicht nur im Hinblick auf wirtschaftliches Wohlbefinden, sondern auch in Bezug auf Landschaftswandel und Umweltverhältnisse. Diese politischen Gegensätze betreffen die landwirtschaftlichen Entwicklungen auf zweierlei Weise: zum einen durch eine Marktkontrolle im Rahmen von Preisstützungsmechanismen und zum anderen durch eine Reihe horizontal ausgerichteter Strukturmaßnahmen, die darauf abzielen, Landwirte in bestimmten Gebieten für die ungünstigen natürlichen Bedingungen, unter denen sie zu wirtschaften haben, zu entschädigen. Der erste Faktor hat einen Prozeß landwirtschaftlicher Intensivierung zur Folge, da die Höhe der finanziellen Unterstützung auf den Umfang der Produktion bezogen ist. Dies wiederum führt unausweichlich nicht nur zu Überproduktion und zur Anhäufung von Überschüssen an Nahrungsmitteln, sondern außerdem zu Umweltbelastungen. Die Auswirkungen, die das Bereitstellen großer Geldsummen aus dem FEOGA-Fond auf die Landwirtschaft hatte, sind besonders auf dem Sektor der agrarischen Marktproduktion sehr deutlich gewesen. So ist als Antwort auf Maßnahmen der EG zum Beispiel die Zahl der Schafe in den letzten Jahren dramatisch angewachsen, was zu Problemen der Überweidung und zu Erosion geführt hat. Wirtschaftsweisen nach Maß haben zu regionaler Spezialisierung einiger Agrarbetriebe geführt, besonders in der Schweine- und Geflügelhaltung. Dies hat, unglücklicherweise, durch das Anfallen großer Mengen an Viehdung und der folgenden Verschmutzung von Flüssen schädliche Effekte auf die Umwelt ausgelöst. Andere Aspekte der Intensivierung, wie zum Beispiel der zunehmende Gebrauch an Düngemitteln und besonders der Ersatz der Heugewinnung durch Silage, haben ebenfalls zu Problemen der Wasserverschmutzung geführt. Auch können strukturfördernde Mittel des FEOGA, die in marginale Agrargebiete gelenkt werden, um diese produktiver zu machen, negative Auswirkungen auf empfindliche Umweltverhältnisse haben. Das sogenannte 'Western Package', bestimmt zur Anregung agrarischer Entwicklung im westlichen Irland wie auch das 'Western Drainage Scheme' sind Beispiele EG-unterstützter Maßnahmen, die schädliche Effekte auf die Umwelt ausgelöst haben.

Die irische Forstwirtschaft erfährt momentan eine umfangreiche Expansion mit einer Verdoppelung der jährlichen Planungsraten von 15 000 auf 30 000

Hektar. Dieser vorher nie dagewesene Entwicklungsgrad geht weitgehend auf Zuschüsse zurück, unterstützt durch Mittel der EG im Rahmen des 'Forestry Operational Programme'. Einige Folgewirkungen der forstwirtschaftlichen Entwicklung in Irland sind die Übersäuerung der Oberflächengewässer, ein Rückgang der natürlichen Fischerei, die Zerstörung bedeutender Ökosysteme in Niedermooren des Tieflandes sowie die Veränderung noch weitgehend natürlicher Landschaften von bemerkenswerter Naturschönheit.

Seit Mitte der achtziger Jahre hat sich der Schwerpunkt von der intensiven Landwirtschaft wegverlagert, teilweise als Antwort auf die Notwendigkeit einer Reduzierung der Agrarproduktion in der Gemeinschaft, teilweise auch wegen der umweltschädlichen Auswirkungen.

Diese Entwicklung hat zu einer Serie neuer radikaler Maßnahmen geführt, in denen die doppelte Rolle der Landwirte als Nahrungsmittelproduzenten einerseits und als Landschaftspfleger andererseits betont wird, politische Grundsätze, von denen die Umwelt ohne Zweifel profitieren wird. Gleichzeitig wird sich in diesem Zusammenhang die Verstärkung der EG-Umweltpolitik mit Maßnahmen wie der 'Environmental Impact Assessment Directive' und der 'Habitats Directive' als nützlich erweisen. Für Irland jedoch werden die regionalen Entwicklungsfonds, die großzügig erweitert worden sind, eine der größten möglichen Umweltbedrohungen darstellen. Es bleibt abzuwarten, ob die Überzeugung, die Umwelt zu schützen, wohl fundiert ist.

Die Umwelt hat großen Einfluß auf den Gesundheitszustand der Menschen. Cosimo Palagiano (La Sapienza, Rom, Italien) untersucht in seinem Beitrag 'Umwelt, Gesundheit und Gesundheitswesen: Ein europäischer Vergleich und eine italienische Fallstudie' (Kap. 13) die Art und Weise, in der die EG Gesundheit und Gesundheitspflege in der Gemeinschaft beeinflußt hat. Die EG-Gesundheitspolitik ist ein Gebiet, das zu analysieren vernachlässigt worden ist, obwohl die Gemeinschaft zunehmend in gesundheitsrelevante Angelegenheiten hineingezogen wurde, zum Beispiel durch die politischen Umweltgrundsätze, durch die vorgesehenen Rechtsvorgaben im Vertrag von Maastricht sowie durch politische Entscheidungen zur Intensivierung wie auch Extensivierung der Landwirtschaft.

Die Ziele dieses Beitrags sind folgende: erstens sollen die Gesundheitsbedingungen in der EG kritisch dargestellt werden, unter Anwendung einer Reihe von Indikatoren bezüglich Dienstleistungen im Gesundheitswesen wie auch des allgemeinen Gesundheitszustandes. Die Ergebnisse machen deutlich, daß noch immer Unterschiede in der Lebenserwartung und auch im Auftreten von Krankheiten bestehen, selbst in dieser weitgehend homogenen Gruppe recht wohlhabender Staaten.

Zweitens soll das fortdauernde Auftreten von Unterschieden in den Gesundheitsverhältnissen innerhalb der einzelnen Länder beleuchtet werden. Italien wurde als Fallstudie gewählt, weil es zum einen in diesem Lande fortwährende tiefgreifende regionale Unterschiede gibt und zum anderen, weil über die dortigen Gesundheitsverhältnisse bisher verhältnismäßig wenig Material in englischer Sprache vorhanden ist (im Vergleich etwa zu den nördlichen Staaten). Zum Schluß wird noch die Frage nach der jetzigen wie auch der möglichen zukünftigen Wichtigkeit von Fragen bezüglich der Gesundheit in der EG aufgeworfen.

In der Schlußbetrachtung 'Eine sich wandelnde Landkarte und neue Prioritäten—die EG an der Schwelle zum 21. Jahrhundert' (Kap. 14) werfen Allan Williams und Mark Blacksell (Exeter, England) einen Blick auf die Richtungen, in die sich die EG möglicherweise auf dem Weg ins 21. Jahrhundert entwickeln könnte, und auf den Einfluß, den diese Veränderungen auf die Politik der Gemeinschaft haben könnten, vornehmlich unter dem Gesichtspunkt der ökonomischen wie auch der ökologischen Entwicklung.

Η ΕΥΡΩΠΑΪΚΗ ΠΡΟΚΛΗΣΗ: ΓΕΩΓΡΑΦΙΑ ΚΑΙ ΑΝΑΠΤΥΞΗ ΣΤΙΣ ΕΥΡΩΠΑΪΚΕΣ ΚΟΙΝΟΤΗΤΕΣ

Η δημιουργία των Ευρωπαϊκών Κοινοτήτων (ΕΚ) ήταν το πιο σημαντικό γεγονός για την οικονομική, πολιτική και κοινωνική γεωγραφία της Ευρώπης στο δεύτερο ήμισυ του εικοστού αιώνα. Βρίσκουμε τις απαρχές της στη δεκαετία του 1950 με τη Συνθήκη των Παρισίων (1952), οπότε ανέκυψε η Ευρωπαϊκή Κοινότητα Άνθρακος και Χάλυβος, και αργότερα στις δυο Συνθήκες της Ρώμης (1958), που συνέστησαν την Ευρωπαϊκή Οικονομική Κοινότητα (ΕΟΚ) και την Euratom. Πιο πρόσφατα, με την Ενιαία Ευρωπαϊκή Πράξη (1986) που ανοίγει το δρόμο για την Ενιαία Αγορά το 1993, και τώρα με τις κοπιώδεις και φορτισμένες διαπραγματεύσεις για τη Συνθήκη του Maastricht και την πλήρη νομισματική ενοποίηση, οι ΕΚ εξελίχθηκαν σε σύνθετη πολιτική ενότητα, που σήμερα επηρρεάξει πλέον κυρίαρχα και καθοριστικά το μέλλον των δώδεκα Ευρωπαϊκών κρατών-μελών.

Η αυξανόμενη θεσμική πολυπλοκότητα των ΕΚ συμβάδισε με την αύξηση των μελών τους. Για μια περίπου εικοσαετία, από το 1952 μέχρι το 1973, υπήρχαν μόνο έξη μέλη—Βέλγιο, Γαλλία, Ομοσπονδιακή Δημοκρατία της Γερμανίας, Ιταλία, Λουξεμβούργο και Ολλανδία— όλες βιομηχανικές χώρες στην καρδιά της δυτικής Ευρώπης, που ανορθωνόταν οικονομικά μετά από δυο καταστροφικούς παγκόσμιους πολέμους το πρώτο μισό του εικοστού αιώνα. Η πρώτη διεύρυνση το 1973 προσέθεσε τρία ακόμα κράτη-μέλη—Δανία, Ιρλανδία και Ενωμένο Βασίλειο—όλα βορειοευρωπαϊκά και αλληλένδετα από οικονομική άποψη, τόσο μεταξύ τους, όσο και με τα ιδρυτικά κράτη-μέλη. Η συνένωσή τους μετέβαλε τη φύση των ΕΚ: τα προβλήματα που σχετίζονται με την περιφερειακότητα αναπόφευκτα οξύνθηκαν και η γεωγραφική συνοχή των Κοινοτήτων, αρχικά πηγή μεγάλης δύναμης, υπονομεύθηκε από την προσθήκη δυό κρατών-νησιών, από τα οποία το Ενωμένο Βασίλειο αντιπροσώπευε περισσότερο από 20% του συνολικού πληθυσμού. Τη δεκαετία του 1980 συναντάμε περαιτέρω διευρύνσεις, με την Ελλάδα το 1981, την Ισπανία και την Πορτογαλία το 1986. Ακόμα μια φορά, η αθροιστική επίπτωση αυτής της Μεσογειακής διεύρυνσης θα μετέβαλε ριζικά τη φύση των ΕΚ. Και τα τρία νέα κράτη-μέλη διέφεραν από το βιομηχανικό πυρήνα της δυτικής Ευρώπης, τόσο από άποψη γεωγραφική, όσο και από οικονομική.

Στο αγροτικό τοπίο κυριαρχούσαν ακόμη παραδοσιακοί αγρότες και κατάλοιπα, ενώ κανένα από τα νέα μέλη δεν αποτελούσε πλήρες μέρος της κυρίως Ευρωπαϊκής αστικής-βιομηχανικής οικονομίας, εκτός από τον ρόλο του ως πηγής φτηνού εργατικού δυναμικού από μετανάστες.

Τη δεκαετία του 1990 μεταβάλλεται, πάλι, η εστία του μετασχηματισμού των ΕΚ. Η ενοποίηση της Γερμανίας το 1990 σήμανε την ένταξη (άν και μέσω απορρόφησης), ενός ανατολικοευρωπαϊκού μέλους, της πρώην Λαϊκής Δημοκρατίας της Γερμανίας (DDR), η οποία προσέθεσε μια νέα διάσταση στον περιφερειακό οικονομικό χάρτη. Πώς να συμπεριληφθούν μέλη των οποίων οι βιομηχανικές οικονομίες είχαν αναπτυχθεί μέσω ενός κεντρικά σχεδιαζόμενου, και τώρα κατά τα φαινόμενα χρεωκοπημένου, συστήματος; Η ενοποιημένη Γερμανία μάλλον θα ενσωματωθεί τελικά στις ΕΚ χωρίς θεμελιώδεις αλλαγές, αλλά αν προστεθούν άλλες ανατολικοευρωπαϊκές χώρες—Πολωνία, Ουγγαρία, Τσέχικα και Σλοβάκικα κράτη που ανακύπτουν από την πρώην Τσεχοσλοβακία, καθώς και η Σλοβενία, Κροατία και οποιαδήποτε άλλα κράτη επιβιώσουν από τα ερείπια της Γιουγκοσλαβίας—τότε ολόκληρη η οικονομική και πολιτική λογική των Κοινοτήτων θα πρέπει να μεταβληθεί.

Και δεν είναι η πολιτική αναστάτωση στην ανατολική Ευρώπη ο μόνος φορέας αλλαγής. Μια μεγάλη ομάδα χωρών της δυτικής Ευρώπης, που για οιονδήποτε λόγο δεν είχαν τη δυνατότητα να ενσωματωθούν στην Κοινότητα αρχικά, τώρα περιμένουν να γίνουν δεκτές. Το 1991 η Ευρωπαϊκή Ζώνη Ελευθέρων Συναλλαγών (ΕΖΕΣ, European Free Trade Association, EFTA) και επτά χώρες—Αυστρία, φινλανδία, Ισλανδία, Λίχτενσταϊν, Νορβηγία, Σουηδία και Ελβετία—υπέγραψαν μια συμφωνία με τις ΕΚ να σχηματίσουν την Ευρωπαϊκή Οικονομική Περιοχή (European Economic Area, EEA), δηλ. να διευρύνουν τη ζώνη ελευθέρου εμπορίου σε ολόκληρη τη δυτική Ευρώπη. Στη συνέχεια, η Αυστρία, η Ελβετία και η Σουηδία πήγαν ακόμα μακρύτερα, με τις αιτήσεις τους για πλήρη ένταξη στις ΕΚ, και υπάρχει το ενδεχόμενο ότι και άλλες χώρες της EEA θα ακολουθήσουν.

Τέλος, υπάρχουν και άλλα κράτη που επιθυμούν να γίνουν μέλη στο απώτερο μέλλον. Η Τουρκία, η Μάλτα και η Κύπρος ελίσσονται με σκοπό την ένταξη εδώ και τριάντα περίπου χρόνια, και τώρα πολλές από τις δημοκρατίες που συναποτελούσαν το δυτικό τμήμα της Σοβιετικής Ενωσης αρχίζουν να δείχνουν ζωηρό ενδιαφέρον. Οποιο αποτέλεσμα κι αν έχουν αυτές οι απόπειρες, το σίγουρο είναι ότι οι ΕΚ θα πρέπει να συνεχίσουν να προσαρμόζονται, ανταποκρινόμενες στις οικονομικές και κοινωνικές απαιτήσεις μιας μεταβαλλόμενης πολιτικής γεωγραφίας.

Η ΔΟΜΗ ΤΟΥ ΒΙΒΛΙΟΥ

Αυτό το βιβλίο, γραμμένο από γεωγράφους επτά διαφορετικών χωρών των ΕΚ, ξεκινά να ερμηνεύσει τις επιπτώσεις που είχαν οι ΕΚ στο κοινωνικο-οικονομικό τοπίο των κρατών-μελών. Στην εισαγωγή, οι Mark Blacksell και Allan Williams (Πανεπιστήμιο Exeter, Ενωμένο Βασίλειο), συζητούν την 'Ανάπτυξη των Ευρωπαϊκών Κοινοτήτων: η γεωγραφική τους σημασία' (Κεφάλαιο 1), εξηγούν τον τρόπο με τον οποίο οι ίδιες οι ΕΚ θεώρησαν το ζήτημα της οικονομικής ανάπτυξης, και εκθέτουν τους τρόπους με τους οποίους μεταβλήθηκε η περιφερειακή τους πολιτική, ανταποκρινόμενη σε διαδοχικές αυξήσεις των μελών τους και στις διαρκείς ανακατατάξεις στο εμπόριο, τόσο μέσα στην Ευρώπη, όσο και στον υπόλοιπο κόσμο.

Όταν οι ΕΚ αποτελούσαν μια κοινότητα έξη στενά συνυφασμένων χωρών στην καρδιά της βιομηχανικής δυτικής Ευρώπης, δεν υπήρχαν ενδείξεις καθ' εαυτό περιφερειακής πολιτικής. Ο στόχος των Κοινοτήτων ήταν η προώθηση της οικονομικής ανάπτυξης μέσω του ελεύθερου εμπορίου, του ανταγωνισμού και της απουσίας κεντρικού σχεδιασμού και διαχείρισης. Αν και στην πράξη έπρεπε να γίνουν ειδικές ρυθμίσεις, από περιφερειακή άποψη για την υποστήριξη του **Mezzogiorno** στη νότια Ιταλία, και από τομεακή άποψη για τη διατήρηση της γεωργίας με τη μορφή του οικογενειακού κλήρου, η γενική οικονομική επιτυχία που συνόδευσε τις δεκαετίες του 1950 και 1960 στην Ευρώπη, επιβεβαίωσε την πεποίθηση σε μια πανάκεια για την οικονομική και πολιτική πρόοδο.

Αυτή η ευφορία υπονομεύθηκε με την πρώτη διεύρυνση των ΕΚ το 1973. Τα ατίθασα προβλήματα που αντιμετώπιζαν οι φθίνουσες παλιές βιομηχανικές περιφέρειες στο Ενωμένο Βασίλειο και, όλο και περισσότερο, και σε άλλες περιοχές της Κοινότητας, οδήγησαν σε αύξουσες απαιτήσεις από τα διαρθρωτικά ταμεία να αντιμετωπίσουν τις δυσκολίες που απειλούσαν αυτές τις αστικές περιοχές, πόρους παρόμοιους που ήταν, θεωρητικά, διαθέσιμοι μέσω της Κοινής Αγροτικής Πολιτικής (ΚΑΠ, CAP) για τις αγροτικές περιοχές. Το 1975 εγκαθιδρύθηκε το Ευρωπαϊκό Ταμείο Περιφερειακής Ανάπτυξης (ΕΤΠΑ, ERDF) με τον εκφρασμένο στόχο να συμπληρώσει τις κρατικές περιφερειακές χρηματοδοτήσεις και τα επενδυτικά προγράμματα. Αν και τα διαθέσιμα ποσά ήταν περιορισμένα (3% του προϋπολογισμού των ΕΚ), αυξήθηκαν, πάντως, σταθερά. Ακόμα πιο σημαντική ήταν η έμμεση αναγνώριση, μέσω του ΕΤΠΑ, ότι οι δυνάμεις της αγοράς από μόνες τους δεν θα αντιμετώπιζαν ποτέ ικανοποιητικά την αδικία των περιφερειακών ανισοτήτων.

Η προσάρτηση της Ελλάδας, της Ισπανίας και της Πορτογαλίας στο πρώτο ήμισυ της δεκαετίας του 1980, ισχυροποίησε περισσότερο την ανάγκη περιφερειακής πολιτικής, αποκαλύπτοντας τις ανεπάρκειες των τομεακών πολιτικών. Και οι τρεις χώρες υποφέρουν από πολλαπλή στέρηση σε μια κλίμακά που βρίσκει κανείς μόνο σε μεμονωμένους θύλακες αλλού στην Κοινότητα. Για την αντιμετώπιση των προβλημάτων τους, απαιτείται περιφερειακή αρωγή σε κλίμακα μεγαλύτερη από αυτήν που εφαρμόσθηκε μέχρι σήμερα, η οποία μάλιστα, για να έχει κάποια χρησιμότητα, πρέπει ν' αποτελέσει τμήμα μιας ολοκληρωμένης συνθετικής προσέγγισης στην οικονομική ανάπτυξη γενικότερα. Η ανταπόκριση των ΕΚ κινήθηκε σε δυό επίπεδα. Πρώτα, καταβλήθηκε συστηματική προσπάθεια για την αύξηση του συνολικού ποσού της διαθέσιμης περιφερειακής αρωγής και για την μεταστροφή περισσότερης από αυτήν προς τις Μεσογειακές χώρες. Δεύτερον, επινοήθηκε ένα πλαίσιο Μεσογειακών Ολοκληρωμένων Προγραμμάτων (ΜΟΠ) για να συντονίσει και να καταστήσει πιο συνεπή την χρήση της περιφερειακής αρωγής.

Η επαναβεβαίωση της περιφερειακής πολιτικής των Κοινοτήτων ενισχύθηκε από την Ενιαία Ευρωπαϊκή Πράξη. Η δέσμευση-κλειδί της Πράξης, να επιτύχει την Ενοποιημένη Αγορά το 1993, προϋπέθετε μια εκ βάθρων νέα προσέγγιση και για τα δώδεκα κράτη-μελη των ΕΚ, κι όχι μόνο για την Μεσογειακή περιφέρεια, αν ήταν επιθυμητό να αποφευχθούν ανυπόφορες περιφερειακές ανισότητες. Το 1989 τα τρία υπάρχοντα διαρθρωτικά ταμεία, το ΕΤΠΑ, το Ευρωπαϊκό Κοινωνικό Ταμείο (ΕΚΤ, ESF) και το Ευρωπαϊκό Γεωργικό Ταμειο Προσανατολισμού και Εγγυήσεων (ΕΓΤΠΕ, FEOGA) της ΚΑΠ, άρχισαν να συγχωνεύονται σε ένα μόνο Ταμείο Συνοχής, που θα εχρησιμοποιείτο για την επίτευξη πέντε στόχων πολιτικής (στην πραγματικότητα, έξη, διότι οι 5α και 5β διακρίνονται σαφώς μεταξύ τους). Οι σκοποί και οι στόχοι είναι πλέον στη θέση τους και η διασαφήνιση των παλιότερων διακεκριμένων διαρθρωτικών Ταμείων, καθώς και η αντικατάστασή τους με ένα μοναδικό και ολοκληρωμένο, είναι τώρα δρομολογημένη.

Υπάρχει μια ακόμα πολύ σημαντική άποψη για την μεταρρύθμιση των διαρθρωτικών ταμείων. Προηγουμένως, η Επιτροπή των ΕΚ μπορούσε να εργασθεί μόνο μέσω των εθνικών κυβερνήσεων, παρέχοντας πρόσθετη βοήθεια για προγράμματα που είχαν ήδη ξεκινήσει. Με το νέο σχήμα, ένα ποσοστό (περίπου 9%) των διαθεσίμων περιφερειακών πόρων θα προορίζεται για Κοινοτικές, σε διάκριση από τις εθνικές, πρωτοβουλίες, μέσω προγραμμάτων όπως τα STAR, VALOREN και RESIDER, που αφορούν, αντίστοιχα, τις βιομηχανίες ενέργειας, σιδήρου και χάλυβα. Αυτό αποτελεί ένα μικρό αλλά σημαντικό βήμα προς την πραγματική ολοκλήρωση και την ανάδυση μιας Κοινοτικής προσέγγισης στην περιφερειακή ανάπτυξη.

Οι συνθήκες στις πόλεις

Περίπου το 80% του πληθυσμού των ΕΚ διαμένει σε πόλεις, έτσι ώστε οι μεταβολές που συντελέστηκαν στο αστικό περιβάλλον από τότε που ιδρύθηκαν οι Κοινότητες, αφορούν με τον πιο άμεσο τρόπο τους πολίτες τους. Ο Pierre Laborde (Καθηγητής στο Πανεπιστήμιο Bordeaux III, Γαλλία) στο 'Χωρική ανάπτυξη των δυτικοευρωπαϊκών πόλεων 1950–1990' (Κεφάλαιο 2) εξετάζει τις γεωγραφικές επιπτώσεις της ταχείας ανάπτυξης του αστικού πληθυσμού της Ευρώπης μέχρι τα μέσα της δεκαετίας του 1970. Εκείνη την εποχή έπαυαν οι πόλεις να είναι συμπαγείς και ενδοστρεφείς και εξερράγησαν προς τα έξω, έτσι ώστε να μεταβληθούν οι υπάρχουσες αστικές περιοχές και να δημιουργηθεί μια νέα αστικοποιημένη περιφέρεια που ακόμα επεκτείνεται, παρ' όλο που η ίδια η πληθυσμιακή ανάπτυξη έχει επιβραδυνθεί δραματικά.

Οι πρακτικές αστικού σχεδιασμού έχουν μεταβληθεί κατά τη διάρκεια του δεύτερου μισού του εικοστού αιώνα. Τις δεκαετίες του 1950 και 1960, συρμό αποτελούσε η συστηματική αναβάθμιση (comprehensive redevelopment), γνωστή με διάφορους τρόπους, όπως 'η ανάπτυξη της μπουλντόζας' στη Γαλλία, 'Βρυξελλοποίηση' στο Βέλγιο και ανανέωση αντικατάστασης' στην Ισπανία. Καθώς άρχιζε να εξαφανίζεται ο ιστορικός πυρήνας ακόμα και εκείνων των πόλεων που δεν είχαν καταστραφεί από τους πολεμικούς βομβαρδισμούς, αναπτυσσόταν μια αντίδραση εναντίον τέτοιων δραστικών λύσεων, ιδιαίτερα στη Γαλλία, και η συντήρηση και ανανέωση (conservation and renovation) του υπάρχοντος ιστού έγινε η νέα ορθοδοξία. Σε τελευταία ανάλυση, όμως, καμμία από τις διαφορετικές προσεγγίσεις στην αναβάθμιση των κέντρων των πόλεων δεν κατάφερε να αντιμετωπίσει τα προβλήματα που τίθενται από τη γήρανση του αστικού ιστού και τη χρόνια ακαμψία του μπροστά στη δημογραφική και οικονομική αλλαγή.

Η πιο ορατή παράδοση στον αστικό ιστό της ταχείας πληθυσμιακής ανάπτυξης, είναι η προαστιακή διάχυση που περιβάλλει όλες τις πόλεις. Αρχικά, η περισσότερη από την προαστιακή ανάπτυξη ήταν για οικιστικούς σκοπούς, χαμηλού ύψους και με μεγάλες απαιτήσεις σε γη. Ακόμη κι εκεί όπου κτίζονταν πολυόροφα κτίρια κατοικίας, όπως τα 'μεγάλα συγκροτήματα' (grands ensembles) στη Γαλλία, χωρίς εξαίρεση χωροθετούνταν σε αγροτικές περιοχές, συνεισφέροντας έτσι περισσότερο στην απώλεια γεωργικής γης. Σταδιακά, με την πάροδο του χρόνου, άρχισε και το εμπόριο, η βιομηχανία, οι υπηρεσίες και άλλες δραστηριότητες να αναχωροθετούνται στην αστική περιφέρεια, κατά κύριο λόγο σε χαμηλά κτίρια.

Πιο πρόσφατα, η εκτατική ανάπτυξη των αστικών περιοχών ενισχύθηκε, όχι από την αύξηση του πληθυσμού, αλλά από κοινωνικές, τεχνολογικές και πολιτικές αλλαγές. Ο αριθμός των νοικοκυριών αυξήθηκε δραματικά, αλλά το μέσο τους μέγεθος συρρικνώθηκε, λόγω παραγόντων όπως μεγαλύτερα ποσοστά διαζυγίων και αυξημένη προσδοκία ζωής. Η εξάπλωση της ιδιοκτησίας αυτοκινήτου σημαίνει ότι οι άνθρωποι μπορεί να επιλέξουν να ζήσουν σε προαστιακές τοποθεσίες χωρίς να θέσουν σε κίνδυνο τις δουλειές τους. Και οι πολιτικές σχεδιασμού που βασίζονται στην αρχή της αποκέντρωσης ενθαρρύνουν, από την πλευρά των κυβερνήσεων, την τάση για μεγαλύτερη φυγή προς τα προάστια. Οι πολιτικές των ΕΚ είχαν μόνο περιθωριακές επιπτώσεις σ' αυτές τις αλλαγές. Παρ' όλο που περιφερειακές πολιτικές, απευθυνόμενες σε υποβαθμιζόμενες βιομηχανικές περιοχές, και η χρήση υψηλοτέρων περιβαλλοντικών προτύπων, ενσωματώθηκαν στην οργανωμένη αστική αναβάθμιση, θα ήταν δύσκολο να θεωρηθούν αυτά ως τμήμα κάποιας συστηματικής πολεοδομικής πολιτκής.

Το τελικό αποτέλεσμα όλων αυτών των διαρθρωτικών αλλαγών ήταν να προκύψουν περισσότερο διαφοροποιημένες χρήσεις γης στις πόλεις, που αντανακλούν κατά κύριο λόγο τις διαφορές στις αξίες γης ανάμεσα στον πυρήνα και την περιφέρεια. Στη Γαλλία, οι δημοτικές αρχές έχουν τώρα αρχίσει να προσπαθούν να διαχειρισθούν αυτές τις αλλαγές πολύ πιο ενεργά, αλλά οι διαφορές στην πολιτική δομή δυσκολεύουν τις γενικεύσεις για τις προσεγγίσεις στην Ευρώπη στο σύνολό της.

Τα προβλήματα της γενίκευσης για τη φύση της αστικής αλλαγής και της διαχείρισης της αστικής γης διαγράφονται καθαρά από την Λίλα Λεοντίδου (Αναπλ. Καθηγήτρια, Εθνικό Μετσόβιο Πολυτεχνείο, Αθήνα, Ελλάδα) στο 'Μεσογειακές πόλεις: τάσεις απόκλισης στην ενωμένη Ευρώπη' (Κεφάλαιο 3). Οι πόλεις είχαν πάντοτε έναν κεντρικό πολιτιστικό ρόλο στη Μεσογειακή Ευρώπη, κι αυτό ακόμα ισχύει στα τέλη του εικοστού αιώνα, με αποτέλεσμα να μην συναντάμε εδώ την τεχνολογικά δημιουργημένη διασπορά που χαρακτηρίζει τις βορειοευρωπαϊκές πόλεις. Οι πόλεις της Μεσογείου είναι πιο συμπαγείς από αυτές της υπόλοιπης Ευρώπης. Η πρόσφατη μάλιστα αποκέντρωση οικονομικών δραστηριοτήτων προς την μητροπολιτική περιφέρεια, δεν συμπαρασύρει πληθυσμούς σε αξιόλογη κλίμακα. Τα λαϊκά προάστια δεν είναι ιδιαίτερα απομακρυσμένα, ενώ ο πυρήνας της πόλης ήταν πάντα, και παραμένει, περιοχή υψηλής ποιότητας κατοικίας στη Ρώμη, Αθήνα, Μαδρίτη, Βαρκελώνη, Λισαβώνα. Οι εργατικές περιοχές τείνουν να διασκορπίζονται γύρω στην περιφέρεια–

με κάποιες εξαιρέσεις, ασφαλώς. Η κοινωνική και οικονομική αποσυγκέντρωση, τόσο τυπική στη Γαλλία, τη Γερμανία και το Ενωμένο Βασίλειο, είναι πολύ λιγότερο εμφανής στη Μεσόγειο.

Αναπόφευκτα, η επίπτωση των ΕΚ στην ανάπτυξη ήταν μέχρι τώρα ελάχιστη. Από τις Μεσογειακές χώρες, μόνο η Ιταλία ήταν ιδρυτικό μέλος, ενώ η Ελλάδα, η Ισπανία και η Πορτογαλία δεν εντάχθηκαν παρά τη δεκαετία του 1980. Αυτό όμως δεν αποτελεί παρά μέρος της εξήγησης: πολλές από τις σχετικές πολιτικές που προέρχονται από τις ΕΚ και επιδρούν στις αστικές περιοχές, διαμορφώνονται με τρόπο άσχετο με τη δομή των Μεσογειακών πόλεων. Για παράδειγμα, οι δείκτες της φτώχειας που βασίζονται σε ποσοστά αστέγων, έχουν μικρή χρησιμότητα εδώ που οι φτωχοί στεγάζονται μεν, αλλά συχνά συνωστίζονται σε πρόχειρες, αυτοφυείς παραγκουπόλεις. Αυτό υπογραμμίζει την απλή αλήθεια, ότι οι συνολικές εκ των άνω πολιτικές, ακόμα και μέσα σε μια ομάδα χωρών τόσο φαινομενικά ομοιογενών όπως οι χώρες της Ευρώπης των 12, είναι απίθανο να επιτύχουν τους στόχους τους εαν δεν είναι ειδικά ευαίσθητες στις τοπικές συνθήκες.

Διαρθρωτική αλλαγή

Η δημιουργία των ΕΚ μετέβαλε το οικονομικό και κοινωνικό πλαίσιο της Ευρώπης και προκάλεσε βαθειές διαρθρωτικές αλλαγές σε πολλές περιοχές, τόσο με συνειδητές πρωτοβουλίες πολιτικής, όσο και με αθέλητες προσαρμογές. Ο Jean-Paul Charrié (Πανεπιστήμιο Bordeaux III, Γαλλία), στο 'Η δομή της βιομηχανίας: ευρωπαϊκότητα και διεθνισμός' (Κεφάλαιο 4), παρουσιάζει έναν λεπτομερή πίνακα των θεμελιωδών αλλαγών που συντελούνται τώρα σε μια ομάδα χωρών, από τις οποίες η μεγαλύτερη αποτέλεσε και την κοιτίδα της βιομηχανικής επανάστασης τον δέκατο ένατο αιώνα. Η Ευρώπη παραμένει μια μεγάλη βιομηχανική δύναμη στον κόσμο, αλλά η ανωτερότητά της αναπόφευκτα αλλάζει εκ βάθρων εν όψει ενός ανταγωνισμού, που ποτέ δεν ήταν πιο αδυσώπητος.

Πολλές από αυτές τις αλλαγές στο διεθνές βιομηχανικό κλίμα ανέσκηψαν μέσα στα σαράντα χρόνια μετά την ίδρυση των Κοινοτήτων. Οι ΕΚ είναι πλούσιες σε άνθρακα και σίδηρο, και απολαμβάνουν τεράστιο παραγωγικό δυναμικό σε πολλούς κλάδους-κλειδιά, όπως ο σίδηρος και ο χάλυβας, τα ναυπηγεία και οι χημικές βιομηχανίες, που είδε τη χρυσή του εποχή τη δεκαετία του 1950. Δεν είναι συμπτωματικό, ότι οι πρώτες επιτυχίες πήγαζαν από την Ευρωπαϊκή Κοινότητα Άνθρακος και Χάλυβος. Σε μιαν ήπειρο ταλαιπωρημένη από πέντε χρόνια συγκρούσεων, η Συνθήκη των Παρισίων έθεσε τα θεμέλια μιας περιόδου συντηρούμενης οικονομικής ανάπτυξης, που διακόπηκε μόνον από την πετρελαϊκή κρίση του 1973.

Οι Κοινότητες έπρεπε να προσαρμόσουν τις μεθόδους βιομηχανικής παραγωγής στην αυξανόμενη σημασία του πετρελαίου και στην κατακόρυφη αύξηση της τιμής του, κι έπρεπε να προσαρμοστούν στην παρακμή των βασικών εκείνων βιομηχανιών που αποτελούσαν τις κορωνίδες αυτής της αρχικής επιτυχίας, καθώς και στην παράλληλη ανάπτυξη τομέων υψηλής τεχνολογίας.

Οι αλλαγές αυτές συντελούνται στο πλαίσιο ενός ανερχόμενου ανταγωνισμού από τις Νεοβιομηχανοποιούμενες χώρες. Η απειλή από την Ιαπωνία είναι προφανής, ιδιαίτερα εφ' όσον τα βιομηχανικά της προϊόντα ανταγωνίζονται άμεσα τις παραδοσιακές εξωτερικές αγορές της Ευρώπης, ιδιαίτερα τη Βόρειο Αμερική. Ταυτόχρονα, οι Ιάπωνες βιομήχανοι επενδύουν άμεσα στις ΕΚ, προσπαθώντας να αντιπαρέλθουν τους κανονισμούς που αποσκοπούν στον περιορισμό της εισροής Ιαπωνικών εισαγωγών στην Ευρώπη. Επιπροσθέτως, εμφανίζεται αυξανόμενο ενδιαφέρον από τις Νεοβιομηχανοποιούμενες Χώρες για την Ασία, ιδιαίτερα από τη Νότια Κορέα, που πρώτη εισήλθε στην αγορά ετοίμων ενδυμάτων αλλά τώρα ταχύτατα διαφοροποιεί την παραγωγή της.

Όλες αυτές οι διάφορες αλλαγές έχουν ένα προσθετικό αποτέλεσμα στη βιομηχανική καρδιά της Ευρώπης. Οι παραδοσιακές βιομηχανικές περιφέρειες φθίνουν, επειδή υποφέρουν από αυξανόμενο αριθμό μειονεκτημάτων και χρειάζονται άμεσα μέτρα που που θα τις βοηθήσουν να προσαρμοσθούν. Κατά τα άλλα, τα μεγαλύτερα αστικά συγκροτήματα βρίσκονται σε καλλίτερη θέση και προστατεύουν με μανία αυτήν τους την υπεροχή.

Η Επιτροπή και τα άλλα όργανα των ΕΚ, ενώ για πολλά χρόνια δεν είχαν δυνατότητες να προχωρούν σε μεμονωμένες παρεμβάσεις, ιδιαίτερα σε μέτρα προστασίας για φθίνουσες περιφέρειες ή προβληματικούς τομείς και εργοστάσια, τώρα αρχίζουν να παίζουν έναν απίστευτα σημαντικό ρόλο στη βιομηχανική πολιτική. Οι ΕΚ αποτελούν σημαντικό παράγοντα στο αναδυόμενο βιομηχανικό τοπίο, αφού παρέχουν συγκεκριμένη βοήθεια σε επιλεγμένους τομείς, συντονίζουν ερευνητικές προσπάθειες, και ηγούνται σε μια αναζωογονούμενη περιφερειακή πολιτική. Επιπροσθέτως, η ολοκλήρωση της Ενιαίας Αγοράς θα έχει πολύ σημαντικό αντίκτυπο σ' ολόκληρο τον βιομηχανικό ιστό της Ευρώπης.

Οι μεταφορές και συγκοινωνίες έχουν από παλιά αναγνωρισθεί από τις κυβερνήσεις ως ένας από τους τομείς-κλειδιά, που χειρίζονται τη δυναμική των βιομηχανικών κοινωνιών, και οι ΕΚ ήταν πάντα ιδιαίτερα ευαίσθητες σ' αυτό το γεγονός, ακόμα και αν δεν το τόνισαν στο Κοινοτικό επίπεδο με την δύναμη που θα αναμενόταν. Οι James Killen (Trinity College Dublin, Ιρλανδία) και Austin Smith (Πανεπιστήμιο Ulster, Ενωμένο Βασίλειο), στο 'Πολιτική μεταφορών στις Ευρωπαϊκές Κοινότητες με ειδική αναφορά στην Ιρλανδία ως περιφερειακή χώρα' (Κεφάλαιο 5), εξετάζουν τον τρόπο με τον οποίο η πολιτική μεταφορών των ΕΚ, ή η έλλειψή της, επηρρέασε το νησί της Ιρλανδίας στο σύνολό του.

Οι εθνικές κυβερνήσεις κατά παράδοση έχουν προσπαθήσει να επηρρεάσουν τα συστήματα μεταφορών και λειτουργιών μέσα στις χώρες τους με δυό κυρίως τρόπους. Πρώτον, υπήρξαν κύριοι ρυθμιστές της κυκλοφορίας θέτοντας, για παράδειγμα, όρια ταχυτήτων και συνθήκες κάτω από τις οποίες μπορούν να εκδίδονται άδειες διαφόρων τύπων. Στην Ευρώπη έχουν συνήθως αναλάβει έναν άμεσο ρόλο στη λειτουργία των σιδηροδρομικών εξυπηρετήσεων και, σε μερικές περιπτώσεις, των λεωφορειακών και οδικών βαρειών μεταφορών, δίνοντάς τους τη δυνατότητα να ελέγχουν άμεσα το βαθμό ανταγωνισμού ανάμεσα στα διάφορα μέσα. Δεύτερον, οι κυβερνήσεις έχουν προσπαθήσει να επηρρεάσουν το επίπεδο και τη φύση των επενδύσεων σε κυκλοφοριακή υποδομή, ιδιαίτερα με αναφορά στα χρηματικά ποσά που επενδύονται σε σύγκριση με άλλους τομείς της οικονομίας, και στον τρόπο με τον οποίο δαπανώνται τα ποσά που κατανέμονται στις μεταφορές.

Πριν από την υπογραφή της Συνθήκης της Ρώμης, η πολιτική μεταφορών στην Ευρώπη ήταν στη δικαιοδοσία κάθε κράτους σχετικά ανεξάρτητα από τα γειτονικά του. Θεωρητικά, η συνεργασία σε Ευρωπαϊκό επίπεδο ήταν δυνατή μέσω του Ευρωπαϊκού Συμβουλίου των Υπουργών Μεταφορών, που δημιουργήθηκε το 1953 αλλά δεν είχε ουσιαστική επιτυχία. Στη Συνθήκη της Ρώμης υπήρχε σαφής δέσμευση να εφαρμοστεί μια Κοινή Πολιτική Μεταφορών, αλλά το γεγονός ότι κάθε χώρα ήδη είχε την δική της, καθιστούσε πολύ δύσκολη μια πολιτική σε Ευρωπαϊκό επίπεδο. Ενα παράδειγμα ευρύτερης συνεργασίας είναι η ανάπτυξη του δικτύου των Ευρωπαϊκών Σιδηροδρόμων Μεγάλης Ταχύτητας (Trans European Express, TEE ή Train a Grande Vitesse, TGV). Ο κύριος στόχος του κεφαλαίου αυτού είναι να δείξει πώς οι σχετικά αδύναμες συμφωνίες που επιτεύχθηκαν στους διάφορους τομείς–οδικές, σιδηροδρομικές, θαλάσσιες και εναέριες μεταφορές–έχουν επηρρεάσει την Ιρλανδία, που βρίσκεται στην απώτερη περιφέρεια όλων των μεγαλύτερων δικτύων μεταφορών της Ευρώπης.

Παρ' όλες τις κρατικές και περιφερειακές παραλλαγές, οι ΕΚ στο σύνολό τους διέθεταν ένα αξιοζήλευτο δίκτυο μεταφορών, που συνεισέφερε σε μεγάλο βαθμό στην συνεκτικότητα των Κοινοτήτων. Διευκόλυνε επίσης την κινητικότητα του εργατικού δυναμικού, που συντηρούσε σε μεγάλο βαθμό την οικονομική επιτυχία της Ευρώπης στο σύνολό της. Ο Russell King (Καθηγητής στο Trinity College Dublin, Ιρλανδία) στο 'Μετανάστευση και η Ενιαία Αγορά για το Εργατικό Δυναμικό: ένα ζήτημα περιφερειακής ανάπτυξης' (Κεφάλαιο 6) εξετάζει τη συμβολή της διεθνούς μετανάστευσης από τα τέλη της δεκαετίας του 1950 στη μεταβαλλόμενη οικονομική και κοινωνική γεωγραφία της Ευρώπης. Οι εργάτες μετανάστες υπήρξαν ένας σημαντικός παράγοντας για την ανάπτυξη των Ευρωπαϊκών βιομηχανικών και μεταβιομηχανικών οικονομιών κατά τις δεκαετίες του 1960 και του 1970. Αν και οι αριθμοί τους, σε όρους συνολικών αφίξεων, μειώθηκαν μετά την πρώτη πετρελαϊκή κρίση του 1973-4, τα μέλη των οικογενειών τους συνέχισαν να εισρέουν. Αυτά, μαζί με τα νέα κύματα μεταναστών που κατέφθασαν τις δεκαετίες του 1980 και 1990, περιέπλεξαν τις εκτιμήσεις που τοποθετούν το σύνολο του πληθύσμού των μεταναστών στην Ευρώπη σήμερα στα 20 εκατομμύρια περίπου, με την πλειοψηφία τους μέσα στα όρια των ΕΚ.

Έπειτα από μια περίπου δεκαετία, όταν η διεθνής μετανάστευση εθεωρείτο παρεμπιπτόντως ως ένα μείζον Ευρωπαϊκό πολιτικό ζήτημα, πρόσφατα η συζήτηση για τη μετανάστευση έχει προσελκύσει ξανά την προσοχή σε ολόκληρη την Ευρωπαϊκή επικράτεια. Οι ροές εργατικής μετανάστευσης άρχισαν πάλι να εντείνονται από τα τέλη της δεκαετίας του 1980, αρχίζοντας σε ορισμένες χώρες (Γερμανία, Ολλανδία) ήδη από το 1985. Αλλά το πιο σημαντικό έναυσμα για τη γένεση νέων ροών μαζικής μετανάστευσης ήταν η κατάρρευση του σοσιαλισμού στην Ανατολική Ευρώπη από το 1989. Τα εκπληκτικά γεγονότα των τελευταίων τριών χρόνων δείχνουν ξεκάθαρα την ανάγκη να είμαστε προσεκτικοί σε κάθε πρόβλεψη διεθνών μεταναστευτικών τάσεων: λίγοι θα προβλέπαμε το 1988 τις δραματικές εξελίξεις που ξετυλίχτηκαν, λίγο αργότερα, ακόμα και μ' ενδείξεις όπως οι δειλές μεταναστευτικές διαρροές από την πρώην Λαϊκή Δημοκρατία της Γερμανίας προς την προ της ένωσης Ομοσπονδιακή Δημοκρατία της Γερμανίας και από την Ουγγαρία—εναύσματα που πυροδότησαν ολόκληρη τη διαδικασία αλλαγής.

Αν δεν αρκούν αυτά τα γεγονότα, σήμερα αντικρύζουμε καινούρια σύννεφα στον δημογραφικό ορίζοντα της Ευρώπης. Σε ολόκληρη την υδρόγειο, εκατομμύρια ανθρώπων βρίσκονται σε μετακίνηση, ανασχηματίζοντας τον κόσμο με τα ταξίδια τους. Ο αριθμός των προσφύγων και των αναζητούντων άσυλο, που φτάνουν στην Ευρώπη, έχει διογκωθεί δραματικά κατά τη δεκαετία του 1980, και τώρα αυτό το ζήτημα πρέπει να αντιμετωπισθεί ευθέως στο επίπεδο τόσο της Κοινοτικής όσο και της εθνικής πολιτικής, ειδικά στο φώς της συμφωνίας του Schengen για την απάλειψη των συνοριακών ελέγχων στις ΕΚ και την καθιέρωση της Ενιαίας Αγοράς.

Ένα ειδικό πρόβλημα που σχετίζεται με τους διεθνείς μετανάστες, τόσο από το εσωτερικό όσο και από το εξωτερικό της Κοινότητας, είναι η παράνομη εργασία, ζήτημα που περιγράφεται ζωηρά από την Solange Montagne-Villette (Πανεπιστήμιο Poitiers, Γαλλία) στο 'Κινητικότητα, μυστικότητα και παράνομη εργασία στην ΕΟΚ' (Κεφάλαιο 7). Το να δουλεύουν άνθρωποι κρυφά, και συνήθως παράνομα, δεν αποτελεί νεωτερισμό στις χώρες των ΕΚ. Αυτό άρχισε στα πρώτα χρόνια του αιώνα μας, όταν εγκαθιδρύονταν μοντέρνες διοικητικές δομές σε όλες τις πλούσιες βιομηχανικές χώρες, κι επεκτάθηκε σταθερά παράλληλα με τα συστήματα κοινωνικής ασφάλισης. Σήμερα, σε ορισμένες χώρες, τέτοια παράνομη εργασία αποτελεί μέρος της παράδοσης και θεωρείται από πολλούς ως τμήμα του εθνικού πολιτισμού. Αντίθετα, η παράνομη εργασία στο επίπεδο της Ευρώπης, όπως αυτή που συναντάμε στις ΕΚ και πέρα απ' αυτές, έχει κάποια πρωτότυπα χαρακτηριστικά που μέχρι σήμερα δεν έχουν προσεχθεί επαρκώς, εν μέρει επειδή το φαινόμενο είναι πολύ πρόσφατο. Η αυξημένη κινητικότητα του εργατικού δυναμικού, της βιομηχανίας και των επιχειρήσεων, έχει δημιουργήσει τελείως νέες πρακτικές παράνομης εργασίας, οι μορφές των οποίων είναι στενά συνυφασμένες με την πολιτική, την οικονομική και τη νομική δομή των ΕΚ.

Οι εργάτες από τις φτωχειές χώρες των ΕΚ, που αναζητούν απασχόληση σε άλλες χώρες-μέλη, η αναχωροθέτηση και/ή οι υπεργολαβίες παράνομων βιομηχανικών δραστηριοτήτων στις Μεσογειακές χώρες της Ευρώπης, άνθρωποι προερχόμενοι από χώρες εκτός των Κοινοτήτων, που εργάζονται εδώ παράνομα, αποτελούν όλα ενδείξεις της αυξανόμενης κυριαρχίας πρακτικών παράνομης εργασίας. Όσον αφορά τις ΕΚ, ολόκληρο το ζήτημα των μεταναστών εργαζομένων υπήρξε πάντα δύσκολο να προσδιοριστεί. Ορισμένα κράτη-μέλη, ιδιαίτερα το Ενωμένο Βασίλειο, δείχνουν πραγματική απροθυμία να αποδεχθούν ότι ο έλεγχος των συνθηκών εργασίας, κι άλλες απόψεις καινωνικής μηχανικής, είναι συμβατός με την ελεύθερη αγορά, στην οποία όλοι αποσκοπούν.

Αγροτική προσαρμογή

Μια πολιτική, η ΚΑΠ, ήταν κυρίαρχη στις ΕΚ για 30 περίπου χρόνια, και σε κάποιο στάδιο καταβρόχθιζε περισσότερο από 90% του προϋπολογισμού τους, ενώ ακόμα σήμερα αντιπροσωπεύει πάνω από 60% . Οι πολιτικές συνθήκες γι' αυτού του είδους την κατάσταση είναι γνωστές και δεν αποτελούν αντικείμενο αυτού του βιβλίου, αλλά οποιαδήποτε σοβαρή μελέτη των ΕΚ πρέπει να αφιερώσει ένα μεγάλο ποσοστό της προσοχής της στη γεωργία. Η υπερβολική έμφαση στη γεωργία μέσα στις ΕΚ αρχίζει τώρα να ξεθωριάζει, αλλά κι αυτό το γεγονός θα έχει σοβαρές, και μεγάλου βεληνεκούς επιπτώσεις στην αγροτική οικονομία και το τοπίο. Ο Dietrich Denecke (Καθηγητής στο Πανεπιστήμιο Göttingen, Γερμανία) στο 'Εκ περιτροπής καλλιέργεια, πληθυσμιακή μείωση και προγράμματα αγρανάπαυσης: η εμβέλεια της προστασίας του τοπίου στην Ευρώπη, με ειδική αναφορά στη Γερμανία' (Κεφάλαιο 8) αναλυει τις συνέπειες αυτών των επερχομένων αλλαγών στην αγροτική πολιτική των ΕΚ για το τοπίο και το περιβάλλον, αντλώντας παραδείγματα από τα ειδικής ευαισθησίας αγροτικά τοπία της Γερμανίας, όπου ακόμα συνυπάρχουν οι καλλιεργητές αγρότες και η σύγχρονη γεωργία. Μέχρι και τον παρόντα αιώνα, η γενική έλλειψη αγροτικών προϊόντων και υλικών διατροφής συνεπαγόταν την κατά το δυνατό εντατική χρήση και καλλιέργεια της αγροτικής γης. Τα τελευταία 20 χρόνια άρχισαν όμως σταδιακά να συντελούνται ριζικές αλλαγές.

Η υπερπαραγωγή οδήγησε στην εισαγωγή εναλλακτικών καλλιεργειών, προγραμμάτων εκτατικότητας, βοσκής και αγρανάπαυσης και, τελευταίο αλλά όχι έσχατο, στην εγκατάλειψη αγροκτημάτων και αγροτικής γης. Αυτές οι αλλαγές και οι πολιτικές που τις επέφεραν κυριαρχούν τώρα σε μεγάλο βαθμό στην ανάπτυξη του πρωτογενούς τομέα της Ευρώπης. Ταυτόχρονα, ο αριθμός των αγροκτημάτων εξορθολογίζεται και τόσο η κτηνοτροφία όσο και η καλλιέργειες ολοένα εντατικοποιούνται, με καταστροφικές παρενέργειες. Και οι δυο αυτές διαδικασίες συνεισφέρουν στην αναστάτωση της ευαίσθητης οικολογικής ισορροπίας στο γεωργικό τοπίο, η διατήρηση του οποίου, μέσω παραδοσιακών μεθόδων καλλιέργειας, έχει γίνει πεποίθηση στις ΕΚ. Η εκτίμηση των δυνατοτήτων για την πραγματική επίτευξη μιας οικολογικά αποδεκτής γεωργίας, που θα προωθήσει τους στόχους της προστασίας του τοπίου, έχει γίνει, γι' αυτό το λόγο, ένα κρίσιμο ζήτημα για την ανάπτυξη των Κοινοτήτων, με σημαντικές διακλαδώσεις για ολόκληρη τη διαδικασία διαπραγμάτευσης μιάς αναμορφωμένης ΚΑΠ.

Αν και η ΚΑΠ έχει τώρα αρχίσει να αλλάζει και η πολιτική της ενίσχυσης της αγροτικής παραγωγής, άσχετα με το κόστος ή τις άμεσες ανάγκες, να αμφισβητείται ολοένα και περισσότερο, αποτελεί, πάντως, ακόμα τον θεμέλιο λίθο της πολιτικής των ΕΚ. Ο Manuel Corbera (Πανεπιστήμιο Cantabria, Ισπανία) στο 'Η Κοινή Αγροτική Πολιτική και η ανάπτυξη της γεωργίας: προβλήματα και προοπτικές' αξιολογεί την ΚΑΠ από την πλευρά της Ισπανίας, μιας χώρας με πολύ μεγάλο αγροτικό τομέα, η οποία ενώθηκε με τις ΕΚ μονο πρόσφατα, το 1986. Σε γενικούς όρους, η Ευρώπη αποτελεί την κύρια παγκόσμια αγροτική δύναμη, κυρίαρχη παραγωγό γαλακτοκομικών προϊόντων, οίνου, ζάχαρης και κρέατος, και δεύτερη στην παραγωγή σιτηρών και κριθής. Είναι επίσης αυτάρκης σε όλα τα τρόφιμα ευκράτων κλιμάτων, με την εξαίρεση των φρέσκων φρούτων, του αραβοσίτου, του αρνίσιου και του κατσικίσιου κρέατος.

Αυτή η αξιοζήλευτη κατάσταση αντανακλά, εν μέρει, τις εξαιρετικά ευνοϊκές φυσικές συνθήκες και τη συμπληρωματικότητα του Ατλαντικού, του ηπειρωτικού και του Μεσογειακού περιβάλλοντος. Μεγάλη σημασία έχουν επίσης οι παραγωγικές διαδικασίες που αναπτύχθηκαν: εντατική χρησιμοποίηση της γης, συστήματα καλλιεργειών προσαρμοσμένα στις φυσικές συνθήκες, αποτελεσματικές αγροτικές δομές, και υψηλά επίπεδα εκμηχάνισης, που δίνουν τη δυνατότητα για υψηλές αποδόσεις. Παρ' όλα αυτά όμως, η επιτυχία της γεωργίας στις ΕΚ αντανακλά κυρίως την επιτυχία της ΚΑΠ, που διατήρησε και διήγειρε την ανάπτυξη του τομέα αυτού για μια ολόκληρη γενιά. Με την απουσία της ΚΑΠ κανένα από τα κράτη-μέλη δεν θα είχε τον πρώτο παγκόσμιο ρόλο στη γεωργία μόνο του, και η πολιτική πρέπει να αξιολογηθεί με βάση αυτό το γεγονός. Παρ' όλα τα πολλά της προβλήματα και την εμφανή ανάγκη μεταρρύθμισης, ήταν και παραμένει επιτυχής.

Παρά την επιτυχία της αγροτικής πολιτικής σε όρους παραγωγής ειδών διατροφής, πολλές αγροτικές περιοχές διέρχονται κρίση. Δεν υπάρχει πλέον τόση ανάγκη για γη, ιδιαίτερα περιθωριακή γη, που να χρησιμοποιείται για παραγωγή τροφίμων και πρέπει να βρεθούν εναλλακτικές λύσεις, τόσο για την ίδια τη γη, όσο και για τους ανθρώπους που παραδοσιακά την καλλιεργούσαν. Η απόσυρσή της από την παραγωγή και η προστασία του τοπίου είναι μια από τις εναλλακτικές λύσεις, που συζητήθηκε παραπάνω, αλλά αυτό ανοίγει ολόκληρα ερωτήματα, όπως είναι η οικονομική ανέχεια που συσσωρεύεται σε κοινότητες κατά τα άλλα σταθερές και κοινωνικά συμπαγείς. Η πιο προφανής εναλλακτική λύση είναι να κεφαλαιοποιήσει κανείς στο τουριστικό δυναμικό των αγροτικών περιοχών, ιδιαίτερα στις παραλιακές και ορεινές περιφέρειες της Ευρώπης.

Οι Allan Williams και Gareth Shaw (Πανεπιστήμιο Exeter, Ενωμένο Βασίλειο), στο 'Τουρισμός: ευκαιρίες, προκλήσεις και αντιφάσεις στις ΕΚ' (Κεφάλαιο 10) εξετάζουν το τουριστικό φαινόμενο στο σύνολό του στην Ευρώπη. Από τότε που ανέκυψε ο μαζικός τουρισμός τη δεκαετία του 1960, ο τουρισμός μπορεί να περιγραφεί ως θεμελιώδες νήμα στον οικονομικό και κοινωνικό ιστό των ΕΚ. Έχει μεγάλη οικονομική σημασία, αφού απασχολεί περισσότερο από έναν στους 20 εργαζόμενους, και συνεισφέρει μεγάλο ποσοστό του ΑΕΠ και του διεθνούς εμπορίου, τόσο μέσα όσο και εξω από τις Κοινότητες. Ο τουρισμός αποτελεί, ακόμα, όργανο κοινωνικής αλλαγής, αφού επηρρεάζει την μεταβίβαση αξιών και τρόπων ζωής και προσφέρει ένα από τα λίγα πιθανά κανάλια για μαζική παγκόσμια αλληλεπίδραση ανάμεσα σε ανθρώπους και πολιτισμούς στις Κοινότητες. Αποτελεί, βέβαια, πολυσυζητημένο ερώτημα, κατά πόσον υπάρχει κάποια Ευρωπαϊκή πολιτιστική ταυτότητα και, αν υπάρχει, πώς συμβάλλει σ' αυτήν ο τουρισμός. Τέλος, ο τουρισμός βρίσκεται στην καρδιά των διασυνοριακών διεθνών μετακινήσεων μέσα στις Κοινότητες, την κυρίως περιοχή απελευθέρωσης για το πρόγραμμα της Ενιαίας Αγοράς. Η συνολική σημασία του για τις Κοινότητες μπορεί να συνοψισθεί με ένα μόνο στατιστικό μέγεθος: 64% όλου του διεθνούς τουρισμού στον κόσμο, εμφανίζεται μέσα στην Ευρώπη, και οι ΕΚ έχουν μεγάλο μερίδιο αυτής της αγοράς. Ο τουρισμός είναι θεμελιώδης για την παραγωγή και την κατανάλωση σε αστικές και αγροτικές περιοχές των ΕΚ, περισσότερο ίσως από ό, τι για οποιαδήποτε άλλη περιοχή στον κόσμο.

Περιβαλλοντικές επιπτώσεις

Το ζήτημα του περιβάλλοντος αγνοήθηκε τελείως στις συνθήκες του Παρισιού και της Ρώμης, καθιστώντας δύσκολη την δικαίωση της όποιας Κοινοτικής πολιτικής για την κατάστρωση λύσεων, παρ' όλη την άνοδο της συνειδητότητας και της ανησυχίας των πολιτών για την περιβαλλοντική υποβάθμιση κι εξάντληση των πόρων καθ' όλη τη διάρκεια των δεκαετιών του 1960 και 1970, και παρά την αναδυόμενη πεποίθηση ότι δεν ήταν ρεαλιστικό να αντιμετωπίζονται αυτά τα ζητήματα σε καθαρά εθνικά πλαίσια. Η ίδιες οι ΕΚ, καθώς διευρύνονταν το 1958–86 από 6 σε 12 μέλη και παρουσίαζαν μιαν όλο και πιο κατακερματισμένη και δυσκίνητη γεωγραφική δομή, δεν αποτελούσαν, βέβαια, κατά κανένα τρόπο κάποια 'φυσική' χωρική ενότητα για την κατάστρωση λύσεων σε όλο και πιο σύνθετα και ποικίλα προβλήματα περιβάλλοντος και διαχείρισης πόρων. Το κύριο πλεονέκτημα των ΕΚ ως φορέα διαχείρισης του περιβάλλοντος ήταν ίσως, κατά τους πολίτες τους, ο εκφρασμένος τους διεθνισμός, που υπογράμμιζε την προφανή παγκοσμιότητα μιας μεγάλης σειράς ζητημάτων που σχετίζονταν με την προστασία του περιβάλλοντος.

Ο Mark Blacksell (Πανεπιστήμιο Exeter, Ενωμένο Βασίλειο) στο 'Περιβαλλοντικές πολιτικές και διαχείριση πόρων' (Κεφάλαιο 11) εξετάζει τον δύσκολο δρόμο προς την συνειδητοποίηση ολόκληρης της σειράς των περιβαλλοντικών πολιτικών που αποτελούν σήμερα ένα ολοένα και πιο σημαντικό τμήμα της πολιτικής των ΕΚ. Είναι τώρα ξεκάθαρο ότι οι καλλίτερες λύσεις σε πολλά από τα πιο πιεστικά περιβαλλοντικά ζητήματα, όπως ο έλεγχος της ρύπανσης της ατμόσφαιρας και των υδάτων και η διαχείριση των σκουπιδιών, ποικίλουν πολύ ανάμεσα στα κράτη της Ευρώπης, και αποδείχθηκε δύσκολο να επιτευχθεί πολιτική συναίνεση για τους τρόπους αντιμετώπισής τους. Οι πλουσιότερες κοινωνίες είναι ευκολότερο να πεισθούν για τα πλεονεκτήματα των μακροχρόνιων περιβαλλοντικών ωφελειών σε σύγκριση με τα βραχυχρόνια οικονομικά ωφέλη. Αυτό δημιούργησε υποβόσκουσες εντάσεις ανάμεσα στις μεγάλες βιομηχανικές χώρες στον πυρήνα των ΕΚ και μερικά από τα πιο πρόσφατα μέλη στη βόρεια και τη Μεσογειακή περιφέρεια. Χώρες-νησιά όπως το Ενωμένο Βασίλειο και η Ιρλανδία, με βραχείς ποταμούς με γρήγορη ροή, τείνουν να μην ενδιαφέρονται για τη χρήση τους ως αγωγών ακαθάρτων, σε αντίθεση με ηπειρωτικές χώρες όπως η Γαλλία και η Γερμανία, που διασχίζονται από μεγάλους διεθνείς ποταμούς. Με τον ίδιο τρόπο, η ατμοσφαιρική ρύπανση που εξανεμίζεται βολικά από τους πνέοντες ανέμους για να προσγειωθεί σε γειτονικές χώρες στο πέρασμά τους, βρίσκει διαφορετική αντιμετώπιση από τον ρυπαντή και τον ρυπαινόμενο. Γενικά, τα κράτη-μέλη στο δυτικό περιθώριο των ΕΚ είναι έτοιμα να δεχθούν επίπεδα εκπομπών στην ατμόσφαιρά τους που θεωρούνται ως σοβαρές περιβαλλοντικές απειλές από τους εταίρους τους στα ανατολικά, αν και τέτοιου είδους ευαρέσκειες εξανεμίζονται όλο και πιο γρήγορα, καθώς οι επιστήμονες κατανοούν τις ανεπαίσθητες επιπτώσεις της μακροχρόνιας ατμοσφαιρικής ρύπανσης. Τις τέσσερις δεκαετίες της ύπαρξής τους, οι ΕΚ έπρεπε να διαβούν ένα δύσκολο μονοπάτι ανάμεσα στους περιορισμούς που τους επιβάλλονταν από τη Συνθήκη, τις συγκρουόμενες στάσεις του αυξανόμενου αριθμού κρατών-μελων, κι ένα όλο και πιο ανεξάρτητο σώμα Ευρωπαϊκής κοινής γνώμης, που υποβοηθήθηκε και ενθαρρύνθηκε από το 1979 από την Ευρωβουλή. Αρχικά, οι επιδρομές στην επικράτεια της περιβαλλοντικής πολιτικής συνδέονταν ανοιχτά με οικονομικά ζητήματα και μέτρα αποφυγής διαστρεβλώσεων του ελεύθερου ανταγωνισμού. Μετά το 1972 όμως, στο κλίμα του Συνεδρίου του ΟΗΕ για το Ανθρώπινο Περιβάλλον, έγιναν προοδευτικά διακρίσεις και διαχωρισμοί. Μια σειρά Προγραμμάτων Περιβαλλοντικής Δράσης κατέληξαν στην ενσωμάτωση του περιβάλλοντος ως περιοχής Κοινοτικής πολιτικής στην Ενιαία Ευρωπαϊκή Πράξη.

Από τότε που τέθηκε σε ισχύ η Πράξη, οι ΕΚ ανέλαβαν έναν πολύ πιο κυρίαρχο και επιβεβαιωτικό ρόλο στην κατάστρωση και εφαρμογή της περιβαλλοντικής πολιτικής. Για την σωστή κατανόηση της αλλαγής, πρέπει να αξιολογηθούν τέσσερα ζητήματα-κλειδιά: πρώτον, η έννοια της Πράξης και η αλληλεπίδρασή της με την εθνική νομοθεσία των κρατών-μελών· δεύτερον, το βεληνεκές των περιβαλλοντικών ζητημάτων που αντιμετωπίζονται σε τέσσερα Προγράμματα Περιβαλλοντικής Δράσης και περισσότερες από 180 Οδηγίες και άλλους τύπους νομοθετικής επικοινωνίας· τρίτον, περιοχές περιβαλλοντικής πολιτικής, κυρίως συνδεδεμένες με την Κοινή Αγροτική Πολιτική, που έχουν εξελιχθεί εκτός των ορίων της περιβαλλοντικής πολιτικής και, τέλος, τα πολιτικά ζητήματα της εφαρμογής της πολιτικής, του ελέγχου και της επιβολής της.

Προφανώς, η δραστικότητα αυτών των περιβαλλοντικών πολιτικών μπορεί να κριθεί μόνο με βάση την αποτελεσματικότητά τους στην πράξη, και ο Michael Quigley (Trinity College Dublin, Ιρλανδία) στο 'Οι επιπτώσεις της πολιτικής των ΕΚ στο αγροτικό τοπίο και το περιβάλλον της Ιρλανδίας' (Κεφάλαιο 12) προβαίνει σε λεπτομερή αξιολόγηση ορισμένων από τις πολιτικές αυτές σε σχέση με την Ιρλανδία, μια χώρα της οποίας το τοπίο είναι κατά κύριο λόγο αγροτικό, κι όπου η γεωργία, ιδιαίτερα οι ποιμενικές καλλιέργειες, είναι η πιο σημαντική μοναδική οικονομική δραστηριότητα. Η Ιρλανδική γεωργία επεκτεινόταν και εκσυγχρονιζόταν ήδη πριν από την ένταξη της Ιρλανδίας στις ΕΚ το 1973, αλλά ο ρυθμός και η κατεύθυνση της αλλαγής συνδέθηκαν ολοένα και πιο στενά με τις πολιτικές που προέρχονταν από τις Βρυξέλλες. Η χρήση της αγροτικής γης και η ποιότητα του περιβάλλοντος επηρρεάζονται από τρεις διαφορετικές απόψεις της Ευρωπαϊκής πολιτικής: πρώτον, και προφανέστερα, από την ΚΑΠ, που επηρρεάζει όλες τις απόψεις των αγροτικών χρήσεων γης· δεύτερον, από διαρθρωτικά μέτρα που, αν και δεν αφορούν αυστηρά τη γεωργία, παρέχουν χρηματοδότηση για μια ποικιλία επιχειρησιακών προγραμμάτων μέσω του Κοινοτικού πλαισίου στήριξης, έτσι ώστε να επηρρεάζουν και το αγροτικό τοπίο· και τρίτον, από την αγροτική πολιτική και νομοθεσία, που λειτουργούν είτε για να ελέγξουν αρνητικές παρενέργειες άλλων πολιτικών, είτε θετικά για να προστατεύσουν διάφορες απόψεις του περιβάλλοντος.

Η ΚΑΠ με όλες τις διακλαδώσεις της, ειναι ιδιαίτερα καθοριστικός παράγοντας για την Ιρλανδία, όχι μόνο για την οικονομική ευμάρεια, αλλά και για την αλλαγή του τοπίου και την κατάσταση του περιβάλλοντος. Επηρρεάζει τη γεωργική ανάπτυξη με δυο διαφορετικούς τρόπους: πρώτον, με τον έλεγχο της αγοράς μέσω μηχανισμών υποστήριξης των τιμών και δεύτερον, μέσω μιας ποικιλίας μέτρων για οριζόντια αναδιάρθρωση που στοχεύουν στην αποζημίωση των καλλιεργητών σε ορισμένες περιοχές για τα φυσικά μειονεκτήματα της κατάστασης μέσα στην οποία λειτουργούν.

Το πρώτο από τα παραπάνω στοιχεία πολιτικής οδηγεί σε μια διαδικασία γεωργοκτηνοτροφικής εντατικοποίησης, αφού το επίπεδο της οικονομικής ενίσχυσης σχετίζεται με τον όγκο της παραγωγής. Αυτό με τη σειρά του οδηγεί αναπόφευκτα, όχι μόνο σε υπερπαραγωγή και συσσώρευση πλεονασμάτων τροφίμων, αλλά και σε υποβάθμιση του περιβάλλοντος. Τα αποτελέσματα σημαντικών χρηματοδοτήσεων από το ΕΓΤΠΕ στην αγροτική οικονομία έγιναν ιδιαίτερα εμφανή στον τομέα των εμπορευματικών γεωργικών και κτηνοτροφικών καλλιεργειών. Με τα κίνητρα από τις ΕΚ, ο αριθμός των προβάτων αυξήθηκε δραματικά τα πρόσφατα χρόνια, κι αυτό οδήγησε σε προβλήματα υπερβοσκής και διάβρωσης. Οι οικονομίες κλίμακας οδήγησαν σε περιφερειακή εξειδίκευση ορισμένων κτηνοτροφικών επιχειρήσεων, ιδιαίτερα χοίρων και πουλερικών. Δυστυχώς αυτό έχει καταστροφικές περιβαλλοντικές επιπτώσεις με την αποβολή μεγάλων ποσοτήτων ρύπων και την συνακόλουθη ρύπανση των ποταμών. Αλλες αποψεις της εντατικοποίησης, όπως αυξημένη χρήση λιπασμάτων και ιδίως η αντικατάσταση των αχυρώνων με παραγωγή φορβής οδήγησαν, επίσης, σε προβλήματα ρύπανσης των υδάτων. Ταυτόχρονα, διαρθρωτικοί πόροι από το ΕΓΤΠΕ που κατανέμονται σε περιθωριακές περιοχές καλλιεργειών με στόχο να τις κάνουν πιο παραγωγικές, ενδέχεται να έχουν αρνητικές επιπτώσεις σε ευπαθή περιβάλλοντα. Το Δυτικό Πακέτο, που στοχεύει στην διέγερση της γεωργικής ανάπτυξης στη Δυτική Ιρλανδία, καθώς και το Σχέδιο Δυτικής Αποστράγγισης, αποτελούν παραδείγματα μέτρων Κοινοτικής βοήθειας που είχαν ολέθριες περιβαλλοντικές επιπτώσεις.

Η ιρλανδική δασοπονία πρόσφατα επεκτείνεται θεαματικά, με διπλασιασμό των στόχων της ετήσιας φύτευσης από 15 000 σε 30 000 εκτάρια. Αυτό το πρωτοφανές επίπεδο ανάπτυξης προκαλείται, σε μεγάλο βαθμό, από επιδοτήσεις, υποστηριζόμενο από Κοινοτικούς πόρους με βάση το Δασικό Επιχειρησιακό Πρόγραμμα. Ορισμένες από τις επιπτώσεις της ανάπτυξης της δασοπονίας στην Ιρλανδία, ήταν: η οξείδωση των επιφανειακών υδάτων, η υποβάθμιση των φυσικών τόπων αλιείας, η καταστροφή σημαντικών βιοτόπων ή προφυλασσόμενων ελωδών πεδινών οικοσυστημάτων, και η αλλοίωση των άγριων τοπίων μεγάλου φυσικού κάλλους.   Από τα μέσα της δεκαετίας του 1980, η έμφαση στην εντατικοποίηση του πρωτογενούς τομέα άρχισε να μεταβάλλεται, εν μέρει ανταποκρινόμενη στην ανάγκη μείωσης της παραγωγής τροφίμων στις Κοινότητες και εν μέρει λόγω των καταστροφικών επιπτώσεων στο περιβάλλον. Αυτό κορυφώθηκε με μια σειρά ριζικών νέων μέτρων που τόνιζαν τον διττό ρόλο των καλλιεργητών ως παραγωγών τροφίμων και ως διαχειριστών της υπαίθρου. Πρόκειται για μια πολιτική που, αναμφίβολα, θα ωφελήσει το περιβάλλον. Ταυτόχρονα, η ενίσχυση της Κοινοτικής περιβαλλοντικής πολιτικής με μέτρα όπως η Οδηγία Εκτίμησης Περιβαλλοντικών Επιπτώσεων και η Οικιστική Οδηγία, θα πρέπει να αποδειχθεί χρήσιμη απ' αυτήν την άποψη. Για την Ιρλανδία όμως, οι πόροι για περιφερειακή ανάπτυξη, που έχουν επεκταθεί πολύ, μπορεί να αποβούν μια από τις μεγαλύτερες πιθανές απειλές στο περιβάλλον. Μένει να δειχθεί εαν η πεποίθηση στην προστασία του περιβάλλοντος έχει γερά θεμέλια.

Το περιβάλλον αποτελεί έναν από τους τομείς-κλειδιά για την υγεία των πληθυσμών, και ο Cosimo Palagiano (Καθηγητής στο Πανεπιστήμιο La Sapienza Roma, Ιταλία), στο 'Περιβάλλον, υγεία και περίθαλψη: Ευρωπαϊκές συγκρίσεις και μια Ιταλική περίπτωση (Κεφάλαιο 13) εξετάζει τον τρόπο με τον οποίο επηρρέασαν οι ΕΚ την υγεία και την περίθαλψη στην Ευρώπη. Οι ΕΚ έχουν παραμελήσει αυτόν τον τομέα, αν και αυξάνουν την συμμετοχή τους σε ζητήματα που σχετίζονται με την υγεία, για παράδειγμα μέσω των περιβαλλοντικών τους πολιτικών, του προτεινόμενου Κοινωνικού Χάρτη (Κοινοτικού Χάρτη θεμελιωδών κοινωνικών δικαιωμάτων των εργαζομένων) στη Συνθήκη του Maastricht και πολιτικές εντατικοποίησης και εκτατικοποίησης του πρωτογενούς τομέα.

Οι στόχοι του κεφαλαίου είναι τρεις. Πρώτον, η επιθεώρηση των συνθηκών υγείας στις ΕΚ με χρήση ποικιλίας δεικτών παροχής υπηρεσιών και συνθηκών υγείας. Τονίζεται εδώ ότι συνεχίζουν να υπάρχουν διαφορές στην προσδοκώμενη ζωή και στην εμφάνιση ασθενειών, ακόμα και μέσα σ' αυτή τη σχετικά ομοιογενή ομάδα εύπορων κρατών. Δεύτερος στόχος είναι η εικονογράφηση της συνεχιζόμενης ποικιλίας συνθηκών υγείας μέσα στις διάφορες χώρες. Επιλέγεται να μελετηθεί η περίπτωση της Ιταλίας, για δυο λόγους: λόγω των διαρκών και βαθύτατων περιφερειακών ανισοτήτων που υπάρχουν στη χώρα αυτή, και λόγω της σχετικά περιορισμένης αγγλόφωνης βιβλιογραφίας για τις συνθήκες της υγείας εδώ, σε σύγκριση, για παράδειγμα, με βόρειες Ευρωπαϊκές χώρες. Τέλος, αντιμετωπίζεται το ερώτημα της πραγματικής και δυνητικής σημασίας των ζητημάτων υγείας στις ΕΚ.

Στο συμπέρασμα του βιβλίου, οι Allan Williams και Mark Blacksell (Πανεπιστήμιο Exeter, Ενωμένο Βασίλειο) στο 'Ένας μεταβαλλόμενος χάρτης και νέες προτεραιότητες: οι ΕΚ στο κατώφλι του 21ου αιώνα' (Κεφάλαιο 14) εξετάζουν τους τρόπους με τους οποίους ενδέχεται να μεταβληθεί η Ευρώπη κατά την καμπή προς τον 21ο αιώνα και τις επιπτώσεις αυτών των μεταβολών στις πολιτικές των ΕΚ, ιδιαίτερα όσον αφορά την οικονομική ανάπτυξη και το περιβάλλον.

La sfida europea: Geografia e sviluppo nella Comunità Europea

La fondazione della Comunità Europea rimane senza dubbio il fatto di maggiore importanza per la geografia economica, politica e sociale dell'Europa della seconda metà del XX secolo. Dai suoi inizi nei primi anni '50—con il Trattato di Parigi (1952) e la nascita della Comunità Europea del Carbone e dell'Acciaio (CECA)—fino ai due Trattati di Roma (1958), che posero le basi della Comunità Economica Europea (CEE) e dell'Euratom, all'Atto Unico Europeo (1986), che ha aperto la strada al Mercato Unico del 1993, e più recentemente ai negoziati un po' tortuosi, ma ricchi di prospettive, sulla completa unione monetaria, punto caratterizzante del Trattato di Maastricht, la Comunità Europea si è trasformata in un'entità politica sempre più complessa e determinante per lo sviluppo ulteriore dei dodici stati europei.

La complessità istituzionale della Comunità va aumentando a mano a mano che nuovi stati vi aderiscono. Per oltre un ventennio, dal 1952 al 1973, essa è stata costituita solo da sei stati membri—Belgio, Francia, Germania Occidentale, Italia, Lussemburgo e Paesi Bassi—tutti paesi industrializzati, situati nel cuore dell'Europa occidentale ed in fase di rinascita economica dopo le devastazioni delle due guerre mondiali, che avevano dominato la prima metà del XX secolo. Nel primo ampliamento del 1973 entrarono a far parte della Comunità altri tre stati membri—Danimarca, Irlanda e Regno Unito—tutti appartenenti all'Europa settentrionale e strettamente legati, dal punto de vista economico, sia tra di loro che con gli stati fondatori. L'adesione dei nuovi stati cambiò sostanzialmente la natura della Comunità Europea: i problemi regionali a causa della posizione periferica divennero certamente più acuti, mentre la coesione geografica della Comunità, che all'inizio era stata il maggiore elemento di forza, fu minata dall'aggiunta di due stati insulari, uno dei quali, il Regno Unito, deteneva più del 20% della popolazione totale. Gli anni '80 videro un ulteriore allargamento dell'associazione, con l'adesione dapprima della Grecia, nel 1981, e poi della Spagna e del Portogallo nel 1986. Anche questo secondo ampliamento, questa volta nel mondo mediterraneo, ebbe l'effetto cumulativo di mutare radicalmente la natura della Comunità Europea. Tutti e tre questi nuovi stati membri erano poco legati al nucleo industriale dell'Europa Ocidentale, sia dal punto di vista geografico che da quello economico. Questi paesi erano ancora caratterizzati, per quanto riguardava il paesaggio agrario, da una struttura che era in qualche modo retaggio della lunga tradizione di origine feudale; per quanto riguardava l'economia industriale e la struttura urbana, non erano ancora entrati nell'alveo della grande corrente europea, se si fa eccezione tuttavia del contributo da essi dato, attraverso l'immigrazione, di una manodopera a basso costo.

Negli anni '90 la Comunità Europea compì un altro passo verso il cambiamento. Con l'unificazione della Germania nel 1990 avvenne di fatto l'annessione—sia pure per 'assorbimento'—di un paese dell'Europa Orientale, l'ex DDR, e così la carta geografica economica regionale venne ad assumere una dimensione completamente nuova. Come sarebbe stato possibile accettare come membri della Comunità certi paesi, le cui economie industriali si erano sviluppate in un sistema di pianificazione centralizzata, che aveva chiaramente denunciato il suo fallimento? La Germania unificata ha probabilmente voluto aderire alla Comunità Europea senza tentare alcun cambiamento strutturale, ma se vi si dovessero aggiungere altri stati dell'Europa Orientale (come la Polonia, l'Ungheria, gli stati ceco e slovacco dell'ex Cecoslovacchia, la Slovenia, la Croazia e qualsiasi altro paese che eventualmente nascerà dalle rovine della Iugoslavia), si verrebbe a modificare l'intera logica economica e politica della CEE.

Lo scompiglio politico dell'Europa Orientale non ètuttavia il solo fattore che spinge al cambiamento. Un buon gruppo di stati dell'Europa Occidentale che, all'inizio, per un motivo o per l'altro, non avevano ritenuto opportuno entrare nella Comunità Europea, fanno ora la fila per esservi ammessi. Nel 1991 l'Associazione Europea di Libero Scambio (EFTA), costituita da Austria, Finlandia, Islanda, Lichtenstein, Norvegia, Svezia e Svizzera, ha firmato per creare l'Area Economica Europea (AEE), un accordo con la Comunità Europea grazie al quale la zona di libero scambio viene estesa a tutta l'Europa Occidentale. Inoltre, Austria, Svizzera e Svezia hanno compiuto un ulteriore passo in avanti, presentando una richiesta formale di adesione come stati membri della Comunità Europea, ed è molto probabile che altri membri dell'AEE ne seguiranno l'esempio.

Infine, in un futuro meno prossimo, aderiranno alla Comunità altri stati che hanno espresso il desiderio di farne parte. Turchia, Malta e Cipro stanno tutt'e tre cercando di aderire alla Comunità Europea nei prossimi trent'anni, e così pure molte delle repubbliche, in cui si è scissa la parte occidentale dell'Unione Sovietica, cominciano a dimostrare un concreto interesse per una possibile adesione. Comunque vadano questi tentativi, un fatto è tuttavia certo: la Comunità Europea dovrà in futuro continuare ad adattarsi alle istanze economiche e politiche di una geografia politica in trasformizione.

Struttura del volume

Con questo volume, gli autori—tutti geografi di sette differenti paesi della
Comunità Europea—hanno voluto interpretare l'impatto che la Comunità
Europea ha avuto sul paesaggio socio-economico degli stati membri. Nell'intro-
duzione, Mark Blacksell e Allan Williams (Exeter, Regno Unito) affrontano
il problema dello 'Sviluppo della Comunità Europea: il significato spaziale'
(Capitolo I) e illustrano come la stessa Comunità Europea abbia prospettato
l'intero processo di sviluppo economico e come le politiche regionali siano
cambiate a causa dei successivi ampliamenti dell'associazione e dei continui
cambiamenti del commercio, sia all'interno dell'Europa che in tutto il
mondo.

La Comunità Europea, fin tanto che è rimasta una Comunità di solo sei
paesi, ben accentrati nel cuore dell'Europa Occidentale industrializzata, non
ha dato alcuna rilevanza alla politica regionale. Tutti i suoi interessi erano
indirizzati a promuovere lo sviluppo economico mediante il libero commercio
e la concorrenza, mentre nulla veniva tentato in direzione di una politica di
pianificazione e organizzazione centralizzata del territorio. Per la verità
qualcosa era stato fatto, sia dal punto di vista regionale, come il sostegno
all'economia del Mezzogiorno italiano, che da quello settoriale, come l'incen-
tivazione alle aziende agricole di tipo familiare, e i risultati complessivi che
questi tentativi avevano conseguito negli anni '50 e '60, erano sembrati assai
promettenti per lo sviluppo economico e politico dell'Europa.

Questa impressione positiva fu però scossa al momento del primo ampliamento nel 1973. I problemi insolubili che dovettero affrontare le vecchie
regioni industriali in crisi del Regno Unito, ma a poco a poco quelle di tutti
i paesi della Comunità, resero indispensabile, per alleviare le difficoltà in cui
si erano venute a trovare le aree urbane di questi paesi, la creazione di fondi
strutturali, un po' come quelli che erano stati resi in teoria disponibili a favore
delle aree rurali, attraverso la Politica Agraria Comunitaria (PAC). Nel 1975
fu creato il Fondo Europeo per lo Sviluppo Regionale (FESR) con il
proposito dichiarato di integrare gli aiuti regionali nazionali e i programmi
di investimento. I fondi, all'inizio limitati axsolo 3% del bilancio della
Comunità Europea, aumentarono in seguito progressivamente; il fatto più
importante, tuttavia, fu il riconoscimento dell'obiettivo del FESR e cioè che
la dinamica del mercato non avrebbe mai potuto da sola risolvere in modo
soddisfacente le iniquità delle disuguaglianze regionali.

Agli inizi degli anni '80, l'adesione di Grecia, Spagna e Portogallo rese più
pressante la necessità di una politica regionale, una volta che si erano
dimostrate del tutto inadeguate le politiche settoriali. Tutti e tre questi paesi
si erano, per tanti versi, nelle stesse difficili condizioni in cui si trovavano

alcune aree isolate della Comunità. Per risolvere i loro problemi regionali sarebbe stato necessario che gli aiuti fossero concessi in maggior quantità che in precedenza e in ogni caso sarebbe stato indispensabile che questi aiuti facessero parte di un più coordinato approccio dello sviluppo economico nel suo insieme. Le soluzioni della Comunità furono di due tipi: in primo luogo essa si preoccupò di accrescere l'ammontare totale degli aiuti regionali disponibili e di indirizzarne parte verso i paesi del Mediterraneo, in secondo luogo predispose un Progetto Integrato Mediterraneo per assicurare più coordinamento e coerenza all'impiego dei fondi concessi.

Il riassestamento della politica regionale comunitaria diede un ulteriore rilancio all'Atto Unico Europeo. Tuttavia, se proprio si volevano eliminare le intollerabili disuguaglianze regionali, l'obiettivo dell'Atto, che è poi quello di raggiungere il Mercato Unico nel 1993, doveva essere dotato di un nuova forma di base destinato non solo agli stati periferici del Mediterraneo, ma anche a tutti i dodici stati membri della Comunità Europea. Nel 1989 i tre fondi strutturali esistenti, il FESR, il Fondo Sociale Europeo (FSE) e il Fondo di Sostegno e di Garanzia all'Agricoltura (FEOGA) della PAC, furono riuniti in un solo fondo, che doveva essere usato per raggiungere cinque (ma in realtà sei, in quanto il 5a e il 5b sono del tutto distinti) obiettivi politici. Gli scopi e gli obiettivi dunque sono ora chiari: i vecchi fondi strutturali sono stati eliminati e sostituiti da un solo fondo integrato.

D' altro canto un altro importante aspetto dei fondi strutturali va riformato. All'inizio, la Commissione della Comunità Europea poteva operare solo attraverso i governi nazionali, fornendo aiuti complementari ai programmi in corso. Nel quadro del nuovo schema, una percentuale (circa il 9%) dei fondi regionali disponibili sarà assegnata dalla Comunità, indipendentemente dalle iniziative nazionali, attraverso i programmi STAR, VOLEREN, RESIDER e RENAVAL, che si interessano rispettivamente delle industrie energetiche, del ferro e dell'acciaio e cantieristiche. Si tratta di un piccolo ma egualmente importante passo in avanti verso l'integrazione e la nascita di un approccio comunitario allo sviluppo regionale.

La situazione urbana

Dal momento che circa l'80% della popolazione della Comunità Europea vive in grandi e piccole città, le modificazioni che sono avvenute nell'ambiente urbano da quando è sorta la Comunità Europea sono quelle che riguardano in modo più diretto la maggior parte dei suoi cittadini. Pierre Laborde (Bordeaux III, Francia), in 'Evoluzione spaziale delle città dell'Europa Occidentale dal 1950 al 1990' (Capitolo 2), considera gli effetti geografici della rapida crescita della popolazione urbana della Comunità Europea fino alla metà degli anni '70. Essa ha determinato la fine della struttura fortemente compatta e centripeta delle città e l'inizio della loro esplosione verso l'esterno. Ciò non solo ha modificato le aree urbane esistenti, ma ha anche creato una nuova periferia urbanizzata, tuttora in fase di espansione nonostante che la crescita della popolazione stessa abbia, negli ultimi tempi, subìto un netto rallentamento.

Le forme del nuovo sviluppo urbano sono andate progressivamente modificandosi nel corso della seconda metà del XX secolo. Negli anni '50 e '60 era di moda il nuovo sviluppo comprensivo, variamente noto come 'sviluppo bulldozer' in Francia, 'Brussellizzazione' in Belgio e 'rinnovamento per sostituzione' in Spagna. Molti centri storici, perfino di quelle città che, in tempo di guerra, non erano state danneggiate dai bombardamenti, furono dunque distrutti, provocando, specie in Francia, una forte reazione contro simili drastici provvedimenti, mentre, secondo i dettami della nuova ortodossia urbanistica, bisognava conservare e rinnovare gli edifici esistenti. Alla fine, comunque, nessuno dei diversi approcci al nuovo sviluppo dei centri delle città è stato utilizzato per risolvere i problemi posti dalle vetustà degli edifici urbani e dalla loro cronica incapacità ad adeguarsi alle vicende demografiche ed economiche.

La più ragguardevole testimonianza della rapida crescita della popolazione delle città è l'espansione delle aree suburbane che circondano quasi tutti i grandi e piccoli centri. Inizialmente, la maggior parte dello sviluppo suburbano era dovuto a motivi residenziali ed era prevalentemente caratterizzato da case basse e forte richiesta di spazi. Ma perfino ladddove venivano costruiti alti edifici, come i 'grands ensembles' in Francia, questi erano invariabilmente collocati in aree verdi, con la conseguente perdita di molto terreno agricolo. Tuttavia, anche le attività commerciali e industriali, assieme ai servizi, a mano a mano che si localizzavano in periferia, andavano ad occupare edifici bassi.

Più recentemente, invece, lo sviluppo topografico delle aree urbane è stato determinato, non dall'incremento demografico, ma da modificazioni sociali, tecnologiche e politiche. Il numero delle unità familiari è cresciuto notevolmente: le famiglie sono molto più piccole, per l'aumento sia dei divorzi che dell'età media; si posseggono più automobili e quindi ciascuno può scegliere di vivere nelle aree suburbane senza rischiare di perdere il posto di lavoro; anche le politiche di pianificazione basate sulla logica del decentramento hanno incoraggiato gli amministratori pubblici a favorire la creazione di aree suburbane. Le politiche della Comunità Europea hanno avuto un effetto del tutto secondario in queste modificazioni. Infatti, anche se le politiche regionali si occupano delle aree industriali in crisi e nel nuovo sviluppo delle città, si sono messi a punto più elevati standard ambientali, queste decisioni non possono essere considerate parti integranti di una complessiva politica urbanistica.

Il risultato immediatamente conseguente a questi cambiamenti strutturali è stato dunque quello di produrre un modello più differenziato di uso del suolo nelle città, determinando così grandi differenze di valorizzazione tra il centro e la periferia. In Francia, le autorità municipali stanno ora cominciando ad occuparsi con maggiore attenzione di questi cambiamenti, ma è davvero impossibile estendere questi metodi a tutta la Comunità Europea, soprattutto a causa delle differenti strutture politiche.

Dei modelli di trasformazione delle città e delle pianificazioni urbanistiche si occupa in modo chiaro Lila Leontidou (Istituto Universitario Tecnico Nazionale di Atene, Grecia) in 'Città mediterranee: tendenze divergenti in un'Europa unita' (Capitolo 3). Per lungo tempo le città hanno avuto un'importante funzione culturale nell'Europa mediterranea e questo fenomeno è ancora presente in questi ultimi anni del XX secolo; e quella considerevole dispersione tecnologica, che ha caratterizzato le città dell'Europa settentrionale, comincia a diffondersi anche nel sud. Il centro della città è sempre stato, ed è, la principale area residenziale a Napoli, Atene e Barcellona, mentre le classi lavoratrici tendono a spostarsi verso la periferia. La disgregazione sociale ed economica, così tipica in Francia, Germania e Regno Unito, è dunque meno evidente nei paesi del Mediterraneo.

Inevitabilmente l'impatto della Comunità Europea sullo sviluppo urbanistico è stato minimo. Tra i paesi mediterranei solo l'Italia è membro fondatore, mentre Grecia, Spagna e Portogallo non hanno aderito prima degli anni '80. Questa è comunque solo una spiegazione parziale: molte politiche di rilievo emanate dalla Comunità Europea relative alle aree urbane, così come sono formulate, sono di scarsa importanza per le città mediterranee. Per esempio, infatti, gli indicatori di povertà basati sulla mancanza di abitazione non possono essere utilizzati in alcun modo, dal momento che i poveri abitano in baracche e abitazioni precarie costruitesi da soli. Bisogna dunque sottolineare l'ovvia verità che le politiche globali, anche all'interno di un gruppo di stati apparentemente omogenei come quelli della Comunità Europea, non possono raggiungere i propri obiettivi se non prestando la massima attenzione alle condizioni locali.

I cambiamenti strutturali

La nascita della Comunità Europea ha alterato il contesto economico e sociale dell'Europa e ha prodotto un profondo cambiamento strutturale in molte aree, sia attraverso precise iniziative politiche, sia attraverso adattamenti involontari. Jean Paul Charrié (Bordeaux III, Francia), in 'Modello dell'industria: Dall'Europeizzazione alla globalizzazione' (Capitolo 4), delinea un quadro dettagliato dei principali cambiamenti che stanno avvenendo in un gruppo determinato di paesi, il maggiore dei quali costituì la culla della Rivoluzione Industriale nel XIX secolo. La Comunità Europea è ancora una potenza industriale mondiale, ma la sostanza della sua supremazia si è dovuta modificare di fronte ad un livello di concorrenza mai così spietata.

Molti cambiamenti nel quadro industriale generale sono avvenuti nei quaranta anni successivi alla fondazione della Comunità. La Comunità Europea, ricca di carbone e di ferro, ha rivolto la sua enorme capacità produttiva in molti settori chiave, come quello del ferro, dell'acciaio e della chimica. Il suo potenziale ha raggiunto l'apice negli anni '50 e non è un caso che i primi successi le siano derivati dalla CECA. In un continente afflitto da cinque anni di conflitti, il Trattato di Parigi portò alla costituzione di un periodo di crescita economica che fu interrotto solo dalla crisi petrolifera del 1973. La Comunità ha dovuto imparare ad adattare i suoi metodi di produzione industriale non solo alla crescente importanza del petrolio e all' incredibile lievitazione del suo prezzo, ma anche al risanamento di quelle industrie di base ora in crisi, che erano però state le pietre miliari del suo successo iniziale e della contemporanea crescita del suo settore di alta tecnologia.

Tutti questi cambiamenti sono inoltre avvenuti mentre aumentava la concorrenza da parte dei paesi di recente industrializzazione. La minaccia rappresentata dal Giappone è chiara ed è anche molto temibile, in quanto i beni prodotti in questo paese sono in diretta concorrenza con i tradizionali mercati d'oltremare, nell'America Settentrionale soprattutto, della Comunità Europea. Nel contempo gli industriali giapponesi investono direttamente nella Comunità Europea in modo da aggirare i regolamenti da questa stabiliti al fine di limitare il flusso delle importazioni giapponesi in Europa. Desta inoltre preoccupazione la concorrenza dei Nuovi Paesi Industrializzati (NPI) dell'Asia, in particolare quella della Corea del Sud, che si sono affermati prima di altri nel mercato dell'abbigliamento e che ora stanno rapidamente diversificando la loro produzione.

Tutti questi vari cambiamenti purtroppo stanno avendo un impatto cumulativo sul cuore industriale dell'Europa. Le regioni tradizionalmente industriali sono in crisi, perché sono afflitte da un numero sempre crescente di problemi, che possono essere risolti solo con urgenti provvedimenti. D'altra parte i maggiori centri urbani, che si trovano in una condizione più favorevole, difendono accanitamente la propria supremazia.

Per molti anni la Commissione e le altre istituzioni della Comunità Europea non hanno avuto grande potere, potendo intervenire solo in casi isolati, in gran parte con misure per proteggere nelle regioni in crisi i singoli settori e le industrie in difficoltà, ma ora gli interventi stanno cominciando ad avere una funzione sempre più importante nella politica industriale. La Comunità Europea è una componente importante del paesaggio industriale in sviluppo, in quanto fornisce aiuti specifici in particolari settori, coordina gli sforzi di ricerca e assume la direzione nella politica regionale in espansione. Inoltre, quando entrerà in funzione, il Mercato Unico avrà importantissime ripercussioni sulla struttura generale della Comunità.

I governi hanno da tempo considerato i trasporti come una delle chiavi per modificare le dinamiche delle società industriali e la Comunità Europea è sempre stata attiva su questo punto, anche se non ha potuto, a livello comunitario, perseguirlo con quella forza che ci si sarebbe potuti aspettare. James Killen (Trinity College di Dublino, Irlanda) e Austin Smith (Ulster, Regno Unito), in 'Politica dei trasporti della Comunità Europea con particolare riferimento all'Irlanda come regione di periferia' (Capitolo 5), dimostrano in quale modo la Politica dei Trasporti della Comunità Europea, o la sua assenza, abbia interessato l'Irlanda nel suo insieme.

Per tradizione i governi nazionali hanno cercato di influire sui sistemi di trasporto e sulle relative operazioni all'interno dei loro paesi sostanzialmente in due modi. In primo luogo essi hanno avuto una parte significativa nel regolare i trasporti, ponendo, ad esempio, limiti di velocità e condizioni per ottenere permessi di vario tipo. In Europa, in genere, i governi hanno svolto una funzione importante nell'attività dei servizi ferroviari e, in taluni casi, dei trasporti su strada, preoccupandosi di controllare direttamente il grado di concorrenza tra le diverse modalità. In secondo luogo questi governi hanno tentato di determinare il livello e la natura degli investimenti nelle infrastrutture dei trasporti, avendo particolare cura che questi investimenti fossero fatti tenendo conto di quelli destinati agli altri settori dell'economia e che i fondi destinati ai trasporti fossero ben spesi.

Prima della firma del Trattato di Roma, la politica dei trasporti in Europa era seguita da ciascuno stato in modo più o meno indipendente da quella degli altri paesi membri. In teoria la cooperazione a livello europeo fu resa possibile dalla Conferenza dei Ministri dei Trasporti, che ebbe luogo nel 1953, ma i risultati concreti ottenuti furono scarsi. Un esempio di cooperazione a livello europeo è lo sviluppo della rete di treni espressi Trans Europe Express (TEE). Nel Trattato di Roma vi è un esplicito impegno per la costituzione di una politica comune dei trasporti, ma il fatto che ciascun paese ne abbia già una rende improbabile l'accordo per una politica comunitaria unica. Il principale obiettivo di questo capitolo è quello di dimostrare come gli scarsi risultati ragginuti finora nei vari settori—strada, ferrovia, mare e aria—abbiano favorito in particolar modo l'Irlanda, una regione della Comunità alla estrema periferia rispetto alle principali reti di trasporto.

Nonostante le inevitabili differenze nazionali e regionali, la Comunità Europea nel suo insieme possiede un'invidiabile rete di trasporti che ha notevolmente contribuito alla sua coesione. Essa ha anche facilitato quella mobilità del lavoro che ha offerto il maggior contributo al successo economico dell'Europa. Russell King (Trinity College di Dublino, Irlanda), in 'Migrazione e mercato unico del lavoro: un problema dello sviluppo regionale' (Capitolo 6), considera il contributo che la migrazione internazionale ha dato, a partire dalla fine degli anni '50, al cambiamento della geografia economica e sociale della Comunità Europea. La migrazione dei lavoratori è stato un importante fattore della crescita delle economie europee industriali e post-industriali alla fine degli anni '60 e all'inizio degli anni '70. Il numero di immigrati, certamente diminuito dopo la prima crisi petrolifera del 1973-'74, ha però contemporaneamente subìto un notevole aumento dovuto soprattutto al ricongiungimento in massa degli altri membri della famiglia. Tutti questi dunque, insieme con le nuove ondate di immigrati della fine degli anni '80 e dell'inizio degli anni '90, possono oggi far stimare approssimativamente la popolazione totale di immigrati in Europa intorno ai 20 milioni, una gran parte dei quali è nella Comunità Europea.

Recentemente, quasi dopo un decennio, si è nuovamente ricominciato ad attribuire grande importanza al dibattito riguardante la migrazione internazionale. I flussi migratori di lavoratori cominciarono ad intensificarsi verso la fine degli anni '80, ma in alcuni paesi (Germania e Paesi Bassi) erano iniziati già nel 1985. Il vero incentivo alle correnti migratorie di nuove masse è stato però il collasso del socialismo nell'Europa Orientale a partire dal 1989. Gli avvenimenti formidabili degli ultimi tre anni ci inducono, tuttavia, ad essere più cauti nel prevedere gli andamenti della migrazione internazionale: poche persone nel 1988 avrebbero potuto prevedere i drammatici avvenimenti che si sarebbero poi svolti, anche se il continuo passaggio di gruppi di persone dalla DDR nella Repubblica Federale di Germania prima dell'unificazione e la miccia scoppiata alla frontiera dell'Ungheria avrebbero potuto far presagire il processo di cambiamento in atto.

Ma questi avvenimenti sono destinati a non restare un fatto isolato: altre nuvole si affacciano ancora all'orizzonte demografico dell'Europa. Milioni di persone sono in movimento intorno al mondo, trasformandolo con i loro viaggi, e l'Europa non fa eccezione. Negli anni '80 sono aumentati notevolmente in Europa i profughi e le persone che chiedono asilo politico. Questo problema va ora risolto coraggiosamente, sia a livello di politica comunitaria che a quello delle politiche nazionali, particolarmente in vista dell'accordo di Schengen sui controlli delle frontiere 'colabrodo' della Comunità Europea e dell'avvio del Mercato Unico.

Un problema particolarmente importante, connesso con le migrazioni internazionali, sia all'interno che all'esterno della Comunità Europea, è il lavoro illegale, vivacemente descritto da Solange Montagné-Villette (Poitiers, Francia) in 'Mobilità, segretezza e lavoro nero nella Comunità Europea' (Capitolo 7). La gente che lavora in segreto, e in genere in modo illegale, non è una novità nei paesi della Comunità Europea. Questo fenomeno, infatti, ebbe inizio nei primi anni di questo secolo, al momento della formazione delle strutture amministrative in tutti i ricchi paesi industriali e si intensificò di pari passo con i sistemi di sicurezza sociale. Oggi, in alcuni paesi, il lavoro nero fa parte di una tradizione ben consolidata ed è visto da molti come parte della cultura nazionale. Il lavoro nero a livello 'comunitario' invece, come quello che si svolge nella Comunità Europea e al di fuori di essa, ha assunto varie caratteristiche originali che non sono state però attentamente considerate, probabilmente perché il fenomeno è troppo recente. La mobilità notevolmente accresciuta della forza lavoro, l'industria e gli affari hanno creato nuove e illegali pratiche di impiego, con forme connesse strettamente con la struttura politica, economica e giuridica della Comunità Europea.

Lavoratori dei paesi poveri nella Comunità Europea che cercano impiego negli altri stati membri, trasferimento e/o subappalto di attività industriali illegittime nei paesi mediterranei dell'Europa, persone provenienti da paesi esterni alla Comunità che vi lavorano illegalmente, sono tutte manifestazioni della crescente prevalenza di pratiche di lavoro nero. Per quel che riguarda la Comunità Europea, il problema del lavoro degli immigrati è uno dei più difficili da comprendere. Vi è stata una vera e propria riluttanza da parte di qualche stato membro, particolarmente il Regno Unito, ad ammettere che il controllo delle condizioni di lavoro e di altri aspetti dell'ingegneria sociale sia compatibile con il libero mercato al quale tutti aspirano.

L'adattamento dell'agricoltura

Una sola politica, la PAC, ha dominato la Comunità Europea per quasi trent'anni, inghiottendo più del 90% del bilancio della Comunità, e controllandone ancora oltre il 60%. Le scelte politiche che sono alla base di questo stato di cose sono ben note, ma questa non è la sede per illustrarle. Tuttavia, tutte le ricerche che affrontano con serietà i problemi della Comunità Europea dedicano una buona parte della loro attenzione al settore agricolo. La straordinaria importanza che si è data finora all'agricoltura nella Comunità Europea sta pian piano diminuendo, ma questa minore attenzione avrà sicuramente ripercussioni gravi e di ampia portata per l'economia rurale e il paesaggio. Dietrich Denecke (Göttingen, Germania), in 'Conversione agricola, spopolamento e programmi di abbandono: lo scopo della conservazione del paesaggio in Europa, con particolare riferimento alla Germania' (Capitolo 8), analizza le conseguenze che questi cambiamenti in atto nella politica agricola della Comunità Europea stanno avendo nei riguardi del paesaggio e dell'ambiente e porta inoltre esempi di paesaggi rurali della Germania, particolarmente vulnerabili a causa della coesistenza, ancora presente, dell'impresa contadina e della moderna agricoltura. Fino a questo secolo la generale scarsità di prodotti agricoli e la mancanza di cibo hanno portato a un uso eccessivo dello spazio rurale. Negli ultimi venti anni, comunque, si è assistito ad un cambiamento radicale. La sovrapproduzione ha consentito di piantare colture alternative, di estendere le colture estensive e il pascolo, di mettere da parte i programmi e, non ultimo, di abbandonare i poderi e le terre. Tutti questi cambiamenti e le politiche che li comportano stanno ora modificando i sistemi di attività agricola in Europa. Nel contempo vi è stata una razionalizzazione del numero dei poderi, e l'intensificazione della produzione agricola e dell'allevamento hanno prodotto effetti secondari di degrado ambientale. Entrambi questi processi contribuiscono allo sconvolgimento del delicato equilibrio ecologico del paesaggio rurale, il cui mantenimento, attraverso i tradizionali metodi di coltivazione è divenuto quasi un atto di fede per la Comunità Europea. Il raggiungimento di un'agricoltura accettabile dal punto di vista ecologico, che deve essere poi lo scopo della conservazione del paesaggio, è perciò divenuto un problema cruciale dello sviluppo della Comunità, con importanti interconnessioni per l'intero processo di revisione della PAC.

Sebbene la PAC stia ora per essere sostituita da una politica che vada incontro ad una produzione agricola senza costi apparenti o alle immediate necessità, essa costituisce ancora la pietra miliare della politica della Comunità Europea. Manuel Corbera (Cantabria, Spagna), in la 'Politica Agricola Comune e lo sviluppo dell'agricoltura: problemi e prospettive' (Capitolo 9), giudica la stessa PAC dal punto di vista della Spagna, un paese con una grande attività agricola e che ha solo da poco (1986) aderito alla Comunità Europea. In termini generali, la Comunità è la principale potenza agricola mondiale, il primo produttore di latte, burro, formaggio, vino, zucchero e carne bovina e il secondo produttore di grano e orzo. Essa è anche autosufficiente per tutti i prodotti di clima temperato, ad eccezione di frutta fresca, granturco e carne ovina e caprina.

Questa invidiabile situazione è in parte un riflesso delle condizioni estremamente favorevoli e della complementarietà dei suoi ambienti atlantico, continentale e mediterraneo. I processi di produzione che vi si svolgono sono di considerevole importanza: utilizzazione intensiva della terra, sistemi di coltivazione che si adattano bene alle condizioni naturali, strutture agricole efficienti e alti livelli di meccanizzazione rendono possibili raccolti continui e abbondanti.

Ad ogni modo, il successo dell'agricoltura nella Comunità Europea si deve soprattutto all'effetto della PAC, che ha sostenuto e incoraggiato lo sviluppo dell'attività per una generazione: senze la PAC nessuno degli stati membri avrebbe potuto ottenere un primato mondiale per proprio conto e questi fatti vanno valutati nella loro giusta luce. Nonostante i molti problemi e l'evidente esigenza di una riforma, possiamo affermare che la sua azione è stata e continua ad essere positiva.

Il successo della politica agricola dal punto di vista della produzione di generi alimentari non può farci tuttavia ignorare la crisi alla quale devono far fronte molte regioni agricole. Non è necessaria tanta terra, specialmente terra marginale, da usare per la produzione di alimenti: sono state sperimentate anche colture alternative, sia per la terra stessa, sia per la popolazione che l'ha finora coltivata tradizionalmente. La semplice esclusione di essa dalla produzione e la preservazione del paesaggio sono scelte discusse in precedenza, ma questo richiede d'altra parte che tutta la questione della mancata coltivazione sia affidata a comunità stabili e coerenti dal punto di vista sociale. L'alternative più ovvia è di puntare sul potenziale turistico delle aree rurali, specialmente delle regioni costiere e montane dell'Europa.

Allan Williams e Gareth Shaw (Exeter, Regno Unito), in 'Turismo: opportunità, sfide e contraddizioni nella Comunità Europea' (Capitolo 10), esaminano l'intero fenomeno turistico della Comunità. Dalla nascita del turismo di massa negli anni '60, questo settore può essere considerato un elemento essenziale nella costruzione economica e sociale dell'Europa. Esso ha in primo luogo una grande importanza economica, poiché impiega più di un ventesimo della forza lavoro e concorre, con una notevole percentuale, alla formazione del prodotto interno lordo e al commercio internazionale, sia all'interno che all'esterno della Comunità. Il turismo è inoltre un mezzo di promozione sociale, perché effettua il trasferimento di beni e di stili di vita, e perché rappresenta uno dei pochi canali di interazioni internazionali di massa tra popoli e culture nella Comunità. Possiamo discutere se esista una identità culturale europea, ma, se è così, il turismo offre certo il suo contributo. Infine il turismo è alla base dei movimenti internazionali transfrontalieri nella Comunità Europea, la principale area di liberalizzazione del programma del Mercato Unico. L'importanza generale del turismo nella Comunità è dimostrata da un semplice dato statistico: il 64% di tutto il turismo internazionale mondiale avviene in Europa e la Comunità Europea partecipa per una grande percentuale e questo mercato. Più che in ogni altra regione del mondo, nella Comunità Europea il turismo è essenziale per la produzione e il consumo delle aree urbane e rurali.

La risposta ambientale

L'ambiente in quanto tale è stato completamente ignorato nei Trattati di Parigi e di Roma, e spesso la politica della Comunità Europea ha formulato soluzioni difficili da giustificare a questo riguardo, nonostante che a cominciare dagli anni '60 e '70 la gente sia andata sempre più prendendo coscienza con inquietudine del degrado ambientale e dell'esaurimento delle risorse, e nonostante che si andasse ormai diffondendo l'opinione che non fosse più possibile considerare questi problemi in un contesto esclusivamente nazionale. La stessa Comunità Europea tuttavia, pur essendo cresciuta come ha fatto da sei a dodici membri e pur avendo presentato sempre un modello geografico frammentario e lento nel suo processo di sviluppo, costituisce comunque una unità spaziale 'naturale' per la soluzione di una serie sempre più varia e complessa di problemi ambientali e di utilizzazione delle risorse. La gente pensava che la Comunità Europea potesse essere lo strumento più appropriato per la pianificazione dell'ambiente, grazie forse al suo dichiarato multinazionalismo che sottolineava l'apparente universalità di tutta una serie di questioni legate alla protezione ambientale.

Mark Blacksell (Exeter, Regno Unito), in 'Politiche ambientali e organizzazione delle risorse' (Capitolo 11), considera il cammino, piuttosto faticoso, che ha portato alla realizzazione di tutta la gamma delle politiche ambientali che costituiscono, attualmente, una parte importante della politica della Comunità Europea. Si capisce bene come le soluzioni più adeguate ai molti pressanti problemi ambientali, ad esempio quello del controllo dell'inquinamento dell'aria e dell'acqua e dello smaltimento dei rifiuti, varino molto tra uno stato e l'altro nella Comunità Europea e come, per questo, il consenso politico su come risolverli abbia incontrato non poche difficoltà. Le società a più elevato livello di benessere comprendono bene che i vantaggi dei miglioramenti ambientali a lungo termine sono preferibili ai vantaggi economici a breve termine e pertanto vi è continua tensione tra i maggiori stati industriali del centro della Comunità Europea ed alcuni membri di nuova adesione delle periferie settentrionale e mediterranea. Allo stesso modo, gli stati insulari come l'Irlanda e il Regno Unito, con piccoli fiumi dal rapido corso, non sono tentati ad usarli come fogne per i rifiuti come fanno invece gli stati con grandi superfici continentali come la Francia e la Germania, attraversati dai maggiori corsi d'acqua internazionali. Così l'inquinamento atmosferico, che da una parte è adeguatamente spazzato via dai venti dominanti e dall'altra discende sul territorio di altri stati sottovento, tende ad essere visto in modo molto differente da inquinatori e inquinati. In generale gli stati situati sui margini occidentali della Comunità Europea accettano, senza rimostranze, quegli stessi livelli di emissione nell'atmosfera, che sono visti invece come serie minacce ambientali da parte degli altri stati situati più ad oriente, sebbene gli studiosi abbiano già compreso e messo in guardia sui subdoli effetti dell'inquinamento atmosferico a lungo termine.

Oggi, a oltre quattro decenni dalla sua costituzione, la Comunità Europea deve dunque ancora percorrere un difficile cammino tra limitazioni poste dai suoi trattati, atteggiamenti conflittuali dovuti all'aumento continuo degli stati membri e la pubblica opinione europea, che è sempre più indipendente e che dal 1979 è sorretta e guidata dal Parlamento Europeo. Inizialmente i suoi interventi in fatto di politica ambientale erano ben connessi con i problemi economici e con le misure prese per eliminare qualsiasi distorsione alla libera concorrenza, ma dopo il 1972, sulla scia delle conclusioni della Conferenza delle Nazioni Unite sull'Ambiente Umano, questi interventi divennero progressivamente più chiari e indipendenti. Una serie di Programmi di Azione culminò con l'inclusione dell'ambiente nell'Atto Unico Europeo come area di competenza della politica della Comunità Europea.

Da quando pertanto l'Atto Unico è entrato in vigore, la Comunità Europea ha assunto una funzione molto più decisa e positiva nella formulazione e nella esecuzione della politica ambientale. Per comprendere in modo appropriato questa inversione di tendenza sono necessarie quattro chiavi di interpretazione: (1) significato del decreto e sua interazione con la legislazione nazionale degli stati membri; (2) portata dei problemi ambientali presentati in quattro Programmi di Azione Ambientale e in più di 180 Direttive e altri tipi di interventi legislativi; (3) aree di intervento politico ambientale, in particolare collegato con la Politica Agraria Comune, che è stata elaborata al di fuori dei limiti della stessa politica ambientale; e infine (4) questioni politiche reguardanti elaborazione delle politiche di monitoraggio e di applicazione.

Ovviamente, l'efficacia di queste politiche ambientali può essere valutata solo per quel che riguarda la loro efficienza di base. Michael Quigley (Trinity College di Dublino, Irlanda), in 'Effetti della politica della Comunità Europea sul paesaggio rurale e sull'ambiente in Irlanda' (Capitolo 12), fa un esame dettagliato di alcune di queste politiche con particolare riferimento all'Irlanda, un paese il cui paesaggio è prevalentemente rurale e dove l'agricoltura, specialmente il pascolo, è l'unica attività economica davvero importante. L'agricoltura irlandese era già in corso di espansione e modernizzazione quando il paese aderì alla Comunità Europea, nel 1973, ma dopo questa data il cambiamento, per velocità e direzione, si è progressivamente adeguato alle politiche emanate da Bruxelles. L'utilizzazione dello spazio rurale e la qualità dell'ambiente sono interessate da tre differenti aspetti della politica europea. Il primo aspetto è dato dalla PAC, che influisce su tutte le forme di utilizzazione dello spazio agricolo; il secondo aspetto è costituito dalle misure strutturali che, sebbene non agricole in senso stretto, procurano fondi per una varietà di programmi operativi, che, attraverso il programma di aiuti della Comunità, sono diretti al paesaggio rurale; ed il terzo aspetto è offerto dalla politica e dalla legislazione ambientale, che operano, da una parte, per controllare gli effetti negativi delle altre politiche e dall'altra per conservare tratti dell'ambiente da salvaguardare.

Per quanto riguarda l'Irlanda, la PAC, con tutte le sue ramificazioni, è una determinante particolarmente importante, non solo del benessere economico, ma anche della trasformazione del paesaggio e dello stato dell'ambiente. Essa interessa lo sviluppo agricolo in due differenti modi: (1) controllando il mercato attraverso il meccanismo di sostegno ai prezzi; (2) attraverso una serie di misure di ristrutturazione orizzontale, finalizzate a compensare gli agricoltori di certe aree per gli svantaggi naturali nei quali essi si trovano ad operare.

Il primo fattore della PAC porta a un processo di intensificazione agricola, in quanto il livello del sostegno finanziario è in rapporto al volume della produzione. Questo a sua volta porta inevitabilmente non solo alla sovrapproduzione e all'accumulazione delle eccedenze dei prodotti alimentari, ma anche al degrado ambientale. Le consistenti somme di danaro elargite dal FEOGA hanno avuto effetti positivi nel settore agricolo commerciale. Grazie agli incentivi della Comunità Europea, il numero degli ovini è aumentato notevolmente negli ultimi anni, con la conseguenza, tuttavia, di una eccessiva pratica del pascolo e quindi dell'erosione. Le economie di scala inoltre, hanno portato alla specializzazione regionale di alcune imprese agricole, soprattutto per l'allevamento dei suini e del pollame. Sfortunatamente, ciò ha avuto effetti di degrado ambientale con la produzione di grandi quantità di rifiuti e con l'inquinamento dei fiumi. Altri aspetti di intensificazione, quali il crescente uso di fertilizzanti, e specialmente la sostituzione della fienagione con la produzione di foraggi conservati in silo, hanno ulteriormente contribuito all'inquinamento delle acque.

Nello stesso tempo, i fondi strutturali del FEOGA, elargiti per rendere più produttive le aree agricole marginali, potrebbero avere effetti negativi sugli ambienti più fragili. Ad esempio, il Pacchetto Occidentale, che tende a promuovere lo sviluppo agricolo nell'Irlanda Occidentale e il Progetto di Drenaggio Occidentale, entrambi misure di assistenza della Comunità Europea, hanno avuto effetti deleteri sull'ambiente.

La silvicoltura irlandese è ora in forte espansione, con raddoppio degli obbiettivi di impianto annuale da 15.000 a 30.000 ha. Questo livello di sviluppo mai raggiunto in precedenza è in gran parte sostenuto dai fondi della Comunità Europea per il Programma Operativo per le Foreste. Lo sviluppo forestale in Irlanda ha, tuttavia, avuto conseguenze negative: l'acidificazione dei corsi d'acqua superficiali; il degrado della pesca naturale; la distruzione della coltre superficiale di importanti ecosistemi acquitrinosi di pianura, e l'alterazione di paesaggi selvaggi di grande bellezza naturalistica.

Fin dalla metà degli anni '80, le coltivazioni agricole sono diminuite d'intensità, in parte per la necessità di ridurre la produzione di colture alimentari nella Comunità, in parte per gli effetti dannosi sull'ambiente. Ora, grazie ad una politica caratterizzata da una serie di nuove misure radicali tendenti a mettere in evidenza la duplice funzione degli agricoltori come produttori di alimenti e organizzatori degli spazi rurali, l'ambiente ne beneficerà indubbiamente. Tanto più che la politica ambientale della Comunità Europea, che è stata rafforzata da misure come la Direttiva dell'Accertamento dell'Impatto Ambientale e la Direttiva sull'Habitat, potrebbe tornare utile a tale riguardo. Per l'Irlanda invece una delle maggiori minacce all'ambiente potrebbe essere costituita dai fondi di sviluppo regionale che sono stati elargiti in grande quantità. Viene il sospetto che non vi sia una seria convinzione di proteggere l'ambiente.

L'ambiente è una delle chiavi di lettura delle condizioni di salute delle comunità e Cosimo Palagiano (La Sapienza di Roma, Italia), in 'Ambiente, salute e cura della salute: confronti europei e il caso di studio italiano' (Capitolo 13), spiega in che modo la Comunità Europea abbia influenzato la salute e la cura della salute negli stati membri. La Comunità Europea è un'area di analisi relativamente trascurata, sebbene essa sia andata sempre più interessandosi dei problemi relativi alla salute attraverso le sue politiche ambientali, ad esempio con la proposta di una Carta Sociale nel Trattato di Maastricht, e le sue politiche per un'agricoltura intensiva ed estensiva.

Gli obiettivi del capitolo sono di tre tipi: primo, esaminare le condizioni di salute nella Comunità Europea, usando una varietà di indicatori sulla consistenza dei servizi e delle condizioni di salute. Si deve sottolineare che persistono ancora differenze per quanto riguarda la speranza di vita e l'incidenza delle malattie anche in questo relativamente omogeneo gruppo di stati ricchi. Secondo, illustrare il persistente divario delle condizioni di salute all'interno dei singoli paesi. L'Italia è stata scelta come caso di studio per due motivi: a causa delle forti differenze regionali che esistono nel paese e perché sulle sue condizioni di salute il materiale in lingua inglese è scarso, in confronto a quello degli stati dell'Europa Settentrionale. Infine, vengono esaminati i problemi della salute nella Comunità Europea, al momento attuale e in proiezione futura.

Nella conclusione Allan Williams e Mark Blacksell (Exeter, Regno Unito), in 'Una carta geografica in evoluzione: la Comunità Europea allo scorcio del XXI secolo' (Capitolo 14), delineano le possibilità di cambiamento della Comunità Europea allo scorcio del XXI secolo e l'impatto che questi cambiamenti potrebbero avere sulle sue politiche, in particolare per quel che riguarda lo sviluppo economico e l'ambiente.

El Fúturo Europeo: Geografiá y Desarrollo en la Comunidad Europea

La creación de la Comunidad Europea (CE) ha sido el acontecimiento que más significativamente ha marcado la geografía económica, social y política de Europa en esta segunda mitad del siglo XX. Desde sus inicios en los primeros años cincuenta, tratados como el de París de 1952—que dió lugar a la Europa del Carbón y del Acero (CECA)—, el de Roma de 1958—con el que se constituyó la Comunidad Económica Europea (CEE) y el Euratom—, el Acta Única Europea (1986)—cuyo objetivov fue preparar el camino para la formación del Mercado Único en 1993—, o el problemático Tratado de Maastricht, han ido desarrollando un complejo sistema político comunitario cuya influencia sobre el futuro de los doce estados miembros resulta cada vez más dominante.

La complejidad en su desarrollo institucional ha ido en aumento conforme aumentaba el número de socios comunitarios. Durante más de veinte años, entre 1952 y 1973, huberon sólo seis miembros—Bélgica, Francia, Alemania, Italia, Luxemburgo y Holanda—todos ellos estados muy industrializados, que formaban parte del corazón de la Europa occidental y que habían resurgido económicamente tras los efectos devastadores de las Guerras Mundiales que habían dominado la primera mitad del siglo XX. La primera ampliaión en 1973 añadió tres nuevos miembros—Dinamarca, Irlanda y el Reino Unido—todos ellos del norte de Europa y bastante vinculados económicamente, tanto entre sí como con los estados miembros fundadores. Sin embargo, esta amplicación cambió e carácter de la CE: aparecieron nuevos problemas regionales asociados debidos en parte, a la situación periférica de los nuevos socios. La cohesión de la Comunidad—que inicialmente había constituido su fuerza principal—se vió de cierto modo socavada, sobre todo por la entrada de los dos estados insulares, uno de los cuales, el Reino Unido, contaba con más del 20 por ciento de la población total. Durante los años ochenta, una nueva ampliación dió entrada, primero a Grecia (1981) y más tarde a España y Portugal (1986). Con esta ampliación Mediterránea la Comunidad cambió radicalmente de. La carácter estructura socioeconómica y las características geográficas de los nuevos socios, tenían, y aún tienen, poco que ver con el corazón industrial de la Europa occidental. En ellos, aparece, el paisaje rural por lo menos en algunas de sus regiones, dominado todavía por explotaciones campesinas y estructuras agrarias arcaicas pues ninguno de ellos tomó parte de forma plena en la corriente de industrialización y urbanización europea, a no ser como fuente de mano de obra barata inmigrante.

Durante los años noventa nuevas adaptaciones serán imprescindibles. La unificación de Alemania en 1990 dió lugar al acceso, aunque por absorción, de un miembro de la Europa del Este, la anterior República Democrática Alemana, lo que ha dado una nueva dimensión al mapa económico regional. El problema ahora es integrar a un miembro cuya economía industrial se ha desarrollado bajo condiciones de planificación centralizada. Ciertamente es probable que la unificación de Alemania se pueda llevar a cabo sin cambios fundamentales en la estructura de la CE, pero si otros estados de la Europa del este—Polonia, Hungría, los estados Checo y Eslovaco surgidos de la anterior Checoslovaquia, y Eslovenia, Croacia y cualquier otro estado que pueda surgir de las ruinas de Yugoslavia—se incorporasen, sin ninguna duda toda la lógica política y económica de la Comunidad tendría que cambiar.

Pero además, no es la confusión política en el este de Europa el único agente que induce al cambio. Todos los estados del oeste de Europa que, por una u otra razón, no se encuentran incluidos en la CE hacen ahora cola para ser admitidos. En 1991 la Asociación Europea de Libre Comercio (EFTA)— Austria, Finlandia, Islandia, Liechtenstein, Noruega, Suecia, y Suiza—firmó un tratado con la CE para formar el Area Económico Europea (AEE), extendiendo el comercio libre a todala Europa del Oeste. Con posterioridad, Austria, Suiza, y Suecia han ido solicitando el apoyo de todos los miembros de la EC, y, con toda probabilidad pronto les seguirán otros miembros de la AEE.

Finalmente, en un futuro algo más lejano, hay otros estados impacientes por ser miembros. Turquía, Malta y Chipre llevan casi treinta años persiguiendo la incorporación, y ahora, muchas de las repúblicas de lo que fue el oeste de la Unión Soviética están también mostrando un interés activo. Sea lo que fuere el resultado de todos estos intentos, de lo que no cabe duda es de que la CE tendrá que seguir adaptándose a los imperativos económicos y sociales y a los cambios geopolíticos.

La estructura del libro

Este libro, escrito por geógrafos de siete paises de la CE, quiere ser una aproximación a la valoración del impacto que la CE ha tenido en el fondo socioeconómico de los estados miembros. En la introducción, Mark Blacksell y Allan Williams (Exeter, RU) tratan 'El desarrollo de la Europa Comunitaria: su significación espacial' (Capítulo 1), explicando el modo que la propia CE en ha contemplado los resultados del desarrollo económico y la forma en que las políticas regionales han cambiado a consecuencia de las ampliaciones sucesivas y de las revisiones continuas de los términos del tratado.

Cuando la CE era una comunidad de tan solo seis paises, estrechamente agrupados en el corazón de la Europa occidental industrializada, la política regional como tal apenas existía. La totalidad de las propuestas de la Comunidad iban dirigidas a promover el desarrollo económico a través del comercio libre sin ningún tipo de ordenación o planificación centralizada. Aunque en la práctica si se tomaron algunas medidas especiales tanto regionales—apoyando la economía del Mezzogiorno en el sur de Italia—como sectoriales—sosteniendo la agricultura bajo la forma de explotación familiar—, en general los éxitos económicos de los años cincuenta y sesenta parecían confirmar la creencia de que por ese camino el progreso económico y político era ilimitado.

Pero esta confianza comenzó a ser menos firme tras la primera ampliación de la CE en 1973. Los problemas espinosos derivados del decline de las regiones industriales más antiguas del RU y de otras regiones de la Comunidad, dió lugar a una creciente demanda de fondos estructurales que se dirigieran a resolver los problemas de estas áreas urbanas, siguiendo el modelo que se venía pràcticando en las áreas rurales con la Política Agraria Común (PAC). En 1975 se creó el Fondo Europeo de Desarrollo Regional (FEDER) con el fin expreso de suplementar las ayundas y los programas de inversiones regionales de los estados socios. Aunque las cantidades de dinero manefados por este Fondo eran pequeñas (3 por ciento del presupuesto de la CE), se han ido incrementando con regularidad. Pero lo que resulta más importante es el reconocimiento implícito que comporta la creación del FEDER de que la economía de libre mercado nunca podrá resolver por sí misma y de forma satisfactoria las desigualdades regionales.

La entrada de Grecia, España y Portugal en los años ochenta, reforzó aún más la necesidad de una política regional, manifestando lo inadecvado de las políticas sectoriales. En general, los tres países presentaban condiciones económicas que sólo era posible encontrar en forma de pequeñas bolsas aisladas en el resto de la Comunidad. Para resolver sus problemas regionales, se requiere una ayuda a mayor escala que antes, que además debe ser eficaz, lo cual se trate de conseguir mediante programas integrados que persigan el desarrollo económico en su totalidad. Por tanto, la solución propuesta por la CE ha sido doble. Primero, el aumento de ayuda efectiva para las regiones, diriqundo dichas ayvdar en mayor medida hacia los países Mediterráneos. Y en segundo lugar, se han creado los Programas Integrados Mediterráneos, que pretenden coordinar y dar coherencia a la aplicación de las ayudas al desarrollo regional.

El Acta Unica Europea ha dado un impulso nuevo a la política regional comunitaria. Dado que el objetivo del Acta es la formación del Mercado Unico en 1993, el documento ha traido aparejado una revisión de la política regional, en el sentido de que ya no es suficiente impulsar ésta en los países Mediterráneos, sino que ahora se trata de eliminar las desigualdades regionales en toda la Comunidad. En 1989 los tres fondos estructurales existentes, el FEDER, el Fondo Social Europeo (FSE) y la Sección de Orientación del Fondo Europeo de Orientación y Garantía Agraria (FEOGA) de la PAC, se han fusionado para resolver cinco (en realidad seis, ya que el 5a y el 5b son bastante distintos) objetivos políticos. Esta delimitación de los objetivos y la reorganización de los viejos fondos reunidos ahora en uno sólo, hace eperar una mayor eficacia en la política de desarrollo regional.

Hay también otra importante faceta en la reforma de los fondos estructurales. Anteriormente la Comisión de la CE sólo podía actuar a través de los gobiernos nacionales, proporcionando ayudas adicionales a programas que ya funcionaban. Sin embargo ahora, una parte de los fondos regionales disponibles (alrededor de 9 por ciento) serán destinados por la Comunidad directamente, independientemente de los programas nacionales, a iniciativas propias, tales como los programas STAR, VALOREN, RESIDER y RENEVAL, relacionados respectivamente con la energía, hierro y acero, y la construcción naval. Se trata de un pequeño pero importante paso hacia la verdadera integración y el surgimiento de una Comunidad con menores desigualdades regionales.

La condición urbana

Casi el 80 por ciento de la población de la CE vive en ciudades, de tal forma que los cambios que se han producido en el entorno urbano desde que se formó la Comunidad han repercutido de forma inmediata sobre la mayor parte de los ciudadanos. Pierre Laborde (Bordeaux III, Francia) en 'La Evolución Espacial de las Ciudades del Oeste de Europa 1950–1990' (Capítulo 2) revisa los efectos geográficos del rápido crecimiento de la población urbana de la CE hasta mediados de los años setenta. Los tejidos urbanos, se vieron transformados, dejaron de presentar una forma compacta explotando hacia el exterior, no sólo modificando las áreas urbanas existentes, sino también creando una nueva periferia urbanizada que se encuentra todavía en expansión, a pesar de que el crecimiento de población ha disminuido. De todas formas, los comportamientos en el desarrollo urbano han cambiado en el curso de la segunda mitad del siglo XX. En los años cincuenta y sesenta el desarrollo se produjo en forma de ola violenta que arrasó todo lo anterior para levantar algo nuevo. En Francia se calificó este período como 'desarrollo bulldozer', en Bélgica como 'Bruselización' y en España como 'sustitución renovación'. De pronto los centros históricos de aquellas ciudades, incluso los de las que no habían sido afectados por los bombardeos de la guerra, comenzaron a desaparecer, provocando una reacción en contra tan drástica (sobre todo en Francia) que la renovación del tejido urbano existente llegó a ser la nueva ortodoxia. Ultimamente, sin embargo, ninguana de las diferentes alternativas que se vienen dando para ordenar el centro de las ciudades parece poder resolver los problemas de la antiguedad del tejido urbano y su inflexibilidad crónica de cara a los cambios demográficos y económicos.

La huella más visible del crecimiento rápido de la población en el tejido urbano es la extensión circundante suburbana que aparece en casi todas las grandes ciudades. Inicialmente, la mayor parte del desarrollo suburbano tenía una función residencial, con viviendas bajas demandadoras de una gran cantidad de espacio. Incluso donde los edificios eran más altos, como sucedía en los 'grandes conjuntos' en Francia, estaban invariablemente localizados en amplias zonas verdes, contribuyendo igualmente a la disminución del espacio propiamente rural. Gradualmente, actividades comerciales, industriales y de servicios, también comenzaron a relocalizarse en la periferia, que ya tenía un carácter residencial con predominio de viviendas bajas.

Más recientemente, la expansión de las áreas urbanas ha venido determinada, no por el incremento de la población, sino por los cambios sociales, tecnológicos y políticos. El número de unidades familiares ha aumentado considerablemente, pero éstas son más pequeñas, debido a factores como la mayor proporción de divorcios o el incremento de la longevidad; la generalización en la propiedad del autómovil ha permitido a un sector de la población la posibilidad de elegir donde vivir, sin que la localización urbana de su puesto de trabajo lo condicionase; y las políticas de planeamiento basadas en la ética de la descentralización han proporcionado el estímulo oficial a las tendencias de crecimiento suburbano. Las políticas de la CE han tenido sólo un efecto marginal en estos cambios. Las políticas industriales parecen apuntar a un debilitamiento de las árcas industriales y se han incorporado mayores exigencias ambientales dentro del desarrollo urbano, pero resulta difícil considerar estas cuestiones aisladas como parte de una política urbana global.

El resultado de todos estos cambios estructurales ha sido el producir una mayor diferenciación entre los modelos para uso del suelo urbano, lo que se ha traducido también en una más amplia diferencia entre los valores del suelo del centro y la periferia. En Francia, las autoridades municipales han comenzado a intentar ordenar estos cambios, pero las diferencias en las estructuras políticas hace difícil poder generalizar en el conjunto de la CE.

Los problemas de la generalización sobre la naturaleza de los cambios urbanos y sobre la ordenación de los usos urbanos están claramente ilustrados por Lila Leontidou (National Technical University Athens, Grecia) en 'Ciudades Mediterráneas: tendencias divergentes en una Europa unida' (Capítulo 3). En la Europa Mediterránea el centro ha jugado desde la antigüedad un papel cultural importante que se conserva aún en la actualidad, por lo que las tendencias hacia la dispersión observadas en las ciudades del norte de Europa no se han dejado sentir de igual manera en el sur. El interior de la ciudad ha sido siempre, y continúa siéndolo, el área residencial principal en Nápoles, Atenas y Barcelona, mientras las áreas en las que viven las clases trabajadoras aparecen dispersas en la periferia. La desagregación social y económica, tan típica de Francia, Alemania y el Reino Unido, es mucho menos evidente en el Mediterráneo.

Inevitablemente, el impacto de la CE en el desarrollo ha sido mínimo. De los paises Mediterráneos, sólo Italia fue socio fundador, mientras que Grecia, España y Portugal no se unieron hasta los años ochenta. Pero esto es, sin embargo, sólo parte de la explicación. Más importante es el hecho de que muchas de las políticas procedentes de la CE y que afectan a las áreas urbanas, están formuladas de tal manera que las hacen irrelevantes para las ciudades Mediterráneas. Por ejemplo, indicadores de pobreza basados en la proporción de los que carecen de casa son de poca utilidad cuando el pobre tiene una vivienda pero construida en precario, en áreas de libre construcción, en áreas de chabolismo. En definitiva, resulta enormemente difícil que las políticas globales lleguen a cumplir sus objetivos, incluso dentro de un grupo de estados tan aparentemente homogéneos como los de la CE, a menos que estén muy sensibilizados con las condiciones locales.

Cambio estructural

El nacimiento de la CE ha alterado el contexto económico y social de Europa y ha inducido a profundos cambios estructurales en muchas áreas, bien a través de iniciativas políticas conscientes, bien a través de adaptaciones involuntarias. Jean-Paul Charrié (Bordeaux III, Francia) en 'El modelo de industria: Europeización versus internacionalización' (Capítulo 4) describe un cuadro detallado de los cambios fundamentales ocurridos recientemente dentro de un grupo de paises, la mayor parte de los cuales experimentaron su Revolución Industrial en el siglo XIX. La CE es aún la mayor potencia industrial del mundo, pero las bases de su supremacía han tenido inevitablemente que cambiar frente a un nivel de competencia que nunca había sido tan fuerte.

Muchos de esos cambios hacia una internacionalización industrial ocurrieron en los años cuarenta, desde la fundación de la Comunidad. La CE es rica en carbón y mineral de hierro y tiene una capacidad enorme de producción en muchos sectores clave, tales como el siderúrgico, la construcción naval o la química. Todo ello forma un potencial que tuvo sus mejores días en los años cincuenta, por lo que no es casualidad que los primeros éxitos se consiguieran precisamente desde CECA (Comunidad Europea del Carbón y del Acero). En un continente destrozado por cinco años de conflicto, el Tratado de París sentó las bases para un período de crecimiento económico sostenido, interrumpido solamente por la crisis del petróleo de 1973. La Cmunidad ha tenido que adaptar sus métodos de producción industrial a la importancia creciente del petróleo y la incremento fuerte precio que del se ha tenido que pagar por él, y, de igual modo, ha tenido que ir ajustándose al declive de aquellas industrias básicas que fueron las piezas claves de su éxito inicial, impulsando paralelamente el crecimiento del sector de alta tecnología.

Estos cambios están ocurriendo frente a la competencia creciente de paises más recientemente industrializados. La industria japonesa es evidentemente la que supone una mayor amenaza, ya que sus productos ofrecen una alta calidad y compiten en los mercados tradicionales de ultramar de la CE, principalmente Norte América. Al mismo tiempo, los industriales japoneses están invirtiendo directamente en la CE como un modo de evadir los intentos de regulación y limitación a las importaciones japonesas. Tampoco se puede olvidar la amenaza de competencia de los Paises de Nueva Industrialización (PNI) en Asia, especialmente Corea del Sur, que por el momento parece limitarse sobre todo al sector de la confección, pero que está diversificando rápidamente su producción.

Todos estos cambios están teniendo un impacto acumulativo en el corazón industrial de Europa. Las regiones industriales tradicionales están en declive económico, afectadas por un creciente número de problemas y requieren medidas para adaptarse a la nueva situación. Por otro lado, los mayores centros urbanos están en mejor posición y defienden enérgicamente su superioridad.

La Comisión y las otras instituciones de la CE han estado durante muchos años limitadas a hacer intervenciones aisladas, principalmente medidas de protección a regiones en declive o a sectores o ramas en dificultades, pero ahora comienzan a jugar un papel importante en la política industrial. La CE constituye una fuerza importante en el paisaje industrial emergente, ya que puede incidir dirigiendo ayudas específicas a sectores seleccionados, coordinando los esfuerzos de investigación y revitalizando la política regional. Además, el establecimiento del Mercado Unico tendrá importantísimas repercusiones en el tejido industrial de la Comunidad.

Los gobiernos siempre han reconocido que el transporte es una de las claves para incidir en la dinámica de las sociedades industriales y la CE ha sido siempre muy activa a este respecto, aunque sin el vigor que podía haberse esperado. James Killen (Trinity College Dublin, Irlanda) y Austin Smyth (Ulster, RU) en 'Política de transporte en la Comunidad europea con particular referencia a Irlanda como región periférica' (Capítulo 5) consideran el modo en que la política de transporte de la CE, o la auscencia de ella, han afectado al conjunto de la isla de Irlanda.

Los gobiernos nacionales siempre han perseguido controlar los sistemas y operaciones de transporte de sus países, principalmente a través do dos caminos. En primer lugar, siendo los mejores reguladores del transporte, estableciendo, por ejemplo, los límites de velocidad y las condiciones y características de los distintos tipos de carnés y licencias. En Europa, ellos han asumido habitualmente un papel directo en los servicios de ferrocarril y, en algunos casos, de autobuses y de carga por carretera, lo que les ha llevado a establecer los mecanismos para controlar directamente el grado de competencia entre los diferentes servicios. En segundo lugar, han tratado de influir a través de las inversiones en infraestructuras de transporte, tanto a través de las cantidades de capital asignadas en comparación con otros sectores de la economía, como a través de la manera en que se orientan los gastos.

Antes de la firma del Tratado de Roma, la política de transporte en Europa se llevaba a cabo en cada estado de forma más o menos independiente de sus vecinos. En teoría, la cooperación a nivel europeo era posible a través de la Conferencia Europea de Ministros de Transportes, fundada en 1953, pero los resultados obtenidos pocos fueron, si exceptuamos el ferrocarril Expreso Trans Europeo. En el Tratado de Roma se establecía un compromiso explícito de crear una Política Común de Transporte, pero el hecho de que cada estado ya contase con la suya propia hacía este propósito muy difícil. El objetivo principal de este capítulo es el de mostrar como los relativamente pocos acuerdos que se han conseguido en varios sectores—carretera, ferrocarril, mar, y aire—han beneficiado a Irlanda, una parte de la Comunidad en la periferia más exterior de las principales redes de transporte.

A pesar de las inevitables diferencias nacionales y regionales, la CE en conjunto tiene una envidiable red de transporte, la cual ha contribuido decisivamente a dar coherencia a la Comunidad. Ha facilitado también la movilidad de la mano de obra permitiendo el éxito económico sostenido del conjunto de Europa. Russell King (Trinity Colle Dublin, Irlanda) en 'Migraciones y mercado único de trabajo: una salida al desarrollo regional' (Capítulo 6) considera el papel que jugo la migración internacional en los últimos años cincuenta como contribución al cambio económico y social de la CE. Igualmente, las migraciones de trabajo han sido un factor importante en el crecimiento de la Europa industrial y postindustrial durante los años sesenta y setenta. Aunque su número, en términos de nuevas llegadas, disminuyese después de la primera crisis del petroleo de 1973–4, nuevas oleadas de inmigrantes han llegado hacia fines de los años ochenta y al principio de los noventa, estimándose que hoy la población inmigrante de Europa es de alrededor de 20 millones, la mayoría de los cuales están en la CE.

Después de aproximadamente una década en la que las migraciones internacionales fueron consideradas como una de las principales cuestiones políticas europeas, parece surgir ahora el debate sobre su conveniencia, sobre todo en la derecha europea. Estos últimos flujos migratorios comienzan ya a finales de los ochenta y en algunos paises (Alemania y Holanda) desde el año 1985. Pero el estímulo realmente significativo de las nuevas migraciones ha sido el colapso de los regímenes de la Europa del Este desde 1989. Los acontecimientos de los últimos tres años parecen aconsejar prudencia en previsión de una aceleración en la tendencia de las migraciones internacionales: casi nadie podía preveer en 1988 la dimensión que podía llegar a alcanzar el fenómeno, ni siquiera después de conocer el goteo migratorio que desde el principio de la crisis en el Este se venía produciendo desde la República Democrática Alemana y Hungría a la República Federal Alemana, antes de la unificación sin embargo, estos hechos sirvieron entonces para que surgieran las nuevas posiciones.

Pero como si estos acontecimientos no eran suficientes, en la actualidad aparecen nuevas nubes en el horizonte democrático de Europa. En todo el globo, millones están en movimiento, y sus viajes están cambiando el mundo, incluida Europa. Durante los años ochenta llegó a Europa una oleada de refugiados y buscadores de asilo y este fenómeno necesita ahora ser regulado honradamente tanto a nivel de la Comunidad como de la política nacional, particularmente en lo que se refiere a los acuerdos sobre control de fronteras en la CE en el inminente Mercado Unico.

Un problema particular asociado a las migraciones internacionales, dentro y fuera de la CE, es el del trabajo ilegal, abordado por Solange Montagné-Villette (Poitiers, Francia) en 'Movilidad, y trabajo secreto e ilegal en la CE' (Capítulo 7). La existencia de trabajo secreto e ilegal en los paises de la CE no es ninguna novedad. Se pueden encontrar antecedentes en los primeros años del presente siglo, cuando ya se estaban estableciendo las estructuras administrativas modernas en los estados industriales ricos y se iban afianzando los sistemas de seguriudad social. Hoy, en algunos paises, parece formar parte de la tradición y es visto por muchos como parte de la cultura nacional. Al contrario, a nivel de la 'Comunidad', tal como se encuentra en la CE (y más allá), tiene una serie de rasgos originales que hasta ahora han recibido poca atención, posiblemente porque se trata de fenómenos muy recientes. El gran incremento de la movilidad de la fuerza de trabajo, ha generado prácticas completamente nuevas de empleo ilegal en la industria y en los servicios, algunas de las cuales se encuentran vinculadas a la estructura legal, política y económica de la CE.

Trabajadores en los paises pobres de la CE que buscan empleo en otros estados miembros, relocalización y/o subcontratación de actividades industriales *ilegítimas* en los países de la Europa Mediterránea, personas de fuera de la Comunidad que trabajan en ella ilegalmente, todas son manifestaciones del cada vez mayor predominio de las prácticas de empleo ilegal. Por lo que concierne a la CE la solución del problema de las migraciones de trabajo ha tardado en ser comprendida. Y ha sido particularmente difícil para algunos estados miembros, principalmente el RU, aceptar que el establecimiento de algunas condiciones de control del trabajo, y otros aspectos de la ingeniería social, pudiesen ser compatibles con el mercado libre al que todos aspiran.

La adaptación rural

La PAC ha sido la política principal de la CE durante casi treinta años, llegando a consumir más del 90 por ciento del presupuesto comunitario y aún hoy consume más del 60 por ciento. Los mecanismos de esta política son bien conocidos y no son materia de este libro, pero ningún estudio serio de la CE puede dejar de dedicar una parte sustancial de su atención a la agricultura. El énfasis abrumador que se dedicó a la agricultura dentro de la CE está ahora comenzando a disminuir, pero precisamente este hecho está teniendo repercusiones serias y transcendentales en el paisaje y en la economía rural. Dietrich Denecke (Göttingen, Alemania) en 'Abandono de tierras, despoblación del paisaje en Europa, con particular referencia a Alemania' (Capítulo 8) analiza las consecuencias que están teniendo estos cambios de la política agraria de la CE para el paisaje y el medio ambiente, aportando ejemplos referidos a los paisajes rurales de Alemania particularmente sensibles, donde las explotaciones campesinas y modernas coexisten todavía. Hasta bien entrado el presente siglo, la insuficiencia de productos agrarios y de productos alimentarios en general, favorecieron un régimen de cultivo lo más intensivo posible. Pero en los últimos veinte años se ha venido produciendo lentamente un cambio radical. La superproducción ha llegado a buscar alternativas a los cultivos hasta entonces plantados, a introducir la extensificación, la transformación en pastizales, los programas de retiro de la agricultura, y, por último, el abandono de explotaciones y de tierras de cultivo. Estos cambios y las políticas que los han motivado dominan ahora la agricultura en Europa. Mientras, al mismo tiempo, un número reducido de explotaciones está siendo racioanlizada, incrementando aún más la intensificación de su producción agraria o ganadera y con ella los efectos contaminantes. Por tanto, ambos procesos están contribuyendo a trastornar el delicado balance ecológico en el paisaje agrario, a pesar de que para la CE su conservación a través de los metodos de explotación tradicionales ha llegado a ser casi un artículo de fe. Valorar el alcance que realmente podría tener el sostenimiento de una agricultura ecológicamente aceptable, que principalmente tuviera como fin la conservación del paisaje, resulta imprescindible para el desarrollo de la Comunidad y puede tener consecuencias importantes en la revisión de los acuerdos de la PAC.

Aunque la PAC está ahora comenzando a cambiar y la política de subvenciones a la producción agricola a través de los precios está siendo cada vez más cuestionada, hoy sigue siendo la piedra angular de la política de la CE. Manuel Corbera (Cantabria, España) en 'La Política Agrícola Común y el desarrollo de la agricultura: problemas y perspectivas' presenta una nueva valoración de la PAC desde la perspectiva de España, un país con un sector agrario aún muy importante y que se ha incorporado a la CE hace relativamente poco tiempo (1986). En términos generales la Comunidad es la principal potencia agrícola mundial, la primera productora de leche, mantequilla, queso, vino, azucar y carne de vacuno, y la segunda en la producción de trigo y cebada. Es autosuficiente en los productos alimenticios del área templada, si exceptuamos los frutos secos, el maíz y la carne de ovino y caprino.

Esta envidiable situación es en parte el reflejo de condiciones naturales bastante favorables a nivel general y, además, permiten una complementari edad dados los matices atlánticos, mediterráneos y continentales que reune. Pero también ha tenido una importancia crucial la modernización del sector: intensificación, transformación estructural, mecanización, etc.

Además de estos factores favorables, la agricultura de la CE es también, y quizás principalmente, el resultado de la PAC, que la ha sostenido y estimulado en su desarrollo a lo largo de una generación. Si la PAC no hubiera existido ninguno de los paises que componen la Comunidad se hubiese destacado como líder mundial en ninguna producción agrícola y, posiblemente, tampoco hubiese alcanzado el nivel de desarrollo del sector que hoy detenta. A pesar de los muchos problemas y de la manifiesta necesidad de reforma, la PAC parece haber cumplido al menos sus objetivos económicos.

Pero este éxito de la política agraria en términos de producción de alimentos no puede enmascarar la crisis por la que atraviesan muchas regiones rurales. Como consecuencia de la superproducción cada vez se hace más necessario retirar de la producción agraria una parte de la tierra, principalmente la marginal, sin embargo, es necesario encontrar verdaderas alternativas, tanto para la tierra misma como para la población que tradicionalmente ha vivido de ella. Y el problema es más grave en aquellas atrasadas en el proceso de modernización y 'excedentarias'. Una de las alternativas que más se airea es la del desarrollo del potencial turístico de las áreas rurales, especialmente para las regiones europeas costeras y de montaña.

Allan Williams y Gareth Shaw (Exeter, RU) en 'Turismo: oportunidades, desafíos y contradicciones en la CE' (Capítulo 10) examina el fenómeno turístico en general en la Comunidad. Desde los comienzos del turismo de masas en los años sesenta, éste ha llegado a constituir uno de los hilos fundamentales del tejido social y económico de la CE. Emplea más de 5 por ciento de la fuerza de trabajo y constituye una proporción sustancial de PIB y del comercio internacional, tanto en el interior como en el exterior de la Comunidad. El truismo es también un instrumento de cambio social, a través del que se transfieren valores y modos de vivir, y ofrece una de las pocas vías de interacción entre los pueblos y culturas de la Comunidad. Se ha discutido muchas veces si existe una identidad cultural europea, pero desde luego, si es así, el turismo contribuye a ella. Finalmente el turismo es una pieza clave para la liberalizacion de los movimientos fronterizos dentro de la CE, y así se ha contemplado en el programa de Mercado Unico. La importancia del conjunto de la actividad turística de la Comunidad puede resumirse con una simple estadística: el 64 por ciento del turismo internacional mundial se produjo dentro de Europa y la CE absorbió la mayor parte de ese mercado. Más que en ninguna otra región del mundo, el turismo resulta esencial para la producción el consumo tanto de las áreas urbanas como rurales de la CE.

Respuesta ambiental

El medio ambiente, como tal, fue ignorado absolutamente en los Tratados de París y Roma, lo que ha llevado a la CE a tener que alcanzar compromisos políticos directos sobre estos aspectos que a veces no eran fáciles de justificar, a pesar de la creciente conciencia pública sobre la degradación ambiental y la reducción de recursos durante los años sesenta-setenta, y de la cada vez más afianzada convicción de que los problemas ambientales no se podían abordar desde un marco puramente nacional. No obstante, la CE parecía ser una unidad espacial 'natural' para buscar soluciones a los cada vez más complejos y variados problemas medioambientales y de recursos, ya que el territorio de los doce estados miembros unidos presentaba un modelo espacial muy variado, fragmentado y difícil de manejar. En ello radicaba la principal atracción de una política ambiental comunitaria, porque además subrayaba la aparente universalidad de las cuestiones de protección del medio ambiente.

Mark Blacksell (Exeter, RU) en 'Política ambiental y gestión de recursos' (Capítulo 11) examina las diferentes políticas ambientales que han ido ganando importancia dentro de la política general de la CE y el tortuoso camino que han tenido que recorrer hasta su aprobación. Hasta ahora, la mejor solución de la mayor parte de los problemas ambientales, tales como la contaminación del aire o del agua o la eliminación de residuos, era distinta para los diferentes estados de la CE, por lo que alcanzar consensos sobre como abordarlos conjuntamente resulta difícil. Las sociedades más ricas reconocen con más facilidad las ventajas a largo plazo de una protección ambiental sobre las ventajas económicas a corto plazo lo cual está provocando tensiones entre la mayor parte de los estados industriales del centro y otros de la periferia norte y mediterránea. Igualmente, los estados insulares como Irlanda y el RU, cuyos ríos son cortos, están menos interesados en una política de regulación de los vertidos que estados continentales como Francia o Alemania, cuyos ríos se encuentran conectados por canales. De la misma forma, los vientos dominantes hacen sentir el problema de contaminación del aire de manera distinta a los estados del oeste que a los del este, aunque, en este caso, los nuevos conocimientos científicos sobre los efectos a largo plazo de la contaminación del aire están reduciendo las diferencias.

Durante las cuatro décadas de su existencia la CE ha tenido que superar dificultades procedentes de las limitaciones impuestas por el tratado, las actitudes conflictivas de su creciente número de estados miembros y la opinión pública, representada en el Parlamento Europeo desde 1979. Inicialmente, sus incursiones en la política ambiental estaban explícitamente unidas a los resultados económicos, que tienen por objeto evitar las distorsiones del comercio libre, pero a partir de 1972, tras la Conferencia sobre Medio Ambiente de la UNU, las medidas llegan a ser cada vez más independientes. Una serie de Programas de Acción Ambiental han permitido incorporar los aspectos ambientales como un área específica de la política de la CE en el Acta Unica Europea.

El Acta ha reforzado el papel de la CE para formular y aplicar la política ambiental. Las claves que permiten apreciar este cambio son cuatro: primero, el significado del acta y como ésta se compatibiliza con las políticas nacionales de los estados miembros; segundo, la extensión de los resultados en legislación ambiental comunitaria que se manifiesta en cuatro Programas de Acción Ambiental y más de 180 Directivas y otros tipos de comunicaciones legislativas; tercero, disposiciones ambientales que afectan a otra política, principalmente a la Política Agrícola Común, que se ha desarrollado fuera de la política ambiental propiamente dicha; y, finalmente, los mecanismos de implementación y control.

Por supuesto, la eficacia de esta política medioambiental sólo puede ser valorada a la luz de su aplicación sobre el terreno. Michael Quigley (Trinity College Dublin, Irlanda) en 'Los efectos de la política de CE en el paisaje rural y el medio ambiente de Irlanda' (Capítulo 12) lleva a cabo una valoración de algunas de estas aplicaciones a Irlanda, un país cuyo paisaje es predominantemente rural, y donde las práticas agrícolas, especialmente el pastoreo, es casi la única actividad económica. La agricultura irlandesa había alcanzado ya un nivel de modernización bastante alto antes de su ingreso en la CE en 1973, pero el ritmo se aceleró considerablemente al quedar incluida en el ámbito de aplicación de las políticas procedentes de Bruselas. El uso del suelo rural y la calidad ambiental quedaron afectados por tres aspectos distintos de la política europea: primero, y obviamente, por la PAC, cuya influencia se extiende a todos los usos de tierras de labor; segundo, las medidas estructurales, que aunque no estrictamente agrarias, suministra fondos a varios programas operativos a través de los cuales la Comunidad sostiene el sistema que afecta al paisaje rural; y tercero, la política y legislación ambiental, tanto en lo que se refiere a las disposiciones destinadas al control de los efectos de otras políticas, como a las dirigidas directamente a la conservación de aspectos del medio ambiente.

Para Irlanda, la PAC, con todas sus ramificaciones, resulta especialmente determinante, no sólo en lo que se refiere al bien-estar económico, sino tambien en los cambios del paisaje y el estado del medio ambiente. El desarrollo de la agricultura le afecta por dos vías diferentes: primero, a través del control sobre el mercado, llevado a cabo con la política de apoyo a los precios; y segundo, a través de una importante variedad de medidas estructurales dirigidas a la compensación de los agricultores en ciertas áreas desfavorecidas.

La primera de estas vías conduce a un processo de intensificación de la agricultura, ya que el nivel de apoyo financiero obtenido está determinado por el volumen de producción. Además no sólo a la superproducción y a llega la acumulación de excedentes, sino también a la degradación ambiental. Los efectos en la economía agrícola de las considerables sumas de dinero proporcionadas por el FEOGA han sido evidentes en el sector de la agricultura comercial. Como respuesta a los incentivos de la CE, el número de ovejas se ha incrementado dramáticamente durante los últimos años, lo cual ha llegado a una expansión de los pastos y a problemas de erosión.

Economías de escala han impuesto como ventajosa una especialización regional de algunas empresas agrícolas, especialmente de cerdos y aves de corral. Desgraciadamente, ellos han tenido efectos ambientales negativos, debido a la utilización de grandes cantidades de productos contaminantes que acaban en los rios. Otros aspectos de la intensificación, tales como el incremento en el uso de fertilizantes y en el del heno, han dabo lugar, igualmente, a problemas de contaminación del agua.

Al mismo tiempo, los fondos estructurales del FEOGA, dirigidos a las áreas marginales y cuyo objetivo es el de hacerlas más productivas, puede tener también efectos negativos sobre su frágil medio ambiente. El Paquete Oeste, dirigido a estimular el desarrollo agrícola en el oeste de Irlanda, y la Disposición para el Drenage del Oeste, son ejemplos de medidas de ayudas-CE que han tenido efectos ambientales perjudiciales.

La silvicultura irlandesa está también experimentando actualmente una gran expansión, doblándose los objetivos de plantación anual que han pasado de 15 000 a 30 000 ha. Este nivel de desarrollo sin precedente es la consecuencia de las ayudas procedentes del Programa Forestal de la CE. Entre las consecuencias del desarrollo forestal en Irlanda están: acidificación de la superficie de los cursos de agua; degradación de los pozos naturales de pesca, destrucción de importantes ecosistemas en tierras pantanosas; y alteración de paisajes silvestres de gran belleza natural.

Desde mediados de los ochenta, el énfasis en la intensificación de la agricultura ha comenzado a cambiar, en parte como consecuencia de reducir la producción de alimentos en la Comunidad, en parte por los efectos perjudiciales sobre el medio ambiente. Ello ha culminado con el estableci-miento de nuevas medidas radicales que reconocen en el agricultor un papel dual, el de agricultor y el de conservador del campo, lo que sin duda tendrá efectos beneficiosos para el medio ambiente. Al mismo tiempo, el reforza-miento de la política ambiental de la CE con medidas tales como la Directiva de Evaluación del Impacto Ambiental y la Directiva de Habitat, constituyen instrumentos útiles al respecto. Pero para Irlanda, una de las mayores amenazas potenciales al medio ambiente pueden ser los fondos de desarrollo regional, que se han incrementado considerablemente. Queda por verse si las manifestadas intenciones de proteger el medio ambiente son realmente ciertas.

El medio ambiente es una de las claves que explica las condiciones de salud de las comunidades. Cosimo Palagiano (La Sapienza, Roma, Italia) en 'Medio ambiente, salud y cuidado de la salud: comparación europea y un caso de estudio italiano' (Capítulo 13) examina las vías por las cuales la CE ha influido la salud y el cuidado de la salud en la Comunidad. Relativamente, la CE ha descuidado este área de análisis, a pesar de que su política está cada vez más implicada en asuntos que tienen que ver con la salud, como por ejemplo, sus políticas ambientales, el propósito de la Carta Social en el Tratado de Maastricht y las políticas de intensificación y extensificación de la agricultura.

El propósito de este capítulo es triple. Primero, revisar las condiciones de salud en la CE a través de una serie de indicadores. La primera conclusión es la de que la esperanza de vida y la incidencia de las enfermedades presentan diferencias incluso entre un grupo tan aparentemente homogéneo de estados prósperos. Segundo, ilustrar las continuas variaciones en las condiciones de salud dentro de los paises. Italia es elegido como caso de estudio por dos razones: por la persistencia de la profunda división regional que existe en este país y porque existe poco material en inglés de sus condiciones de salud, comparado con el que existe para los países del norte de Europa. Por último, se aborda la importancia actual y potencial de los asuntos de salud en la CE.

En la conclusión Allan Williams y Mark Blacksell (Exeter RU) en 'Un Cambio de mapa y nuevas prioridades: la CE a la vuelta del siglo 21' (Capítulo 14) observan las tendencias que presentan los cambios y el impacto que estos cambios pueden tener en la política de la Comunidad, particularmente con respecto al desarrollo económico y del medio ambiente.

PART II

Introduction

Introduction

This section provides the context for the individual chapters that form the core of the book. It begins with a brief description of the political evolution of the EC and its emergence as the most important supranational institution in Europe. There follows an analysis of the mosaic of regional problems within the Community and the effect of successive enlargements—from six to nine to ten and now twelve member states—on centre–periphery tensions. To what extent have enlargement and increased political and economic integration benefited the individual regions? Has the gap between rich and poor grown? Or has integration enabled the benefits of economic growth in the richer core regions to spread generally throughout the Community?

The conclusions are mixed. Economic integration and the removal of restrictions on the movement of people, goods, and services has clearly brought many benefits, but developments, like the conclusion of the Single Market in 1993, have also left some of the weaker regions of the EC extremely vulnerable. Freedom of movement has also made it imperative to reform, strengthen, and unify the various structural funds (European Social Fund, the guidance section of the Common Agricultural Policy, the European Regional Development Fund), so that the Community can assist those regions adversely affected. Whether it will prove possible to manage the economic structure of Europe in this way is still an open question, but some of the pointers to the likely direction of change up to the beginning of the twenty-first century and beyond are considered.

Finally, the logic and structure of the book are explained, providing a guide through the varied perspectives on the EC that exist in the different member states and which are manifestly apparent in this text.

1 The Development of the European Community: Its Spatial Dimension

Mark Blacksell and Allan M. Williams

The evolution of the EC

The creation of the European Community (EC) has been the most significant event for the economic, political, and social geography of Europe in the second half of the twentieth century. From its beginnings in the early 1950s with the Treaty of Paris (1952) and the emergence of the European Coal and Steel Community (ECSC), to the two Treaties of Rome (1958) setting up the European Economic Community (EEC) and Euratom, on to the Single European Act (1986) paving the way for the Single Market in 1993, and now the tortuous, and fraught, negotiations over full monetary union at the heart of the Treaty on European Union (Maastricht Treaty), the EC has evolved into an increasingly complex political entity. It is now the dominant influence in shaping the future of twelve European states.

Growing institutional complexity has gone hand in hand with a growth in membership. For more than twenty years, from 1952 to 1973, there were only six members—Belgium, France, Germany, Italy, Luxembourg, and the Netherlands—all states with well-developed industrial bases at the heart of a Western Europe, economically resurgent in the wake of the two devastating World Wars that had dominated the first half of the twentieth century. The first enlargement in 1973 added three more member states—Denmark, Ireland, and the UK—all north European and closely linked economically, both to each other and to the founder member states. Their accession did change the nature of the EC: the regional problems associated with geographical peripherality inevitably became more acute and the cohesion of the Community, initially a major source of strength, was undermined by the addition of two island states, one of which, the UK, accounted for more than 20 per cent of the total population. The 1980s saw a further growth in membership, with first Greece joining in 1981, followed by Spain and Portugal in 1986. The cumulative effect of this Mediterranean enlargement radically changed the nature of the EC. All three new member states—but especially Greece and Portugal—were less wedded to the industrial core of

Western Europe, both in terms of geography and economic make-up. Semi-subsistence peasant agriculture and latifundia still dominated the rural landscape and none was fully part of the mainstream European urban industrial economy. Indeed, in the 1960s and early 1970s one of their principal roles was as a source of cheap immigrant labour.

In the 1990s the focus of change in the EC is once more shifting. The unification of Germany in 1990 saw the accession, albeit by absorption, of an East European member, the former DDR, thus adding a new dimension to the regional economic map. There is also the more general question of how to accommodate potential new members whose industrial economies had developed under a centrally planned, and now manifestly failed, system. The unified Germany is proving acceptable without fundamental institutional change to the EC, if only because Germany itself will bear the brunt of the costs. However, if other central and Eastern European states— Poland, Hungary, the Czech and Slovak states emerging from the former Czechoslovakia, and Slovenia, Croatia, and whatever other states eventually struggle out of the ruins of Yugoslavia—join, then the whole economic and political logic of the Community will have to change.

Nor is the political turmoil in Eastern Europe the only agent for change. A group of states in Western Europe, which for one reason or another did not feel able to join the EC initially, is now queuing up to be admitted. In 1991 the European Free Trade Association (EFTA)—Austria, Finland, Iceland, Liechtenstein, Norway, Sweden, and Switzerland—signed an agreement with the EC to form the European Economic Area (EEA), extending the free trade zone, excluding agriculture, throughout the whole of Western Europe. Subsequently, Austria, Finland, Norway, and Sweden have all applied for full membership of the EC, and there is every likelihood that other EEA members will follow suit.

Finally, in the more distant future, there are other states eager to become members. Turkey, Malta, and Cyprus have been manœuvring, separately, to join for nearly thirty years and now many of the republics in what was the western part of the Soviet Union are also beginning to show an active interest. Whatever the outcome, it is certain that the EC will have to continue to adapt in response to the economic and social imperatives of a changing political geography. The ability of the Community to do so is partly an institutional question, but also depends on the potentials and limitations of a diverse set of member states and their constituent regions.

The mosaic of regional problems

Regional disparities are a structural feature of the EC. The ten least developed regions of the Community, nearly all of them in the two least developed states, Greece and Portugal, have an annual per capita income of less than one-third that of the ten wealthiest regions. Furthermore, whatever measure of development is chosen the picture is broadly the same, making it relatively straightforward to pick out the truly disadvantaged regions of the EC, even though the handicaps they face vary. All the most recent studies indicate that the disparities between the rich and poor regions are growing, especially as far as employment is concerned, because of the general economic crisis and the effect it is having on manufacturing industry (Commission of the European Communities 1991*d*). Virtually all the most deprived regions are in the south and west of the EC but, in addition to the difficulties being faced by these essentially rural regions, there are also the problems confronting the older industrial regions in the centre of the Community, not to mention the five German *Länder* that used to form East Germany (DDR).

Regional policy has never been completely absent from the deliberations of the EC, but it began to assume a new importance after the mid 1970s, as a result of the first enlargement of the Community and the slowdown in the level of economic activity, linked to two successive huge increases in the world market price of crude oil. However, it has been the commitment to the unified Single Market from January 1993 that has really forced the Community to take the whole issue of intervention seriously. Without effective policy instruments of its own, the EC would be unable even to attempt to combat regional inequalities and guard against the very real danger that a single market would further reinforce the weak position of the poorest regions.

The European Regional Development Fund (ERDF) provided 24 billion ECUs for distribution between 1975 and 1987, but this is still less than 10 per cent of the total EC budget, paling into insignificance when compared with the sums spent on the Common Agricultural Policy (CAP) (Commission of the European Communities 1990*c*). The present reform of the structural funds, the drawing together of the European Social Fund (ESF), the ERDF, and the guidance section of the CAP, should provide the Commission with new powers and much greater financial clout. The three structural funds now account for 20 per cent of the total budget, offering the prospect of improved cohesion in regional policy amongst an ensemble of European states that has to cope with regional disparities considerably greater than those found in the United States.

The contribution of successive enlargements of the EC to the growing economic crisis

There is no direct reference to regional policy in the Treaty of Rome, other than a passing mention in the sections on transport policy to aid for member states. In practice, the closest the Treaty came to addressing the issue was the European Investment Bank (EIB), its main purpose being to promote regional development. The apparent lack of interest and the professed belief that market mechanisms will eliminate disparities, other than in the short term, sit strangely with the individual commitment by the six original member states to national intervention policies for their own regions. The contrast is greatest in Italy, where southern Italy, the Mezzogiorno, received massive long-term state aid via the 'Cassa per il Mezzogiorno' from its foundation in 1950 up to its demise in the late 1980s.

The favourable economic climate of the 1950s partly explains why regional problems were not high on the agenda when the EC was founded. Growth was particularly rapid and the prevalent belief was that 'trickle down' effects would spread the benefits. Even the most disadvantaged areas seemed to be able to attract new investment, a fact well illustrated by the Mezzogiorno, where a whole new heavy industrial structure was created: iron and steel at Taranto and Naples, and chemical industries at Brindisi, Augusta, and Taranto. With the benefit of hindsight, it is now clear that very little private investment was attracted to the region and that its economy had become heavily polarized. Potential regional tensions at the time were further reduced by the large-scale migration from the poorest areas of Europe to the main urban and industrial centres of industry in the north (see Chapter 6). Had this not occurred, then arguably chronically high levels of unemployment in the least industrialized regions could have led to more serious social and political discontent.

The first enlargement of the Community in 1973 presented the EC with the problems of a number of new regions with known persistent, and chronic, economic difficulties, like the west of Ireland and the older heavy industrial areas in the UK. In a sense, the timing of the expansion could not have been worse, for it coincided with a sustained period of weak growth and crisis in the European economy. The effects of the dramatic rises in oil prices during the 1970s were felt most in the least-developed regions, and the sharp fall-off in immigration in the major industrial countries also penalized these same areas, contributing to a rapid rise in the level of unemployment. The situation was aggravated even further by a crisis of accumulation, leading to reduced investment everywhere, but especially in the least-developed regions. Finally, the restructuring of manufacturing industry in the face of growing internationalization continued to affect traditional industries in the older industrial regions and also contributed to the urban economic crisis in cities such as London, Rotterdam, and Paris, the major conurbations at the heart of Europe (Keeble 1989).

These different factors, taken together, threatened not only further progress in integration, but the very survival of the Community and contributed to the member states adopting more interventionist policies. The ERDF came into operation in 1975 and, although it was designed partly to compensate for the anticipated UK budget deficit, its two main objectives were to reduce overt regional disequilibria and to stimulate renewed growth in the declining older industrial areas. For the most part, these regions corresponded to the areas covered by national programmes of regional aid. Member states had difficulty in extending the scope of the areas involved, because of the very limited funds available from the EC. As a general rule, the ERDF contributed an amount equal to 50 per cent of public expenditure in infrastructural works, or in investment in manufacturing industries or services, so long as it was directed towards sustaining, or increasing, jobs. At the same time as the ERDF came into existence, both the Agriculture Guidance and Guarantee Fund (FEOGA) and the European Social Fund (ESF) also began to be used much more explicitly to address regional problems.

When Greece joined the Community in 1981, followed by Spain and Portugal in 1986, the whole question of the coherence of the Community was raised again in an even more acute way. The Community responded to this crisis with the Integrated Mediterranean Programme and pre-accession aid packages. Subsequently, integration of the former East Germany (DDR) has added another economically weak region with hitherto unique problems of adjustment. After almost twenty years of the ERDF, there is a growing realization that the EC is a group of states with a number of, structurally, chronically disadvantaged regions. The long-term impact of the Single Market and monetary union on these regions is still uncertain, but it is difficult to be optimistic about the outcome.

The centre and the periphery

Most of the measures used to define and explain regional disparities use the contrasts between a dynamic 'centre', despite evidence of decline in the older industrial areas, and a weak 'periphery' characterized by a combination of low per capita incomes, relatively high levels of unemployment, smaller numbers of people in the higher, professional, socio-economic groups, and larger numbers employed in agriculture. These are indications of a poor capacity for innovation and sustained growth and they have been drawn together and generalized by the EC itself to produce an index of peripherality a map of which is reproduced in Fig. 1.1.

If the regions outside the 'centre' of the EC are assumed to be those with a per capita GDP of less than 70 per cent (measured in standard purchasing power) of the Community average, then they can be divided roughly into two groups. Ireland and most of the regions in Spain and Italy are close to the 70 per cent threshold. Greece and Portugal on the other hand are nowhere near, barely rising above 50 per cent of the Community average. The former East Germany (DDR) is a special case and is not included in this analysis.

The Mezzogiorno in Italy, despite having benefited greatly from Community aid via the ERDF, has still not really closed the gap. Between 1975 and 1987, Italy received nearly 7 billion ECUs, three-quarters of it for infrastructural improvements, and Ireland more than 1 billion ECUs. The impact of this investment in terms of development are rather difficult to interpret. In Ireland the catching-up process did not really begin until 1985, when a more rigorous programme of budgetary controls was introduced, whilst in Italy economic disparities actually widened up to 1987.

Greece's entry into the EC caused virtually no serious economic disruption to the EC itself. However, there was little significant structural improvement in the economy of the new member either. Over the past decade, per capita income has fallen and the country's economy often seems locked into perpetual crisis, partly as a result of weak economic management, which itself has been linked to ineffective and unstable political leadership. Inflation has been high, the level of indebtedness intolerable, and unemployment has risen. The situation in Portugal has improved sharply since 1986, due to both greater political stability and the inflow of EC funds. With some of the highest growth rates and lowest levels of unemployment in the whole of the OECD group of nations, it has begun to close the gap with the rest of the EC and its GDP per capita has now risen above that of Greece. Nevertheless, it still lags far behind the EC average and there is growing concern over the impact of the Single Market programme.

In addition to these structural problems, there are the constraints imposed by distance from the 'centre', a fact that goes some way towards explaining the lack of development in most of the peripheral regions. In virtually every case the infrastructure is inadequate, if not downright obsolete, lacking higher-order rail and road connections, modern port facilities, comprehensive airline links (see Chapter 5), and IT networks. Distance in terms of time is often more serious than distance in terms of kilometres. The coefficient of proportionality between these two parameters is nearly 2 for Athens and Dublin, and around 1.5 for Madrid, Lisbon, and Rome. Clearly, those countries with elongated, or island, geographies will have some regions where the distance–time problem is particularly acute, as in the Greek islands, western Ireland, or southern Italy.

The above analysis enables the broad changes since 1975 to be sketched out, but does not explain the fundamental lack of competitiveness in the less-developed regions. Recent EC company-level surveys clearly reveal that the cost of credit, a lack of risk capital, inadequate facilities and money for research and development, less diffusion of innovation, and the lack of skilled labour, all contribute to the unattractiveness of these regions (Commission of the European Communities 1991d). Three-quarters of the investment in research in the EC is concentrated in France, the UK, and Germany (see Chapter 4). Not only is there less money spent on research in the peripheral regions, but what expenditure there is tends to be highly concentrated in the most dynamic pockets of activity: the Madrid conurbation, Lisbon, and Dublin. Furthermore, the real cost of borrowing is often much higher in the periphery than it is in the industrial heartland of the Community.

The Single Market and the reform of the regional funds

Ever since the 1985 Cockfield White Paper on the Single Market and the 1986 Single European Act, progress towards economic and monetary union has gathered pace. Even though the final stages of political and monetary integration, proposed in the 1991 Treaty on European Union (Maastricht Treaty) are not expected to be completed until the turn of the century at the earliest, most frontier controls should have disappeared by the beginning of 1993. There are doubts whether this huge integrated market can survive without imperilling the overall cohesion of the Community, if regionalism continues to be a potent social and political force. It is for this reason that the Commission and the Council of Ministers decided to reform the various regional funds, so that the less-developed regions would stand a better chance of catching up, helped by a completely redesigned Community aid programme (Commission of the European Communities 1990d). More cynically, we can also note that this was the political price that had to be paid to secure the agreement of the less-developed member states to the process of greater integration.

The probable regional impact of the Single Market

The spatial dimensions of economic development are still imperfectly understood. For the neo-liberals economic integration should be marked by convergence; the liberalization of trade, capital, and labour are expected to narrow disparities in incomes and profitability. Others claim that integration encourages divergence, by reinforcing the locational advantages of the most-developed areas, especially in the large conurbations where there are aggregate economies of scale and higher-level contact networks. The EC's own research into this question suggests that the most-deprived regions ought to gain from the general liberalization of trade, because they will be able to exploit their specific advantages and seek out markets outside their normal trading area (Cecchini 1988). Nevertheless, research on the potential handicaps such regions face suggests that such a view may be over-optimistic.

The impact on the regions may be measured by the resilience of their industries in the face of the increased competition that will be the inevitable consequence of the unified internal market. Experts have predicted that about forty sectors are likely to be directly affected, representing nearly half of the total employment in manufacturing industry and an eighth of all employment in the EC (Commission of the European Communities 1991d). While the adversely affected industries only account for between 45 and 52 per cent of employment in the member states in the 'centre', the equivalent figures for Greece and Portugal are in excess of 60 per cent (see also Chapter 4).

Industry is not destined to disappear from the most-disadvantaged regions, but, if a substantial loss of jobs is to be avoided, it can be argued that it is essential to set in train a radical restructuring process. From Greece to Ireland, industry on the periphery is dogged by low levels of productivity, a lack of skilled labour, and poor innovative capacity. Turning to the role of the public sector in the economy, the reduction or elimination of state procurement and other restrictive, or protective, measures as part of the Single Market programme runs the risk of exposing many public and semi-public companies to greater competition from within the periphery and from the 'centre'. The reshaping of the international division of labour will almost certainly see economic control, and possibly some production of goods and services, being displaced from the periphery to the centre. It is, of course possible that the periphery will attract industries, but this is most likely to be because of the availability of cheap and flexible labour. Even if the grudging introduction of the measures in the Social Chapter in the Treaty on European Union (Maastricht Treaty) does not nullify any such comparative advantage, 'success' in these terms would be an admission that only the regions in the 'centre', especially those in the major conurbations, have a capacity to innovate and generate new technology and products. The periphery could face the gloomy future of being fragmented into pockets of manufacturing, relying on comparative labour-cost advantage. In the long term, such a scenario could only widen the gap between regions and increase the dependence of the periphery on the 'centre'. Furthermore, there is considerable theoretical and empirical scepticism concerning development strategies based on external capital. At the very least it is essential that there is also parallel endogenous economic development (Garofoli 1992). However there is little in the Single Market programme that seems likely to be conducive to endogenous development. This is implied by the Community's belated creation of a 'small firms policy' and the introduction of stronger anti-monopoly legislation.

The reform of the structural funds and the increased scope for EC intervention

By the mid-1980s the ERDF and regional policy generally were universally accepted as part of the EC's remit, and this was explicitly referred to in the Single European Act. A framework regulation, and specific actions, came into force at the beginning of 1989. The main feature of the reform was to spell out a series of priorities over the medium term, backed up by the funds to put them into practice. In 1975 the total amount allocated to structural funds was 6 per cent of the Community budget but, by 1990, the proportion had risen to 20 per cent; this was equivalent to 10 billion ECUs and was set to continue to rise until 1993. This reform has given the Commission the opportunity to take a more active role in co-ordinating national and Community policies, and the overall impact of these policies has been enhanced by the merging of the original three separate structural funds (ERDF, ESF, and FEOGA).

The reform has also created a more direct partnership with the regions, enabling pluriannual programmes to be devised and implemented. The qualifying criteria are now set by the Commission, so that the ERDF is not the sum of national regional policies, as it was in the 1970s and early 1980s. All regions where per capita GDP is 25 per cent or more below the Community average come within the terms of Objective 1, the main purpose of which is to enhance the level of economic development (Fig. 1.1). They include the whole of Ireland, Greece, and Portugal, as well as 57 per cent of the Spanish and 36 per cent of the Italian populations. Somewhat less than 3 per cent of the populations of the UK and France will also be eligible, mainly because of the specific economic problems faced by some of their offshore islands. Objective 1 will absorb the bulk of the money available for regional policy from the EC, probably 36 billion ECUs in 1993, 80 per cent of the resources of the ERDF.

Objective 2 covers the declining industrial areas (Fig. 1.1) and is less well resourced with an allocation of little more than 2 billion ECUs in the first four years. In order that the available aid may be used as effectively as possible, a twofold categorization has been introduced, distinguishing

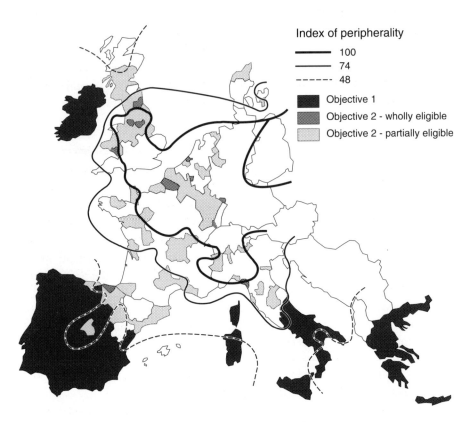

FIG. 1.1. Economic disparity and regional policy in the EC

Source: Based on data from the Commission of the European Communities (1990*d*).

between those areas that are fully and those that are only partially eligible. Most of the areas covered by Objective 2 are in the traditional industrial states. In Belgium, Luxembourg, and the UK more than a third of the population is included and although the coverage is more restricted elsewhere, regions like the Basque country in Spain and the Nord-Pas-de-Calais in France are also covered.

Regional policy extends to rural areas as well under the terms of Objective 5b. It encompasses 80 per cent of the EC in terms of area, but only a third of the population and it is proposed that nearly 3 billion ECUs be injected into these predominantly rural regions by 1993. Half the eligible areas are also included within Objective 1, which will give them a priority to the detriment of rural regions in France and Germany.

Although 43 per cent of the Community's population benefits from the new integrated regional policy, it is concentrated primarily in four countries. In Ireland and Portugal 100 per cent of the population is included, as it was prior to the reform, but the same now also applies to Greece, while in Spain the proportion has risen to 80 per cent. The UK and Italy have lost out somewhat in the reallocation, but the other members of the EC, the most prosperous countries, have seen massive reductions in their eligibility for assistance.

As well as redrawing the geographic map of intervention, the Commission has also introduced more severe eligibility criteria for Community aid. In practice, it is now a matter of joint negotiation between the Commission, the competent national authorities and the regions concerned. The Community aid agencies (BICs) make initial proposals with the aim of ensuring that the available resources, both from the member states and from the Community, have the maximum impact on development. Even though the basic economic infrastructure remains the first priority, the Commission is increasingly concerned with the actual means of production, and with promoting local development initiatives like, for example, industrial support services and local labour-market measures. Evidence of the more proactive role of the Commission is to be seen in the fact that some of the BICs were radically restructured in 1989, because they had not observed sufficiently closely the new EC rules. Finally, the Commission is insisting that all member states respect the principle of additionality (that is, that Community aid should not be seen as a substitute for state programmes).

The reform of the structural funds in 1989 for the first time enabled the EC to pursue effectively 'Community initiatives' to tackle persistent regional economic problems and allowed it to oversee the implementation of these common policies in the regions affected. Although the discretionary finance available will only represent 9 per cent of the total structural fund, even by 1993 (5.5 billion ECUs), the list of Community programmes is still impressive and is evidence of the Commission's determination to initiate more integrated policies. So far there are four programmes in operation—STAR, VALOREN, RESIDER, and RENEVAL—dealing respectively with the problems of the energy, iron and steel, and ship building industries (see Chapter 4), but there are a dozen other 'Community initiatives' still in the pipeline. Of these, three are particularly noteworthy: ENVIREG, which will try to combat the environmental problems facing the Mediterranean; INTERREG, which will seek to speed up trans-border co-operation after the disappearance of frontier controls; and STRIDE, which will attempt to enhance the scientific research potential of the more backward regions in the Community.

Into the twenty-first century

The EC has now reached a critical point in its development. As a political entity it has matured, with its own potentially autonomous government and institutions, but it still has to define satisfactorily its relationship with the governments of its individual member states. The process began in earnest with the Single European Act and has continued with the debate over the fate of the Treaty on European Union (Maastricht Treaty). The Maastricht agreement is essentially about the redistribution of power between national governments and EC institutions and, now that it has eventually been ratified, intergovernmentalism rather than federalism will increasingly characterize Community decision-making.

Now that the Single Market is well on the way to being realized, even if the original 1985 concept has become somewhat diluted, social and regional disparities will become one of the Commission's main priorities. The EC remains a body of diverse member states and even more diverse regions and its long-term cohesion depends to no small degree on reducing, or at least checking, these disparities, although there can be no illusion about the obstacles to such an objective within an essentially liberal market framework. For a region with a per capita GDP 70 per cent that of the Community average to raise itself by 20 percentage points, it will have to grow 1.25 per cent faster than the overall Community average for twenty years. If the required growth is not forthcoming under market conditions, then it will necessitate massive state intervention to redistribute resources from the more prosperous to the poorer social groups, regions, and countries. It is difficult to be optimistic about the chances of realizing such an ambitious goal and the evidence in this book shows what a formidable task lies ahead.

The difficulties are made even more forbidding because finances dictate that EC policies may only provide a small addition to the intervention strategies of the individual member states and there are likely to continue to be wide national variations in the way that redistribution issues are addressed. As far as regional policy is concerned, Germany, the richest country in the EC, is also the one that spends most on regional aid. Generally, it would seem that the availability of aid depends more on the relative state of health of the national budget, than on the severity of the structural problems in any absolute sense. It follows that the gap between the rich and the poor regions in the Community as a whole will inevitably, and inexorably continue to widen, unless there is a fundamental change in the relationship between the EC and its member states. This disturbing fact has recently led the Commission to try to persuade the German government to limit its aid from the public purse to the five new *Länder* which formerly constituted East

Germany (DDR). Similarly, the Commission has asked France to modify its aid programmes, so that they only benefit those regions shown as eligible on the new and more restricted Community map of regional assistance.

As in many other areas, regional policy is a test of the willingness of member states to cede part of their traditional sovereignty to the Commission. This was the underlying aim of the reform of the structural funds in 1989. There are still many obstacles to be overcome before it can be claimed that the regional cohesion of the Community has been truly strengthened. Overcoming the claims of national sovereignty and facilitating greater direct EC intervention will, at best, be a long haul and quite conceivably may prove impossible.

The structure of the book

This book takes as its starting point the political changes caused by the emergence of the EC in its present form over the past four decades and the legacy of regional disequilibria that the whole process has bequeathed. Its aim is to consider how the social, economic, and political geography of the twelve member states, and their regions, have changed since their accession. The text has been written by fourteen geographers from seven different member states and considers the changes within the context of four broad themes: the urban condition, structural change, rural adaptation, and environmental response.

The urban condition

This theme is recognition of one of the key features of the geography of the EC: the fact that nearly 80 per cent of the population lives in towns and cities. The changes to the urban environment since the Community was formed are of the most immediate concern to most of its citizens and Pierre Laborde (Bordeaux III, France) in 'The spatial evolution of West European cities 1950–1990' (Chapter 2) considers the geographic effects of the rapid growth in the urban population of the EC up until the mid-1970s and the subsequent period of consolidation that has followed. Cities have changed from being tightly-knit and inward-looking and have exploded outwards. Not only have the existing urban areas been modified, a new urbanized periphery has been created that is still expanding because of changes in taste and building technology, despite the fact that population growth itself has now slowed dramatically.

The problem with broad generalizations about any aspect of socio-economic change is that they almost inevitably mask regional and local variations. This is clearly illustrated by Lila Leontidou (National Technical University Athens, Greece) in the second chapter in this section, 'Mediterranean cities: Divergent trends in a united Europe' (Chapter 3). Cities have long had a central cultural role in Mediterranean Europe, but much of the technologically-led dispersal that has characterized the urban areas of northern Europe has yet to be felt in the south. For example, in Naples, Athens, and Barcelona the inner city remains the prime residential area, with working-class suburbs scattered around the periphery. The social and economic disaggregation, so typical of France, Germany, and the UK, is as yet much less in evidence in the Mediterranean.

Inevitably the impact of the EC has so far been minimal: only Italy was a founder member; Greece, Spain, and Portugal did not join until the 1980s. It remains to be seen whether the distinctiveness of urban areas in the Mediterranean will survive the greater centralization of policy-making which membership of the Community inevitably brings with it.

Structural change

Part IV examines the broader underlying infrastructural and socio-economic adaptations that EC membership has induced, both consciously through regional and other policies and involuntarily through having to accommodate the greater freedom of movement of goods and services. Jean-Paul Charrié (Bordeaux III, France) in 'The pattern of industry: Europeanization versus globalization' (Chapter 4) paints a detailed picture of the industrial transformation in the EC, a group of countries that includes many which were the cradle of the Industrial Revolution in the nineteenth century. He demonstrates that the Community is still a major industrial force in the world, but to survive the basis of its supremacy is having to alter in the face of unprecedented global competition. The EC is an important force in the emerging industrial landscape, providing specific aid to selected sectors, especially those at the leading edge of technological change, co-ordinating research efforts, and taking the lead in a revitalized regional policy. In addition, the completion of the Single Market will have very important repercussions for both the competitiveness and the overall industrial fabric of the Community.

When it comes to manipulating the dynamics of industrial societies governments have long recognized that transport is one of the keys. The EC has always been alive to this fact, even if it has not so far pursued it with the vigour that might have been expected. James Killen (Trinity College Dublin, Ireland) and Austin Smyth (Ulster, UK) in 'European Community transport policy with particular reference to Ireland as a peripheral region'

(Chapter 5) consider the way in which the EC Common Transport Policy, or lack of it, has affected development in the island of Ireland as a whole. It is an aspect of development where the benefits of co-ordination at a European level would have been enormous, but one where the combined political will has never quite measured up to the challenge.

Nevertheless, whatever its shortcomings, the EC as a whole benefits from an extensive transportation network that is much envied elsewhere in the world. It has contributed immeasurably to the coherence of the Community and, *inter alia*, facilitated the mobility of labour which has been an important dynamo powering much of the sustained economic success of Europe over the past forty years. Russell King (Trinity College Dublin, Ireland) in 'Migration and the single market for labour: An issue in regional development' (Chapter 6) examines the economic contribution that some 20 million immigrant workers have made and the growing, and ever more serious, political problems that such new arrivals now pose. One of the great challenges facing the EC is how to accommodate swelling numbers of economic migrants from the erstwhile Communist states in Eastern Europe within a domestic labour market that seems set to be saturated well beyond the turn of the century.

One particular problem associated with international migrants, from both inside and outside the EC, is illegal labour, an issue described vividly by Solange Montagné-Villette (Poitiers, France) in 'Mobility and illegal labour in the EC' (Chapter 7). Illegal working is no novelty in Europe, it began in the early years of this present century and grew steadily in parallel with the development of modern social-security systems. The emergence of the EC, however, has provided a new dimension: the increased mobility of the labour force, as well as industry and business, has given rise to a range of illegal employment practices, closely linked to the political, economic, and legal structures of the EC.

Rural adaptation

This theme acknowledges that in one area, agriculture, Community policy has overshadowed national policies for nearly thirty years, at one stage devouring more than 90 per cent of the EC's budget and still accounting for more than 60 per cent. The politics of this state of affairs are well-known and not the subject of this book, but any serious study of the EC must devote a substantial proportion of its attention to agriculture. In fact, the over-whelming emphasis on farming and farmers is now beginning to wane, but this in itself is going to have serious and far-reaching repercussions for the rural economy and landscape. Dietrich Denecke (Göttingen, Germany) in

'Set-aside and landscape preservation: The German experience' (Chapter 8) analyses the consequences of these coming changes to EC agricultural policy for landscape and environment, drawing examples from the particularly sensitive rural landscapes of Germany where peasant farming and modern agriculture still manage to coexist.

However, although the CAP is beginning to change, and the policy of subsidizing agricultural output apparently regardless of cost, or immediate need, is being increasingly questioned, it remains the cornerstone of EC policy. Manuel Corbera (Cantabria, Spain) in 'The Common Agricultural Policy and the development of agriculture: Problems and perspectives' (Chapter 9) reassesses the CAP itself from the perspective of Spain, a country with a very large agricultural industry, which only recently in 1986 joined the EC. Purely quantitative measures of production can no longer be taken as the sole tokens of success; the difficult question of, 'Production for what?' has to be asked and the answer shows unequivocally that much marginal land in the EC is no longer required for agriculture. Alternative uses are having to be found, one of the most important of which is recreation and tourism. Allan Williams and Gareth Shaw (Exeter, UK) in 'Tourism, opportunities, challenges and contradictions in the EC' (Chapter 10) examine the whole burgeoning tourist phenomenon in the Community. Ever since the emergence of mass tourism in the 1960s, tourism can be described as an essential thread in the economic and social fabric of the EC. It is of major economic importance, employing more than one in twenty of the workforce and constitutes a substantial proportion of both GDP and international trade, both within and without the Community. More than any other major region in the world, tourism is now essential to production and consumption in rural, and urban, areas in the EC.

Environmental response

This underlines the important reality that the EC has been as much shaped by events as it has dictated them. The environment, as such, was ignored completely in the Treaties of Paris and Rome, making direct EC policy involvement in formulating solutions difficult to justify, despite growing public awareness and disquiet about environmental degradation and resource depletion throughout the 1960s and 1970s, as well as an emerging appreciation that it was unrealistic to view these global issues in a purely national context. Mark Blacksell (Exeter, UK) in 'Environmental policies and resource management' (Chapter 11) considers the rather tortuous path to realizing the gamut of environmental policies that are now an important part of EC policy as a whole. Over the four decades of its existence the Community has had to tread a difficult path in environmental matters between the limitations imposed on it by treaty, the conflicting attitudes of its growing number of member states, and an increasingly independent body of European public opinion, aided and abetted since 1979 by the European Parliament. However, the revision of the EEC Treaty by the Single European Act in 1986 formally brought the environment within the legal competence of the Community and it has subsequently taken a much more assertive role in environmental matters, ranging from water quality to food hygiene.

Obviously, the efficacy of these environmental policies can only be judged fully in terms of their effectiveness on the ground and Michael Quigley (Trinity College Dublin, Ireland) in 'The effect of EC policy on the rural landscape and environment of Ireland' (Chapter 12) makes a detailed assessment of some specific policies with respect to Ireland, a country whose landscape is predominantly rural and where agriculture, especially pastoral farming, is the most important single economic activity. Economic change has done much to upset the fine environmental balance at the heart of the rural economy and managing the unwanted side-effects is an issue of growing political importance.

At a more general level, the quality of the environment is one of the keys to the overall health of communities and individuals. Cosimo Palagiano (La Sapienza Rome, Italy) in 'Environment, health, and health care: European comparisons and an Italian case study' (Chapter 13) examines the way in which the EC has already influenced health and health care in the Community through its environmental policies, the Social Chapter in the Maastricht Treaty, and the policies to intensify and extensify agriculture. Yet despite the centralization of policy and decision-making inherent in the EC, significant variations in such indicators as life expectancy and the incidence of disease remain. It will be fascinating to see whether closer political and economic integration succeed in reducing such discrepancies in the future.

Finally, in the conclusion, Allan Williams and Mark Blacksell (Exeter, UK) in 'Development, distribution, and the environment: Future challenges for Europe' (Chapter 14) look at the ways in which the EC is likely to change as the turn of the twenty-first century approaches and the impact that these changes are likely to have on its policies. The political turmoil throughout Eastern Europe, from the Aegean to beyond the Arctic Circle, the fragility of the world economic system based on free trade, and the growing appreciation of the potentially catastrophic consequences of environmental mismanagement will all combine to ensure that any prescriptive policies must constantly be reviewed in the light of new and even more pressing imperatives.

Further reading

There are a number of books which provide an overview of the development of the EC. One of the most recent is A. M. Williams (1991), *The European Community: The Contradictions of Integration* (Oxford), which looks at a periodization of the evolution of conflicts and contradictions within the EC. Other, more specialized perspectives, are provided by L. Tsoukalis (1991), *The New European Economy: The Politics and Economics of Integration* (Oxford); A. H. Dawson (1993), *A Geography of European Integration* (London); R. W. Vickerman (1992), *The Single European Market: Prospects for Economic Integration* (New York); and J. R. Lodge (ed.) (1993), *The European Community and the Challenge of the Future*, 2nd edn. (London).

Useful reviews of uneven regional development, and of EC structural policies, are provided by titles such as L. Rodwin and H. Sazanami (eds.) (1991), *Industrial Change and Regional Economic Transition: The Experience of Western Europe* (London); M. Hebbert and J. C. Hansen (eds.) (1990), *Unfamiliar Territory: The Reshaping of European Geography* (Aldershot); W. Molle and R. Cappellin (eds.) (1988), *Regional Impact of Community Policies in Europe* (Aldershot); D. Pinder (1983), *Regional Economic Development and Policy: Theory and Practice in the European Community* (London); and D. Keeble (1989), 'Core–periphery disparities, recession and new regional dynamics in the European Community', *Geography*, 74: 1–11.

The Commission produces a constant stream of statistics on the regions via EUROSTAT, as well as periodic views of regional policy as a whole and of programmes in particular countries. A good summary is provided by the Directorate General for Regional Policy (1992), *The EDRF in 1990* (Brussels).

PART III

The Urban Condition

The urban condition

The growth of towns and cities has been one of the most notable features of recent social and economic change throughout the EC and makes it a natural starting point for analysing the processes at work. This section considers the nature and form of spatial evolution in Western European cities, a process dominated by the replanning of the historic urban fabric, and by the unprecedented expansion and dispersal of the built-up area. The dynamics of the spatial changes are the results of a combination of both general and local factors, which have produced a range of intractable economic and social disequilibria in urban areas. These processes are illustrated with a wide range of examples from many different European countries, though with detailed reference to France, a country where the growth of major cities at the expense of rural areas has been particularly marked in the second half of the twentieth century.

In any large and complex region the dangers of distortion through over-generalization are always present and geographers, in particular, need to be sensitive to regional variations. On the southern periphery of the EC, along the Mediterranean, the urban tradition is somewhat different from that in northern Europe and historically more deeply rooted—a journey from *polis* to *metropolis*. Though the cultural importance of the central city remains, there is less evidence of the rigid functional segregation now so characteristic of the north.

Nevertheless, in recent years cities in all the Mediterranean countries have experienced a period of rapid and far-reaching change. The democratization of the body politic in Greece, Portugal, and Spain has opened the way for new, and more responsive, local government structures. The tightening of north European labour markets has resulted in much greater pressure to create jobs in the domestic economies, thus further increasing the rate of expansion in many towns and cities. And the explosive growth of tourism has sparked fundamental social change and frequently led to rising tensions in the population.

The EC has so far had little direct influence on the process of urban transformation in its member states. It remains to be seen if it can translate its acute analyses of the problems into policies which forestall a two-speed Europe, divided between north and south.

2 The Spatial Evolution of West European Cities, 1950–1990

Pierre Laborde

The nature and form of the spatial evolution

Beginning in the 1950s and until 1975 the populations of West European cities went through a period of rapid growth. Subsequently, the rate of expansion has slowed down markedly, but nevertheless the effect has been to modify fundamentally the historic fabric of built-up areas and to create a new urbanized periphery, which still continues to extend outwards. Increasingly, high land-use intensities in the existing urban fabric and extensions beyond the original built-up area are the two chief physical manifestations of the overall process of urban growth. Historically, these two processes have sometimes occurred separately and sometimes simultaneously: peripheral growth has either been a direct consequence of redeveloping the existing urban core (the present situation), or it has happened independently (the most common situation in the past), or both have occurred at the same time, as happened in the years between 1950 and 1980.

Replanning the historic urban fabric

From the earliest times, cities have grown and developed at the locations where they were founded and in every period the most dilapidated parts of the fabric have been demolished and under-utilized land has been reclaimed to allow new buildings to be erected. For example, the old city of Bordeaux has a plan that reflects a mixture of the Roman and medieval heritage, but the buildings for the most part date from the seventeenth and eighteenth centuries. The process of renewal may perhaps be best described as unevenly continuous, but after World War II it gained a certain momentum, especially in the major European cities. The same process was also apparent on a lesser scale in the larger towns, but was almost completely absent from small ones.

The problem of how to reconstruct areas destroyed by the bombing was paramount immediately after World War II. In some cases, such as

Chapter translated by Mark Blacksell.

Nuremberg (Germany) and St-Malo (France), they were faithfully rebuilt. Elsewhere, for example in Coventry (UK), Le Havre (France), Rotterdam (Netherlands), and Hannover (Germany), what remained was demolished and replaced by completely new districts. Except for such unusual instances, the process of renewal can best be understood as a struggle against decay and a drive to maximize economic returns. Whole districts, or even just blocks, of slum property, empty warehouses and factories, and dilapidated public buildings, such as hospitals, prisons, or barracks, were cleared away. They were replaced by various different kinds of residential estate, ranging from public housing to exclusive villa developments, by new public buildings, by offices and, rather less frequently, by parks and other planned open spaces. Manchester (UK), where more than 200 ha were redeveloped, is a good example of this process. In practice, the greatest transformation occurs when all the different aspects of renewal are concentrated in one small area. It allows the road system to be completely reconstructed; old streets can be abandoned, new main roads superimposed, and a system constructed which separates the different forms of traffic. The volume, the height, and the architecture of these modern buildings is in stark contrast to older buildings in the surrounding blocks. When redevelopment succeeds in combining office and retail activities, it often enhances both the visual impact of the architecture and the degree of functional success. The 'Front de Seine' in Paris, 'Manhattan' in Brussels, 'North-West City' along the Mainzer Straße in Frankfurt, and the 'Part-Dieu' in Lyons are all outstanding examples of new development schemes, which combine housing with public service functions, high-rise office buildings, retail centres, and cultural facilities. This type of brutal redevelopment, marked by the demolition of everything that was there before, from substandard housing to historic buildings, is known as 'bulldozer renovation' in France, as 'Bruxellisation' in Belgium, and as 'substitution renovation' in Spain.

The whole question of renovation has frequently made a public issue out of the history and the historic fabric of entire quarters and, in some cases, whole towns. In the 1950s and 1960s, popular movements were spawned to protect the historic heritage as a whole, something that had hitherto been rather scorned and limited to specific listed monuments. It enabled André Malraux, the French Minister, to have passed a law enabling zones to be designated in French cities, incorporating all the historic quarters of high urban and architectural quality. In these zones demolition, new construction, or even replanning could only be sanctioned by an officially recognized Architect for French Buildings. Since the law came into force, thirty towns have created *secteurs sauvegardés*, their size varying from 150 ha in Bordeaux

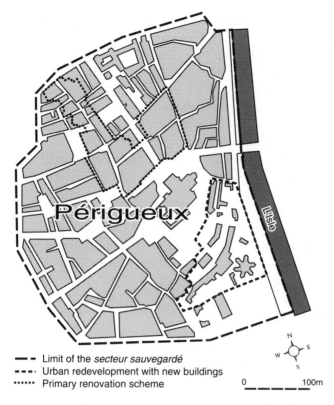

— - Limit of the *secteur sauvegardé*
--- Urban redevelopment with new buildings
····· Primary renovation scheme

0 _____ 100m

FIG. 2.1. The *secteur sauvegardé* in Perigueux, France
Source: Genty (1986).

and 126 ha in the Marais in Paris, to only 2 ha in Sarlat (Fig. 2.1). In Great Britain the Civic Amenities Act 1967 enabled Conservation Areas to be designated to protect individual buildings, or whole areas, of particular historical or architectural interest. Large parts of Bath, Chester, and York have been protected under the terms of this Act. The city of Bologna is well known for having adopted an ambitious policy for restoring and revitalizing its ancient centre. Rather late in the day, a 1977 German federal law enabled the conservation of old housing to be guaranteed when it was being modernized. However, protecting the relics of the past is not always easy, as is illustrated by Dublin's experience, where virtually the whole of historic Wood Quay has fallen victim to office construction. Only one small piece, listed in 1978, was saved, the first ever such action in Ireland.

The unplanned proliferation of new housing estates and comprehensive redevelopment schemes, nearly all sanctioned solely to maximize financial returns, have now mostly been replaced by policies directed towards conserving the historic housing heritage. Restoring the economic value of these districts, has also had the welcome additional effect of halting their progressive dereliction and helping them to be revitalized. From the mid-1970s, the amount of new construction in the old urban fabric declined and there was a considerable upsurge in rehabilitation. A by-product of this, for both public and private development, was to update quality standards for unmodernized and dilapidated housing. It is not uncommon to find efforts being made to reinstate former architectural and aesthetic values in housing as part of an overall restoration programme. Such 'gentrification' is having the effect of modifying the outward appearance of many old historic quarters in city centres. Further actions, like banning traffic and parking, creating pedestrian-only streets, repairing pavements and improving lighting, providing street furniture, complement the rehabilitation of the buildings. The arrival of new residents from different social groups and the introduction of alternative types of commercial activity change even more completely the social and functional character of individual districts.

Restoration schemes have, on occasion, come into conflict with the needs of contemporary town planning. Until 1986 the renovation of the ancient centre of Colmar, begun in the early 1960s, was undertaken alongside the development of a large, modern, commercial and business centre, whereas a quite different future was originally envisaged for the old tannery district and 'Little Venice' when a *secteur sauvegardé* was created in 1966. The plan was to create conditions which would enable Colmar to retain the outward appearance of 'an ancient town with a rich historic inheritance' (Nonn 1986: 395–407). The effects of policy changes are just as obvious in some larger cities. In Frankfurt, for example, the planners first of all opted to rebuild the city in its original style, but in the 1960s this policy was overriden by the construction of multi-storey office blocks. More recently, with the economic downturn, priority has been accorded once more to the restoration of old buildings.

Ultimately, all these different approaches to city-centre redevelopment are attempts to cope with the problems posed by the ageing of the urban fabric and its chronic inflexibility in the face of population growth and general economic expansion. However, none has proved capable, either of eliminating substandard housing, or of enabling the people who formerly lived in the city centres to remain. It follows, *a fortiori*, that they have also not succeeded in attracting many new residents, other than very specific groups.

The expansion and dispersal of the urbanized area

The demands of all the many urban land uses simply could not be met in the city centre and its immediate surrounds and the doubling, or even trebling, of urban areas in the course of the last two or three decades is by no means exceptional. Cities, which in 1950 had hardly reached the adjoining *communes*, find themselves today at the centre of conurbations spread over whole groups of *communes*, many of which are now completely urbanized. In 1954 Toulouse was accommodated entirely within the *commune* of the same name. By 1962 it covered 21 *communes*, by 1968 29, by 1975 36, and by 1982 47. Between 1948 and 1954 Madrid annexed 13 *communes*, increasing its area from 68 km² to 607 km² in the process. When the metropolitan area was created in 1963 it encompassed 22 *communes* in addition to the capital itself. In the UK, the designation of seven conurbations in 1956 was a form of official recognition of the contemporary extent of urbanization.

The search for new sites concentrates first of all on the empty spaces left behind by earlier periods of growth. These spaces are very often the visible signs of past speculative gambles that have failed. The search then moves to peripheral sites on the edge of the continuously built-up area. Finally, urban shoots begin to appear at varying distances beyond the central city itself, continuing the process of peri-urbanization. These peripheral urban creations are, of course, on a completely different scale when they take the form of new towns, as in Great Britain after 1946 and around Paris after 1965.

Most of the land is devoted to housing, every different type having its own peculiar features and impact. Public housing in the tower blocks of *les grands ensembles* devours the most land, because it is invariably built on green-field sites. The 200 or so *grands ensembles* built in France as part of the Priority Urban Zone Programme (ZUP) cover nearly 20 000 ha; similar developments around German cities (Garath south of Düsseldorf and Perlach near to Munich, for example), Italian cities (Gallarate near Milan), or Spanish cities are similarly demanding of space. On the other hand, the space requirements for individual houses are related only to the gardens in which they are set (on average 1500 m² in rural *communes* and 430 m² in large cities). This is the main type of housing in Great Britain and it is gradually becoming so in France and Germany, but is still little in evidence in Italy and Spain.

Even though it takes up relatively little urban space in comparison with housing, except in major industrial regions, the economic sector is becoming more demanding (Fig. 2.2). Around most towns, one or more industrial estates, ranging in size from a few hectares to well over 100 ha have been built along the main lines of communication; 60 000 ha were designated for this purpose in France alone between 1965 and 1975. They have been built

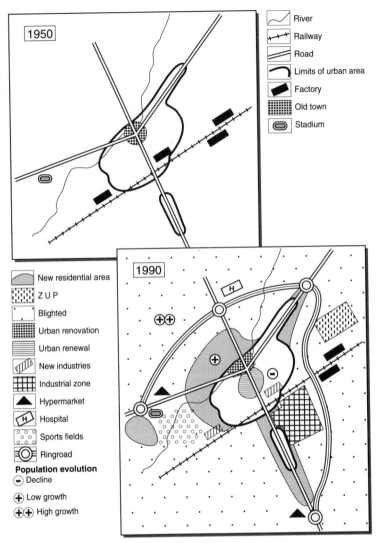

Fig. 2.2. A model of the evolution of a typical medium-sized French town, 1950–1990

Source: Author.

on the initiative of local authorities, public bodies, and private enterprise and, in recent years, trading estates, science parks, and technology centres have been mushrooming as speculative ventures on the fringes of virtually every city. They have a distinctive character: a small scale, a high quality environment, low-rise modular buildings, etc. However, these specialized estates have not eliminated isolated, individual, developments.

On the periphery of the very largest cities, there have been huge new developments incorporating a wide range of tertiary activities: examples include, La Défense to the west of Paris (160 ha, 650 separate enterprises, and more than 100 000 jobs: the biggest centre for business in Europe); Geschäftstadt Nord covering 120 ha in Hamburg where there are more than 35 000 salaried employees; and EUR in Rome. Elsewhere such new concentrations of tertiary activities are on a smaller scale. Until recently commerce was overwhelmingly confined to the streets of the city centres, but now there has been a veritable explosion of new activities on the periphery of towns with the introduction of supermarkets, hypermarkets, and retail centres selling a wider range of goods, and with the opening of large sites devoted to specialized retail services (furniture, DIY, garden-centres, etc.). These vast new developments are located more or less continuously along the main roads spreading out from the city and attract people from outside the immediate urban region. Mérignac-Soleil in the suburbs of Bordeaux with 53 000 m², accounts for 27 per cent of the sales area of the whole conurbation, including the centre, Woluwe on the outskirts of Brussels, and the Main-Taunus Centre near Frankfurt are similar examples. However, Italy, Spain, and even Great Britain have relatively few such retail complexes in comparison with Germany, the Netherlands, Belgium, or France (Merenne-Schoumaker 1983: 63–78), although they are now beginning to catch up rapidly. Wholesale activities (the huge markets supplying the food for urban areas, the *Marchés d'Intérêt National* in France, private-sector warehousing) are also concentrated mainly in the periphery, as are exhibition complexes that have moved out of the centre. The inner cities have also lost their monopoly on hotels and leisure facilities, which have likewise migrated to sites on arterial routes or near to airports.

The expansion of public services has also led to a shift to the urban periphery, a change that applies as much to universities in the larger cities as to tertiary colleges in the large towns and schools in small towns. The same has also happened to major hospital developments, private clinics, and nursing homes. The growing demand for leisure space is also making it essential to have more land specifically designated for recreation and sport; the urban park in Brême covers 1140 ha and as long ago as 1980, the one in Ferrare was planned to cover 1000 ha. As a broad generalization, it is fair to say that green space has become as much of an integral part of the urban structure as any of the other major functions.

Alongside these different forms of land use must also be included the burgeoning traffic network. In order to avoid towns being swallowed up, diversions have been signposted around them and ring roads built linking into the inter-urban motorways, with slip roads into the city centres. Economic necessity has dictated too that railway marshalling yards and passenger stations have also been built on the outskirts of all the larger towns, while passenger airports have been constructed near to all the major cities, even the less important ones.

To summarize, development during the past few decades has been characterized by a marked dispersal of both living space and economic activity; it is both a cause and a consequence of the general transformation in society and of the current urban and regional dynamism.

The dynamics of spatial change

To understand these spatial changes they must be seen in the context of the population growth and economic development of the period 1950–75. However, in response to the multiple needs of urban society, the process of expansion is still continuing, despite the slow-down in the rate of population growth and the difficulties caused by the economic crisis of the 1970s.

General factors

The urban population of Europe grew by more than 46 million between 1965 and 1984, necessarily engendering a steady expansion of the urban area. By the early 1990s, nearly 248 million people (79.5 per cent of the total population) lived in towns and cities and their surrounding peri-urban satellites.

The exodus from rural areas was for a long time the main explanation for peripheral growth in much of Europe, but today its contribution is of little significance. Natural increase and internal migration have taken over as the main causes. Between 1975 and 1982 the population of central Paris fell by 124 000, that of the inner suburbs by 173 000, but the outer suburbs grew by 454 000. In Spain, the population of the urban periphery was 0.9 times that of the centre for the years 1970–5, but the ratio rose to 1.06 times for the years 1975–81, and to 2.69 times for the years 1981–6.

The main causes of this spatial growth are the changes that have taken place in the nature of society. The transformation in the nature of the family, the rise in living standards, the reduced amount of time spent working and the increase in the amount of leisure time, individual car ownership, the encouragement given both by the state and by the banks and the building societies to home ownership, etc., have all profoundly altered life-styles and the way in which people live. There is greater emphasis on comfort, the need for labour-saving appliances, and for more space in residential accommodation; in Germany the latter amounted to 76 m² in 1960 and 109 m² in 1980. There is also more stress on environmental quality, while the nature of consumption has changed with more emphasis on consumer goods and leisure, etc. Other factors have also contributed to greater residential fluidity: the separation between place of work and place of residence, professional mobility, the way in which space is perceived, and the fact that leisure is now as important as work in contributing to quality of life.

Urbanization is not determined solely by the scale of population growth and the social variables described above; it is also affected by the mechanisms driving the economic system. Not a single sector has been immune to technological change. Commerce has been fundamentally altered, both with respect to the means of distribution and the way in which products are marketed. Supermarkets with ample parking, the collapse of small-scale retailing, rapid development of occasional and specialized retailing, and the emergence of large-scale, non-food, retailing have all contributed to the process of change. Problems of access and the lack of scope for expansion have driven wholesalers to relocate on the fringes of cities. As for retailing, it has followed its customers, who have moved to new peripheral housing estates, driven either by the inadequacy of their old accommodation in the centre, or by the overwhelming pressure for office expansion. Universal education and the raising of the school-leaving age, as well as the improvement of health services, have necessitated the construction of vast specialized complexes, which simply could not be accommodated within the existing urban fabric, even by modifying and extending buildings at existing locations.

Industry too has changed profoundly. On the one hand, there has been the decline of what is known as traditional manufacturing (textiles and footwear in particular), and the obsolescence of industries born in the Industrial Revolution (mining, iron and steel). On the other, there has been the rise of new industries (electronics, computing, petrochemicals), the explosive growth of tertiary industries, and the spread of improved working conditions. These changes, many of which are the result of the crises in the coal, and iron and steel industries in the 1960s and the more general economic crisis that followed after 1973, have had a severe impact on urban areas. No town or city has escaped the consequences of deindustrialization, but the effects have been particularly serious in those that owed their very existence to the Industrial Revolution. The result of old and often dilapidated firms closing has been the creation of wastelands, especially in the zones immediately beyond the urban centres. Other factors have also encouraged industry to move, including the growing pressure on land, land-use planning policy, and urban renewal. The land released has been used instead for new housing projects, retail development, and the like. At the same time, industry has been expanding beyond the built-up area, a process of deurbanization encouraged by a general desire for modernization and new development.

The evolution and modernization of transportation systems has also led to important changes. The prime example is the advent of road haulage, which has liberated industry from its former dependence on the railways, enabling a large range of new sites to be developed. Improvements in merchant shipping have led to traditional ports being abandoned and the docks closest to the city centres becoming new urban wastelands (London Docklands). The car is now an everyday item of household equipment and its widespread use has led to the relocation and dispersal of housing. Finally, the filling out of the transportation infrastructure has made it possible to separate workplace and housing.

Political factors must also be taken into consideration. After World War II there was a severe housing shortage, caused by a combination of war damage, a lack of maintenance, almost no new building (this dated back even further to the economic crisis of 1930), and rapid population growth. As a result, the public sector became effectively the only source of new housing for rent. Since 1950 a law has been in force in Germany which obliges the state and local authorities to finance and promote housing construction. In France, the government has given bodies such as the *Office d'Habitation à Loyer Modéré* (HLM) the job of building housing for the most deprived sections of the population, requiring that it be made available at affordable rents and built to minimum standards. Everywhere new building has progressed, facilitated by industrialization and standardization, which lowered production costs and allowed in labour, materials, and land. Finally, in all countries the expansion of the built-up areas has been helped by administrative changes which made the necessary land available for development. The archetype of the new approach to town planning was the *grand ensemble*, or the high-rise public housing estate, but after 1965 governments generally began to relinquish their direct responsibility for housing, and new construction became increasingly a matter for the private sector. At the same time, there was a rapidly growing demand for individual houses, previously the exclusive preserve of a minority, although both Italy and Spain were exceptions to this trend. It represented a rejection of high-rise public housing and encouraged the emergence of construction firms offering new homes for sale from catalogues.

National governments also pursued planning policies aimed at reducing regional inequalities. This led in the 1950s to a policy of decentralization, which encouraged entrepreneurs to leave selected major cities, so as to create new development poles. More generally, national governments introduced measures to help and promote industrialization. In particular, they all pursued social policies which promoted measures to refurbish hospitals, universities, and schools, thereby modernizing the public service sector as a whole in many towns and cities. Finally, all governments introduced some form of town-planning doctrine, throughout their countries. Nevertheless, although these applied to all urban areas, irrespective of size, there were still important differences between them in practice.

Local factors

Not all towns shared equally in the general growth in population and economic activity. In France, for example, urban population growth between 1975 and 1982 varied from 2.5 per cent for towns with less than 20 000 inhabitants, to 0.8 per cent for those between 20 000 and 200 000, and even less for the largest cities (1.2 per cent above 200 000 generally, but only 0.09 per cent for the Paris conurbation). Between 1982 and 1990, the rate of growth of small towns slowed to 1.8 per cent per annum, while that of medium-sized towns remained stable. In the major cities of over 200 000 there was an increase of 0.4 per cent, rising to 0.5 per cent in Paris. Similarly, the changes in the nature of economic activity and the consequences of the global economic crises were not everywhere felt equally. Similarly, policies relating to housing and public services were also modified by specific local considerations.

Individual municipalities had at their disposal town-planning regulations, for which they themselves were in part responsible. Nearly everywhere, plans or schemes for land use and town planning were used to decide the overall direction of spatial development and land use, determining how individual plots of land were to be used and thus becoming the overwhelming influence on how urban areas evolved. It was the policy adopted by the municipality that determined which historic quarters were protected and which were selected for renovation. They also exerted a decisive influence over the precise form of urban growth. All kinds of different situation were to be found coexisting side by side. One mayor might favour the *commune* being completely urbanized, whilst a neighbour might be totally opposed to any development, and a third might try to promote some development, but also preserve the area's original rural character. Problems arise when the area being urbanized reaches the boundaries of a *commune*. The perimeter of many conurbations extends *de facto* along the boundaries of several *communes*, each with the same rights to decide its own administrative, town-planning, and fiscal policies. For the largest and most complex cases, attempts have been made to overcome the inevitable difficulties that this causes by creating special administrative entities. Examples include the Greater London Council in Great Britain (but abolished in 1986 and its responsibilities taken over by 26 districts); the metropolitan areas in Spain, the communities (Bordeaux, Lyons, etc.) and urban districts (Bayonne, Rennes, etc.) in France.

As well as town-planning regulations, local fiscal measures, which often differ considerably from one *commune* to another, can favour or discourage new economic initiatives and investment decisions, so much so that the communal political map can sometimes directly affect locational policy. In responding to the needs of developers, some municipalities look favourably on the creation of industrial trading-estates and the arrival of new factories. Others oppose them on political grounds, fearing changes to their social structure, damage to the environment, or a reduction in the quality of life. The way the built-up area is organized politically, how it has grown, and its physical characteristics also influence residential development.

Structural considerations combined with the nature of the local environment play a critical role in shaping development. The physical quality of a site is, in practice, often the determining factor; if it is in some way limited, then any development will be subordinated to carrying out the necessary public works, even when superficially there is no bar to further expansion into areas that topographically look much the same. The pattern of holdings inherited from the previous agricultural owners sets the framework for future urbanization, with large blocks favouring comprehensive programmes, both public and private, whilst a division into small lots lends itself best to individual houses, and spontaneous small-scale ventures. In all towns the road network, especially the motorways and their interchanges, channel and direct the pattern of growth, and in the conurbations and larger cities the traditional influence of the railways remains undiminished.

Local factors are for the most part paramount in shaping development and membership of the EC has done little to change this. To all intents and purposes, there is no such thing as a Community town-planning policy, despite the fact that many of the rules and regulations in the member states are very similar. In practice, the process of urbanization, and the way in which the problems associated with it are tackled, vary considerably from one country to another, as the following examples clearly illustrate. In Great Britain the nineteenth-century new towns created without any formal plans contrast starkly with those of continental Europe, where the urban development generated by the Industrial Revolution was confined, for the most part, within existing towns. As a result, the evolution of their centres and immediately surrounding areas is very different. In the second half of the twentieth century, Germany and France have increasingly begun to adopt the British model of building individual private houses on the periphery, but Italy and Spain still remain wedded to mass-apartment buildings. Life in these two countries is quite different from that in the countries of northern Europe. Noise levels, cleanliness, living conditions, and the way they are organized, all bear very little comparison.

Although the EC has had very little impact on urban politics, some of its actions have affected towns and cities (see Chapter 3). For instance, ERDF measures to plan the rundown of certain industries and to lessen regional disparities have had a direct impact on the towns in the areas concerned. The same is true with respect to the environment, as a result of the need to harmonize national legislation, and to implement EC directives on air and water quality, and the elimination of waste. These measures have an effect on urban planning, but the harmonization and implementation of the various regulations are still very far from being complete. Another relevant facet of EC policy is the drive to harmonize living standards and working conditions, an essential element of which is the requirement that member states provide all their citizens with an acceptable level of housing. Elsewhere, the Council of Europe has tried to awaken public opinion through information campaigns to initiatives, such as European Architectural Heritage Year in 1979 and the European Campaign for City Renaissance, launched in 1980. The aim of both these programmes has been to improve the quality of the environment, to renovate historic buildings, to generate policies for providing amenities, and to raise the level of awareness amongst local authorities to the problems facing urban areas. Nevertheless, municipal governments still enjoy a great deal of local discretion, unless they are overruled by EC or national legislation and the wishes of their local inhabitants.

The consequences of spatial change

The urban phenomenon can no longer be described simply by reference to a neatly delimited town. It is now characterized by an urbanized envelope the reality of which is very different, assuming the form of a conurbation, whose configuration and structure have become increasingly complex.

Intra-urban disequilibria

Urbanized space is neither homogeneous nor static and the way in which it evolves depends on its land and property values. The highest land values are to be found in the centre, in isolated islands of historic buildings that have been renovated or which are in the process of renovation, and in areas known for their healthy living conditions, their physical aspect, or their environment. To some extent the same applies to areas that are easily accessible to the centre, or to other employment concentrations, and to cultural amenities or sporting facilities. On the other hand, rundown districts, abandoned industrial zones, and areas plagued by specific nuisances, either actual (noise, smells, etc.) or perceived (cemeteries, factories, wasteland, etc.), suffer from depressed land values. There is, therefore, great variation, with land and locational values directly influencing the nature of development and land use. The variations in the values attached to land means that certain social groups occupy high quality locations, while others are relegated to less salubrious areas. Some districts experience depopulation, or are even in the process of being abandoned, while others are attracting new inhabitants or being renovated. Despite the fact that new housing is continually being built and a pool of unoccupied accommodation, the housing crisis persists in large cities because of land speculation and inadequate amounts of public housing to ameliorate the effects of inequalities in income. As a result, one of the most marked tendencies in the developing European urban mosaic is for social space to become more and more highly differentiated.

Economic space in cities today is also highly differentiated, economic activity being distributed around the urban area in a way that reflects a combination of land values and special needs of individual sectors. Tertiary activities are found mainly in the centre, but as far as retailing is concerned most cities now have at least two types of shopping complex, one in the centre for high-value speciality goods and one on the periphery to accommodate large-scale hypermarkets and the like. Other parts of the urban fabric attract industrial enterprises. The old-established areas generally comprise dilapidated buildings housing metal-products and heavy-engineering firms, many of which are now defunct. They are found side by side with residential areas that are equally antiquated and of low quality, unless there have been recent public-housing programmes. The industrial zones developed outside the cities, beyond the residential areas, look quite different, with low-rise buildings set amongst car-parks and tree-lined green spaces.

Economic and social segregation is on the increase. Nevertheless, the conflict between the centre and the periphery is still the main distinguishing feature of intra-urban disequilibrium. Land use in the centre is becoming increasingly dominated by high-rise development, driven by the high land prices and its attractions for big business, and by the expected high economic returns. The periphery offers development that is much more dispersed and at lower densities, partly because land values are lower, and partly because of a desire to be closer to nature and to enjoy a better quality of life. In the intercensal period 1975–82, nearly one million people left French towns to live in nearby rural communities and, although the flight slowed somewhat and was even reversed in the big cities between 1983 and 1990, this outward movement reflects a rejection of urban values and a general redistribution of population towards the periphery, or even beyond the confines of the conurbations altogether. Both the centre and the periphery run the real risk of physical degradation or, at the very least, of being fundamentally altered. The threat in the centre is to the architectural and historic heritage; on the periphery it is to the 'natural' environment.

Despite all this change, the centre is still where the excitement of high-density living is to be found. Not only is it bound up with the history, the self-image, and the culture of the city, but it is also where recreational amenities and tertiary activities are located, and where decision-making and government reside. The periphery is characterized by dispersal, modernity, large-scale retail complexes, theme parks, a disjuncture between the employment opportunities it offers and the people who actually live there, and population growth. Nevertheless, the required level of interdependence will necessitate the relocation of labour, a high price to be paid for installing services and providing public transport, large-scale investment in infrastructure, and the over-eager abandonment of agricultural land.

In short, during the past forty years developments in transportation, rapid economic and technical change, as well as fundamental reassessment of social expectations, have led to widespread dispersal of both people and economic activity. It has led to a lowering of the population densities in city centres, a massive growth in the extent of the urban periphery, and a marked differentiation in the land-use pattern. Both the physical size and the role of the city centre have been reduced in favour of a rapidly expanding periphery. The latter has managed to achieve a certain independence, thanks to the emergence of secondary centres and to a proliferation of different types of economic activity. It has been the main beneficiary of what is known as counter-urbanization and the more diffuse urban structures that have accompanied it.

Inter-urban disequilibria: Some examples from France

These general trends must not be allowed to mask the way in which growth rates have varied depending on the size of the conurbation and the impact that this has had on spatial form. Even the smallest towns have not escaped the dispersal of activities and people. There too, they are leaving the core, because its buildings are antiquated and inconvenient for the periphery. Out-migration means that these districts cannot look forward to growth and are unlikely to become fully fledged towns. They function as diffused entities, frequently trespassing on to the territory of neighbouring communities. Since the 1950s, the small towns of Aquitaine in south-west France, mostly with between 3000 and 5000 inhabitants, have experienced spectacular growth. Previously they covered between a dozen and twenty hectares, about a third of which encompassed the historic medieval core. By the beginning of the 1980s the built-up area of these small towns had extended to 100, 150, or even 200 hectares (Charrié et al. 1992).

Medium-sized towns have clearly been part of the processes described above, but their growth has been limited to an area sufficiently small to ensure that they have not had to cope with serious diseconomies of scale. Castres, about 80 km from Toulouse, which has doubled its population and quadrupled its area, illustrates the kinds of development that have occurred, both in the structure of local society and in the urban area, in the face of the general economic and political changes, partially filtered through local actors (Jalabert 1989).

The larger towns and cities exaggerate these phenomena, making the effects of dispersal more marked, weakening the traditional central functions as other *communes* on the periphery become 'dominant'. Take for example Merignac, a town of 51 000 as compared with Bordeaux which has just over 200 000 (the conurbation as a whole has 640 000 inhabitants). Its demographic dynamism, its spatial structure, its modern and expanding industrial and commercial firms, its sporting and socio-cultural amenities, all reinforce its separate communal identity and sense of autonomy and make it fit less and less easily within the confines of the core–periphery model (Augustin and Pailhé 1989).

Since 1975 there has been a slow-down in the rate of both population and economic growth. Urbanization, for so long driven by industrialization, is today increasingly a response to the tertiary sector, favouring the expansion of the towns and cities of the south at the expense of those in the north and north-east. The towns in those areas most affected by the economic crises of recent years are those least able to adjust. Mining towns, like Béthune and Lens, and traditional industrial towns, like Denain and Longwy, contrast starkly with towns dependent on modern electronics industries (towns in the west such as Angers), or on computer industries (the sunshine towns of the Midi like Montpellier and Nice), or high-tech (near to good skiing like Grenoble). The dynamism and the quality of the environment are the main attractions and, almost incidentally, lead to increased urbanization.

Municipal policies vary, with some towns believing in strict controls on house building and industrial and business development. After World War II the city of Rennes operated a voluntary code of practice for urbanization. Since the 1970s it has been followed rigidly within one part of the city and has become a dynamic policy for creating new districts on public land that previously had little development. The result is mixed housing schemes serving the needs of a range of social groups, enabling new inhabitants to be accommodated within the existing urban area (Binet 1986). On the other hand, there are also cases where there is no overall development policy of any kind for a conurbation, with each *commune* doing exactly as it likes. For example the *Communauté Urbaine de Bordeaux* is 'a conurbation becoming progressively more diluted as the strength of the core declines'. In 1967, immediately before it was created, the central city of Bordeaux housed half the total population; by 1982 it had little more than a third and had also lost numerous industrial and commercial activities. The core no longer generates the necessary organizational vigour and has become little more than a battleground, the outcome of the conflicts decided by the relative dynamism of the economic actors' (Dumas 1990). There is also no over-arching structure for planning the Paris conurbation as a whole and the lack of a new regional development plan will encourage fragmented planning at the level of the *communes*, generating incoherent and badly organized development.

Elsewhere, there are examples of municipalities with bold urban development plans, seeking to give a good impression to the outside world and thereby increasing their attractiveness (Laborde 1986). The case of Montpellier is particularly striking. Here, under the direction of the architect Ricardo Bofill, the historic centre has effectively been extended into the Antigone district, following the same monumental town-planning and architectural principles, but incorporating modern building techniques and materials and thereby maintaining a flattering comparison between the old and the new (Brunet 1990: 315).

Conclusion

The physical structure of towns and cities, both 'within the walls' and in the periphery has changed dramatically over the last forty years, but the rich subtleties which make up a town's character are to be found elsewhere. Differences persist in the way individual towns have been redeveloped and in the way they have expanded outwards. The most obvious sign of change is the rapid growth in the extent of the urban area, often apparently out of control despite policies designed to tame it. The cities have changed from being highly centralized entities to polynuclear structures and it is this, more than anything, that explains their present territorial incoherence and lack of social cohesion.

Further reading

For those wishing to find out more about recent developments in the urban geography of Western Europe, the following should be useful sources. Two general works on the whole process of urbanization and the so-called 'urban crisis' are G. Di Méo (1986), *Les Démocraties industrielles, crise et mutations de l'espace* and P. Laborde (1989), *Les Espaces urbains dans le monde* (Paris). Particular national perspectives on urban development in France and Spain respectively are to be found in P. Barrère and M. Cassou-Mounat (1980), *Les Villes Françaises* (Paris) and J. Estibanez-Alvarez (1988), *Las Cuidades* (Madrid). More general and international overviews are given in the special edition of *Éspaces, Populations, Sociétés* vol. 1, published in 1986, and in R. Kain (1981), *Planning for Conservation, an International Perspective* (London). The first concentrates on housing issues, the second on urban conservation. Finally, the EC perspective is clearly explained in the Community's own publication (1988*a*) *Urban Problems and Regional Policy in the European Community* (Luxembourg).

3 Mediterranean Cities: Divergent Trends in a United Europe

Lila Leontidou

Introduction

Urban restructuring in Mediterranean Europe (as delineated by Braudel 1966: 232, to include Portugal), has gone through many transitional phases. Layers of history have bound these cities together and then have torn them apart, only to make their *rapprochement* more important during the next cycle of the *longue durée*. Braudel's concept and the resulting view of history, is particularly appropriate for the cities of Mediterranean Europe. Whether closed to the world, within their walls, or open to the globe through expansionist wars or explorations, the Mediterranean city states have been connected, at times, by bonds of peace and rifts of war, by figures of emperors, conquerors, explorers, discoverers, and religious leaders, in long cycles of urban development. In other periods, however, their trajectories diverged dramatically. The coincidence of preparing this paper with the celebration of the 500th anniversary of Columbus's departure from Spain to the New World, provides an opportunity to recall this long-lasting Mediterranean creativity, its imperialistic expansionism, but also the divergence between the western and the eastern part of the region for centuries. Constantinople was besieged and the Levant was falling into Ottoman hands a few decades before Columbus sailed off to the New World, in 1453 and 1492 respectively.

Now the face of Europe is changing, after the demolition of the Berlin wall, even to the point where new maps are needed. European integration processes keep speeding up. Other centres of creativity have emerged within the core of European development, the proverbial 'blue banana'. Urban core–periphery hierarchies are relatively sharp in Europe today. Athens, Lisbon, and Dublin, the cities on the three edges of the EC, are outside its umbrella in many respects—ranging from geography and accessibility, to policy formulation. The core-case study of the following paper, Greater Athens, highlights weaknesses in the new European order: Greek cities are diverging dramatically from others, with which until the 1980s they used to move in parallel trajectories, and form the basic focus of this paper.

The initial theme is a summary of post-war developments which have bound together productive restructuring and residential change in large Mediterranean cities, and an illustration of their parallel transition during the mid-1970s. The nature of the 'urban crisis' was then transformed. An effort is being made to compare southern cities among themselves and to stress contrasts with northern Europe. In the first part, common characteristics will be outlined, which set Greece, Italy, Spain, and Portugal together against the rest of Europe as a group. We will then show that parallel processes have been at work until the 1980s in the large cities of all southern countries, on several levels—political, social, economic, geographical, environmental—irrespective of the timing of EC integration. The period studied in the first and second part is prior to the integration of the largest part of the Mediterranean into the European Community. It could not be otherwise, given that Spain and Portugal joined only in 1986 and Greece in 1981, while only Italy joined the Community in 1958. Community policy has hardly influenced the development of the most basic aspects of urban restructuring, even in Italy; but now, during the 1990s, we can discern economic, cultural, and political forces, partly due to European integration, which are changing the picture dramatically. This will be argued in the third part of the paper, which aims to show that the common trajectories of Mediterranean cities have been disturbed as we enter the 1990s.

From polis to metropolis: A review of basic urban attributes

In contemporary Europe, the Mediterranean countries are distinctive for being interspersed with so many former city states. Although most of these have lost their capital status, they have retained their dynamism and strong symbolism, and owe much of their aura to their monumental past. However, not all the cities can build upon this heritage during a period of urban competition and place marketing. Some common urban patterns, outlined in this part, introduce what may be termed Mediterranean peculiarities.

The city-centred cultural heritage and its spatial impact

By the sixteenth century there were cities with populations of about half a million in Europe, led by Constantinople, which was inhabited by 700 000 people, double the size of Paris (Braudel 1966: 345). But like many glorious city states, it lost its glamour under Ottoman rule, and as recently as 1923 surrendered capital status to Ankara, the most 'artificial' of Mediterranean capitals. It is also one of the very few cities that has lost its name. But this is not quite accurate; even if the Turks named it Istanbul, this is a phonetic rendering of the Greek expression Εις την Πόλη, i.e. 'to the Polis'. In fact, for long centuries it was *the* City (Polis), dominating the urban network after the glory of Rome had dimmed. But again, Rome is unparalleled as 'the city that died and was resurrected so many times' (Gore Vidal in Fellini's *Roma*). Athens may also deserve such a characterization. Today this most peripheral of southern cities is also the most problem-ridden one.

After the mid-nineteenth century, when the walls of the old cities were pulled down and the modern metropolis arose, Mediterranean cities passed through diverse development stages. Convergence could be observed only after World War II. Its most striking manifestations were unstable politics (with the exception of Italy, where Fascism was not resurrected in the post-war period), which isolated them from the rest of Europe; migration to northern Europe originating in every one of the four countries including Italy, despite its 'economic miracle' and early integration in the EC. Other important similarities mostly stem from the coexistence of modernity and informality (both traditional and post-modern), on many levels (Leontidou 1990: 3).

Their urban dynamism, to the point of primate distributions in Greece and Portugal, and their urbanization models, were parallel, ranging from the populations of the capital cities to more structural aspects. By 1971 Rome, Madrid, and Athens, as well as Barcelona, had 2.6–3.5 million inhabitants. Although nationwide rates of growth were homogenously moderate, at about 1 per cent, the three capital cities grew at similarly rapid annual rates in 1951–71: 2.8 per cent (Rome), 3.3 per cent (Madrid), and 3 per cent (Athens) respectively (Leontidou 1990: 10–11). Demographically, these are all new cities. The native-born population of Rome dropped from 47 per cent in 1921 to 20 per cent in the 1960s (Fried 1973: 82–3); that of Athens was even smaller since, in 1960, 56 per cent of the population were migrants who had arrived during the post-war period alone (Leontidou 1990: 103). There were also similarities of urban morphology and of rapid, unplanned expansion. This paper has begun with an emphasis on urban traditions and urban dynamism in order to highlight a long-standing antithesis: that between the urban-oriented cultures in the Mediterranean, as opposed to Anglo-American idealization of nature and the countryside (Leontidou 1990: 257–9). This is reflected in urban patterns: the compact and dense cities of the Mediterranean contrast sharply with the low-density ones in the north, cities with large parks and remote suburbs. In addition, in the Mediterranean cities wealthier groups cluster at the centre while the periphery is abandoned to the poor.

This is the 'inverse-Burgess' spatial pattern of the peripheral cities in general, where social-class levels usually correlate with land-rent and density gradients. The affluent classes are more represented in the centre around the CBD, and the working classes in the periphery. The same is true in southern European large cities. In Italy, Milan has been structured in this way since the late nineteenth century (Lyttleton 1979: 253–60). In Rome, social rank is low in the *suburbi* and still lower in Agro Romano on the urban fringe (Fried 1973: 94), and highest in the *rioni*, in the old city centre (McElrath 1962: 389–90). In Venice, there is continuing out-migration of the working classes (Costa *et al.* 1980: 404). In Turin, a central high-status area coexists with old slums north of the centre, but the most extensive working-class areas are on the northern and southern outskirts. Similar patterns are to be observed in Iberian cities. In Spain, the areas of the earliest nineteenth-century suburban expansion of the *ensanche* on the north of the centre of Barcelona, are still inhabited by affluent social classes (Ferras 1977*a*), and the city is encircled by many working-class districts. Madrid represents a concentric-zone distribution, where central areas and inner nineteenth-century suburbs have the highest socio-economic status (Abrahamson and Johnson 1974: 526–7). In Lisbon, various social classes live in the centre in close proximity although in different subdistricts; but the current tendency is for there to be an increase in the proportion of the middle classes (Gaspar 1976: 131–5). The periphery is flooded by waves of urban poor. The same is true of Athens.

At the same time, these cities manifest a sectoral development model, with some more peripheral bourgeois 'garden suburbs' in Athens and Rome, in both cases since the 1920s (Regni and Sennato 1973: 922; Leontidou 1990: 11, 79–80). The northern and western sectors of Rome are inhabited by higher-income groups than are the eastern ones, where popular housing has developed amongst factories, railway yards, and the cemetery (Fried 1973: 93–5). The same east–west divide also exists in Spanish cities, while the inverse exists in Athens, where more affluent residents inhabit the eastern sectors of the city. In general, the inverse-Burgess pattern is not non-existent north of the Mediterranean (e.g. in Paris or Vienna), but nowhere is it so systematic (Leontidou 1990: 10–11 and chapter 7).

The proletariat is distributed throughout the urban fabric, but is usually concentrated in the periphery. Central pockets of poverty exist: for example, the whole inner city of Naples, but especially the area around the Via Roma (Allum 1973); Trastevere, Ponte, Parione, etc. in Rome (Fried 1973: 93), although these have recently been gentrifying; Alfama in Lisbon; Sant Cugat del Rec and Barrio Chino in Barcelona (Ferras 1977*a*), where artisans have concentrated since the nineteenth century. However, poor populations are increasingly being displaced through urban renewal programmes and creeping gentrification (Ferras 1977*b*: 193–4). By contrast, working-class housing is still growing in the urban periphery, and has a positive correlation with industrial concentrations. In Anglo-American geography these traits have triggered off superficial connections between southern European cities and pre-industrial ones. However, although the inverse-Burgess spatial pattern does go back in history, this does not justify such references; post-modernism is rather more plausible (Leontidou 1993b). The interpretation of urban structure should be based on a combination of material conditions and cultural traditions, that is, industrial location, fragmentation of landowner-ship, land prices and controls, on the one hand, and cultural values focused on urbanism, on the other.

The great diversity of landownership patterns in Mediterranean cities precludes a comparative treatment. Diversity of size derives from the involvement of several types of landlordism—private, large and small, state, church. In any case, large properties are rare and the fragmentation of urban landownership and piecemeal urban redevelopment is rather more system-atic. There seems to exist a division between Spain and Italy, on the one hand, and Portugal and Greece, which are smaller and less developed, on the other (Leontidou 1990: 248). In the latter, large urban properties are rarer, while, in Greece, no land registration systems exist. In general, the control of peripheral urban land seems to have been much looser in the Mediterranean than in northern Europe. Large real-estate entrepreneurs seem to have emerged only rarely in Italian and Spanish cities. It is notable that the same looseness seems to have been practised in Latin America by the Spanish and Portuguese, during the sixteenth century. These colonial governments introduced the Western concept of property, as well as a dual system of land rights (Evers 1975: 125; Leontidou 1985).

The cultural values around urbanism have been stressed inadequately in geographical research. In the walled Mediterranean cities, the centre was always the heart of the city and urban areas were compact, with high densities and small piazzas, ornamented with cultural buildings and surrounded by offices, shops, and bourgeois residences. These urban-oriented cultures are not fading today, with new waves of suburbanization, as is argued later (see also Leontidou 1990: 259–61).

Informality in urban life: Industry and housing

The other important difference between Mediterranean urban morphology and that of Anglo-American cities is the diversity of spatial distributions. There is a patchwork of economic activity and social classes throughout the urban fabric, with a few but important exceptions. This contrasts with zoning of economic activity and segregation of social classes in the north.

Mixed land uses predominate, and the informal sector of the economy is dispersed through various areas in a disorderly urban tissue. The southern European working class lives in socially mixed communities, while the more affluent social classes tend to cluster together and exclude other social groups from these areas. Again this is a contrast with Anglo-American social geography, where working-class areas tend to be the most segregated and socially homogeneous zones. The mixture of middle and working classes in Mediterranean cities is due to several factors. What should be stressed are the alternatives to community segregation, which are not encountered in the north. The most widespread alternative is *vertical differentiation* in multi-storey apartment buildings (Leontidou 1990: 12–13, 132–3).

Mixed land use is usually attributed to real-estate speculation and the lack of planning and land-use control. In fact, urban planning seems to have faded in history (Wynn (ed.) 1984*a*), and today ranges from the comprehensive planning carried out for the Olympic Games in Barcelona, through the municipal socialism of Bologna, to the largely free-market or unplanned urban development in the cities of Portugal and Greece. However, there are more factors leading to a spatial patchwork and to piecemeal urban development besides the weak role of public planning: as already pointed out, large developers are rare and landownership is fragmented. The housing production system is *dual*, but the public–private sector dichotomy has been irrelevant in the Mediterranean until the 1970s, to varying degrees, because of the small size of the public sector and the lack of planning in the postwar period. In place of the public–private divide, the formal–informal, capitalist and speculative owner-built (often illegal) dichotomy predominated (Leontidou 1990: 20–3, 252–4). Throughout the region, a speculative real-estate market coexists with an informal land and housing sub-market. Piecemeal urban redevelopment on the one hand, and illegality on the other, are all pervasive, involve all social groups, and are conducive to the development of popular, spontaneous urban movements.

The disorderly urban tissue is thus not only due to unplanned development, as most analysts of these cities suggest, giving a negative overtone to their assessment. Disorderliness can also be attributed to spontaneity and informality, as structural, socio-economic features. Popular self-built settlements on the urban periphery, mixed land uses, and the interpenetration of so-called tradition and modernity, are only some of the manifestations of the informality, which permeates many spheres of urban life in the Mediterranean. In the housing sector, Gramsci's concept of spontaneity is especially relevant. Self-built settlements are not a residual characteristic of pre-capitalism; on the contrary, we can argue for an alternative culture underlying such patterns, which is close to post-modernism as defined today in geography (Leontidou 1993*b*).

A distinction has been proposed between two types of informalization, the traditional and the modern (Leontidou 1990: 38), and another between the black and lighter sides of the informal sector. However, the inhabitants of Mediterranean cities have always manifested ingenuity in the development of the 'lighter' side of the informal sector (Leontidou 1990: 19–22), as well as social polyvalence such as multiple employment (Tsoucalas 1986). 'This many-sidedness was a long-established rule; to engage in several activities was a sensible way of spreading risks' (Braudel 1966: 320).

In the housing sector, informality is evident in peripheral shanty-towns: *bairros clandestinos* in Portugal, *viviendas marginales* in Spain, *borghetti* and *borgate* in Italy, *afthereta* in Greece, and *gececondus* in Turkey (Berlinguer and Della Setta 1976; Fried 1973: 70, 271; Lewis and Williams 1984: 295; Leontidou 1990: 20–3, 252–4; Tsoulouvis 1985: 149; Keles and Payne 1984: 181). The mushrooming of these settlements provides a stark contrast with all the other familiar arrangements of northern cities: the industrial estate, Engels's 'landless proletariat', the central slum familiar from Chicago ecology, and the suburb. These simply did not take root in the Mediterranean. On the other hand, unlike the case of the peripheral city squatters, property rights are respected in southern Europe, but not public land-use regulations (Fried 1973: 271). In turn, public authorities have often left semi-squatter areas without any infrastructure for long periods, even after their 'legalization'. However, the settlements have been upgraded by the families themselves as their savings accumulated. Shacks have been developed into proper houses by extensions or rebuilding in these 'slums of hope' (Leontidou 1990: 87–8).

Common trajectories in the transition of the 1970s

During the early 1970s the Mediterranean cities were in transition. It was then that their half-century long common trajectories were dramatically and vividly illustrated by their simultaneous transformation. Nine points are of particular importance:

1. These least-developed countries in western Europe—even Italy, though a member, had the Mezzogiorno to deal with—developed and depolarized.

2. Again with the exception of Italy (with Mussolini's Fascism in the interwar years), political consolidation was simultaneous: the Portuguese 'revolution of the carnations' where young military officers overthrew

Caetano (April 1974) coincided with the fall of the Greek colonels' junta (July 1974), and a little later in Spain came Franco's death (1975).

3. Emigration to the north slowed, and return migration became more pronounced.

4. Polarization gave way to diffuse industrialization, with the proverbial 'Third Italy' providing the most famous example of flexible accumulation regimes.

5. Similar patterns of tourist demand—the seasonality of 'sun-and-beach' tourism—did not change, but the tourist waves became stronger, and cultural tourism began to expand.

6. Urban dynamism, to the point of primate distributions in Greece and Portugal, gave way to stabilization, while diffuse urbanization animated provincial towns. The situation at the end of the 1990s is shown in Fig. 3.1, which also indicates the wider Mediterranean context.

7. The dual housing market was disturbed by forces and policies leading to the end of spontaneous urban development, with an unusual coincidence which is very telling: the peak and defeat of urban social movements in all four countries took place in the mid-1970s. Dualism thus gradually receded, and speculative, unorganized capitalism became increasingly dominant over the self-built sector in urban development.

8. Cities remained compact and dense, as in the past, with an inverse-Burgess spatial pattern, but new types of suburbanization appeared. The population of popular suburbs stabilized and that of middle-class ones developed, but in a dense and compact pattern which was very different from suburbs in the north.

9. Finally, Mediterranean societies were caught in a sweeping depolarization process, or socio-spatial homogeneization, involving all sectors (e.g. industry, residence), and all spatial scales (e.g. regions, neighbourhoods). In other words, we find in Mediterranean cities the opposite of the polarization, which has been identified by most British, German, French, or Dutch geographers.

Regional depolarization, urban unemployment, and spatial fixity

It would be superfluous to repeat here the well-known case of the 'Third Italy' and its flexible accumulation regime, which led to regional depolarization. It is only necessary to stress that its neighbours went through the same stage by different procedures (Lewis and Williams 1987). Large cities were transformed. Two decades of industrial restructuring and regional depolarization led to the decline of Fordist centres, while deindustrialization was observed on the metropolitan and local level.

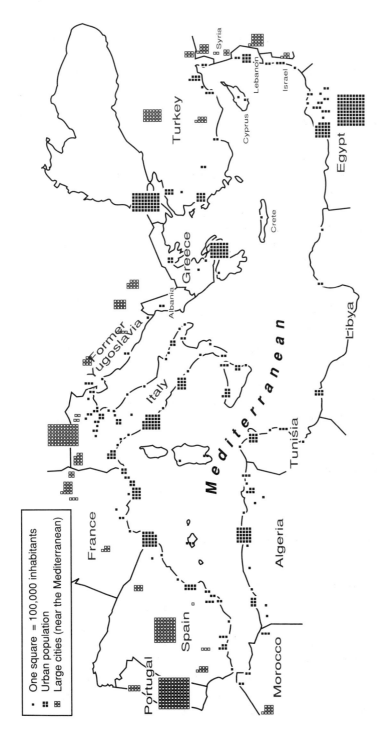

Fig. 3.1. The distribution of the urban population in the Mediterranean basin

Source: Grenon and Batisse (1989).

The inner city shed industrial jobs. In Athens, the concentration of employment along a traditional industrial axis lasted until the late 1960s. Industrial decline in the inner city and along the industrial axis, since 1973, was a novel feature in urban history. This was moderate in absolute terms, since it only involved the loss of 52 000 jobs in certain groups of manufacturing in 1973–84 (while 16 000 were added in other groups until 1978 (Leontidou 1990: 196–7)). However, the decentralization of jobs marked a very important change. Communities located along the traditional industrial axis were responsible for 98.2 per cent of the net job loss in the agglomeration as a whole, and their multiplier effects were considerable: unemployment affected not only those dismissed, but also employees in industry and services dependent on the export base of the city. Restructuring of and crisis in the construction sector has been added to all this.

At this point, a crucial difference between Greek cities and the other southern urban areas is worth stressing: informalization was a metropolitan rather than a provincial phenomenon in Greece during the 1980s (Leontidou 1990: 179–84). In addition, it was located in the heart of the large cities. Industrial decomposition in 1973–84 was spectacular along the traditional industrial axis, where the mushrooming of small manufacturing establishments coincided with employment decline. New small enterprises appeared while earlier industries shed part of their labour force, closed down, or were broken up.

Industrial decentralization in Mediterranean cities affected employment patterns. The study of urban unemployment is very difficult because statistical reliability is limited in this area. It is only feasible therefore to refer to the example of the geography of Greek unemployment. A basic change has been a shift toward urban areas and female populations. Another has been its suburban location. In fact, a more important general North–South contrast is revealed in the intra-urban location of poverty and unemployment. In northern Europe, 'unemployment, overcrowded squalid rented accommodation, lack of amenities, ill-health, and deprivation of all kinds confirm time and time again the polarity between inner-city poor and suburban rich' (Jones 1990: 194–5). In contrast, there are few pockets of poverty and marginality near the urban core in Mediterranean cities. The inverse-Burgess spatial pattern predominates, as the poorer unemployed populations concentrate in peripheral urban areas, especially in popular self-built settlements.

Traditionally, such settlements have been in close proximity to industrial areas. However, this is no longer the case. As industry also relocated from the traditional industrial axis toward the metropolitan periphery, the new zone of factories around cities failed to attract residences. In the case of Athens, the establishment of new industry in the regions around it revealed the stubborn spatial fixity of the urban working class, despite efforts by industrialists and the creation of new estates (Leontidou 1990: 191–201). As traditional industrial areas became more congested and declined, more industrialists sought relocation. Their complaints about labour immobility merged with those of foreign and domestic capitalists unable to attract labour to the provinces. This was an additional force leading to pressures for changes in working-class land allocation patterns in the years that followed.

Home ownership, as such, does not fully explain working-class spatial fixity. This was due to compact social networks operating around owner-built houses on the urban periphery. Structural and friction unemployment, as well as housing problems, institutional gaps, and the weakness of the welfare state, have traditionally been met by the family. One cannot overemphasize its importance in Mediterranean societies. The family is present where the welfare state is absent, in unemployment relief, health care, welfare provision, housing, and the relief of homelessness (as known in northern Europe), and in many other areas of social life. It provides material and moral support to its members. Income sharing is customary. Extended families often create an intricate, self-help network of illegal building, popular owner-occupation and self-help, or of unemployment relief based on personal acquaintances rather than contacts with formal agencies. This is an additional reason for underestimation in the official unemployment figures (Leontidou 1993a).

The house is an important work base in areas where the informal economy predominates. Subcontracting, putting-out systems and home-working rely on using the house as a base, as well as on electricity, sewage, roads, communications, and other technical infrastructure. This is a very important fact, which actually leads to popular and working-class spatial fixity. It should be noted that this is often ignored in urban policy. In other words, it is not owner-occupation as such, or the high housing-transfer tax, which discourage residential mobility. These factors are combined with the importance of family, locality, and the house in informal work (Leontidou 1993a). Owner-occupation means not only shelter, but also work. The home has a central function in life prospects. This, along with the need for proximity to informal work opportunities in the inner city, as well as the important role of income-sharing processes in the family and neighbourhood networks, keeps workers within the city.

Despite the fact that unemployment is rising, then, many of the labourers affected seem to have been reluctant to decentralize to those areas where jobs are offered. Rather they present demands for improvements in their own communities. New types of urban inequality appear in large agglomerations, and new enclaves of unemployment and informalization emerge in traditional suburban working-class settlements. At the same time, filtering-down processes, due to middle-class suburbanization, create new pockets of poverty within the inner city.

It is worth pointing out that the relationship between owner-occupation, population decentralization and job decentralization has been exactly the inverse in Anglo-American cities. On the one hand, 'The growth of owner-occupation from 29 per cent in 1951 to 63 per cent in 1985 has fuelled the outward movement of population' (Robson 1988: 85). On the other hand, in northern Europe, it was population decentralization which attracted jobs to the suburbs and not vice versa. By contrast, despite the decentralization of employment to metropolitan peripheries or even further out, the population of Mediterranean cities is still growing, although at a slower rate than in the 1960s. This contrast is worth stressing. It has been well established that, in northern Europe, population decline in larger cities started earlier and preceded the decentralization of jobs (Robson 1988: 25, 84; Jones 1990: 80–1, 130–2): 'The economic dimension of urban decline has been evident *only more recently*, but it has followed the same pattern as that of population loss; an outward ripple of contractions which has had its worst effects in inner cities and in northern regions' (Robson 1988: 25, emphasis added).

It is a fact, then, that very different sets of forces lie behind the process of 'disurbanization' or 'counter-urbanization' in North America (Berry (ed.) 1976) and Western Europe (Hall and Hay 1980), on the one hand, and urban development trends in Lisbon, Madrid, Barcelona, Bilbao, Athens, Salonika, Rome, and other Mediterranean cities on the other. Diffuse urbanization outwards from the large cities in the Mediterranean followed rather than preceded industrial decentralization, and it was never combined with disurbanization. It was coupled with the decrease in the power of attraction of metropolitan cities, not with flight from the city (Leontidou 1990: 184–8).

The containment of urban social movements

Before moving to developments in the housing sector, we want to argue that the process of land colonization on the fringes of Mediterranean cities has been a long-standing urban social movement. Despite the fact that each family has bought its own plot, the process has never been clearly individual: informal networks have operated for information and mutual aid. The nature of informal house building, as an urban social movement, has often been revealed in popular mobilizations. And this is exactly where Mediterranean common trajectories are clearly illustrated: in the urban social movements which peaked and then declined in all southern cities, almost simultaneously, during the early 1970s (Leontidou 1990: 22–3, 264–7).

It was then that the residents of Rome, Madrid, Barcelona, Lisbon, and other cities mobilized about issues of reproduction, usually housing and service provision, or around the question of housing scarcities and infrastructure (Castells 1983; Pickvance 1985). Popular mobilizations to secure infrastructure provision in illegal areas and to organize squatting in vacant property did not only present urban demands; they also raised political issues. Italian urban movements have attracted international attention because they were advanced, large-scale, and overtly politicized. In 1972–3, urban and labour struggles were unified and became massive and radical in all cities, while various organizations emerged (Della Seta 1978; Lagana et al. 1982; Marcelloni 1979). Bloody clashes and evictions followed. Urban movements in Spain were no less politicized. Besides housing issues, posed by the inhabitants of the urban periphery, opposition was expressed to non-representative government (Castells 1983; Logan 1978). Urban movements were also a focus of political opposition in Portugal, and often focused on specific national issues, such as the colonial wars, but played a weaker role than the Spanish ones. Urban struggles culminated during the revolutionary period 1974–5 (Topalov 1976; Gaspar 1984). In Greece, finally, the colonels were in power when the urban movements exploded in the rest of Mediterranean Europe. Before 1967, however, the proletariat and informal-sector workers did mobilize around urban as well as work conditions: land struggles correlated with broader popular mobilization waves during the mid-1960s (Leontidou 1990: 169–70).

The economy of urbanization and income growth, however, was reaching a threshold by the mid-1970s. In addition, social threats of housing mobilizations were escalating. The informal-housing sector and its accompanying urban social movements had to be controlled. In practice, the first and most successful instance of housing 'modernization' was the suppression of illegal building in Athens and Salonika after 1967. Only a dictatorial government could impose this so effectively, using coercion as well as integration into the city plan. But the rest of the cities followed. Urban social movements declined throughout the Mediterranean during the mid-1970s. In Barcelona shanties were eliminated and replaced with *barraquismo vertical*, substandard dwellings in huge apartment blocks with minimal services (Ferras 1977b: 194–5; Naylon 1981: 245). In Madrid, the authorities assimilated shanty-towns by providing basic amenities as well as periodic demolitions (Castells 1983: 242–7). In Lisbon, shanty residents seem to have preferred to co-operate with government-sponsored SAAL self-help schemes during the mid-1970s (Lewis and Williams 1984), with dependence on the state as the eventual result. It is interesting, however, that as some shanty residents were rehoused, usually in large blocks, new waves of migrants and *retornados* from African colonies immediately invaded the shanties. As for Italian urban movements, the process of their erosion is more complicated, as disagreement among Italian researchers makes evident. The only point of agreement is on their decline.

Through various procedures, then, urban movements declined throughout Mediterranean Europe, and a large part of the informal sector was 'assimilated'. The very slogan of the 1974 rally in Lisbon—*casas, sim: barracas, não* (Lewis and Williams 1984: 321)—is indicative of indignation with poverty and the dependence on the state. As informality rose in productive activity, it declined in the housing sector. Dualism in housing production receded, in favour of a fragmented, competitive capitalism, a speculative market which produced a piecemeal urban development pattern in a context of widespread distribution of landownership and construction capital to many small entrepreneurs. This contrasts, of course, with rationalization and concentration of capital in the north. Meanwhile, Mediterranean peripheral shanty-towns, but also small self-built and gradually evolving houses in the 'slums of hope', now belong to history.

Urban life-cycles: a North–South contrast

Intense exploitation of central urban areas, the expansion of urban capitalism, the suppression of the informal housing sector and industrial decentralization toward the metropolitan periphery and provincial areas, influenced urban structure in a radical manner. Many of the changes are too recent to appear in official statistics. Some aspects of the urban formation, however, responded almost immediately to the transformations discussed.

In the case of Athens, intra-urban population movements have been peculiar: the strong wave of suburbanization toward the popular suburbs in the 1950s was replaced, first by a population explosion in the inner city during the 1960s, and more recently by a middle-class suburbanization wave (Leontidou 1990: 218). For the first time in the history of Athens, a filtering-down process started to operate in certain pockets on the north of the CBD, as the pressure for middle-class suburbanization was felt on the north-eastern and southern suburbs (Leontidou 1990: 236–7). The other surprising pattern, which was less evident during the late 1960s, is socio-spatial homogenization rather than increasing segregation in Athens. Traditional working-class strongholds have been losing their proletarian character. This could be interpreted in the context of social restructuring after deindustrialization and the rise of tertiary activities, if another surprising pattern were not found: the increase of working-class populations in middle-class and mixed inner-ring suburbs on the north-east and the south of Athens. It seems that middle-class suburbs, overbuilt with multi-storey dwellings during the dictatorship, attracted a mixture of social classes living in vertically differentiated flats (Leontidou 1990: 233–6).

The pattern observed in Athens is not unusual in the Mediterranean context, but the missing pieces of this puzzle cannot be filled in unless more focused research on these issues appears. In any case, if we can say little about spatial homogenization, there is evidence of recent urban deconcentration trends in most southern European cities except Italian ones, which are closer to northern Europe, in that deconcentration started early: in Rome, population in the city centre has declined since 1931, after the major housing clearance operation and public works by the Fascist government. Decentralization in Naples effected the reduction of the average inner-city density by one-half in 1951–71 (White 1984: 142–8, 201). Iberian cities are closer to the Athens pattern, where suburbanization is relatively recent. The 1981 population census in Portugal indicated moderate population increase in the cities of Lisbon and Oporto and high rates of increase in their satellite towns (Hudson and Lewis, 1985: 15). Parts of central Madrid started to decline for the first time during the 1970s (Ballesteros 1977). The centre of Barcelona has also been gradually abandoned as a museum for tourists (Barrio Gotico), or a residential ghetto for recent migrants (for example, Barrio Chino), and has been reconstructed in connection with the holding of the Olympic Games.

Urban life-cycles are usually defined through such population movements and, to a lesser extent, through industrial restructuring. In this framework, the phases of urban development evident in Greek as well as Iberian, and to a lesser extent Italian cities, can seem stunning to European students (Leontidou 1990: 222–3). The process of population and employment concentration, which has characterized the Athens development pattern for over a century, peaked in the 1960s during a period when other European inner-city areas were declining. Greek cities experienced two waves of suburbanization, the first of which—popular suburbanization from the 1920s through to the 1960s—preceded centralization. Only in the late 1970s was a new process of middle-class suburbanization, along with lower-class overcrowding in the inner city, observed. This may mark the beginning of a filtering-down process in Athens.

The cities of the north have known neither dualism in the housing and land market, nor popular control of urban expansion, nor centralization, since the beginning of the century (Van den Berg 1982). Suburbanization and the generalization of landownership through mortgage-credit diffusion, closely controlled by the state and large capital, present radically different features and timing than self-built uncontrolled housing development processes described above (Leontidou 1990: 244–5). New towns and satellite settlements are rare in continental Europe (Lichtenberger 1976: 98), but even more so in the south, where city extensions are more usual. The commuting range of about 50 km in Europe, rather moderate by US standards, is too long for Mediterranean ones, except for seasonal commuting. The compact apartment house creates high densities in Mediterranean suburbs.

As for the inner city, there is ongoing gentrification. It is interesting that recent trends of reurbanization and gentrification in the north do not necessarily suggest the rise of urban-oriented cultures, as in Mediterranean traditions. They should be rather attributed to economic forces for centralization. Globalization and new technology recentralize the population in new localities, but also within large cities. Reurbanization is a qualitatively different phenomenon in the rest of Europe.

To sum up, Mediterranean cities present a certain unity and a set of common features, absent or inverted in the cities of the north. We do not encounter different phases in a process of convergence between cities of the two regions, but a different model of urban development. We have proposed to refer to the *Mediterranean* urban development trajectory, and the attendant urban type (Leontidou 1990: 244–5).

To what could this systematic urban development trajectory be attributed? Why is it that until the 1980s one could speak of diffuse urbanization rather than counter-urbanization, of industrial depolarization, of the informal sector expanding in industry and shrinking in housing, of the dual but increasingly unified housing market, of the end of spontaneity in urban development, whether focusing on Greece or Portugal, Spain or Italy? Is it because of their late industrialization, peripherality, migration waves, class relations, land-ownership patterns, urban-oriented cultures, or the legacy of 'the Polis'? In fact, it is all these factors together, and more, which will be gradually unravelled as research on Mediterranean cities takes it course.

'Europe à deux vitesses'? The divergence of Mediterranean cities

Parallel trajectories among Mediterranean cities seem to have lasted until the 1980s. When available, the 1991 census material will show how far these changes have affected the cities. Though it is increasingly difficult to collect reliable information, it seems that the trajectories were still parallel until recently. This was because of economic forces, as well as the sensitivity of democratic governments, in place of authoritarian ones, to social policy for depolarization. However, the picture is changing during the early 1990s. Localities in Europe move at different speeds: but how many?

EC policy gaps and prospects

It is not coincidental that change in the EC has hardly touched large peripheral cities, which follow their own paths of development. Mediterranean cities in particular, have long suffered from a peculiar neglect: much of the research undertaken, the priorities set, and the decisions taken are usually tailored to the problems of the core of Europe. In a sense, all cities are neglected in the EC context, because urban policy has not been a principal area of concern. This is already changing, as EC urban policy is reoriented and inter-urban networks expand. In fact, there was no structured urban policy until recently—just an urban dimension to various sectoral policies— in the same way that today there is no housing policy. But now an urban dimension is being introduced by DG 16 to regional policy (Commission des Communautés Européennes 1991), by DG 5 to poverty policy, by DG 11 to the Green Book, and by DG 12 to the FAST programme. How can they do otherwise, given the importance of cities? However, it is argued here that such decisions and policy assumptions are imperceptibly based on central and northern European experiences. In order to put southern Europe into the picture, it is necessary to compare urban development processes, and to unravel those which are specific to the cities of the south.

The most striking example of EC bias is in poverty policy. Local development assistance is directed toward already dynamic communities, which show at least a level of awareness, if not solidarity, cultural development and leverage *vis-à-vis* EC administration. Indicators used for poverty are not only inadequately quantified (e.g. unemployment), but often irrelevant for the Mediterranean. Homelessness, for example, is almost unknown in the south, where precarious self-built housing shelters the poor. Policy focused on inner cities rather than suburbs, reflects the geographical concentration of the poor in northern metropolitan areas. The inverse development is evident in the south, where poverty is less visible, having been dislocated to popular suburbs from an early period. In addition, the exclusion of the housing sector from policy considerations is more offensive for the south than for the north, as indicated in our analysis, because of its importance in productive activity in Mediterranean popular suburbs. Other examples of EC bias include the treatment of informality in urban life; policy on industrial restructuring, especially with respect to its impact on the metropolitan periphery and the inner city; attitudes toward residential restructuring during the 1980s; a neglect of urban cultural tourism, which has increased in all cities with a few exceptions, such as Athens (Williams and Shaw (eds.) 1991), and which could be supported in order to even-out acute tourism seasonality in the Mediterranean; and many other issues. Themes in the *Green Book for the Urban Environment* (Commission des Communautés Européennes 1990) touch upon issues which are sometimes peripheral to Mediterranean concerns. The diversity in urban restructuring processes in various parts of Europe should be studied in depth if European integration, and in particular EC policy, is to be addressed to southern cities.

Meanwhile, there are important policy areas which are aimed specifically at Mediterranean Europe, such as Integrated Mediterranean Programmes and structural convergence assistance promised as compensation for greater unification. There are also the EC-wide 'sectoral' policies, such as the Social Fund and Objective 1 ERDF policy. In addition, there is the Single Market drive to financial liberalization, which has an effect on the Athens and especially Piraeus' role as a financial centre. The EC's medium-term loans and their limitations on Greek government expenditure also have implications for national policy. All these programmes and policies have important implications for Mediterranean urban development, which are largely neglected. Finally, research interests are usually tailored on the basis of EC priorities. There is a growing concern in various of the DGs for overall reform, rather than the earlier almost exclusive emphasis on the economy. Even our vocabulary is changing. Was there ever discussion in the early 1980s of subsidiarity, sustainability, or synergy? Not as far as I can remember. Today it is inevitable that research interests are shaped by EC concerns, but policy-makers always have different priorities from those of universities, especially as Europe and the world are changing. As always, the social sciences are the most dramatically affected during this major transitional period. In geography, the post-1968 turning point had triggered off the familiar critique against logical positivism. Now we need to question modernism, 'the grand narratives of progress'. Whatever form Lyotard's 'local narratives' will take in geographical analysis, one thing is certain: geography continues its course from universals to diversity. In addition, there is a growing concern about the unintended effects of EC integration— new polarization trends, environmental deterioration, social marginalization, political extremism. We might also see a resurgence of political geography, involving the new geopolitical conditions in the Balkans, new parties of ecologists and the extreme right, and of cultural geography, in the face of regionalism and nationalism re-emerging, and the resentment at the reception of foreigners 'threatening' cities.

Besides marginal localities and success stories within the EC, there is also the question of cities condensing the essence of our transitional period. Asa Briggs (1968) sought 'shock cities' in Manchester of the 1840s, Chicago of the 1890s, and Los Angeles of the 1930s. Which one will it be in the 1990s? Will it be in the restless Balkans? Athens, perhaps, where Eastern European migrants concentrate? Or some city on the western edge of Eastern Europe, in a zone developing rapidly with high in-migrations? Or will it be Berlin, perhaps, a new capital city, the gateway where Western and Eastern Europe meet?

From convergence to divergence in United Europe

Forces for divergence among Mediterranean cities have been creeping in recently, and the extraordinary historical transformations after the tearing down of the Berlin Wall are now changing the European picture completely. They create new types of uneven development in the new 'Europe of the regions'. There are success stories and there is marginalization, enhanced by new communications networks. Athens, for example, used to be a node in the days of air transport. Now, the map of the high-speed rail network shows that only two regions are connected to the EC by boat: Greece and Ireland. And the former is the furthest away from the proverbial European 'blue banana' and in close proximity to the restless Balkans.

New types of peripherality are emerging in the 1990s, which have nothing to do with the familiar process of neo-colonialism. The lowest speed threatens remote localities, while the highest speed develops where headquarters of large enterprises locate. The core has been reshuffled, but there is still a core, because new technology does not only allow for decentralization in the entire world; it simultaneously creates centralization. Economic and political power are concentrated in the Eurotriangle, and there are several gradings in between. Among the forces shaping urban Europe, it is important to stress the technological breakthrough, especially informatics and the high-speed rail network, and the sweeping changes in Eastern Europe. But I would also stress changing life-styles, post-modernism, re-urbanization, environmentalism, new gender (and consequently family) values, leisure activities and tourism turning towards the cities, the aestheticization of everyday life, and also resentment against foreigners and new migrants, resulting in the rise of the extreme right. What is important, in this light, is the rise of urban competition. Cities and localities seek centricity. Globalization aspirations are reflected in 'place marketing' and promotion for the attraction of capital and production of micro-electronics. They are also reflected in efforts to host the growing waves of urban tourism: exhibitions and fairs which culminated in the recent creation of a Disneyland near Paris. There are the glittering cities, but there are also the more moderate success stories of towns outside the core, which managed to find the right form and degree of specialization— such as Bari, Valencia, Seville.

Balances are overthrown in the Mediterranean region. Italy is building on its flexible accumulation regime, while Spain sparkles with successful urban promotion for Seville (Expo 1992), Madrid (European 'city of culture'), and Barcelona (1992 Olympics). But on the eastern edge, Greece is in the middle of an economic crisis, is flooded with East European migrants, is involved in regional disputes, and faces a broader urban crisis. This is not confined to environmental pollution—the proverbial *nefos*, the smog cloud which often darkens the Athens sky—but also to social upheaval and vandalism: frequent strikes by public-utility workers, riots of the young, terrorist attacks, petty theft by incoming minorities, the 'barbarians', as ancient Athenians would call them, who are often treated as unfairly as in our weak ancient democracy.

As globalization sweeps the economic sphere, localities turn from inert spaces to interactive agents. As firms act through networks, so do localities. The Europe of the regions is also a Europe of networks. It even seems that urban hierarchies are tending to recede in favour of urban functional differentiation, competition, and promotion (Commission des Communautés Européennes 1991). Both globalism and localism are rising simultaneously. The former involves the concentration of economic and political power, and will rise further with European interdependence, the Central Bank, and common currency. As Castells has argued recently, this loss of control by localities seems to make people more place-oriented. In fact, it creates solidarity around agents and institutions, a search for identity and tradition in society and in education, the revival of regionalism and nationalism. At the same time, co-operation and networking interconnect cities, localities, institutions, universities, people. Flows of information and flows of people intensify with networks like ERASMUS, ROME, ESF, and even by floating international exhibitions of waterfront developments.

And what about new polarization trends? Do we argue that there is global polarization and local depolarization? This seems to be the case, at least for certain Mediterranean cities. During the 1990s we can again discern Braudel's dichotomy between the West and the Levant, in the long run. Trajectories diverge among cities, which are relatively homogeneous internally. The Mediterranean welfare state is anything but strong; but its weakness does not obstruct depolarization among urban neighbourhoods. These societies have grown wise in regulating crises via informality, diffusion of real-estate property, homogenization, fragmentation of agents of urban development, and so on. Long-standing structures, such as these, create egalitarianism of a type, and a post-modern condition which was always there, as an alternative culture, and therefore is not 'post-', in their case (Leontidou 1993*b*).

At the same time, the new peripheries have pockets of poverty to deal with at the local level. Enclaves of poverty are threatening some cities, especially as waves of migrants from Eastern Europe arrive. Poor localities, too, are more numerous in the south, and very different—as are strategies of integration and local development. At the other extreme, there are several localities affected by the technological destruction of distance, the quaternary sector, tourism, and innovations creating dynamism, and even transforming earlier poor regions into prospering ones.

There are then new polarization trends, dimensions, and intensities, not always more pronounced than in earlier periods. They are just different, and their location changes. They also take different forms on the North and South. 'Europe a deux vitesses', as they say in Brussels? As it seems, the speeds are more than two.

Further reading

There is a relative paucity of literature on Mediterranean urban development during the postwar period, and virtually no sources in the major north European languages on developments in the 1980s after the accession of Greece, Portugal, and Spain to the EC, although the gap is now gradually being filled by articles in journals such as *Urban Studies* and *European Planning Studies*.

The classic work on the history of the Mediterranean is F. Braudel (1966), *The Mediterranean and the Mediterranean region in the Age of Philip II* (London). Other interesting contributions are: C. Pooley (ed.) (1992), *Housing Strategies in Europe, 1880–1930* (London), which has chapters on both Greece and Portugal; I. Malkin, and R. L. Hohlfelder (eds.) (1988), *Mediterranean Cities: Historical Perspectives* (London); and J. de Vries (1984), *European Urbanization, 1500–1800* (Cambridge, Mass).

An overview of postwar urban development with comparative material on Italy, Spain, and Portugal, and a special emphasis on Greece, is provided by L. Leontidou (1990), *The Mediterranean City in Transition: Social Change and Urban Development* (Cambridge).

Chapters in edited volumes only cover the period up to the end of the 1970s. The chapter by J. Gaspar in A. M. Williams (ed.) (1984), *Southern Europe Transformed* (London) is very well worth while reading and the book also includes useful material on regional and sectoral restructuring. Aspects of urban structure with a heavy emphasis on physical planning are discussed in M. Wynn (ed.) (1984), *Planning and Urban Growth in Southern Europe* (London). Italian cities are discussed in ch. 4 of

R. King (1987), *Italy* (London). Spanish, and other, urban social movements are presented in M. Castells (1983), *The City and the Grassroots* (London).

There are fragmentary references to Mediterranean cities in a number of recent books on urban Europe generally. P. Cheshire and D. G. Hay (1989), *Urban problems in Western Europe: An Economic Analysis* (London) includes Italy and Spain in its systematic comparisons, as well as some references to Greece and Portugal. Further references are to be found in H. Clout, M. Blacksell, R. King, and D. Pinder (1993), *Western Europe: Geographical Perspectives* 3rd. edn. (Hemel Hempstead), especially in ch. 2; in D. Pinder (ed.) (1990), *Western Europe: Challenge and Change* (London), especially ch. 8; in M. Wynn (ed.) (1984), *Housing in Europe* (London). Providing one makes allowances for occasional stereotypical descriptions, D. Burtenshaw *et al.* (1991), *The European City: A Western Perspective* (London) and P. White (1984), *The West European City: A Social Geography* are both useful, with a collection of eclectic references to southern European cities.

Interesting case studies of Italian cities are: P. Allum (1973), *Politics and Society in Contemporary Naples* (Cambridge); and R. C. Fried (1973), *Planning the Eternal City: Roman Politics and Planning since World War II* (London). The social anthropology of cities, especially in the 1960s, is discussed in M. Kenny and D. I. Kertzer (eds.) (1983), *Urban Life in Mediterranean Europe: Anthropological Perspectives* (Chicago).

Finally, books on industrial, sectoral, and regional restructuring, which include useful references to urban development, include: R. Hudson and J. R. Lewis (1985) (eds.), *Uneven Development in Southern Europe: Studies of Accumulation, Class, Migration and the State* (London); and E. Mingione (1991), *Fragmented Societies: A Sociology of Economic Life beyond the Market Paradigm* (Oxford).

PART IV

Structural Change

Structural change

Whatever the political vicissitudes of the past forty years, the EC has been a major force behind the economic and social transformation of Europe in the second half of the twentieth century. Profound structural changes have occurred in the patterns of contact between the individual member states, and their links with the world outside the Community. This section of the book examines some of the dynamics behind that transformation.

The successes and failures of industry are at the heart of the changes. The Community remains an industrial giant in world terms, but a weakened one, threatened on a number of different fronts. Many of its traditional industries, such as iron and steel and textiles, are in decline, mere shadows of their former selves and unlikely ever again to dominate world markets as they did so successfully in the nineteenth and early twentieth centuries. The new technologies that have replaced them are by no means exclusively European, so that competition is intense from North America, Japan, and other parts of south-east Asia that are now rapidly industrializing. On the other hand, the countries of the EC are increasingly being seen by non-European industrial nations as lucrative places to invest with the attendant risk that they dictate, rather than follow, EC strategy.

The response of the EC itself has been slow and uncoordinated, partly reflecting the fragmentation inherent in the three founding treaties, which established the European Coal and Steel Community, the European Economic Community, and the European Atomic Energy Community respectively. Each defined specific areas of responsibility, which made it difficult to develop a single, focused, strategy. Only with the Single European Act in 1986 did the situation begin to change. This brought R and D within the Community's brief and stimulated a whole range of development programmes, aimed at promoting high technology industries (e.g. ESPRIT) and introducing new technologies into traditional industries (e.g. BRITE). They have begun to imbue the EC's industrial policy with a much greater sense of direction and purpose, but there is much ground to make up before the competitive advantage of North America and East Asia is effectively neutralized.

The transportation network in the member states of the EC is generally well-developed, but lacks the co-ordination that should be provided by the

Community. There are considerable variations in both quality and comprehensiveness, notably between north and south, and formal mechanisms for joint planning and development have been slow to emerge. The crucial importance of transport has always been recognized and a Common Transport Policy was one of the declared objectives of the EEC Treaty, but rather than a coherent strategy, all that has been achieved are piecemeal operating standards (mainly for motor vehicles) and small amounts of infrastructural investment through the European Regional Development Fund and the European Investment Bank. Ireland is used as a case study to illustrate that the actions taken thus far hardly add up to the kind of coherent strategy needed to help bridge the country's political divide, or to integrate a peripheral member state more closely into the economic heartland of the Community.

Great as are the importance of infrastructure and infrastructural investment, they are not a substitute for the access to labour markets. In this sense, policies on the freedom of movement of workers, and workers' rights, are of crucial importance for the operation of the Single Market. Migrant workers were a key element in driving industry in the heartland of the Community throughout the 1950s, 1960s, and 1970s, but, ironically, just as some of the major sending countries (Greece, Portugal, Spain) prepared to join the EC, the demand for migrant workers began to evaporate. The change was partly a result of a general economic slowdown, and partly because many of the initially temporary migrants became permanent minorities in their host countries, and the true costs of such transfers of population were becoming increasingly apparent. Rather than providing just a short-term solution to labour shortages, many of the migrants and their families have become significant, and frequently isolated, minorities in their host countries, competing for jobs and resources with the rest of the population.

In many of the northern industrial countries of the EC growing disillusion with the benefits of employing migrant labour has not necessarily stifled demand. Opportunities for migrant workers still present themselves, because people from poor countries are in no position to resist illegal undercutting of wages or benefits. The pressures to work clandestinely in richer host countries, or to undertake cut-rate piece-work at home (especially in the textile industry) still abound, even though the conditions may openly flout both EC, and national, regulations.

Since the mid-1980s there has been a renewed influx of migrants, particularly to Germany, from Eastern Europe and the former Soviet Union. These people are driven in part by political persecution, but even more by economic necessity, but whatever their motivation they pose a serious challenge in an already saturated EC labour market.

4 The Pattern of Industry: Europeanization versus Globalization

J.-Paul Charrié

Introduction

The countries of the EC formed the cradle of the Industrial Revolution in the nineteenth century and the Community is still a major industrial force in the world. The basis of this supremacy has altered however in the face of unremitting international competition. The countries that now form the EC developed their industrial strength around a potential that saw its heyday some thirty years ago and as evidence of this one needs only to recall that the first tentative success of the union was the European Coal and Steel Community (ECSC). In a continent bruised by five years of conflict, this agreement hastened the process of economic reconstruction, and laid the foundations for a period of sustained economic growth, that was only interrupted by the oil crisis of 1973.

The EC is rich in both coal and iron ore and endowed with enormous production capacity in many key sectors, such as iron and steel, shipbuilding, and chemicals. In recent years, however, it has had to tailor its methods of production to the growing importance of oil, as well as having to adjust to the profound changes now taking place with the decline of basic industries and the parallel growth of the high-technology sector. These changes are all occurring in the face of growing competition. The established threat posed by Japan is obvious and is accentuated because it competes directly in the EC's traditional overseas markets, notably North America. At the same time Japanese industrialists are investing directly in the EC as a way of circumventing the regulations aimed at limiting the flow of Japanese imports into Europe. In addition, there is growing competition from the Newly Industrialized Countries (NICs) in Asia, especially South Korea, which first of all entered the clothing market but are now rapidly diversifying their production.

All these different changes are having a cumulative impact in the industrial

Chapter translated by Mark Blacksell.

heart of Europe. The traditional industrial regions are in decline, because they are suffering under a growing number of competitive disadvantages. On the other hand, the major urban centres are in a stronger position and are fiercely protective of this.

The role of the Commission and the other EC institutions was for many years limited to isolated interventions, mainly measures to protect declining regions and individual sectors, and factories in difficulties. However, they are now beginning to play an increasingly important role in industrial policy. The EC is an important force in the emerging industrial landscape, providing specific aid to selected sectors, co-ordinating research efforts, and taking the lead in a revitalized regional policy. In addition, the completion of the Single Market will have important repercussions for the overall industrial fabric.

This chapter does not attempt to be comprehensive; instead it uses selected sectors of manufacturing industry to illustrate the underlying dynamic principles.[1] The question of energy is put to one side, even though the present uncertainties surrounding this subject have an important bearing on current industrial developments. Equally, no attempt has been made to deal with the construction sector or public works, even though their contribution to employment is considerable, especially in the less-industrialized areas of the EC.

A weakened industrial giant

Most industrial indicators show that the EC is still one of the major global industrial powers and that many of its companies are world leaders, but there are also contrary indicators. The competitive edge of European products has been blunted and the comparative advantage of whole areas of manufacturing is under threat, particularly from lower labour costs elsewhere. Of course not all restructuring is negative; much of it, a priori, is evidence of a capacity to adapt to contemporary changes and by no means all sectors are endangered. However, these changes are accompanied by a loss of employment with painful social repercussions. More seriously, because there is no effective common research policy, there is a real danger of the gap widening in the high technology sector.

Measures of the industrial power of the EC

The simplest way of demonstrating at a global scale the position of the EC is to compare some of its major industries with those of its principal rivals,

---

[1] Except where indicated otherwise, all the statistics used in this chapter come from official EC publications.

TABLE 4.1 *Manufacturing production in the EC in a world context, 1987*

	EC	(rank)	USA	Japan	US
Manufacturing output					
(value added, $US billion)	625	(2)	803	395	507
Chemical products					
(value added, $US billion)	62.5	(2)	80.3	35.3	—
Textile-clothing					
(value added, $US billion)	45.1	(1)	40	24	—
IAA					
(value added, $US billion)	87.6	(2)	96.4	39.5	—
Steel (million tonnes)	126	(1)	75	93	112
Aluminium (million tonnes)	2.3	(3)	3.3	0	2.4
Automobiles (million)	11.6	(1)	7.8	7.8	1.3

Sources: Author's calculations based on data from 'L' État du Monde' (1990) and 'Eurostat' (1990).

the USA, the former USSR, and Japan (see Table 4.1). In the world rankings, the EC comes second after the USA, but ahead of both the former USSR and Japan. Its position reflects its high standing with respect to traditional industries: first place in textiles, iron and steel, and car production; second place in chemicals and food processing; third place in aluminium production. Despite the lack of new investment in shipbuilding and the accumulated weakness in high-technology industries in comparison with the USA and Japan, European industry remains amongst the most productive in the world.

In fourteen major industrial sectors, EC firms lead the world in four, as compared with eight for the USA and two for Japan. This Community dominance is particularly pronounced in traditional areas, such as iron and steel,[2] textiles, and food-processing, where companies from Germany, the Netherlands, and the UK are strong. One should also add to this list the French company Oréal, which is first in the field of cosmetics (see Table 4.2). Irrespective of who leads, European firms are well represented amongst the twenty top firms world-wide in any given sector, just as they are in other areas where the comparisons are only valid amongst the five or six at the top. The one exception is toy manufacture where there is not a single Community firm amongst the first five.

Closer examination of the turnover figures, however, sheds more light on the relative position of Community firms. If one separates out the oil companies, the turnover of which is comparable to those in the United States,

[2] Today Thyssen is neither the world nor the European leader as a result of mergers that have subsequently occurred in the iron and steel industry.

TABLE 4.2 *The leading world and European manufacturing firms, 1986*

	World	Turnover in billion ECUs	Europe	Turnover in billion ECUs	No. of firms in top 20		
					EC	USA	Japan
Aeronautics	Boeing (US)	17	Aerospatiale (Fr)	5	7	13	—
Food	Unilever (Neth.)	26	Unilever (Neth.)	26	4	14	—
Automobiles	Gen. Motors (US)	106	Daimler/Benz (Ger.)	31	7	3	8
Chemicals/ pharmaceuticals	D. Nemours (US)	28	Bayer (Ger.)	19	9	10	2
Oil	Exxon (US)	72	Shell (Neth.)	67	5	10	2
Computing	IBM (US)	51	Siemens (Ger.)	5	4	11	5
Iron and steel	Thyssen (Ger.)	14	Thyssen (Ger.)	14	8	4	5
Textiles	Courtaulds (UK)	3	Courtaulds (UK)	3	3	11	5

Source: Économie européenne (1989).

there is a gap of between two and three times between the world leader and the largest European company. The gap is even more pronounced in computing where Siemens has a turnover figure a tenth of that of IBM.

The setting up of the ECSC in 1951, followed by the liberalization of trade after the signing of the Treaty of Rome, boosted industrial development in the EC. However, the fact that countries joined at different times, notably the UK which only became a member in 1973, and the narrow nationalism which surrounded much decision-making, has meant that those firms owed their place primarily to domestic activities in their own countries. This is one of the main reasons for the large gap between the turnover figures of European companies and those of the American competitors. The markets are not of comparable size and it is this more than anything that explains the drive to complete the Single Market in 1993.

The overall position of the EC amongst the industrialized countries should not be allowed to hide the fact that the contribution of manufacturing industry to the GDP in each individual country remains limited, being in the range between 15 per cent (Greece) and 30 per cent (Germany). It is generally largest amongst the Mediterranean countries, Greece being an exception in this respect. In France, and the Benelux countries, the proportion is about 20 per cent. However, even though manufacturing industry generally contributes less than a quarter of the GDP in the EC countries, manufactured goods play a dominant role in intra-Community trade, ranging between 73 per cent in Greece to 97 per cent in Germany. Manufactured goods are at the heart of commercial dealings in the core of the EC, just as they are in extra-Community trade.

Faced with the overwhelming industrial strength of North America and the growing strength of Japan and some NICs, the industrial development of the EC has been determined by global economic fluctuations. Strong growth in output up to 1973 benefited Germany, the Benelux countries, and Italy, rather than France and, more especially, the UK, which had chronic structural difficulties. The UK was the only one of the EC countries where the rate of growth before the oil crisis was below that of the USA. Industrial activity in the EC declined sharply after the oil crisis in the mid-1970s, but began to recover strongly in 1985. However, Ireland and Denmark were less affected than other countries between 1980 and 1984. Overall there has been a 13 per cent increase in the level of manufacturing output since 1985, with Portugal, Spain, and Ireland registering the highest rates of growth, and both Greece and the UK falling below the EC average.

In general the economic indicators of manufacturing output for the EC12 show that rates of growth were lower than in either Japan or the USA. The growth that did occur was heavily dependent on the dynamism in the four largest countries, Germany, France, the UK, and Italy, which together accounted for nearly 80 per cent (in terms of value added) of manufacturing output in the EC. At the same time, a number of industrial sectors faced growing difficulties in the face of international competition.

The major industrial sectors of an ageing economic power

The length of time that the EC countries have been industrialized explains the wide diversity of industrial activities. This industrial diversity emerges clearly from the indicators used in Table 4.3. In terms of employment and the relative contribution of manufacturing to GDP, traditional industries still occupy a strong position within the industrial structure of the EC. Of particular note is the fact that food-processing industries contribute 7 per cent of production in terms of value, but employ less than 2 per cent of the labour-force. In general terms, the EC is still characterized by an industrial structure built around heavy industry (iron and steel, and chemicals), cars, and other labour-intensive industries, and food-processing. In contrast, the manufacture of office machines and computers is in last place, representing less than 1 per cent in each of the categories in Table 4.3. It is a reflection of both the recent arrival of these industries on the scene, and the accumulated lack of European investment in this area.

TABLE 4.3 *Three indicators showing the relative importance of the main sectors of industry*

	% of employed work-force	% of total manufacturing output	% of GNP
Textiles, leather, shoes	2.5	2.9	2.0
Electrical goods	2.2	2.8	2.6
Food processing	2.2	7.0	4.1
Heavy engineering	2.1	3.0	2.5
Vehicles	2.1	3.0	2.9
Metal goods	2.0	2.6	2.3
Paper	1.5	2.4	1.8
Chemicals	1.4	4.1	2.4
Other	1.4	1.8	1.2
Mining and quarrying	1.0	1.6	1.3
Rubber and plastics	0.9	1.2	1.0
Minerals	0.8	3.0	1.1
Office equipment/computing	0.6	0.8	0.8

Source: Author's calculations based on data from 'Eurostat' (1990).

Although it is not possible to describe all the different branches of industry in this chapter, it is essential to outline some of their difficulties, using selected examples.

The crisis facing the iron and steel industries

The European industry felt the full force of the economic crisis at the end of the 1970s and the beginning of the 1980s. Depression came after an extended period of growth, which had been helped by the creation of the ECSC and steady growth in demand. The growth in demand reflected, first, the period of reconstruction after World War II and then the buoyant demand from other branches of industry up to 1975. The traditional steel suppliers, Germany, France and, to a lesser extent, Belgium were joined by new producers in Italy (which rose to second place thanks to massive investments in new locations on the coast), the Netherlands, and Spain. The recent crisis in the iron and steel industry was caused primarily by underlying structural problems, that have necessitated vigorous restructuring policies, rather than by the economic uncertainty resulting from the sharp explosion in oil prices, important as this was.

The interventions in the market by individual states, and by the Commission under the terms of the anti-crisis programme, have had quite spectacular results in that the European iron and steel industry had regained its competitiveness by the early 1990s. To achieve this, between 1980 and 1988 production capacity was cut from 195 to 165 million tonnes and the workforce reduced from 672 000 to 410 000. In addition, over the same period, the industry received 40 billion ECUs in aid and 20 billion ECUs of investment.

In addition to the social consequences of such policies, which resulted in the loss of more than 250 000 jobs, the restructuring programme had a wider impact on the traditional, over-specialized, industrial regions. Regions like Wallonia, Nord-Pas-de-Calais and Lorraine in France, Scotland, and even Asturias seemed to have been virtually abandoned, because they contained the bulk of the most obsolete plant. New plants relocated on the coast and new mini steel-making furnaces now form the basis of the EC's reconstituted iron and steel industry.

As a result of this process of reconstruction, the large industrial groups have put their weight behind an EC-wide production programme, though for the most part confining their activities to their individual national territories. The merger between Sacilor and Usinor (France) makes this group the second largest in the world (17 million tonnes in 1987), after Nippon Steel (26 million tonnes), but ahead of another nationalized group, the Italian Finsider. The largest private company, Thyssen of Germany, comes only eleventh in the world rankings (11 million tonnes).

The changing car industry

The changes in the structure of the European car industry are typical of those that have occurred in EC industries in general. Overshadowed by the USA until the 1960s and by Japan up until the mid-1980s, it has emerged from the depths of crisis to occupy first place in the world once again with some 30 per cent of production. Seven EC firms are now in the world's top twenty, the first being Volkswagen in terms of the number of cars produced and Daimler-Benz in terms of turnover. The components industry is more fragmented, even though a process of rationalization is now in train, and Germany and France account for 40 per cent and 20 per cent of production respectively.

The EC car industry makes up 6 per cent of the total value added by manufacturing and 7 per cent of jobs. It is an indication of the importance of the car market, which is still one of the most important in the world after the USA. The car manufacturers export 27 per cent of their production, though 90 per cent of this is within the EC itself. Of the large companies only Volkswagen and Peugeot (PSA) send more than 10 per cent of their vehicles outside the EC itself, though Daimler-Benz and BMW achieve this with their luxury models (see Table 4.4).

During the 1970s the European car industry relied somewhat smugly for its success on its traditional outlets, a combination of a thriving internal market and a captive foreign clientele. Slow progress was made in modernizing factories and productivity remained low, so that the car makers were unprepared for the onset of Japanese competition and the contraction of the market during the economic downturn.

TABLE 4.4 *Structure of the European car market in 1986*

	Sales in Western Europe		Sales outside Europe
	% of sales in domestic market	% of sales in Europe	As % of European sales
Volkwagen/Audi	53	15	22
Fiat/Alfa	67	14	1
Ford	33	12	3
PSA	49	11	11
General Motors	45	11	2
Renault	57	11	9
Austin-Rover	73	4	3

Source: Author's calculations.

The nature of the recovery had important effects on the number of jobs with a reduction in the number employed from 2 200 000 to 1 800 000 between 1980 and 1987. With the exception of Germany, all countries experienced contraction; in the UK, the worst affected by the crisis, it was of the order of 44 per cent. Elsewhere, in other countries with large car industries like France, Italy, and Spain, it was between 25 and 35 per cent. The changes were qualitative as well as quantitative. There was a reduction in the number of unskilled workers, because automation removed first of all the most repetitive manual jobs and then allowed the jobs that had traditionally been the preserve of skilled workers to be taken over by employees with lower qualifications. On the other hand, there was increased demand for better qualified employees to work on the new machines, or in the commercial sector. Finally, 'Fordism' has been progressively replaced by 'Toyotaism' with its much greater emphasis on employee responsibility.

It was the desire to adhere to the Japanese model, especially with respect to productivity and quality, that obliged the European car makers to reorganize their factories. It resulted in a productivity drive based on greater use of computers and robotics. Despite this extensive modernization, the European factories remain less productive than their Japanese counterparts. It takes an average 35 hours to build a car in Europe, as against 20 hours in Japanese factories in the UK, and 19 hours in Japan. Relations with subcontractors have also been modified in the sense that there is now much greater emphasis on quality and 'just-in-time' methods. Dispersal has been another response to the challenge posed by competition. The new European firms have concentrated recent investment in the Iberian peninsula where labour costs are lowest.

The difficulties facing high-technology industries

Today high-technology industries constitute the leading edge of development in most industrialized countries. At first glance the EC seems well established in most branches, if one can measure that in terms of the amount spent on R and D. The industries with levels of expenditure on R and D in excess of 10 per cent of total turnover in rank order are: electrical goods, electronics, aeronautics, and pharmaceuticals. The success achieved by Airbus, the successful satellite-launching programme developed around the Ariane rocket, the strong performance of companies like Philips, Siemens, and Thomson in the electrical and electronics sectors, and the high quality of European pharmaceutical production all appear to support a general picture of well-being.

In fact, high technology in Europe is anything but thriving and this is especially true of electronics. In 1988 the EC as a whole was running a trading deficit of 220 billion French francs in this sector and this is expected to rise to 400 billion French francs by 1994. Within the overall field of electronics, results in the mass-production areas (television sets, video recorders, etc.), office technology, and computing have been little short of disastrous. In the last of these, the German firm Nixdorf has gone into liquidation and Olivetti is losing money, as is the French firm Bull in spite of its takeover of the American firm Zenith. The situation is hardly any better in the components sector. The EC is becoming steadily less competitive year by year in the production of integrated circuits and micro-chip semi-conductors. Given the overall weakness of the Philips group, the goal of producing a new generation of processors within the framework of European programmes such as 'JESSI' is seriously in doubt. Although semi-conductors only account for 6 per cent of the total turnover of the electronics industry, they constitute the core of the electronic components used in all other sectors of industry. In particular, the car industry is more and more dependent on electronics.

The EC still has some strengths. In telecommunications the same companies, together with the French firm Alcatel, ensure that the EC accounts for 35 per cent of world production. Nevertheless, this sector also lost money in 1988. Computer software firms, such as Cap-Gemini-Sogeti, are equally well-placed with 20 per cent of the total world market. Finally, European firms are also world leaders in the production of medical equipment (28 per cent of the market), and in the military applications of electronics.

In spite of these successes, the EC's share of electronics manufacturing fell from 26 per cent of the global total in 1980 to 23 per cent in 1989. The USA saw a similar decline, while the Japanese share grew from 15 to 27 per cent. In terms of electronics manufacturing the European industry is being forced to face up to the full force of international competition.

Competition weakens European industry

During the 1970s the EC felt threatened by the competition from those developing countries with cheap labour costs. It resulted in a policy of overseas investment by those firms that felt most vulnerable, in particular those heavily involved in the textile industry. Now the EC sees the danger coming more from other industrialized countries, principally Japan, especially in the high-technology sector. They now no longer talk only of overseas investment, because the creation of the Single Market in 1993 has encouraged US and Japanese firms to set up branches in the EC. It is now the pre-eminent position of European firms within the EC itself that is under threat.

The decline and dispersal of traditional industries

Faced with growing competition both firms and individual countries chose to specialize in those sectors where the world market was growing fastest. The result was reduced assistance for the most traditional industries and encouragement of massive investment overseas, especially in the textile industry. However, it was not possible to pursue this strategy in every instance. The collapse of shipbuilding provides the best example of the effects of competition from Japan and South Korea on one of the most traditional of European industries. Immediately after World War II the EC was still pre-eminent in shipbuilding, accounting for 85 per cent of ship launches. By 1974 EC shipbuilding only represented 40 per cent of the world total, and Japan has occupied first place ever since. Now, the EC accounts for barely a third of the world fleet of new ships, and the total tonnage has fallen by 15 million tonnes gross since the onset of the recession following the oil crisis. What is more there is now no single country that exceeds 1 million tonnes gross, whilst there were eight in 1974. In the UK the crisis was so severe that the Labour government decided to nationalize the industry, but even this measure could not save the shipyards on Teesside, Glasgow, and Belfast. Of the 26 yards that once provided employment for more than 100 000 workers on the banks of the Clyde only four remain. All of these have been completely modernized, but there is still over-capacity. In spite of state aid, support from the EC, the closure of the most obsolete yards and the continuation of government orders, the shipbuilding industry is still experiencing great difficulties.

If it is difficult to relocate shipyards, it is easy to close factories making textiles, footwear, and electronic consumer goods, or those assembling components, and then to reopen them in countries where labour is cheaper. In 1986 the average hourly wage, including social security contributions, was 11.80 French francs in South Korea, as compared with about 100 French francs in France and Germany. The French multinational Thomson laid off some 1000 employees in France and Germany in 1988 and transferred production to south-east Asia. The firm now has more than 5000 employees in Asia. Nor is it alone, Grundig, Siemens, AEG, and Philips have all done the same. The success the Briton Alan Sugar has made out of selling personal computers is also very significant. Amstrad's dominance stemmed from the fact that it was able to arrange the manufacture, or simply buy ready-made, the components it required in south-east Asia.

With consumer goods, outward investment was the most obvious way for EC industries to respond to competition from Asia, especially as the crisis was particularly severe in textiles and clothing. Between 1971 and 1988 EC output fell in both these areas, but it rose strongly in Eastern Europe, most developing countries and, most dramatically of all, in Asia (240 per cent in the clothing industry). In the clothing industry, the sector most affected, the EC has had an overall trading deficit since 1975 and it has been growing steadily reaching 7 billion ECUs in 1988. The decline has continued, despite the Multi-Fibre Agreements (MFA), specially negotiated outside the framework of GATT, between the EC and the Newly Industrialized Countries.

Nearly every country in the EC has its own textile and clothing industry and, combined, it is the largest in the world in terms of the numbers employed. Roughly 100 000 firms support more than 3 million people with a total turnover of 145 billion ECUs. Flexible and diverse production processes have enabled the industry to manufacture not only man-made and natural fibres, but also carpets, clothes, and specialist machinery. The textile industry is highly capitalized, even though the clothing industry remains highly labour-intensive. This latter characteristic has meant the measures to combat competition from low-wage countries elsewhere in the world have had to be particularly drastic in the clothing industry.

However, not all the EC countries are in the same boat. The newer members, in particular Portugal, have lower costs and, therefore, have remained competitive. Equally, the level of decline in a given branch of the industry reflects, to no small degree, the extent to which it has been able to specialize. Textiles and clothing have always been strong in Italy and there has been a sustained effort to modernize and innovate, enabling the country not only to go on producing, but also to develop and manufacture sophisticated new equipment. In contrast, the German textile industry has specialized very little and has been decentralizing since the 1960s, a process which accelerated sharply in 1973 and 1974. The German government, which was very free-trade minded, supported the principal of subcontracting on the international market via the TPP, while all other members of the EC, especially France, were against it. Under the Community system then in force, German firms were able to benefit from a differential tax, levied only on the value added to semi-finished products that were reimported. German firms tended to favour links with countries in Eastern Europe, especially Yugoslavia, and with the countries of the Maghreb, all of which were closer geographically than the Asian countries. In this way, Germany has been able to build up quite a strong clothing industry, even though it had specialized very little.

The two contrasting examples of Germany and Italy demonstrate clearly that the crisis facing the textile industry in the Community is more complex than would appear at first sight. However, it is true that decentralization from Europe has been the rule and this has gathered pace everywhere since the beginning of the 1980s. Thanks to the introduction of more sophisticated machines, some firms have managed to break back into the undergarment market, though knitwear has declined sharply. In general, labour-intensive industries have only managed to survive if they have undergone radical restructuring. The price of this has been a labour-force reduction, which has hit the highly specialized regions particularly hard.

Foreign investment in the Community: The Japanese threat?

The creation of a huge common market with twelve members, as well as the goal of achieving the Single Market in 1993, have clearly influenced major foreign investors to move into Europe. American firms are long-established and the takeover of Vauxhall and Opel by General Motors dates from the inter-war years. In the 1980s, however, the movement took on a new intensity, though without causing any serious problems so long as a real reciprocity existed. The American market stayed relatively open and European firms were in no way prevented from selling there. The situation with Japanese firms is very different. Its domestic market remained largely closed until recently and its industrial and commercial practices evoked strong reactions amongst the EC member states.

In ten years Japan has invested more than $US14 billion in EC countries (see Table 4.5). From a base of less than $US500 million in the mid-1980s, the level of investment has leapt upwards, causing considerable concern in the member states of the EC. There was a rapid initial rise in 1985, reaching $US5 billion in 1988, and then nearly $US8 billion in the first quarter of 1989.

There are three reasons for this sudden increase in Japanese overseas investment and the concentration on the EC. Clearly the prospect of the Single Market in 1993, at one and the same time, unsettled and attracted Japanese firms. On the one hand the Single Market threatened to infuse European companies with a new dynamism and make them more determined to see off Japanese competition. On the other, the large unified market is a prize worth fighting for, so long as fines and restrictions under the anti-dumping legislation can be avoided. Faced with this threat, the Japanese response was to invest heavily in the EC itself. The rise in the value of the yen has also encouraged Japanese overseas investment. Having invested massively in North America, it is now the EC's turn.

The first Japanese firm to build a factory in Europe was in 1959 when Tankara opened a plant in Scotland manufacturing medical equipment.

TABLE 4.5 *Japanese investment in Europe 1978–1988* ($US million)

	UK	France	Germany (West)	Spain	Italy
1978	66	38	41	22	n.a.
1979	67	41	94	73	n.a.
1980	186	83	110	28	n.a.
1981	110	54	116	39	28
1982	176	102	194	19	19
1983	153	93	117	52	13
1984	318	117	245	140	n.a.
1985	375	67	172	91	n.a.
1986	984	152	210	86	23
1987	2 473	330	403	283	59
1988	3 956	463	409	161	n.a.
TOTAL	8 864	1 540	2 111	994	figures incomplete

Note: n.a. = figures not available.
Source: L'Usine nouvelle (1990).

However, it was not until the 1980s that the number really began to increase with most of the new investment being in the UK, the Benelux countries, and Germany. France initially lagged behind, because of its hostility towards Japanese commercial practices, but by the beginning of 1989 the UK with 116 factories and France and Germany, with just over 80 each, accounted for nearly 60 per cent of total Japanese investment.

Initially, Japanese firms concentrated their efforts on the peripheral regions of the Community in Scotland, Ireland, and Iberia, but the Japanese firms are now equally interested in the industrial heartland of the EC. Germany is the most favoured country because of the reunification, with Mitsubishi establishing a semiconductor factory in Aachen, followed by Hitachi in Munich. As a rule, Japanese firms prefer to use wholly owned subsidiaries, rather than rely on buying into existing European companies although, against the trend, neither the revival of Dunlop, nor the purchases made by Dai Nippon Ink in printing-ink manufacture should be overlooked.

The investment has come mainly from large corporations and has benefited primarily specific sectors of industry, such as electronics and cars. Sixty per cent of those employed by Japanese electronic companies are employed by Sony and Mitsubishi making video recorders or CD players. The Sony factory in Wales has flooded the European market with some 800 000 video recorders. The same thing has happened in the car industry with the growing importance of Nissan and Toyota.

On the whole, this foreign investment should be viewed in a positive light, because it serves to strengthen the overall industrial structure of the EC and create new jobs. It is for these reasons that the UK and, more recently, France have pursued vigorous policies aimed at attracting Japanese companies. In certain areas, however, there is a danger of allowing overcapacity to develop, as happened in the American car industry, leading inevitably to a loss of jobs in those firms in the most direct competition with the new arrivals.

The car industry provides a good example of the advantages and disadvantages. The EC is at the heart of a Japanese marketing strategy and has seen a network of retail outlets set up, car firms partially taken-over and, most recently, the construction of completely new purpose-built assembly plants. Present Japanese capacity in the EC, which is around 300 000 vehicles a year could rapidly be raised to 600 000 as and when the economic recession ends. The UK, whose car industry was decimated during the last economic crisis, has provided the main platform for breaking into the EC market, although research and development are carried out mainly in the Benelux countries. As a result, the warning of the managing director of Peugeot that 150 000 jobs in the car industry are threatened should not go unheeded. One thing is certain, the abolition of quotas in Europe after 1993 will enable the Japanese to consolidate their competitive position. Faced with this potential threat the member states are divided, because many of them are also partners in the new Japanese developments. It is all part of a European dilemma, examined in the next section, and the true impact of these changes on the spatial distribution of industry needs to be properly understood.

Selected changes in the industrial spatial structure

Rapid industrial changes nearly always have an immediate impact on spatial structure. The closure of the older coal and iron-ore mines, the drift of heavy industry towards the coast, and the disappearance of shipyards, all threatened the traditional industrial regions. At the same time, the high-technology industries are usually looking for a scientific environment, mostly to be found in the largest European cities. As a result a new industrial geography is born, no longer based on the old imperatives. In future, market considerations will determine location strategies, whereas up to the 1960s supplies of raw materials were the main determining factor. This has been particularly true of the car and electronics industries in the past twenty years. For all that, the regional industrial map of the EC has not changed fundamentally and there are still deep-seated discrepancies between countries and regions within the Community.

The distribution of industry: A map of enduring inequality

Overall, 33 per cent of employees in the EC are in manufacturing, but there are considerable variations between the different member states. Germany, where 40 per cent of employees are in the secondary sector, is still the country with the strongest industrial base. France, Spain, and Italy all have figures close to the Community average, but the UK is well below average. It may be logical to include Luxembourg in this group of countries, but the argument for Portugal is less clear in view of the less-developed nature of its economy. All the other states have less than 30 per cent of their labour force in the secondary sector.

This crude picture takes no account of variations within each country. An interpretation based on national statistics alone would seriously underestimate the regional disparities within the Community. These are so large that the creation of the Single Market in 1993 can only accentuate the discrepancies and any remedial policy must be based on a clear understanding of their nature and extent.

The contribution of manufacturing to total employment

With the Community average for the economically active population employed in manufacturing standing at 25 per cent, only just over a third of regions have levels in excess of this (Fig. 4.1). The only ones where it exceeds 40 per cent are the Basque region and Emilia Romagna, while in Baden Württemberg and Lomardy, it exceeds 38 per cent. If the expectation is that the older industrial regions will head the list, then it will come as some surprise to find that only in the Basque country is the industrial structure based on metallurgy. The pattern is confirmed when one looks at the fifteen regions where the figure is between 30 and 35 per cent. If the Midlands, North Rhine Westphalia, and perhaps the Sarre, all of which have economies fundamentally dependent on heavy industry, are excluded, traditional industries are in the minority.

Within each member country in the EC there are marked regional differences. Only Germany exhibits a distribution pattern that is reasonably homogeneous and no region has less than 25 per cent of its economically active population in manufacturing. Elsewhere, there are strong contrasts between a few regions with very high levels and a much larger number where the percentages are only very modest; this pattern is particularly marked along the Mediterranean coast. The regions that stand out are the Midlands in the UK, Picardy and eastern France, northern Italy, and some parts of northern Spain and Portugal.

To summarize, the regions with really high proportions of industrial

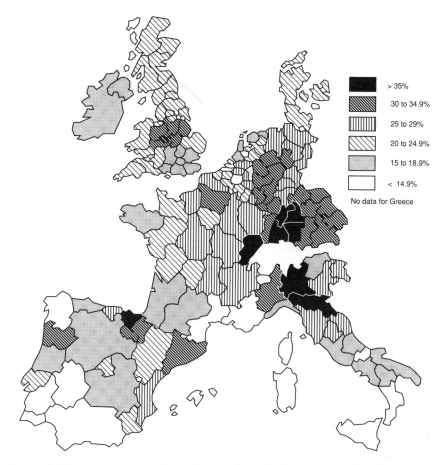

FIG. 4.1. The percentage contributed by manufacturing industry to total employment in the regions of the EC

Source: Based on data from Eurostat (1990).

employment form a rough north–south axis, running from the Rhineland in Germany to northern Italy and embracing Franche-Comté and Alsace. Around this axis there is a series of regions with less than 25 per cent of their work-force in manufacturing, like the Benelux countries and the bulk of northern France. In contrast, the UK and the Mediterranean countries are not well located in relation to this industrial core. Of course the UK maintains close contact with this European Rhineland region, but the physical separation is obvious from the map. More serious still, however, would seem to be the isolation of those important industrial regions in the north of the Iberian peninsula. Catalonia, the Basque country, and Navarre are all cut off from the main industrial region in northern Europe by a vast, under-industrialized, swathe of France stretching from the Atlantic to the Mediterranean coasts. Finally, the position of the most peripheral of all the EC's regions, stretching in an arc from Ireland to Greece should be noted.

These accidents of geography should not necessarily be seen as advantages and handicaps. The fact that some regions are cut off from the industrial heartland by rural tracts is of course limiting, but in an era when the tyranny of location is being reduced by modern communications, no region is a priori unable to contemplate an industrial future. Nevertheless, this spatial pattern underlines how recent the EC economic space is and the extent to which the national system of states and regions impedes international and transfrontier co-operation. Finally, the underlying weakness of the whole structure was further exposed by the delays in admitting the Mediterranean countries to the Community.

The proportion of the total number of jobs in manufacturing in each region

The above analysis does not give a sufficiently detailed insight into the underlying structure of industry, underestimating in particular those regions where the tertiary sector is prominent. One knows, for example that the Île de France and South-East England are among the most important industrial regions in each of their respective countries, but it is the English Midlands and Picardy that are picked out by the previous analysis. This can partly be corrected by examining the contribution of each region to the total level of industrial employment (Fig. 4.2). The new approach produces a pattern that is even more unequal, with an even greater concentration on the Community's core regions, though the basic hierarchy remains. In the earlier analysis, a quarter of the regions equalled or exceeded the EC average, but now there are only eleven accounting for more than 1 per cent of total employment, with a further eight contributing between 0.7 and 0.9 per cent. These twenty regions account for a quarter of all industrial employment in the EC.

If little has changed as far as northern Italy and Germany are concerned, with all their regions still contributing strongly to the industrial base, this is not true of the other countries. Now the true industrial importance of regions such as northern Denmark, Scotland, and South-East England can be seen. Similarly in France the real hierarchy emerges, with the Île de France in first place, ahead of the Rhône-Alpes and Nord-Pas-de-Calais regions. Finally, in the Iberian peninsula only Catalonia has a sufficient number of manufacturing jobs to enable it to stand alonside the regions in the north of the EC.

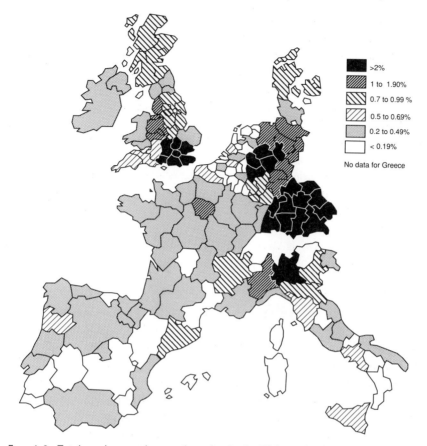

Fɪɢ. 4.2. Total employment in manufacturing in the EC in each of the regions
Source: Based on data from Eurostat (1990).

The disequilibrium between the north and east and the other regions of the community is, once again, clear to see. The industrial heart of the EC extends from England through to northern Italy, with only a small hiatus of regions with rather lower levels of jobs in manufacturing in the Benelux countries. It is in this belt that one finds the highest percentages, headed by North Rhine Westphalia with just over 3 per cent of the EC's manufacturing employment. One can do no more than stress the similarity between the shape of this zone and that encompassing the major conurbations, proof that the expansion of the service sector is partly dependent on the level of industrial development.

On the other hand, the south of the community, enlarged to include nearly the whole of France, seems almost totally without any industrial workers. If

Rhône-Alpes and the Nord are part of the industrial core, then Île de France and, even more so, Catalonia seem like islands isolated in the heart of regions where the level of manufacturing employment never rises above 0.5 per cent of the Community total. The further south one goes, the more regions there are with levels of less than 0.2 per cent, clear signs of low levels of industrial development.

The regional distribution of the main categories of economic activity

A picture based only on the numbers employed in manufacturing is limited, and so it has been supplemented by an analysis of the regional distribution of the three major categories of industry (Fig. 4.3). The 'intermediate'

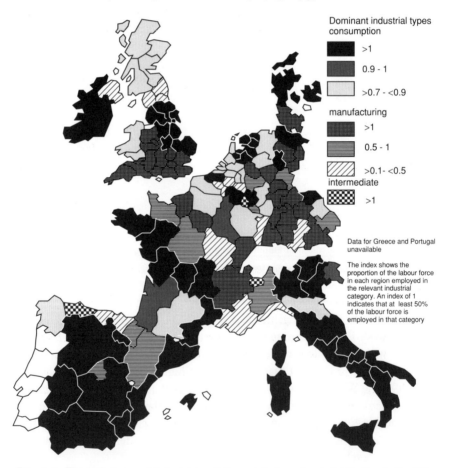

Fig. 4.3. The main types of industrial activity and their regional distribution in the EC
Source: Based on data from Eurostat (1990).

category includes mainly basic industries, such as iron and steel and heavy engineering. The 'manufacturing' category includes the electrical and electronics sectors, as well as all those industries associated with vehicle production and transport. Finally, the 'consumption' category includes agriculture and food, timber, and the huge range of consumer-goods industries (textiles, clothing, leather, etc.). This very crude picture does not enable any distinction to be made between dynamic sectors that are forging ahead and those that are in decline, such details remaining hidden within the broad threefold categorization. Nevertheless, it does highlight generalized regional specialisations.[3]

By the mid-1980s, 'intermediate' industries had sunk to a position of only minimal importance and they dominated only a very small number of regions. To all intents and purposes there are just three remaining: Val d'Aosta in Italy, Luxembourg, and Asturias in Spain. The Val d'Aosta is explained by the heavy dependence of the local economy on extractive industries; the other two reflect a continuing reliance on metallurgy and a lack of success in attempts to diversify.

The most industrialized regions in the EC are dominated by 'manufacturing' industry. They are also the most dynamic, because their development is based on the car, electrical, and electronics industries, the buoyancy of which is renowned. This is confirmed by the picture in Germany where in nearly every region those working in industry are actually in the manufacturing sector. In Hannover, Baden Württemberg, or Bavaria, all of which have a long tradition in this sector and are still building on their reputations for car production and electronics, this is hardly surprising. In North Rhine Westphalia it is a relatively new development, taking over from the traditional dependence on heavy industry. The same pattern can be seen in the London Basin, the central and southern parts of the Paris Basin, the foothills of the Alps, and the northern regions of Spain. In the other regions of this part of northern Europe there is a more or less equal division between, on the one hand, firms supplying other industries and, on the other, consumer goods industries, although the latter are particularly strong in Yorkshire (the woollen industry) and the East Midlands, as well as in the northern parts of the Low Countries and Denmark. Elsewhere there is a mixed picture with no one sector dominating. The former coal-producing regions, like Scotland

[3] We have calculated an index based on the relationship between each category and the two others. A coefficient of 1 indicates that at least 50 per cent of the labour-force works in that category. There are no figures for either Greece or Portugal.

and Wales in the UK, and the Nord-Pas-de-Calais and Lorraine in France, are all good examples of the trend.

The under-industrialized regions of southern Europe are still dominated by consumer-goods industries; this is not necessarily evidence of backwardness, as both Lombardy and Catalonia fall into this category. Nevertheless, one cannot ignore the similarity between this pattern and that of low levels of industrial employment discussed above. The rest of this section will concentrate on the most dynamic aspects of the changes in the spatial pattern, using as examples the programmes to revitalize the older industrial regions, the swing towards car manufacturing, and the impact of introducing new, high-technology industries.

The crisis facing the older industrial regions and the programmes to revitalize them

Just as the level of industrialization was measured by the percentage of the labour-force working in the secondary sector, so the areas of industrial decline can be well picked out by the level of unemployment. It is also the only criterion used by the Community for distributing structural funds. By combining these two indices it is possible to define those regions suffering from industrial decline: northern and eastern France, the central and northern parts of the UK, some parts of the Benelux countries, the north and east of Spain and, finally, part of the Ruhr and the Sarre. Altogether these areas encompass 22 per cent of the labour-force in the EC. In terms of individual countries, the UK, Belgium, and Spain are the worst-off and the situation is best in Germany, because even though all its regions are experiencing unemployment the levels are below the Community average. By contrast, in Spain unemployment was high throughout the country in the late 1980s and industry concentrated in only a small number of regions.

Using unemployment as a measure has the disadvantage that it says little about the severity of the decline and the nature of the problems that have to be faced. Other measures would reveal different aspects of reality, such as progress towards post-industrial systems of production using much less labour, the potential problems caused by the general economic situation, or by differential economic growth between sectors, a global recession being very much more difficult to combat. With reference to this last point, those regions concentrating on textiles and iron and steel are examined in particular detail, because both are in deep recession and this is having a profoundly destabilizing effect on the local economies.

The old textile regions

These are the most widespread of the declining regions. In some cases, as in Nord-Pas-de-Calais, they are to be found in traditional coal-mining areas; the textile factories provided employment for women to complement male employment in the mines. Elsewhere the industry grew up more spontaneously, capitalizing on indigenous advantages, such as sheep-farming in Scotland and Ireland, the quality of the water in the Vosges, the Black Forest, and some parts of the Pennines, and the availability of labour on the edges of the Massif Central, in the Pyrenees, and in central and southern Italy. In most cases this was the only major industry making the effects of the current recession even more severe. Two examples taken from France illustrate the problems facing these textile regions.

The Olmes country around the town of Lavelanet (population 9000) in the Touyre valley in the Pyrenees has been almost entirely dependent on textiles for nearly two hundred years. About seventy entrepreneurs used to provide the infrastructure that enabled spinning and weaving mills, dye works, and other associated factories to survive. Into the heart of this small business community came Roudière, a national company looking to expand its operations, and by 1985 it was employing 2400 people out of a total labour-force in the region of not more than 20 000. Between 1988 and 1989 thirty of Olmes's original businesses went bankrupt; 1500 jobs were lost, in addition to the 750 that Roudière announced would have to be made redundant as part of a rationalization programme. The local economy is so deeply entrenched in the textile industry that it is very difficult for it to diversify.

These problems appear almost insignificant when compared with those facing Nord-Pas-de-Calais. Its textile production is recognized as being of the highest quality, except for silk, for which both Lyons and Milan have better reputations. The wool and linen industries date back to the Middle Ages and to them have been added, first cotton and more recently synthetic fibres, making it a region with an unusually diversified industrial structure. In addition, the industrial processes it embraces are both complex and varied, ranging from carding to the production of ready-made garments, by way of spinning, weaving, and the hosiery trade. At the end of World War II there were 125 000 workers employed in the textile industry in Nord-Pas-de-Calais, half the total for the region. Today there are no more than 25 000 and each new restructuring programme brings with it additional redundancies. The agonies of the Boussac empire have been followed by the difficulties facing Lainière de Roubaix (part of the Prouvost group) and Chargeurs Réunis. Unless there is savage rationalization, further investment, and reductions in the size of the labour-force, the textile industry will not have seen the end of its restructuring. A shrinking market and the need for higher levels of productivity will both ultimately have the same effect. The story of the loss of markets is well known and reflects the ravages of foreign competition. For instance, Lainière de Roubaix has seen 25 per cent of its hosiery outlets disappear, although this has as much to do with the virtual disappearance of home knitting, (which has caused a reduction of 50 per cent in the demand for wool in France) as with foreign competition. At the same time heavy investment has enabled plants to be modernized and production to be concentrated on the top end of the market. The reduction in the size of the labour-force is the price that has to be paid.

Although it has not totally undermined the local economy as in Lavelanet, the economic shock engendered profound changes in attitudes and the look of the local landscape. For the most part, the old-established textile families have lost power to the accountants. The textile industry has started to look for better qualified workers and, to the prospect of redundancy has been added the problems of finding a job at all for anyone who is not properly trained. Finally, the red brick industrial buildings from Tourcoing to Roubaix, which were symbols of the power of the textile industry at the beginning of the century, have become surplus to requirements. Today, the buildings have been renovated and reopened to house a wide variety of different activities—tree nurseries, a telecommunications centre, a cultural centre, and a variety of others.

The crisis in the iron and steel regions

The crisis in iron and steel principally affects the traditional 'black countries', which have lost their comparative advantage in having access to cheap energy in the form of deep-mined coal and have suffered further through a lack of investment in new plant. The UK has suffered most amongst the member states, with Glasgow, the North of England, the East Midlands and Wales all being seriously affected. Even though the crisis started there earlier than elsewhere, the effects are still being felt. France and Belgium are also experiencing similar problems, especially the regions of Pas de Calais, Lorraine, the Borinage, and Creusot. In Germany the Ruhr did not escape the process of restructuring, even if it seems to have survived better than the UK, France, and Belgium. Finally, Asturias, which has seen its mines closing one after another. Examples from each of the countries most affected serve to demonstrate the true dimensions of this crisis.

It is no exaggeration to talk in terms of the tragedy of iron and steel in the UK. The British Steel Corporation (a nationalized industry until 1990) employed 252 000 people in 1971, as compared with less than 100 000 in the 1990s. Teesside in north-east England illustrates the scale of the recession that has hit those regions specializing in metal working. Industrial development in Teesside was built on coal and supported by a whole range of associated engineering industries, iron and steel, and shipbuilding. Iron and steel is a sick industry, for although the Redcar works is one of the most modern and efficient in Europe and enjoys the benefits of a coastal location, all the older plants have been closed. A study by the University of Newcastle shows that the number of new jobs created in small and medium-sized enterprises (SMEs) between 1979 and 1982 was just under 2000, but over the same period 46 000 employees were made redundant, bringing the total number of unemployed to more than 100 000.

Like most other heavy industrial regions, Teesside seems to some extent to be a victim of its own image. Pollution and the lack of alternative skills amongst the former workers in the iron and steel industry has not attracted new, high-technology firms. New developments in nearby Newcastle, many of them connected to the discovery and exploitation of North Sea oil, and to its university, have not been sufficient to make any significant difference. Similarly, Enterprise Zones and other special assistance measures have failed to attract the dynamic and innovative industries that are essential to the region's revitalization.

The city of Liège and the rest of the Belgian industrial region of Wallonia is facing similar problems and is widely known as an 'industrial cemetery'. Here too, the iron and steel industry was the first to be affected by the 1970s economic crisis. Cockerill-Sambre has reduced its work-force by half and now only employs 10 000 people in both Liège and Charleroi together. Overall, the iron and steel industry has seen half of its total work-force in the region disappear. The reasons are identical to those in the UK and in neighbouring Lorraine. Without new investment and modernization the firms were unable to compete in the face of much reduced demand for iron and steel and fierce competition from better equipped plants. It seems that the dispersed nature of the sites was an insurmountable obstacle: in Wallonia a tonne of molten metal could travel as much as 15 km in the course of the production process.

As a result, Wallonia has had a wholesale process of economic restructuring thrust upon it. Derelict land is being converted into parks and green spaces or, where the locations are suitable, transformed into 'industrial parks' mostly employing people in the tertiary sector. Nor should it be overlooked that, for the most part, the workers are very badly prepared for this change. The unions have also found it difficult to adjust to the break-up of large work-places and they have exerted little influence over the move to shift working by the new and dynamic SMEs. Despite all this, Liège still offers at least four significant advantages for potential new employers; a prestigious university that can assist in the development of new, high-technology industries; location at the heart of the EC; the third largest river port in Europe; and the imminent arrival of the Brussels–Cologne TGV rail link.

As far as the Ruhr is concerned, it is now somewhat macabrely being asked whether it is better described as a 'silicosis valley', or a 'silicon valley'. The region is still the core of the European iron and steel industry, producing two-thirds of German steel and employing 40 per cent of those in the industry. But it did not escape the difficulties of the 1970s and 1980s. One out of every two workers in the iron and steel industry has been made redundant and there are now no more than 100 000 workers left in the industry. Like other comparable regions, the Ruhr has lost 40 per cent of its industrial jobs in the period since 1960. As a result, it is not surprising to find that unemployment here, in 1988, was higher than in any other part of what was West Germany; 16 per cent as compared with 11 per cent in North Rhine Westphalia as a whole, and 9 per cent nationally. The levels were even higher in individual cities, such as Dortmund (17 per cent), and they would be worse still if large numbers of people had not already moved away. The Ruhr is going through a period of depopulation and the number of people living there has fallen from 6 to 5 million in the past twenty years, most of those leaving moving to more attractive regions in the south of the country.

Further evidence of the crisis is in the intolerable level of debt that most of the constituent local authorities are carrying as a result of having instituted generous social security schemes when continued economic growth seemed assured. Now there is little money available, either to help the local population, or to revitalize the ravaged landscape. Factory closures leave behind huge areas of derelict land, as at Hoesch in Dortmund, which once covered an entire suburb. The Ruhr also suffered from the effects of bad planning during the years of growth; a particularly blatant example of which is its dense network of motorways, conceived as a way of improving the urban fabric, but now an obstacle to urban redevelopment.

The Ruhr, like all other single industry regions, suffers from a whole series of ills: over-specialization, the paternalism of employers, a lack of training opportunities for employees, low wages which act as a disincentive to newer industries requiring high levels of skill in their labour-force, and an absence of universities prior to the opening of that at Bochum in 1961. Nevertheless, when it came to restructuring the Ruhr had a number of significant advantages in comparison with other regions. The iron and steel industry was able to relocate on the banks of the Rhine and thus enjoy some of the benefits of the coastal plants. In the central part of the conurbation which was steadily abandoned, restructuring policies were adopted very early on and were helped by the existence of a well-financed administrative agency covering the whole of this core zone, the SVR.[4] However, as has been shown by a study undertaken by the University of Duisburg, the scale of the international competition overshadowed all the attempts at restructuring. The aid tended to go to those sectors that were in crisis and declining, rather than to the dynamic new industries. A great deal of money went into social programmes, rather than into the creation of new jobs. As a result, the reconstruction of the Ruhr is still awaiting completion, because the resources required have simply been too great. In too many instances as well, initiatives were isolated and poorly co-ordinated. Finally, the real efforts that have been made to improve the quality of life must be recognized. The SVR fought hard to conserve woodland (72 000 ha today as compared with 80 000 ha in 1920), to reduce the ugliness of the slag-heaps, to convert some of the factories and mines into museums, and to reduce the levels of pollution in the rivers. The River Ruhr is no longer the sewer it once was, but has clear water and lakes that are a major recreational resource.

Changing a deeply entrenched image is no easy task and surveys have shown that Germans still consider a move to the Ruhr a demotion. All the above examples have underlined that the restructuring of these old industrial regions will be a slow process. They are unlikely ever again to employ the large numbers of people they did in the past, though steady outmigration may eventually make employment provision easier to manage.

New industrial strategies and their implications for the regions

If industries are classified on the basis of the extent to which they incorporate modern technologies and rely on research, then a fourfold grouping emerges. The first group, comprising those processes involved with primary-metal working, is heavily reliant on raw materials and remains the mainstay of the old industrial regions that have just been discussed. Nevertheless, there has been a steady shift to coastal locations, which provide sites near the sea that are sufficiently vast to enable enormous integrated iron and steel complexes to be brought together, such as are to be found at Dunkirk in France, Port Talbot in the UK, Taranto in Italy, and Ghent in Belgium. For identical reasons, Rotterdam, Antwerp, Le Havre, and Marseilles are four of the most important refinery locations in Europe. The second group, those industries

---

[4] The Siedlungsverband Ruhrkohlenbezirk—The Ruhr Regional Planning Authority.

manufacturing intermediate goods, also tends to be governed by the same sorts of factors and are moving to similar locations.

The situation is quite different for the third group, those industries primarily engaged in assembling finished products. The same is true of the fourth group, the high-skill industries where raw materials form an even smaller part of the overall costs, but where there is heavy dependence on research and access to research capability. Car manufacture belongs to the third group, while high-technology industries belong to the fourth.

The two latter examples will be used to illustrate the distinct geographical concentrations that are beginning to appear within the Community. The restructuring taking place in the industries in categories three and four is having a profound effect on the dynamics of industrial location in Europe. It also follows that the more those industries in categories one and two begin to be replaced by tertiary industries, the more that dependence on central, 'core' locations will increase. All the available research indicates that the major urban agglomerations are best provided with social infrastructure and contain at least half of all research centres, but that they are much less dominant when it comes to manufacturing. A survey of 2000 firms carried out in the London area revealed that the region accounted for only 30 per cent of manufacturing, but the corresponding figure for research was 50 per cent and for company headquarters 75 per cent. The same is also true of France where office space is disproportionately concentrated in Paris. Only in Germany is this excessive concentration of economic activity a little less marked, the economic structure being slightly more decentralized and activity more evenly spread amongst the major urban centres (see Chapter 1).

The discovery of new products, as well as the process of putting them into production, demands the close proximity of a technological centre with the right sort of environment, in particular, access to sufficient grey matter. On the other hand, once production is up and running, there is a tendency to look for more peripheral locations so as to exploit other advantages, such as a cheaper labour-force. Car manufacturing provides a good example of the way new sites have been developed on sites away from the national centres in the Community; high-technology industries will be used to illustrate the strategies developed in urban areas and the intense rivalries that surround them.

The diffusion of car-assembly plants

Until the end of the 1960s, the location of car-assembly plants was largely determined by historical influences. The Porte de Bourgogne in France (Sochaux) is the ancestral home of the Peugeot family, Oxford in the UK that of the Morris's, and Runelsheim in Germany was the main centre for Opel before it was taken over by General Motors. The subsequent relocation was brought about by the fact that most car components are manufactured in the major urban-industrial regions, which are also the main source of the car industry's labour and its markets.

This is how the huge concentrations of production which characterize the car industry today came about. The London region has Ford at Dagenham, Rover at Oxford, and Vauxhall at Dunstable and Luton. More plants were built at Coventry and Birmingham in the Midlands. In the Paris region, all the main car-makers, with the exception of Peugeot, have plants either in the city itself, like Citroën at Javel wharf, or in the inner suburbs, like Renault at Billancourt, or Simca at Poissy. Despite intense competition from Milan, Fiat has made Turin the car capital of Italy. Finally in Germany, BMW in Munich, Ford in Cologne, Opel in Frankfurt, and Mercedes and Porsche in Stuttgart have all made major contributions to the international industrial standing of their respective cities.

In the 1960s and 1970s, industrial policy-makers used government powers to decentralize the industry as part of a wider industrial strategy. The result was the renewed dispersal of car manufacturing into almost every major region of the Community, and reduced concentration in the major conurbations. Most firms were content to co-operate with the policy as a way of escaping the urban-congestion cost of existing plant and relocating on larger sites, closer to a more flexible potential work-force. It was changes in the conditions of production rather than state policy that eventually proved decisive. The increasing complexity of the assembly process, the flexibility offered by road transport for supply, and the use now made of extended supply networks influenced the decision to relocate. Nevertheless, there were limits to dispersal from the major conurbations, so as to ensure that they did not lose entirely the advantages of central locations.

Citroën built new factories at Aulnay-sous-Bois in the Paris suburbs and at Rennes, the gateway to Brittany, a region where an excellent potential labour-force was available. Renault built most of its plants along the Seine valley at Flins, Cléon (near to Rouen), and Sandouville (near to Le Havre), with others at Caen and Le Mans. Volkswagen has continued to be based at its original site at Wolfsburg, though it now has plants elsewhere in Lower Saxony, in Emden, Brunswick, and Hannover, as well as at Kassel in Hessen. For its part, Mercedes has built a plant at Singelfingen, near Stuttgart, in an area where labour is plentiful, land is available for expansion and there is an excellent road network. BMW has three plants in Munich and is about to open another at Regensburg.

Another facet of the strategy followed by the major producers has been the rapid development of manufacturing capacity in Spain. From nothing in 1950, the industry now ranks fourth in Europe, supports directly more than 100 000 people and, indirectly, half a million more as subcontractors and in parts manufacture. However, Spain is an example of a car industry dominated by foreign manufacturers, developed initially to supply the European market, with 60 per cent of its production going for export. The locations of the new plants reflect the availability of substantial pools of labour and a good communications network.

The first company to begin production in Spain was Renault, which has a 72 per cent stake in FASA and plants at Valladolid, Seville, and Palencia. Peugeot has plants at Orense, Vigo, and Villaverde on the outskirts of Madrid. The American and Japanese producers, although they have arrived more recently, have pursued the same strategy: seeking out cheap labour and locating in a prospective member of the EC. Ford opened its plant at Valencia in 1976 to build the Fiesta, and General Motors' plant for the Corsa in Zaragossa was opened in 1980.

The spread of car manufacturing was also partly influenced by state economic policies. At the end of the 1960s, car manufacturing seemed to offer one solution to the problems of underdeveloped or crisis-prone regions. France, Italy, and the UK were all particularly prominent in offering inducements for relocation, further encouraged by the fact that it would reduce development pressure in the major cities. Aside from Rennes, which has already been mentioned, help was given to Simca to open a new plant in La Rochelle and to Ford in Bordeaux. In the UK, plants were opened at Liverpool on the Mersey estuary and at the new town of Livingstone in Scotland. Finally, there is the Alfa-Romeo plant near Naples, though this has been plagued by persistent high levels of labour absenteeim. Problems of chronic unemployment in the former coal-producing regions have encouraged several governments to try and persuade car manufacturers to relocate there. The former British Leyland (now Rover) was persuaded to open new plants in Scotland at Edinburgh and Glasgow. In Germany, Opel moved to Bochum and Ford to Sarrelouis. In France, the nationalized firms were directed to invest in the Nord (notably at Douai and Valenciennes) and in Lorraine. However, the rapid changes taking place in car manufacturing mean that the industry has not been a panacea for solving regional problems.

High-technology industries associated with the major conurbations
The high-technology industries demand a skilled labour-force and easy access to university or private research laboratories, as well as other high-level

services; as a result, they have tended to be located within the Eurocity network. They have become a symbol of European competition in the run-up to the Single Market, as evidenced by the proliferation of technology and business parks throughout the Community. Even the smallest agglomeration is trying to acquire the image of a development centre, built around high-technology industries. However, although there has been some diffusion to the level of regional centres, these industries remain overwhelmingly concentrated in the major conurbations.

London, Copenhagen, and Paris each account for more than 45 per cent of employment in high-technology industries in their respective countries. Milan and Turin together account for 60 per cent of the Italian total and, if Rome is included, the proportion is 70 per cent. Similar values are found in Randstadt Holland and they are even higher if Eindhoven, home of Philips, is included. As usual, only Germany has a more dispersed pattern, with these industries being important in all the main cities—such as Munich, Stuttgart, Düsseldorf—as well as in second-tier centres like Berlin, Hamburg, and Nuremberg.

In addition to these major centres, there is some evidence of dispersal. Amongst European firms, this is restricted to the central core of the EC, but Japanese firms have been readier to invest in more peripheral regions. British high-technology firms are now spread quite widely throughout the London Basin. Those in Germany prefer the south, not least because it is close to two major centres, Munich and Nuremberg. There is less evidence of dispersal in France, but in addition to the long-established centres in the Rhône-Alpes region, Montpellier, Toulouse, and Bordeaux have all benefited from relocations. All three depend on the presence of multinationals, like IBM at Montpellier and Bordeaux, and Motorola at Toulouse, although the aeronautical industry in Bordeaux and Toulouse has been an important additional source of rapid development.

Catalonia and 'Silicon Glen', and, to a lesser extent, Madrid and Dublin all provide further evidence of the importance of major cites for attracting high-technology industries, initially from North America, but increasingly from Japan. However, much of this new development is insecure, usually being based on 'screwdriver plants', attracted by a combination of cheap labour, government subsidies, and the prospect of unrestricted access to the EC market.

Scotland could justifiably be called the 'aircraft carrier' for American and Japanese interests. It was in the 1950s that the first American firms located in a corridor 11 km long and 5 km wide between Edinburgh and Glasgow, which became known as 'Silicon Glen'. The development has been enormously successful, in that some 400 electronics firms now employ nearly 50 000 people, one of the biggest concentrations in Europe. There has been some direct central government involvement, but the principal credit for the success goes to the Scottish Development Agency, which has its own budget and direct access to the network of new towns. For example, employment in one new town, Livingstone, grew by 150 per cent between 1976 and 1986.

Although lacking any real locational advantages, the Spanish electronics industry has reached agreements with both North American and Japanese firms, as well as with some European ones (Philips and Siemens). Spain has become almost entirely dependent on these foreign firms, since IBM dominates the computer market and Westinghouse the electrical appliance market. The main focus of development has been Catalonia, a region that has long expressed the wish to become 'one of the main springboards for Japanese development in Europe'. Today, in terms of employment, Catalonia with between 80 000 and 100 000 employees is ahead of Scotland, Rhône-Alpes, and Berlin. With their state-of-the-art activities and production methods, and low-level of dependence on supplies of materials, the high-technology industries are the vision of the industrial future. For the moment they have benefited mainly the urban areas, in particular those offering a good quality of life and a high-quality scientific environment. However, not all these new creations deserve the epithet high technology and many, especially in the peripheral regions of the EC, are built on a fragile base.

The Community has come to realize that a successful future for high-technology industries is dependent on the development of a common industrial policy. Nevertheless, European industrial policy has so far been mostly constructed around national policies. The combination of inter-national competition and the coming of the Single Market make better co-ordination essential.

The industrial policy of the Community

Until 1974, industry in the Community went through a period of exception-ally rapid expansion carried along by the general economic growth of the 1960s and the removal of customs barriers. The member states concentrated their efforts on devising a Common Agricultural Policy rather than on industrial policy, believing that rapid industrial development would be an inevitable consequence of an integrated market.

Today it is clear that the industrial growth was the result of national, rather than EC policies, a fact that has been underlined by the recent economic crisis. The intensification of international competition and the completion of the Single Market are both strong arguments for the development of a common industrial policy. Research policy needs to be co-ordinated, help needs to be given to promote mergers between firms in different countries, and regional disparities need to be reduced. The Commission responded by becoming more interventionist in the run-up to 1993, though its enthusiasm has been checked somewhat by the growing fears about its influence amongst the member states, as expressed in the debate over ratification of the Treaty on European Union (the Maastricht Treaty).

Nationally inspired strategies

The way in which the EC worked prior to the adoption of the Single European Act tended to favour national strategies. Individual states pursued policies to protect the independence of their troubled industrial sectors, the Commission only being brought in when the dangers threatened to get out of hand, as in the case of the multi-fibre textile agreements. Companies also introduced different national standards as a form of protectionism and it is this, rather than state interference, which needs to be highlighted. Throughout the early years of the EC, there was little attempt at co-operation between the big multinationals. For the most part they followed the strategy of making exclusive agreements with non-European firms, especially in North America, and were relatively hostile to forming European industrial consortia.

A Europeanization index based on a range of criteria, such as turnover, number of employees in Europe, number of factories, and the proportion of their European assets held outside the country of origin throws some light on the picture.[5] The Swiss firm Nestlé comes at the head of the list, while the rest of the top ten comprises two Dutch conglomerates (Philips and Akzo), three French (l'Oréal, CGE, and Rhône-Poulenc), one in each of Germany (Siemens) and Belgium (Solvay), and two others from outside the EC, the Norwegian firm Norsk Hydro, and the Swiss firm Roche. At the other end of the scale, not a single Italian firm appears in the top thirty, underlining the degree of protectionism within the Italian economy. The survey of the degree of participation by European firms in the wider European economy, based on capital investment outside their country of origin, shows that German and Dutch firms are more open than French ones. Between 30 and 48 per cent of the capital investment in Philips, Siemens, BASF, and Azko comes from outside the country of origin, but the figure is less than 10 per cent for Saint-Gobain, CGE, and Rhône-Poulenc.

The example of high-technology industries provides some indication of the

[5] A classification started in 1988 by the economic journal *L'Expansion*.

weakness of this reliance on national strategies, faced with intensified competition in a single market of more than 300 million people. It is also relevant to recall that, in the 1960s the Commission was unable to persuade European firms to co-operate in the face of the threat of the North American computer firms. The most obvious illustration is the failure of Unidata (formed by the three European market leaders, Siemens, Philips, and CII— a little later to become Bull), as a counterweight to the giant IBM. There were disagreements between the 'three national champions' and their respective member governments who were underwriting them and who, eventually, killed the initiative. The history of the industry is littered with such failures, clear evidence of the decline of the EC relative to the foreign competition, including, recently, the European defeat in the battle for high-resolution television.

In the electronics field, most of the EC countries have adopted a 'national champion', but this policy has fatally undermined their capacity to compete with first the American, and now the Japanese, multinationals. Siemens in Germany, Bull in France, Philips in the Netherlands, and Olivetti in Italy dominate the European market, but they have been unable to assume a dominant position in those countries where the domestic computer industry is weak. IBM dominates the microcomputer industry in Spain, and, in the UK, ICL's hold on its market relies on agreements reached with Fujitsu and other Japanese firms.

However, the steady increase in terms of both value and volume of intra-Community initiatives, by 40 per cent in 1989 alone, shows that changes are afoot. It is possible that part of the explanation for the emphasis on nationally based takeovers is a desire to achieve critical mass before the advent of the Single Market in 1993, arguably only then will firms attempt to show their European credentials. Others, faced with the Single Market are opting for a global strategy, following the American and Japanese lead in this.

Growing Community voluntarism

Since the early 1970s, the EC has become increasingly active in trying to assist those industrial sectors that have found themselves in difficulty. Intervention in the textile industry was the first example of the new policy being pursued by Brussels. In effect the Commission intervened to pre-empt excessive national protection through public subsidy and thus over-capacity. It has also encouraged modernization and restructuring by financing research programmes and providing assistance through the European Regional Development Fund and the European Investment Bank. Finally, it has negotiated a multi-fibre agreement (MFA) within the framework of

GATT to limit textile imports from both the newly industrialized and the non-EC Mediterranean countries.

The effect of EC policies on the iron and steel industry has been even more decisive, because the Commission had a right to inspect built into the ECSC treaty. The Commission was bound, both to ensure competition and to limit productive capacity, while at the same time facilitating the closure of the most obsolete plants. It fixed its own quotas and obliged firms to respect them, despite mutterings of discontent from the Italian and German producers, who were least affected by the crisis. This interventionist policy only came to an end in the latter part of the 1980s when the steel market began to revive, although there are renewed calls for intervention in the face of a further market downturn in the early 1990s.

Industrialists who felt threatened by foreign competition frequently sought the help of the Commission. Under the anti-dumping legislation, the EC was able to limit imports of videos and TVs and it has been asked to do the same for Japanese car imports. This has truly been a Community initiative, but it does not of itself constitute a real industrial policy.

The Single Market, which came into operation in 1993, can make such a claim, even though this does not constitute a comprehensive strategy for manufacturing. To ease acceptance of the policy, the Commission has undertaken a number of studies on the effects of non-tariff barriers on the volume of trade. In the food and food-processing industries, the main obstacles emerged as being: bans on the use of certain ingredients, such as glucose in non-alcoholic drinks in France; regulations governing the purity of pastries in Italy; packaging and labelling; fiscal discrimination, such as the extra duty on beer in the UK; and health regulations, like those in Spain and the UK. In the car industry, technical requirements for vehicle safety are still not standardized and the whole issue remains subject to national, rather than Community, decision-making. Rates of value added tax for vehicles also vary from state to state and marketing arrangements serve to protect national monopolies. Finally, problems in obtaining technical permissions for building and public works, especially in France and Germany, help to protect national markets.

The Commission has commissioned several studies to calculate the eventual impact of the creation of the Single Market on both the Community economy and the individual national economies. As far as industry is concerned, it is clear that the result will be a significant reduction in the most important area, unit production costs, as well as benefits from increased competition and a more rapid diffusion of innovation. These changes will be most apparent in 40 out of the 120 sectors and these can be classified into four groups, based on levels of dependence on intra-Community trade.

First come the high-technology industries linked to the public sector such as computing, telecommunications, and medical equipment. These industries enjoy a high level of national protectionism, but none the less are growing rapidly and use technologies which will benefit, both from the larger market offered by European integration, and from the greater protection that size will offer against North American and Japanese competition.

Groups two and three may be loosely described as the traditional nationalized industries and other industries operating within long-established regulated markets. As far as energy, pharmaceuticals, and railway equipment are concerned, the Single Market should bring about a greater sense of dynamism and also encourage trade, because prices vary between countries by an average of between 15 and 25 per cent. On the other hand, the potential gains in technical efficiency are likely to be smaller in shipbuilding, the electrical appliance industries, and in the food and food-processing industries.

Finally, the fourth group includes the bulk of consumer industries and the car industry, which account for more value added than the whole of the other three groups put together. Competition is already quite strong, intra-Community trade well-developed, and some of the industries involved already organize their operations on a Community-wide scale; these are all reasons for believing that the effects will be limited. Nevertheless, they too will reap the benefits of fewer administrative, tariff, and fiscal barriers.

Despite all the inherent imponderables associated with predictions, there seems little likelihood that the removal of non-tariff barriers will radically change the industrial map. There is unlikely to be much major industrial relocation and reorganization of regional economic activity. For the major industrial member states the stakes are not sectoral competition, but rather their ability to adapt to the more international environment. The outcome may either be a more European industrial structure, or greater domination by the leading national firms. The former depends on co-operation between the member states and progress being made on the adoption of Community-wide legislation.

The major firms themselves expect that the Single Market will lead to mergers, more worker participation and, in passing, co-operative agreements being concluded in virtually every industrial sector. The shape of the future is already apparent: in the three huge consortia that have been formed in the radio and telecommunications industry; in the restructuring now taking place in telecommunications; in the takeover by Siemens of the English electronics firm Plessy; in the arrival in the Community of the Swedish electrical manufacturer ABB; in the numerous agreements made by the car manufacturers to produce components, such as gearboxes and engines; and in the

TABLE 4.6 *Breakdown of mergers and take-overs at national, EC, and international levels* (%)

	Operations			Total number
	National	EC	International	
1982–3	50.5	32.5	17.0	117
1983–4	65.2	18.7	16.1	155
1984–5	70.2	21.2	8.7	208
1985–6	63.7	23.0	13.3	227
1986–7	69.6	24.8	5.6	303
1987–8	55.9	29.0	17.1	383
1988–9	47.4	40.0	12.6	492

Source: *Économie europénne*, (1989: 37).

commercial agreements in the iron and steel industry. The food and food-processing industries have also been involved in radical financial restructuring, usually as a result of takeover bids: for example, the Italian firm Ferruzzi and Lesieur, and the English firm Cadbury and Poulain.

In the less-industrialized member states it seems probable that in future there will be even greater emphasis on specializations that exploit their regional advantages. In practice it will mean the establishment of branch factories in order to take advantage of cheaper labour costs. The relocations will most likely be factories producing consumer goods, with the risk that these countries will specialize in sectors with weak growth prospects and facing growing competition from developing countries. This has already occurred in both Greece and Portugal, but is less true of Spain.

The panoply of Community instruments

In an industrial climate of such comprehensive change, the Community has laid particular emphasis on promoting scientific research and technological development (R and D). Unfortunately, this has not been sufficient to compensate for policy failures elsewhere. Gross expenditure on R and D (65 billion ECUs in 1985), both civil and military, is little more than that of Japan, and half that of the USA with a population of similar size and an equivalent industrial structure. Moreover, the limited scale of the various national R and D efforts is not necessarily the most important statistic; the crucial factors are the dispersal of expenditure and the duplication of research effort—the failure of Euratom is still a painful memory. Joint research achieved relatively little, because each member state decided to follow its own policy when developing its civil nuclear industry.

The Single European Act which came into force in 1987 was a turning point, giving the Community competence in the area of R and D. This part of the Act had two facets. First, the member states agreed, under the unanimity principle, to sanction pluriannual framework programmes for research and technological development, each of which has a clear set of objectives, the necessary resources and guidelines on distribution. Second, the implementation of these framework programmes is in the hands of the Council of Ministers, which decides by qualified majority voting on more detailed working programmes. The concept of framework programmes actually predates the Single European Act, but has been clarified and strengthened by it. For example, the 1987–91 framework programme was funded to the tune of 5 billion ECUs, 40 per cent to be spent on information and communications technology, 25 per cent on energy, and the rest divided between industrial modernization, quality of life, the development of biological and marine resources, and encouraging European scientific and technical co-operation.

Existing European co-operation initiatives, in areas such as aerospace (Airbus, Ariane), and nuclear fusion (JET), have been further helped by a whole series of specific programmes. ESPRIT (European Strategic Programme for Information Technologies), now in its second quinquennial plan, is supposed to help EC competitiveness in the information technology sector. RACE (Research and development in Advanced Communications technologies for Europe) is aimed at helping the adoption of fibre-optic technology and thus furthering the development of telecommunications. BRITE (Basic Research in Industrial Technologies for Europe) is supposed to encourage the diffusion of new technologies in the traditional sectors of industry. Not surprisingly, another programme is targeted at the area of biotechnology, since 40 per cent of manufactured goods are either biological themselves, or made from biological materials. This list of fundamental research programmes is further supplemented by a large number of smaller ones. DRIVE (Dedicated Road Infrastructure for Vehicle safety in Europe), for instance, is a three-year programme, funded to the tune of 60 million ECUs, to develop the technologies, information and telecommunications in the field of road transport.

However, political will is not necessarily a good measure of success, especially as none of the member states wishes to abandon entirely its own R and D programme. The contribution that firms make to these R and D objectives needs to be carefully monitored.[6] The discussion surrounding the

---

[6] The EC research budget only accounts for 2 per cent of the total sum spent on public and private research in the twelve member states.

framework programme for 1990–4 has thrown up important differences, raising, for example, the whole question of whether a European research agency should be formed. The new programme will continue to emphasize communications technologies (55 per cent of the budget), the management of natural resources (36 per cent), and the management of intellectual resources (only 9 per cent); the latter emphasizes, in particular, the mobility of young researchers.

The electronics industry is going through a period of sustained and unrivalled growth and is predicted to take over first place in world trade from the car industry in the near future, but it is in precisely this sector that the EC is falling furthest behind. This explains why communications technologies are emphasized in the framework programmes and why ESPRIT and RACE, in particular, monopolize the available resources.

Starting from the assumption that Europe's poor standing is mostly to be explained by a lack of critical mass, which makes it impossible to achieve economies of scale, ESPRIT aims to promote co-operation between industry, universities, and research laboratories at the 'pre-competitive' stage. It has three fundamental objectives: to provide European industry with the basic technologies necessary to compete in the world market; to develop internationally accepted technical standards; and to implement these. The first phase of the programme, ESPRIT I, had a budget of 1.5 billion ECUs, half of it provided by the EC, and has funded 227 projects involving 526 participating institutions and bringing together more than 3000 researchers. By the end of 1988, 165 projects had produced what were considered significant results. The majority involved either technology transfer, or the marketing of specific products, such as microchips and the computer language Prolog. About thirty succeeded in developing internationally recognized specific standards.

One of the main objects of this first phase was also to encourage co-operation between companies, the majority of which were SMEs employing less than 500. Before ESPRIT I was launched, European firms mostly made technology transfer agreements with American companies. Since 1986, the number of intra-Community commercial agreements has risen eightfold (i.e. 46), equalling the number concluded with the United States. It is also relevant to note that the number of agreements made with Japanese firms (8) has changed little over the same period.

These successes meant that the budget for ESPRIT II was doubled. The second phase is continuing to develop research into micro-electronics, with particular emphasis on improving the ECs position in the manufacture of key components, but in addition concentrating on systems for processing information (software, signals, etc.) and then using these new technologies in business and the home. There were more than 700 applications in the first round and SMEs were even more prominent than previously amongst the 200 that were successful bids in the first round between 1989 and 1990. At the same time, there is disappointment in Brussels that the co-operation between researchers often involves working in parallel, rather than common strategies.

JESSI, the European programme for integrated circuits and part of ESPRIT, illustrates another difficulty. The project is being led by the 'national leaders' Philips, Siemens, and Thomson and they have been slow to involve smaller companies, like STC, Plessey, ES2, and AEG. Restructuring in the sector has also had a prejudicial effect on the process of co-operation. The need for co-operation has become even greater since the Dutch firm Philips has been experiencing serious financial problems, thus reducing its involvement in JESSI. This serves to show that co-operation between Community firms has not been easy to achieve, especially amongst the larger ones.

The close interconnections between European and North American firms ultimately make it hard to envisage agreements that are restricted solely to the twelve member states. It is probably this fact that led to the French initiative EUREKA, a multinational research programme that reaches beyond the Community to include 19 countries and a large number of North American firms. Its 297 projects and a budget of nearly 38 billion francs have enabled it to include most areas of high technology, with electronics accounting for the lion's share.

Not only do the major companies dominate the activities of all the programmes, participation is also uneven amongst the different regions of the EC. In France, the Paris and Rhône-Alpes regions account for most of the firms taking part in EUREKA. Generally the map of research activity shows the same uneven distribution. In the heart of the Community the co-operative links between different firms, especially those in the main European cities, constitutes a veritable spider's web. On the periphery the mesh is much less dense, links are mainly to the centre of Europe and only emanate from the larger agglomerations. The explanation is probably a lack of research expertise, aggravated by lower quality information sources.

EC intervention is also evident, if more indirectly, through its regional policy. This is not the place to go into this subject in much detail (see Chapter 1), but its role does need to be mentioned, especially since the 1989 reform of the structural funds has given the Community more autonomy in this field. The programmes that were started in 1987, STAR (telecommunications) and

VALOREN (endogenous energy potential) have only had a modest impact on industry, but the same is not true of RESIDER and RENAVAL, adopted in 1988. Both have been incorporated into the regional assistance distributed by the Community to revitalize the declining industrial regions through ECSC and the ERDF, a programme that has been running since 1975. RESIDER (revitalizing iron and steel regions) and RENEVAL (revitalizing shipbuilding regions) are supposed to help the economic restructuring of areas over-dependent on a single industry. The programmes are designed to create alternative employment in areas of high unemployment. For example, the Commission has invested 5.4 million ECUs in South Yorkshire and around Scunthorpe in the UK. In France, the départements of Meurthe-et-Moselle (Lorraine) and Le Nord (except for Lille) have been beneficiaries, while the Sarre and several areas of North Rhine Westphalia in Germany have received 64.5 million ECUs.

Support for industry is also provided by the Community's common interest programmes, signed by all the member states of the EC, and by the regional development programmes which have assumed much greater importance as part of the reform of the structural funds. Finally, mention should be made of RECHAR, aimed at the coal-mining areas and the last of the programmes designed to help the older industrial regions.

General conclusions

The growing interest of the Commission in industry and energy, which lay behind the Single Market programme, both seem likely in the medium to long term to strengthen the position of industry in EC 12, better enabling it to withstand international competition. Nevertheless, the EC is faced with at least two major challenges: one is related to the globalization of trade, the other to the uneven distribution of industrial activity.

The policy of firms is often at odds with that of both individual states and the Community. Firms are geared to the international level, thinking in terms of the global market and not exclusively in terms of the Twelve, even though the latter form one of the fastest growing trade blocks in the world. Equally, all the existing and presently planned European programmes have been devised with a purely European context in mind, but they need to be widened to incorporate the full interests of all the multinational companies within the EC, or at least those that have most of their turnover within Europe. However, individual governments are generally resistant to such an idea, especially as far as electronics are concerned. The French are implacably opposed, because they see it favouring the competition, but elsewhere the UK government is more ambivalent, not wishing to marginalize Fujitsu, who have taken over ICL, and the Germans are sympathetic to IBM, with its large financial interest in Siemens.

The uneven distribution of industrial activity needs to be ironed out as a matter of urgency, but it is going to be difficult to achieve this in the face of German dominance. In a crude diagrammatic form the industrial structure of Europe can be thought of as a series of concentric circles centred on Germany. The distribution of employment and firms demonstrates clearly that the most vigorous industrial regions are close to this core and that the level of activity and the number of industrial jobs decreases steadily down the Rhine axis. In addition, the major firms in other countries are usually judged first in terms of their German competitors.

Some commentators believe that the future will belong to some of the regions in the south, unsullied by traditional industrial crises and benefiting from a network of dynamic small and medium-sized enterprises, as well as from the attractive climate. According to some experts, the new European industrial landscape could be organized around an axis running from south Germany, to northern Italy, south-east France, and on to part of northern Spain. This conception derives from the general dynamism of the Spanish and Italian economies (prior to 1992 at least) and the existing industrial strength of cities like Stuttgart, Munich, Milan, Turin, and Barcelona. The prospect has already encouraged some cities to trade on their supposed locational advantages in the scramble to attract investment. On the other hand, cities and regions on the Atlantic coast are beginning to feel in danger of being marginalized.

Industrial Europe is already a reality, its global significance universally recognized, but the dual threats referred to above raise questions about the European infrastructure of the future. Should it protect national autonomy and individual firms, or should it encourage greater co-operation in research, technology transfer, planned production, and the ironing out of regional inequalities in the distribution of employment and the location of new investment? The whole future of the EC in world trade is the prize.

Further reading

Those wishing to go more deeply into this subject should turn first to the general studies published in each member state of the Community by the EC. They all contain one or two chapters on industrial development and energy and are based on a wide variety of, predominantly, national sources. Anyone requiring a more exhaustive treatment should turn to the publications of the EC itself. A wide variety of useful statistical material can be found in *Panorama de l'industrie Communautaire* which is published annually. The issues raised for industry by the advent of the Single Market are dealt with in several issues of the journal *Économie européenne*, notably numbers 35, 40, and 46 and the special edition published in 1991.

5 European Community Transport Policy with Particular Reference to Ireland as a Peripheral Region

James Killen and Austin Smyth

Introduction

Transport is of fundamental importance in facilitating the economic and social life of any region. Economic activity requires the existence of transport systems to bring raw materials to points of production, finished products to markets, and workers to their places of work. Transport systems comprise one of the most visible human-made landscape features. In many instances, the development of a transport facility has itself influenced other locational decisions; for example, between 1968 and 1973, six hundred factories located along the recently completed Italian Autostrada del Sole which runs from Milan to Naples (Hull *et al.* 1988: 207).

At the level of the European Community, transport and the issues surrounding it impinge on many other areas of EC concern. The construction of new transport links often involves substantial environmental impacts and thus has implications for EC environmental policies. The question of how the various regions of the Community can best be linked is obviously of fundamental importance within the context of EC regional policy. Major transport projects, for example aircraft construction, can obviously benefit from Community programmes which encourage co-operation and the sharing of expertise. Transport has a key role to play in progressing the Community's objectives of achieving ever closer political and economic co-operation between member states.

Given the importance of transport, it is not surprising that governments have traditionally sought to influence transport systems and operations at a national level. This influence has been expressed in two main ways. First, government has been the major regulator of transport, setting for example speed limits and the conditions under which licences of various types such as to operate a vehicle may be issued. Government has usually assumed a direct role in the operation of railway services and, in some cases, bus and road freight services as well. This has enabled it to control directly the degree of competition between these modes.

The second major role of government in the transport sphere has been to influence the level and nature of transport infrastructure investment. Two important issues which have arisen in various countries in this context have been, first, the amount to be invested in transport as against other sectors of the economy and, second, the manner in which the money allocated to transport is to be spent. In 1975, for example, 2.3 per cent of GDP was invested in inland transport infrastructure by Austria while the corresponding figure for the Republic of Ireland was only 0.6 per cent (European Conference of Ministers of Transport 1988: Table A, p. 10). In Germany, government policy has dictated that sufficient finance be directed to the railway in order to avert a major programme of closures; in contrast, the railway network in the United Kingdom was considerably reduced in length in the twenty years following World War II, although extensive upgrading of inter-city and certain suburban services also occurred.

Before the signing of the Treaty of Rome, transport policy in Europe was pursued by each state more or less independently of its neighbours. In theory, co-operation at a European level was possible through the European Conference of Ministers of Transport. This body had been set up in 1953 to encourage the rational development of European inland transport links of international importance but, in practice, it had no powers and acted mainly as a research forum (Hull *et al.* 1988: 221). One of the most important European-based transport innovations prior to the signing of the Treaty of Rome was the inauguration in 1957 of the Trans European Express (TEE) network of express trains under the auspices of the International Union of Railways, a body set up to co-ordinate railway operations between national railway administrations.

Given the importance of transport within the overall context of social and economic development, it is not surprising that the establishment and implementation of a common transport policy was perceived at the outset to be a fundamental EC objective. The Treaty of Rome states that 'the Community should establish a common transport policy to enable the free movement of people and goods over national boundaries'. From the beginning, developments in transport were seen at Community levels as an important means by which Community cohesiveness could be increased. The fact that transport policy had been pursued more or less independently by the various member states prior to the Treaty of Rome made the development and implementation of a Community-wide transport policy all the more difficult.

This chapter reviews the evolution of EC transport policy and assesses its impact on one part of the Community. By EC standards, the island of Ireland presents a unique set of geographical circumstances. It is located on the periphery of Europe. With the opening of the Channel Tunnel, the Republic of Ireland will be the only EC country without a fixed land-link to the rest of the EC. The island is small (84 450 km² approximately) and has a relatively low population (5.1 million in 1991). Yet, it contains an international boundary: the six counties in the north-east comprise Northern Ireland which is part of the United Kingdom while the remaining twenty-six counties comprise the Republic of Ireland.

From a transport operator's point of view, a favourable environment in which to run a transport service is one in which there are a number of sizeable urban centres with substantial distances between them. These conditions do not exist in Ireland. Dublin, Belfast, and Cork are the only centres with a population in excess of 100 000 and much of the population is located near the east coast. There are few major indigenous resources, e.g. minerals, which might be expected to generate large freight-traffic flows. Average journey distances are low by European standards: for example, it is estimated that in 1988, only 26.1 per cent of road freight tonnage in the Irish Republic moved a distance in excess of 50 km (*Road Freight Transport Survey*, 1988: 7). Journeys from Ireland to the European mainland and to the United Kingdom (excluding Northern Ireland) require a sea or air journey. These relatively unfavourable conditions pose a particular challenge for EC transport policy.

European Community transport policy: 1958–1986

A number of authors consider EC transport policy in detail, e.g. Abbati (1986), Erdmenger (1983), Gwilliam (1989), Hamilton (1990), and Whitelegg (1988). Throughout, three themes have been of importance:

(1) Harmonization, effectively seeking to bring about a situation whereby the various modes of transport operate under the same conditions throughout the Community, thereby eliminating any unfair advantage between countries or transport modes.

(2) Deregulation, effectively seeking to remove barriers to individual transport operators seeking to enter the market, thereby stimulating competition with a view to increasing overall efficiency.

(3) Transport infrastructure investment, effectively seeking to reduce transport journey times and costs, thereby increasing the cohesiveness of the Community as a unit.

Initially, the emphases in EC transport policy lay in harmonization and deregulation. The former, which was seen as creating the conditions for fair competition, preceded the latter. There was a desire to achieve harmonization in three areas: fiscal, social, and technical. In the fiscal area, there was for example a view that the rules by which national railway operations are subsidized should be standardized, with common practices in such matters as granting of aid to loss-making services deemed to be socially necessary. There was concern that, without harmonization, some member governments might grant large sums of money to their railways thereby giving that mode an unfair advantage while others might starve their railway of cash thereby forcing service reductions. In the fiscal area, there was also a desire to achieve harmony in respect of such matters as excise duties and taxes payable on vehicles and fuel. In the social area, it was intended that a single set of rules in respect of such matters as maximum allowable working hours would ultimately apply throughout the Community. Finally, on the technical side, there was a desire to achieve standardization in respect of such matters as vehicle weights, container dimensions, and the use of tachographs.

Turning to deregulation, it was intended that many of the national regulations, such as those concerning road-freight transport operations, would be abolished. In many of the member countries, road-freight and passenger-bus operations had been restricted, for example, through the issuing of licences. In many cases, this had been done by governments seeking to protect their national railway systems by ensuring that other transport modes operated as an adjunct to them. There was a desire at EC level to bring about a situation whereby freight and passengers could move freely between and within the countries comprising the Community on any chosen carrier, and without the payment of discriminatory taxes or surcharges.

The measures intended under the twin themes of harmonization and deregulation comprised an ambitious programme. Speaking in 1988, the European Commissioner then in charge of competition noted that:

in general . . . the national systems of transport in the Community have traditionally been the bastions of protectionism. It is difficult to identify other sectors where a comparable degree of protectionism has been permitted to reign in general over such a prolonged period. (Sutherland 1988: 107)

Given the foregoing view, it is perhaps not surprising that, for a considerable period, achievements in the area of EC transport policy were modest. By 1969, a procedure for consultation on national transport policies had been set up and some limited measures had been introduced concerning rationalizing railway operations and allocating infrastructure costs.

Ilbery (1986: 92) suggests that one difficulty in making progress related to the rapidly changing relative importances of the various transport modes within the EC at this time. The implementation of a common transport policy was complicated also by the accession to the Community in 1973 of the United Kingdom, Ireland, and Denmark: now the EC comprised more members from whom agreement had to be obtained on any issue, and included two islands which increased the need for policies to deal with sea transport. Gwilliam (1989: 3) suggests that the accession of the UK to the Community increased the emphasis in Community transport policy on deregulation rather than harmonization: the UK road-freight haulage industry had been deregulated prior to EC entry, while long-distance road passenger services in Great Britain were liberalized significantly in 1980.

Early EC transport policy laid little emphasis on the theme of infrastructure provision. Rather, individual governments pursued their own national plans, sometimes with the help of loans from the European Investment Bank which had been set up in 1958 to give assistance, especially to projects of common interest to several member countries, such as the construction or improvement of international transport links. In 1965, the Commission recommended that various key links be added to the European motorway network. A final programme was agreed in 1967 but little progress was made. A further attempt, in 1973, to draw up an optimal transport network in accordance with an agreed master plan also made little headway. The accession to the Community in 1981 of Greece, which is separated from the other members by non-member countries, called for yet more transport policy initiatives.

In summary, while the overall thrust and direction of EC transport policy was clear from an early date, little significant progress was made throughout the 1970s in respect of implementation. Blacksell (1977: 172) concluded that 'transportation remains the preserve of national governments and private enterprise'. Eventually, concern with the relative lack of progress at EC level was such that the European Parliament took the Council of Ministers to the European Court of Justice and, in 1985, the Court found against the Council.

Transport trends and policy: The case of Ireland

Roads and road transport

The period since the formation of the EC has seen steady increases in car and freight-vehicle ownership levels, in traffic levels, and in the level of road investment in all the member countries. In 1976, there were 85 million cars in Europe, of which 71 million were in the EC. This was a 250 per cent increase over 1960 (Ilbery 1986: 86). Car-ownership levels vary considerably throughout the Community: in 1979, for example, there were 427 cars per thousand persons in Luxembourg, 262 cars per thousand persons in the UK, and 194 cars per thousand persons in the Republic of Ireland (Bamford and Robinson 1983: 173). It is estimated that travel by coach and car in the EC plus Switzerland, Austria, and Yugoslavia, grew from 1700 billion passenger-km in 1970 to 2800 billion passenger-km in 1986, an average increase of 3.2 per cent per annum. Over the same period, the length of the motorway network in the same area increased from 14 000 km to 33 000 km. In most instances, the pace of road improvements did not keep pace with traffic increases. It is estimated that traffic congestion now costs 2.6 per cent to 3.1 per cent of GDP in EC countries (Community of European Railways 1989: 7–8).

TABLE 5.1 *Private cars and freight vehicles in the Republic of Ireland and Northern Ireland, 1961 and 1991*

	Republic of Ireland		Northern Ireland	
	1961	1991	1961	1991
Private cars	186 302	836 583	135 273	498 471
Freight vehicles	43 838	148 331	n.a.	18 401

Note: n.a. = comparable figures not available.

Sources: Central Statistics Office (1962): *Statistical Abstract of Ireland* (Dublin) Table 327, 309, and Table XXXVI, 365. Central Statistics Office (1991), *Ireland Statistical Abstract* (Dublin), Table 12.4, 310, and Table XXX, 393.

While Ireland has traditionally had a low level of vehicle ownership by European standards, the period since World War II has been one of vigorous economic development which has led to dramatic increases in vehicle numbers (Table 5.1). This has caused ever-increasing traffic flows, especially within the larger urban centres and on the major roads joining them.

The Irish Republic and Northern Ireland are served by 115 800 km of road. The most important routes in the Republic are designated 'National Primary routes' (Fig. 5.1). They comprise 2.8 per cent of the total road length but were estimated to be carrying 26 per cent of all traffic in 1988. There are less than 15 km of motorway in the Irish Republic. The major routes in Northern Ireland are designated 'all-purpose trunk routes'. These are supplemented by 111 km of motorway (Fig. 5.1). The United Nations Economic Commission for Europe defined in 1975 a set of routes comprising a European road network of strategic importance. These routes are now known colloquially as 'Euroroutes'. The route from Larne Harbour via

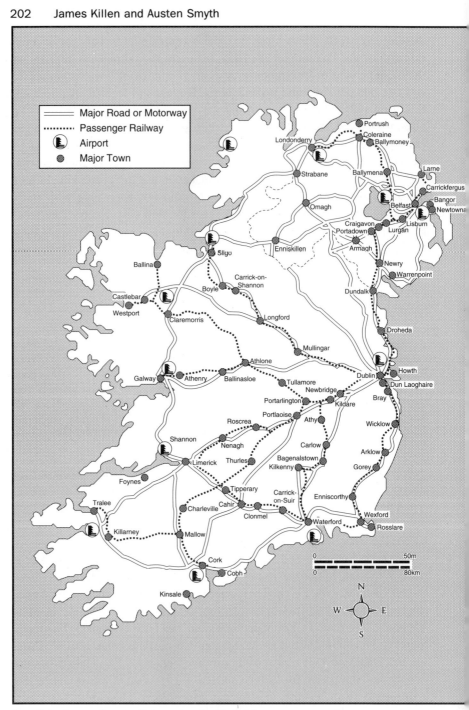

FIG. 5.1. The road and railway network of Ireland

Belfast and Dublin to Rosslare Harbour, together with those from Dublin to Limerick and Shannon Airport, and from Rosslare Harbour to Waterford and Cork, are included in this network.

In general, the quality of the road network in the Republic of Ireland is poorer than that of Northern Ireland. This reflects the fact that for a long period and relative to the length of the road network in each jurisdiction, less finance was provided for road maintenance and improvement in the Republic than in Northern Ireland (Confederation of Irish Industry 1985; Killen and Smyth 1989). Current government policy in the Republic calls for a significant increase in roads expenditure.

To date, the main impact of EC transport policy on roads and road transport has been in two main areas. First, a number of road-building projects have been supported through loans from the European Investment Bank and grants from the European Regional Development Fund. Second, the twin thrusts of EC transport policy towards harmonization and deregulation have brought about important changes, especially within the context of road-freight operations.

In both Northern Ireland and in the Irish Republic, it was decided in the 1930s that road-freight operations should be strictly controlled and operated as an adjunct to the railway. In the case of Northern Ireland, the Northern Ireland Road Transport Board was set up in 1935 and was empowered to take over the various commercial hauliers who were operating at that time. In the Republic, legislation passed in 1932 required road-freight operators to hold a licence in respect of each vehicle operated. Licences (which could be transferred to new vehicles) were issued in respect of each vehicle operating at that time, but no further licences were issued. The railway company, which was effectively exempt from licensing regulations, was empowered to buy out the private operators and was expected to operate its own road-freight business as an adjunct to the railway. By 1969, the railway company in the Republic was operating 1082 road-freight vehicles while the remaining 1094 vehicles available for hire were shared between a large number of operators, the majority of whom had only one or two vehicles (Barrett 1982: 140).

The restrictions placed on the road-freight industry in Northern Ireland and in the Republic did not have the desired effect of supporting the railway. Rather, in the absence of a viable road-freight industry to which they could turn, many of those requiring freight haulage purchased their own vehicles in which to transport their own goods. By 1964, 82.9 per cent of all road freight in the Irish Republic was moving in own-account vehicles as compared to only 43 per cent in Great Britain, where the same restrictions did not apply (Barrett 1982: 141).

From an EC perspective, the foregoing regulations ran counter to the objectives of Community transport policy. In the case of Northern Ireland, the road-freight industry was liberalized in July 1966, after which commercial hauliers could enter the road-freight market provided they could meet criteria relating to such matters as safety. This meant that a number of relatively large and efficient operators were able to emerge there in advance of accession to the EC and to meet the challenge of an expanding market. In the case of the Republic, liberalization of the road-freight sector proceeded more slowly, with full liberalization not being achieved until 1988.

As stated previously, one aim of EC transport policy is to encourage competition and efficiency by ensuring that transport operators compete on equal terms. A comparison of road-freight operations in Northern Ireland and the Republic in 1987 found that operating costs were approximately 16 per cent higher in the Republic as a result of higher vehicle-excise duties, tyre prices, fuel prices, and employers' liability insurance rates (Chartered Institute of Transport in Ireland 1987). It was claimed that the Republic's operators would not be able to compete successfully in the manner intended by the EC until these market distortions were removed. Yet, more recent results (Barrett 1990: 115) suggest that the differential in operating costs has actually increased. This, potentially, has serious implications for the Republic. By the end of 1992, it is intended that the European road-freight market shall be liberalized completely with carriers from one EC country being permitted to carry freight between and within other EC countries.

The Railway

Ireland was provided originally with a very extensive railway network with lines (some narrow gauge) being built in even the remotest parts of the country, often in the belief that the railway would bring prosperity to them. In virtually all instances, this did not prove to be the case. By the mid-1960s, many routes had been closed, including all but one of those crossing the international boundary. Eighty-six per cent of the current railway network is open to passenger traffic (Fig. 5.1). Freight services are available between certain centres in the Republic of Ireland, and from the Republic of Ireland to Belfast and Londonderry. Freight services are not available internally within Northern Ireland.

The major problem which has beset the railway in both the Irish Republic and Northern Ireland has been large recurrent financial losses. Thus the railway in the two jurisdictions has had to rely for many years on grants from government. The main reason for the particularly dramatic shrinkage of the Northern Ireland network in the 1950s and 1960s was that the government at that time was not prepared to give financial support to the relatively extensive railway network; rather, road development was seen as a more effective catalyst for economic progress.

The main area in which EC transport policy has had an impact on the railway has been in respect of the annual subventions by national governments. With a view to seeing that the railways in the various member countries are dealt with in the same manner by their respective governments, the EC in 1969 and 1970 laid down the conditions under which member states can support railway operations: grants may be paid only in order to support passenger services which are loss-making but are deemed to be socially necessary, to enable railway companies to meet employment and pension obligations and to countervail undercharging for infrastructure by other modes. Gwilliam (1989: 9) remarks that, in some cases, these regulations 'were merely used to legitimise the deficits that arose from essentially unconstrained government rail-financing policies'. In the case of the Irish Republic, the railway and associated road-freight business of Iarnrod Eireann showed a profit of £IR3.131 million in 1989, having received state grants under EC regulations of £IR75.4 million, together with a further grant of £IR11.3 million in connection with the Dublin Area Rapid Transit scheme. In Northern Ireland, Northern Ireland Railways showed a profit in 1990–1 of £0.4 million having received grants under EC regulations of £7.3 million.

A development which the EC would like to see in respect of rail transport is the separation of operating costs from infrastructure costs. The view is that railway companies might be responsible ultimately for providing railway services while a government-based authority would be responsible for maintaining the right of way and other elements of infrastructure. The railway company would pay for the use of this right of way and infrastructure, just as road users pay road tax for using the roads infrastructure. While the EC Council of Ministers has accepted the validity of this approach in principle, little has been achieved to date in the area of implementation.

A matter of European-wide interest has been the possibility of developing a high-speed railway network to serve the EC as a whole. Such a scheme would obviously be of limited relevance in Ireland which is physically separated from Great Britain and the European mainland. Nevertheless, a proposal from the Community of European Railways (Community of European Railways 1989) for such a network (Fig. 5.2) includes the route from Belfast to Cork via Dublin. Furthermore, a working party of the Commission of the European Communities has identified the link from Belfast to Dublin (in conjunction with the sea route to Holyhead and the railway route onwards to Crewe) as being one of fourteen key railway routes

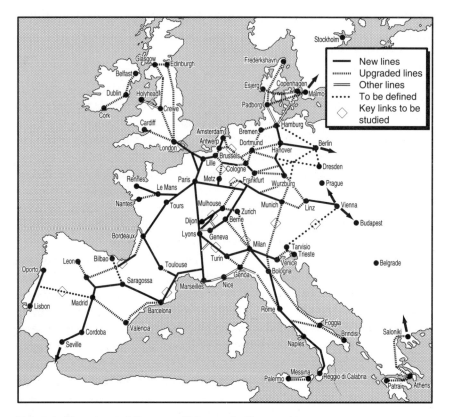

FIG. 5.2. The proposed European high-speed rail network

Source: Based on data from Commission of the European Communities (1991*a*).

in the Community which should be developed as part of such a high-speed network (Commission of the European Communities 1991*c*).

The long-term future of the Irish railway system rests ultimately upon its ability to attract traffic in competition with the other modes and, perhaps more importantly, upon continued political support. The increasing liberalization of the road-freight sector, referred to previously, is likely to place increasing pressure on the railway whose freight carryings in the Republic have remained more or less constant in recent times. The development of long-distance coach services is now providing greater competition in the passenger market. In the Irish Republic, a complete liberalization of the coach industry has been promised which, when complete, will bring increasing pressure to bear on the railway. In Northern Ireland, the underlying problems of political instability have reduced the likelihood of liberalization of the bus industry there, despite the accepted wisdom of such a policy in the remainder of the UK.

Sea transport

An island location means that sea transport and its associated infrastructure is of particular importance to both the Republic and Northern Ireland. In the past, a wide variety of routes was available between Ireland and the United Kingdom, many of these being operated by the railway companies or their subsidiaries. Three main route corridors can be defined: the northern corridor based on Belfast and Larne, the central corridor based on Dublin and Dun Laoghaire and, finally, the southern corridor based on Rosslare and Cork (Fig. 5.1). The passenger-ferry routes (Table 5.2) are supplemented by a number of other routes which are operated for freight traffic alone, either roll-on roll-off (ro-ro) or lift-on lift-off (lo-lo).

In the case of the UK routes, there is considerable competition between the various corridors for traffic. At present, up to 25 per cent of Larne's freight throughflow originates in or is destined for the Irish Republic. Despite the fact that Cairnryan and Stranraer are less centrally located relative to the main UK markets than Holyhead, passage via Larne is often cheaper and more convenient due to lower port charges and ferry fares and a greater service frequency. The fact that goods are cleared through customs at the land boundary between the Republic and Northern Ireland, rather than at the port of arrival, is also considered to be an advantage. It was estimated recently that £IR56 million per annum is being lost to the Republic's economy as a result of freight to and from the Irish Republic being routed via Northern Ireland (Dublin Chamber of Commerce 1990: 14).

TABLE 5.2 *Passenger-ferry services outward from Ireland, April 1992*

	Journey time		Number of sailings
	hrs.	mins.	
United Kingdom routes			
Larne–Cairnryan or Stranraer	2	15	9–13 per day
Dublin or Dun Laoghaire–Holyhead	3	30	5 per day
Rosslare–Fishguard or Pembroke	3	30	
	or 4	15	3–4 per day
Cork–Swansea	10	0	3 per week
European routes			
Rosslare–Le Havre or Cherbourg	17–21	0	3 per week
Cork–Roscoff	14	0	1 per week

Source: Thomas Cook European Timetable (Apr. 1992).

The current role of Larne *vis-à-vis* freight to and from the Irish Republic may alter (General Consumer Council for Northern Ireland 1991). The Republic's government is anxious to encourage the development of a high-frequency low-cost ferry route to the UK via the central corridor. The A55–A5 route serving Holyhead has been upgraded at a cost of £500 million and it would appear that, in the long term, British Rail's freight organization intends to develop this corridor as its primary freight route to serve Ireland as a whole. The identification of the Belfast–Dublin–Holyhead–Crewe railway route as one of fourteen key EC railway routes requiring development is also significant in this regard.

It might be thought that, at EC level, the development of policies to deal with sea transport would have been a priority. Yet, this has not been the case, partly because devising policies did not become important until the accession of two island nations to the Community in 1973. The first moves towards a common shipping policy were not made until 1986 when regulations were introduced to deal with competition in the provision of shipping services within the Community, and between member states and non-Community countries. As in the case of road-freight transport, the overall thrust of these regulations is towards harmonization and deregulation (Council of the European Communities 1989: 3–4).

Murphy (1988), in a discussion of the Irish Shipping Line operation between the Republic and Europe, sets out some of the ways in which governments and shipping companies can and have distorted competition. In the case of governments, these include the granting of subsidies by the state to national shipping lines, such as has occurred in the case of the B. and I. shipping line in the Irish Republic, and the granting of subsidies to national shipbuilders for ships being constructed for national carriers. In the case of the shipping companies, measures which distort competition include the dumping of excess shipping on to other routes, as may happen in the case of the routes to Ireland with the opening of the Channel Tunnel, distortions which arise through the control of ports by shipping companies which could debar competitors (as at Holyhead, Fishguard, and Stranraer traditionally), and the cross-subsidization of fares. In the latter context, it is of interest to note that, in 1988, certain fares from Ireland to Europe via Great Britain were set at a lower level than those for the Great Britain to Europe segment only, presumably in an effort to remove traffic from the direct ferries from the Republic to France. It can be expected that EC sea-transport policy, as it evolves, will address these types of issue.

A further point of concern to the EC, within the context of shipping policy, has been the 45 per cent employment decline in the EC shipping fleet, in the period 1980 to 1986 (Commission of the European Communities 1989*b*: 4). This was due mainly to non-EC companies subsidizing their fleets and to the use of flags of convenience offering a more favourable tax treatment, less-strict operating conditions, and lower labour costs. The Community hopes to take a number of measures to counter this decline, such as the creation of a Community flag and the setting of regulations, for example, concerning the employment of non-Community nationals on EC vessels.

Air transport

Until the 1980s, air travel in Europe operated under guidelines set out in the Chicago Convention (1944). This declared that each state has sovereignty over its own airspace and provided for states to reach bilateral agreements concerning the provision of air services between them. In Europe, most countries developed their own air-transport companies. In the Irish Republic, Aer Lingus commenced operations to Great Britain in 1936 and began services to Europe after World War II. Northern Ireland was served from Great Britain by British European Airways, later British Airways. Thus the status of Dublin and Belfast, the major airports in each jurisdiction, was and is different: Dublin is the headquarters of a national airline and at the centre of its route network whereas Belfast is in effect a regional centre whose route network focuses on London. In June 1980 for example, Dublin was linked by through flights with two centres in the Irish Republic, sixteen centres in the UK, fifteen centres in continental Europe, and three centres in North America, while Belfast only enjoyed through services to one centre in the Irish Republic, sixteen centres in the UK, two centres in continental Europe, and none in North America.

The amount of air travel into and out of Ireland has grown steadily since World War II and especially in the last twenty years. For example, the number of air passengers to and from Northern Ireland went up from 1.37 million in 1979 to 2.71 million in 1989. A major relative loser in this process has been the sea-ferry services, which are carrying a declining number of those passengers travelling without a car: passenger travel by sea to and from Northern Ireland increased from 1.56 million in 1979 to only 1.76 million in 1989. Over the same period, the passenger market share held by sea transport fell from 67 per cent to 39 per cent (General Consumer Council for Northern Ireland 1991: 7).

Hull *et al.* (1988: 212) point out that air travel in Europe does not have the same relative importance as in North America for three main reasons: the fact that the bulk of Europe's population lives in a relatively restricted area; the fact that international boundaries have tended to restrict longer-distance travel over which the air mode is most competitive; and the fact that, as a result of the highly regulated operating environment, fares have traditionally been high. Barrett (1987: Table 1, p. 2) in a comparison of one-way fares charged in Europe and the United States in June 1986 on nineteen routes and eight journey lengths found that, on average, the European fares were three times higher than their United States counterparts.

The European regulatory environment discussed above obviously ran counter to the basic philosophy underlying EC transport policy. Yet, and in part due to the vested interests of some individual governments in maintaining the *status quo*, progress in the directions of harmonization and, more particularly, deregulation has been slow. In 1983, greater freedom in fare setting was allowed on passenger services between non-major airports using small aircraft. The so-called Luxembourg Agreement (for a full summary, see Mullan 1988: 20–2), which became effective in January 1988, allows international carriers (subject to certain restrictions concerning airports used, fares, and passenger numbers carried) to pick up passengers at an intermediate stop in another Community country. Thus, in April 1992, Aer Lingus was operating services from Dublin to Amsterdam, Copenhagen, Paris, and Zurich via Manchester. The Luxembourg package also relaxed certain restrictions on the share of traffic to which a national airline is entitled on a route to and from its home country, on fare setting, and on the conditions under which new competitors can enter the market. Brown and Sorenson (1989) report that, between 1987 and 1989, 127 new European air routes were introduced of which thirteen did not survive; in part these developments reflect the impact of the Luxembourg package although they also reflect the generally favourable conditions for air transport prevailing through this period: increasing traffic volumes, declining aviation fuel costs, and increases in productivity and efficiency.

The overall aim of EC air-transport policy is to achieve full deregulation of air-passenger services and air-freight services (in respect of which no measures have been introduced as yet) by 1993. Given the experience of the United States, where airline services were fully deregulated in 1978, there are likely to be winners and losers in this process. Certainly, deregulation poses the greatest challenge to the smaller airlines. Graham (1990) details the impact of deregulation on domestic air services operating to and from Northern Ireland. A foretaste of what may be in store at a European level is perhaps given by recent experiences on the route between London and Dublin, following the introduction of a revised and extremely liberal bilateral agreement in respect of flights between the UK and the Republic of Ireland. This allows two carriers on all routes and multiple carriers on the busier routes, for example, Dublin to London. Any route may be operated. No capacity restrictions are imposed and the airlines may set any fare except where both governments disapprove. For a long period, Aer Lingus and British Airways operated the Dublin to London route jointly. Then, in May 1986, Ryanair, a low-cost operator, commenced services between Dublin and London (Luton), which had the immediate effect of causing the pre-existing carriers to lower their fares. Later, Virgin Airlines (subsequently replaced by Capital Airlines) and British Midland commenced operations but, more recently, British Airways and Capital have ceased operating to Dublin, the latter having ceased trading. Thus, there are now three operators providing service between the two cities, as was the case in 1986.

A feature of air-transport operations in recent times, and one in which Ireland has participated, has been the development of services from smaller airports (Horner 1991). In 1983, three airports in the Republic had regular scheduled air services: Dublin, Cork, and Shannon. Services now operate from six additional regional airports (Fig. 5.1). In Northern Ireland, the growth of Belfast City Airport is particularly notable: in its year of opening, 1983, 85 000 passengers were handled. By 1990, this had increased to 555 000. In June 1991, the airport was offering direct services to fifteen UK destinations and was being served by four airlines. The need for more direct air links between Belfast and the European mainland has been highlighted (e.g. Smyth 1989: 14) and it may be that the increasing use of small aircraft, coupled with deregulation, will permit developments in this regard.

The Single European Act

The development and implementation of EC transport policy since 1986 has gained considerable momentum as a result of the ratification of the Single European Act (SEA), which became effective in July 1987. The aim of the Act is to facilitate the free movement of capital, persons, goods, and services throughout the Community by the end of 1992, thereby creating a single internal market. When the Act is fully operative, fiscal frontiers will disappear, customs control at national boundaries will be eliminated, and Value Added Tax rates and excise duties will be harmonized. The intention is that the Act will stimulate economic growth while also increasing the social and economic cohesion of the Community. The existence of efficient transport networks, operating in accordance with the principles underlying EC transport policy, is seen as a necessary prerequisite to the successful completion of the internal market.

From the point of view of Irish transport operations, it seems that not all of the impacts of the SEA will be favourable. At present, transport is zero rated for VAT purposes in the Republic of Ireland and in the UK. With the harmonization of VAT rates, the imposition of a rate of between 4 per cent and 9 per cent on transport charges is likely. The airlines are currently lobbying for an exemption in respect of this imposition, at least for trips to destinations outside the Community. Smyth (1989: 6) suggests that when loss of patronage due to the fare increase is taken into account, fares will have to rise by between 10 per cent and 15 per cent in order to preserve earnings. A further probable consequence of the implementation of the SEA will be the abolition of duty-free sales to international travellers undertaking journeys within the Community which will affect the income of certain carriers and airports (Hampson 1988: 99–100).

EC regional-development policy

A stated aim of the SEA is to assist in achieving convergence between the economic and social conditions prevailing in the richer, generally centrally located member states, and the poorer member states, generally located on the periphery. Prior to the signing of the Act, the latter nations argued that this process could be facilitated only through a series of special measures designed to assist them in raising the standard of their infrastructure to a level where they could compete successfully within the single market. Accordingly, it was agreed in 1988 that the level of the European Regional Development Fund (ERDF) and other EC funds used for grant-aiding so-called qualifying regions should be doubled in real terms between 1987 and 1993. These regions include those with a per capita income of less than 75 per cent of the Community average (Objective 1). All of the Republic of Ireland qualifies under this objective. Although it does not meet the per capita income criterion, Northern Ireland has also been included as a qualifying region for 'special' reasons.

Member states with regions qualifying for aid were invited to bring forward and ultimately to agree with the Commission a number of operational programmes for these regions. The operational programmes relate to a number of key areas including transport.

The operational programmes for transport: Northern Ireland and the Irish Republic

The operational programmes for transport for Northern Ireland (Department of the Environment Northern Ireland 1989) and for the Irish Republic (Government of Ireland and Commission of the European Communities

TABLE 5.3 *Operational programmes for transport for Northern Ireland, and the Republic of Ireland: Summary of proposals*

Sector	Main proposals	% of total planned expenditure
Northern Ireland		
Ports	Developments at Belfast, Larne, Londonderry and Warrenpoint	45
Airports	Developments at Belfast International; new terminal buildings at Belfast City and Londonderry	26.6
Railways	Construction of Belfast cross-town link; upgrading of Belfast–Republic of Ireland route; feasibility study of establishment of rail links, to the ports of Belfast, Larne, and Londonderry	17.5
Roads	Certain bypasses and other improvements	10.9
TOTAL PLANNED EXPENDITURE: 211 million ECUs (1989 prices)		
Republic of Ireland		
Ports	Developments at Dublin (ro-ro and lo-lo); Rosslare (ro-ro), Waterford (lo-lo), and Cork (bulk traffic); improvements at Drogheda, Dundalk, Foynes, Galway, and Kinsale	8.2
Airports	Passenger terminal extension at Dublin; Developments at other major and regional, airports	11.5
Railways	Extension of railway to serve additional areas in Dublin port; developments to increase freight carryings by 25 per cent; introduction of commuter service to the west Dublin suburbs	4.4
Roads	Major road building programme; bridge strengthening to allow maximum, vehicle weight of 40 tonnes	75.2
TOTAL PLANNED EXPENDITURE: 1064 million ECUs (1990 prices)		

Sources: Department of the Environment, Northern Ireland (1989); and Government of Ireland and Commission of the European Communities (1990).

1990) were agreed in December 1989 and August 1990 respectively. The total costs are 211 million ECUs (1989 prices) and 1064 million ECUs (1990 prices), respectively, with almost two-thirds of the funding coming from EC sources in each case. The programmes indicate how each administration in

Ireland believes transport infrastructure must be developed in order to meet successfully the conditions which will prevail after completion of the internal market (Table 5.3).

The major differences of emphasis between the operational plans for the Republic and Northern Ireland are highlighted in a comparison of the percentages of total investment it is planned to allocate to each transport mode. The plan for the Republic calls for a massive investment in the road network while that for Northern Ireland allocates more resources, in relative terms, to the railway. In part, this relates to pre-existing differences in the quality of transport infrastructure in the two jurisdictions: Northern Ireland has a higher-quality road network than the Republic while, conversely, the Republic has a more extensive railway network for both passenger traffic and freight traffic. The Northern Irish plan seems to be more optimistic about the future role of the railway: the plan for the Republic in justifying the balance of investment proposed for roads and public transport states that 'it is not expected that the railway will be in a position to substantially increase its market share in the freight or mainline rail passenger markets' (Government of Ireland and Commission of the European Communities 1990: 111). While the Northern Ireland programme provided for investment in the rail link to the Irish Republic, no such investment was contained in the Republic's programme. This was clearly unsatisfactory (Smyth 1991: 15) in view of the strategic importance which has been attached to this link (Commission of the European Communities 1991c; Community of European Railways 1989) and it has now been resolved: it was announced in April 1992 that c.100 million ECUs are to be invested in the Belfast to Dublin railway route over the next five years.

Conclusions

The introduction of a common transport policy was a fundamental principle enshrined in the original Treaty of Rome. Progress with that policy was modest up to the mid-1980s. Since then, the prospect of a single European market and the associated transport-infrastructure expenditure programmes have provided a stimulus for much greater progress although, to date, the extent of this progress has varied both between member states and between the various transport modes. In at least some instances, the reticent stance which has been adopted on the part of some EC members to certain initiatives has reflected an unwillingness to accept an increasing role for the EC in transport-planning and transport-investment decisions.

The prospect of the single market has acted already as a catalyst for various transport investments within the EC, for example, elements of the proposed European high-speed railway network, the Channel Tunnel, and the TGV Nord. As with most such projects, these are extremely expensive schemes which can only be justified financially by the existence of large markets. Such markets exist only in the core areas of the Community. As far as the poorer, peripheral areas are concerned, implementation of such projects in the core is actually increasing their disadvantage relative to core regions in accessibility terms. The provision of enlarged structural funds for infrastructure investment is intended to address this increasing relative disadvantage.

The question which must be asked is whether implementation of the operational programmes will indeed ameliorate the locational disadvantages of the poorer, peripheral regions and enable them to compete successfully within the single market. In seeking to answer this question, it is important to emphasize that these programmes represent just one element in the development of this market and that they do not encompass all of the financial assistance which will be distributed to the disadvantaged regions. They do reflect, at least in theory, the combined view of the Community and the relevant national governments of the challenges which these regions face and the manner in which these challenges should be overcome.

The Cecchini Report (Cecchini 1988) forecasts that the aggregate net benefits arising from the creation of the single European market will be approximately 200 billion ECUs, that is an average of 625 ECUs per person. If Ireland was to receive benefits at the latter rate, these would amount to approximately 3 billion ECUs. While it is not possible to reach a definitive conclusion at this stage, the likelihood is that benefits of this magnitude will not accrue; indeed, the island may ultimately be a net loser. Begg (1989: 373) comments that 'it is probable that the losses suffered by the less-favoured regions will be many times greater than the available structural fund support', and that '. . . completion of the internal market could, perversely, result in the transfer of resources *out* of regions most in need of income support'. Improvements in transport and other infrastructure 'may simply make a disadvantaged area *more* accessible to import penetration, while doing nothing to improve its underlying competitiveness'.

In overall terms, some are pessimistic about the net long-term outlook for the peripheral regions of the EC relative to the core, despite the anticipated positive effects of implementing the operational programmes. Yet, from the point of view of these regions, none can afford not to improve its links with the core regions because to do so would only increase yet further its disadvantage in accessibility terms.

A feature of EC transport–investment programmes is that these programmes are undertaken at national or sub-national level. This militates against co-ordinated planning along complete transportation corridors which often transcend administrative boundaries. The divergence in the transport policies and operational programmes for the Republic and Northern Ireland and the inconsistencies in the treatment of, for example, the Dublin to Belfast railway link is a case in point. The fact that the Republic of Ireland is an independent political entity while Northern Ireland is part of a much larger EC state, the United Kingdom, with its own transport interests, reinforces in particular the difference in the availability of international links emanating from the two jurisdictions with the Republic enjoying, for instance, a substantially greater range of direct international air services.

What is largely missing at present, despite the increasing role of the Community, in transport matters, is the presence of truly co-ordinated strategic transport planning across the Community's internal borders. Even where the EC does take on a proactive role, e.g. through the disbursement of structural funds, its effectiveness in achieving action on the ground is being constrained by such matters as variations in investment appraisal procedures and policies at national level.

A major implication of the foregoing is that politics and, in particular, a political will to succeed will have a key role to play in determining the success or otherwise of EC transport policy and planning initiatives in the future. The further harmonization of legislation and market conditions which will arise with the creation of the single market together with new pressures which are arising from outside the Community, e.g. those caused by the need to build new links with Eastern Europe, could well boost the fortunes of truly European transport policies and projects in the future.

Further reading

While aspects of transport are discussed in many geography books and articles, the number of works devoted specifically to the geography of transport is relatively low. An important recent publication is B. S. Hoyle and R. D. Knowles, (eds.) (1992), *Modern Transport Geography* (London) which contains chapters on all the major transport modes and the environments in which they operate. Another work of general interest is W. Owen (1987), *Transportation and World Development* (London). A recent review of urban transport trends and problems is contained in S. Hanson (ed.) (1986), *The Geography of Urban Transportation* (New York), while the classic work on rural transport is M. J. Moseley (1979), *Accessibility: The Rural Challenge* (London). A recent work which discusses transport deregulation and related topics is P. Bell and P. Cloke (eds.) (1990), *Deregulation and Transport: Market Forces in the Modern World* (London). Those seeking further information concerning the current regulatory environment for European air services should consult F. de Coninck (1992), *European Air Law: New Skies for Europe* (Paris). Transport operations are constantly changing as a result of evolving technologies, operating practices, and regulations, and a number of periodicals aim to keep their readers abreast of these changes, for example, *Modern Railways* (published monthly) and *ITA Press*, the semi-monthly newsletter of the Institute of Air Transport in Paris.

With regard to the specific case of Ireland, the publication R. King (ed.) (1993), 'Ireland and the Single Market', *Geographical Society of Ireland Special Publication*, 8 (Dublin), has appeared since this chapter was written and gives an excellent insight into the impact of EC policies (including transport policies) on Ireland. In addition the government of the Republic of Ireland has set out in the publication (1993) *Employment through Enterprise* (Dublin) its current intentions concerning industrial and development policy. Support for EC transport policies is reaffirmed strongly and major investment in the main-line railway system, with the assistance of EC funds, is anticipated.

6 Migration and the Single Market for Labour: An Issue in Regional Development

Russell King

Introduction

Since the end of World War II, and especially since the late 1950s, international migration has made a major contribution to the changing economic and social geography of Europe. Labour migrants—people who move with the express purpose of finding employment or a better job—have been an important element in the growth of the European industrial and post-industrial economies during the 1960s and the first part of the 1970s. Although their numbers, in terms of new arrivals, slackened off after the first oil crisis 1973–4, family members continued to pour in and these, together with new waves of immigrants arriving in the late 1980s and early 1990s, lead experts to estimate a total immigrant population in Europe today of around 20 million, a majority of whom are found in EC countries.[1]

After a decade or so when international migration was sidelined as a major European political issue, recently the migration debate has received fresh attention right across Europe. Labour migration flows started gathering pace again during the late 1980s, commencing in some countries (West Germany, the Netherlands) as early as 1985. But the really significant stimulus for the generation of new mass migration flows has been the collapse of socialism in Eastern Europe since 1989. The stunning events of recent years clearly demonstrate the need for caution in forecasting international migration trends: few people in 1988 could have predicted the dramatic events which have unfolded, even if the migratory trickles seeping through from East to West Germany and via Hungary were one of the triggers which set the whole process of change in motion.

If these events were not enough, the present time also sees other clouds

---

[1] Statistics on the number of migrants in Europe, indeed anywhere, are always likely to be approximate because of different countries' varying methods of defining and recording foreigners. Nationality and birthplace are the two most common criteria but they can yield completely different figures owing to the variable inclusion of second-generation children born to immigrant parents and of naturalized persons born abroad. Clandestine immigration—by definition unrecorded—is a further problem, notably in France, Italy, and Spain.

on the demographic horizon of Europe. All around the globe, millions are on the move, their journeys reshaping the world, including that of Europe. Numbers of refugees and asylum-seekers arriving in Europe have swelled dramatically during the 1980s and this issue now needs to be faced squarely at the level of both Community and national policy. At home a new demographic revolution is in the making—the transition to a shrinking and ageing population. The contours of this new demographic transition make striking reading. Europe's share of the world's population has halved since the nineteenth century. Today Europe contains 9 per cent of the world's people, a proportion which could fall to 5 per cent in the twenty-first century. Over the past 25 years—less than one generation—there has been a fall in fertility in most European countries from around 2.5–3 children per mother to only 1.3–1.8. In Spain the fall was from 2.5 to 1.3 in just one decade! The majority of European countries now have fertility levels amongst their native populations of below the replacement level of 2.1. Many demographers therefore forecast substantial fresh waves of immigrants in future decades. Given the high levels of both poverty and natural increase in the less-developed world, including countries such as Algeria and Egypt which are on Europe's doorstep, there will be no shortage of candidates for the next wave of immigration.

The limits are more likely to be social and political: the extent to which 'Fortress Europe' becomes a reality. If in the UK the repatriation speeches of Enoch Powell seem a distant echo from the past, the same message comes across loud and clear in recent political rhetoric in other European countries such as France, Germany, and Belgium. Neo-Nazism in Germany, the recent successes of the Flemish *Vlaams Blok* in the Belgian elections of November 1991, and the dangerously charismatic appeal of the French *Front National* leader Jean-Marie Le Pen are just three examples of the enlarging support in Europe for the Extreme Right and its political exploitation of the immigration issue. Moreover, recent Eurobarometer opinion polls carried out for the European Community have revealed widespread unease about the number and rights of immigrants in EC countries.[2] Too often, it seems, immigrants are regarded as a 'problem', whereas in reality they are scapegoats for the failure to resolve more deep-seated social problems.

---

[2] See the recent Eurobarometer polls on *Racism, Xenophobia and Intolerance*, Brussels 1989 and 1991. The 1991 survey indicated that half of the Europeans interviewed thought that there were too many foreigners living in their country, with figures ranging from 63 per cent in Italy, 54–6 per cent in UK, France, Germany and Belgium, to 25 per cent in Spain, 18 per cent in Portugal, and 12 per cent in Ireland. These figures represent significant increases over those recorded in earlier polls.

Immigration, economic structure and Community policy: Two cycles

Having established the general context of immigration, this chapter will present a broadly chronological account of the evolving patterns of labour migration in Europe since the 1950s. This evolution has taken place in the form of two main cycles, each lasting 15–20 years and each corresponding to a different set of economic structures and political and administrative policies.

The first cycle started soon after the end of the war in some countries (France, Belgium, UK) but really took shape during the 15 years or so between the late 1950s and 1973–4. This period saw the industrialized countries of Western Europe draw in millions of migrant workers to staff their factories, and their construction sites, and perform low-grade manual work in the service sector such as office cleaning and refuse collecting. Initially these immigrant workers—called *Gastarbeiter* ('guestworkers') in the German language—were only expected to stay temporarily, but reality proved very different leading to a subsequent phase of family-reunion migration and to a long-lasting impact on the social geography of many large and industrial cities. The institutional contexts of this first migration phase lay in the ex-colonial links which brought migrants from the Caribbean, West Africa, and Southern Asia to France, the UK, and the Netherlands; in the Common Market's Free Movement of Labour provisions for intra-EC mobility; and in a large number of bilateral labour-recruitment agreements with (then) non-EC countries such as Spain, Portugal, Greece, and Turkey. The economic context of this mass migration was rooted in the demand for cheap labour for heavy industries and unattractive service jobs. It was particularly linked to the expansion of large factory complexes, such as car plants, operated on 'Fordist' principles of mass production, integrated flow-line or conveyor-belt methods, and repetitive, low-skill operations for workers on the shop-floor.

The structural circumstances surrounding the second cycle of mass migration are less easy to identify since they are still in the process of unfolding. One key change has been the process of economic restructuring which has shifted the European economy from an industrial to a post-industrial stage and from Fordist to post-Fordist methods of organization based on a higher technological content, more flexible production systems, and the development of a whole range of advanced producer services. This economic restructuring is tending to polarize immigrant labour demand into highly skilled professional and technical personnel on the one hand, and the lowest grades of jobs (building workers, street cleaners, etc.) on the other.

The institutional context of the new phase of European migration is provided by the transition to the Single Market, but in recent years this has been overtaken by more immediate movements from outside the EC such as asylum-seekers, growing numbers of workers from the reforming countries of Eastern Europe and the former Soviet Union, and clandestine migrants from the southern Mediterranean countries and the Third World.

Evolution of the post-war European labour-migration system

Labour migration into the industrial countries of north-west Europe between the 1950s and 1970s is, quite simply, one of the contemporary world's most remarkable and large-scale human phenomena. The framework and details of this post-war migration have been thoroughly described by a number of geographers (e.g. King 1976; Salt and Clout (eds.) 1976). Since the story is so well known, this account will be brief.

The key factor in the evolution of the system was labour demand. This pull factor from the 'host' countries was quite specific since official agencies were set up by the countries of labour shortage to attract foreign workers to plug labour-market gaps. Thus in the early post-war years London Transport recruited from the West Indies and in 1951 the London Brick Company hired workers direct from southern Italy. In continental Europe the earliest bilateral agreements dated from the mid-1950s; they involved France and Greece, and the Netherlands and Spain. During 1960–72 approximately 30 recruitment agreements were signed between France, West Germany, and the Benelux countries on the one hand, and southern Europe (Portugal, Spain, Greece, Yugoslavia, Turkey), the Maghreb states, and francophone West Africa on the other (Salt 1976: 98–100). The push factor for this phase of labour migration was equally clear: the failure of economic development to keep up with demographic growth with the result that increasing numbers of young adults were unable to find work in the still predominantly stagnant peasant economies of their own countries.

The spatial pattern of flows as they developed over the period between the 1950s and 1973–4 depended on a number of factors: geographical and cultural proximity (thus Portuguese and Spaniards migrated mainly to France); the existence of institutional channels such as the recruitment agreements mentioned above; and the more historic links to former colonial territories. Also important were the Free Movement of Labour rules which came in progressively during the 1960s, and allowed large numbers of Italians

(Italy was then the only Common Market country with a large emigration potential) to migrate freely to the other five EC states.[3]

The variable interplay of these factors in time and space produced a complex evolving geography of international migration. The earliest phase—the 1950s—involved mainly intra-EC moves with Italians migrating to industrial and mining areas in Belgium and France. Outside of the Community the Nordic Common Labour Market, set up in 1954, saw Finns emigrate mainly to Sweden, whilst Britain drew on its colonial territories in the Caribbean and on its traditional supplier of cheap labour, Ireland. The 1960s saw two important new trends: the rise of West Germany as the main destination for international labour movements coming into Europe, and the tendency for labour-demand countries to seek their supplies in an ever-widening arc. Thus West Germany, which had satisfied its foreign labour demands from former East Germany before the erection of the Berlin Wall in 1961, turned to Italy in the 1960s, to Yugoslavia in the early 1970s, and to Turkey thereafter (see Fig. 6.1). Outside the EC, the Irish continued to migrate to Britain during the 1960s whilst the West Indian flow, which peaked in 1961, was overtaken by migrants from India and Pakistan. Switzerland was also an important labour-importing country, especially from neighbouring Italy.

Some idea of the changing shape of the flows can be gained from Fig. 6.2 which compares the patterns for 1965 and 1972. Whilst the general periphery-to-core pattern remains constant, significant changes took place. Italy, the main supply country in 1965, no longer features in 1972, which was the first year that Italy became a net gainer of migrants; the Irish flow to Britain dried up (in fact there was a substantial return movement to Ireland during the 1970s); and the major flows into the industrial heartland of Europe were coming from further afield, notably North Africa and Turkey.

Perhaps the most important point to note in conclusion to this section is the comparative irrelevance of the 'free movement' ideology of the EC when set against the rapid augmentation of flows from outside the Community. At this time the power of labour demand amongst the Six (or, rather, five of them) was such that it drew into the labour-market system an increasingly far-flung ring of countries which eventually stretched from Turkey to the Ivory Coast.

---

[3] The Free Movement of Labour regulations were enshrined in Articles 48 and 49 of the Treaty of Rome, mainly on the initiative of Italy which saw them as a solution to its severe unemployment problems. The provisions for free movement came into force progressively between 1961 and 1968. By the latter date workers and their families were allowed to cross internal EC borders freely and were granted equal rights of residence and work (but not to vote). Provision was also made for transferability of social-security rights.

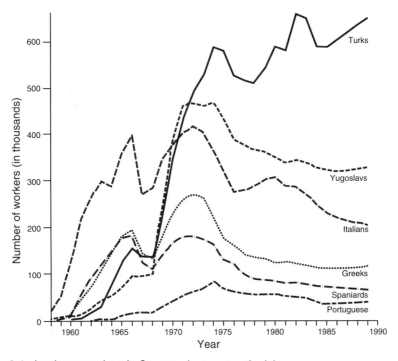

FIG. 6.1. Immigrant workers in Germany, by country of origin

Source: Based on OECD SOPEMI unpublished data.

The *Gastarbeiter* effect: Myths and realities

A very important aspect of the international labour flows into Western Europe in the 1950s and 1960s was that both the public authorities and the migrants themselves (but for different reasons) perceived the migrants' stays as temporary. The term *Gastarbeiter* encapsulates this temporariness by implying that the migrant workers were almost privileged to be guests in the host society. It took some time for the true nature of the guestworker phenomenon to emerge: namely that it involved capital dehumanizing an underprivileged 'reserve army' of labour.

In the beginning, it was assumed by the recruiting countries that the migrants' stay would be strictly short-term, to redress temporary labour shortages in certain key sectors of the labour market. Moreover, from 1950 to about 1970 it was more or less taken for granted that the transfer of labour from Mediterranean countries to the industrial economies of north-west Europe was beneficial to the areas of origin since they were all suffering from

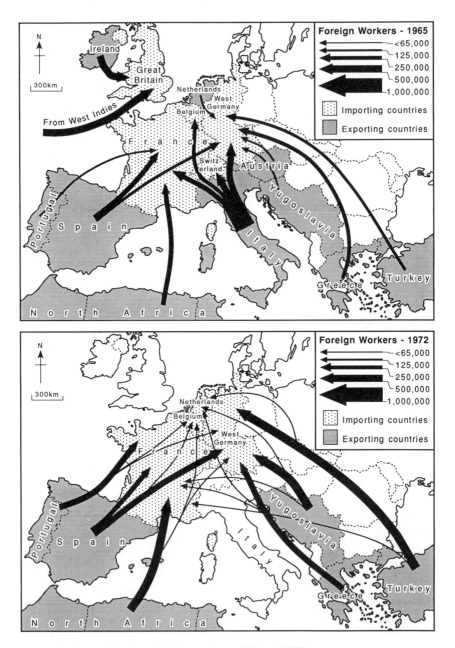

FIG. 6.2. The destination of foreign workers, 1965 and 1972

Source: Based on OECD SOPEMI unpublished data.

acute unemployment. The arch-priest of this view was Charles Kindleberger (1967) who argued that only with an elastic labour supply could fast industrial growth be achieved. The economic success of West Germany, using first migrants from the East and then Turkish *Gastarbeiter*, represented the paradigm of the Kindleberger thesis. Kindleberger also argued that the migrant labour system benefited the source areas through migrants' remitted income which provided valuable foreign exchange, with additional benefits accruing when returning migrants brought back newly acquired industrial skills and modern attitudes to the world of work. Thus emerged the view that the recruitment of migrant workers constituted a form of development aid to the Mediterranean countries of origin.

During the 1970s, however, an alternative interpretation emerged. Castles and Kosack (1973) and Piore (1979) argued that migrant labour of the *Gastarbeiter* type was fundamentally exploitative at the personal level and that, for the sending society, the economic and social costs outweighed the benefits. It was the sending society, not the receiving one, which bore the costs of reproducing (feeding, clothing, housing, educating) migrant labour. Since many of the migrants ended up by staying away for good, this investment in human capital was never recouped. The migrants who did return failed for the most part to exert any beneficial effect on the economic health or social structure of their regions of origin. Reversing the conclusion above, Castles and Kosack (1973: 8) claimed that emigration was 'a form of development aid given by poor countries to rich countries'.

It was the explicit intention of countries like Germany and Switzerland to use migrant labour as a shock absorber against cyclical economic fluctuations. This was the *Konjunkturpuffer* or 'buffer theory' approach (Salt 1985). For a time this approach worked: migrants were admitted only on short-term contracts, were not allowed to bring in dependants, and were housed in densely packed hostel accommodation. When the West German recession of 1966–7 struck, the open unemployment effects were cushioned by a backflow of migrant labour to the countries of origin (Kayser 1972). This effect is clearly visible in Fig. 6.1. By 1968, however, the German authorities were recruiting foreign labour faster than ever before and numbers climbed steeply, especially during the years 1969–72. Also by this time, the German government was following the French and Dutch in liberalizing the regulations on length of stay and immigration of family members. A significant change also took place in the attitudes of the migrants themselves: intending originally to migrate temporarily, they increasingly tended to prolong their stays. Several reasons lay behind this behavioural shift. The progressive extension of unemployment benefit and other social welfare rights made a big difference. Many migrants found that the cost of living in Europe was higher than they anticipated and thus their rate of savings was reduced, necessitating a longer stay. But perhaps the most important reason for staying was the realization of the pointlessness of a quick return to a rural peasant environment which still offered them so little in terms of material progress. And finally the migrants stayed because they made themselves indispensable. Far from being a temporary floating work-force, they had transformed themselves into a permanent structural feature of the labour market of post-industrial Europe, doing the jobs that no one else wanted to do (Böhning 1974).

From labour migration to family reunion

At the time of the so-called 'recruitment-stop' in 1973–4, the numbers of foreign workers employed in EC countries were as follows (the figures in brackets represent the migrants' percentage in the total labour-force): West Germany had 2.6 million (12 per cent), France 2.3 million (10 per cent), Belgium 200 000 (7 per cent), the Netherlands 80 000 (1 per cent), Luxembourg 33 000 (30 per cent), and Italy also 33 000 (but only 0.3 per cent). The UK, which joined the EC in 1973, had about 750 000, Switzerland had 600 000, and Sweden 220 000. It should be emphasized that these figures are approximate because of different ways of recording immigrants and the underestimation of clandestine migrant workers. The main national groups of immigrant workers in EC countries in January 1973 were from Italy (858 000), Spain (527 000), Portugal (469 000), Yugoslavia (535 000), Greece (332 000), Turkey (582 000), and North Africa (701 000). The main immigrant group in Britain at that time was the Irish (471 000).

The halt in labour recruitment by the European Community's receiving countries is commonly 'explained' by the economic crisis. White (1986) has shown that this is a grossly oversimplified interpretation, on two counts. First there were many other factors involved such as the rising social tension surrounding the immigration issue and the political significance of hardening public opinion against large-scale inflows of foreigners. Signs of 'migrant saturation' were already evident before the economic crisis struck. Even the economic arguments were not that clear-cut, for most countries resumed high rates of economic growth (but not of immigrant workers) in 1976. The second aspect of oversimplification was that immigrant labour was not completely blocked. Italians were still free to move, with the result that Italy resumed for a while its earlier role of prime supplier of migrant workers to EC countries. Other countries' worker-migrants also continued to enter, albeit in much smaller numbers. Total immigration flows fell even less, since the 1970s became the 'decade of family reunion' for migrants in Europe.

The EC experience shows how quickly temporary labour migration led to longer-term settlement, and eventually to the establishment of permanent ethnic communities (King 1990). A fundamental weakness of migration policy in the 1960s was to treat migrants as mechanical units of labour and not as human beings: hence the desire for family reunion was not spotted in time for appropriate plans to be formulated. The changing character of the migration flow had important economic implications. Single, fit labour migrants were distinctly profitable for the receiving economy, but when families arrived costs—of schooling, health services, etc.—rose (Salt 1989: 449). In most EC countries regulations favouring family reunion were already in place by 1973, but it was the restrictive legislation on worker migration which perhaps did most to actively encourage family migration. Many workers were reluctant to return home since they feared they would not be allowed back in if they wanted to re-emigrate; hence they brought their families into the EC instead.

Some idea of the changing character of the stocks and flows of migrants in the EC during this critical period can be gained from the following data, taken from SOPEMI Annual Reports.[4] Figures for the Netherlands are presented in Table 6.1 based on three representative years across the 1973–4 threshold. The table shows that worker migration from the Mediterranean countries (chiefly Morocco and Turkey) fell from more than four-fifths of the flow to just one-tenth, and the sex balance of the flow became normal with the onset of predominantly family migration after 1974. The French case is summed up in Fig. 6.3 which graphs the annual inflows of migrant

TABLE 6.1 *Immigration into the Netherlands, 1970–1981*

%	1970	1976	1981
Male	61.0	50.8	51.6
Economically active	53.3	30.6	27.2
Economically active amongst immigrants from Mediterranean	82.8	22.5	10.8
TOTAL IMMIGRANT INFLOW	90 829	82 853	80 183

Source: White (1986:70).

[4] The SOPEMI bureau, a monitoring unit for international migration trends, is part of the OECD Directorate of Social Affairs, Manpower and Education. SOPEMI distributes an annual mimeographed report which is a valuable source on the evolution of stocks and flows of migrants and their families in most West European countries (curiously Ireland is excluded). For further information on SOPEMI and on the quality of its data see Salt (1987).

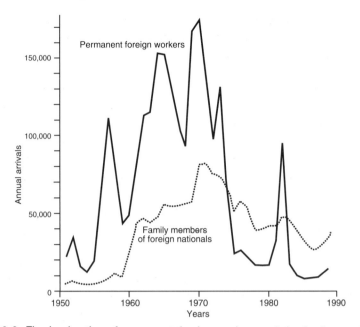

FIG. 6.3. The immigration of permanent foreign workers and the family members of foreign nationals into France

Source: Based on OECD SOPEMI unpublished data.

workers and family members for the period 1951–89. The sharp fall in worker immigration after 1973 is clear (the peak in 1982 was due to a 'regularization' of illegally present workers carried out in that year). Unlike some other countries, the French government tried to prevent the immigration of family members after 1973. This proved impossible to administer, with the result that family immigration remained at 30 000–50 000, well above worker immigration, throughout the late 1970s and 1980s, raising the total immigrant population in France to at least 4 million.[5]

Legacy of immigration in the social geography of Europe

In a chapter which is mainly concerned with the interaction between immigration, the labour market, and European integration, many of the

---

[5] French immigration statistics are a minefield because of clandestine migration, naturalization, 'regularizations' of illegal immigrants, the status of overseas French territories like Martinique and Guadeloupe, the numerous complications of Algeria, and the fact that the Census and the Ministry of the Interior issue significantly different figures. The 1982 Census recorded 3.68 million foreigners and 1.43 million 'French by naturalization' whereas the Interior Ministry gave 4.22 million. For attempts at clarification see George (1986); Ogden (1991).

social contexts of immigration have to be passed over. Here we will simply mention three issues: the impact of immigration on the social geography of European cities; the demographic significance of immigrants and their families; and some brief remarks on social structure.

Far from being a temporary phenomenon, labour migration has left a lasting legacy. At the human scale, the immigrants have literally changed the face of many European cities, and indeed of the European populations themselves. White (1984, 1993) has provided excellent overviews of the impact of foreign migrants on European urban populations, synthesizing a wealth of studies published in various languages ranging, for example, from the widely dispersed and nearly assimilated Irish in Great Britain to the highly concentrated and segregated Islamic Africans in Paris. In between, a whole variety of situations can be observed, depending, amongst other things, on the numerical size of the emigrant community, the length of time it has been established, its 'cultural distance' from the host society, and the housing policies of the receiving country. Generally the immigrant concentrations of the 1960s in German *Wohnheime* (factory hostels) and French *bidonvilles* (peripheral shanty-towns) are a thing of the past: now most immigrants and their families live in inner-city districts or in working-class suburbs near to the main industrial zones.

Inner-city migrant accommodation has been mainly in the privately rented sector, a fluid market where recently arrived immigrants move from one tenancy or sub-tenancy to another, often using pre-emigration kinship and friendship links to find improved facilities. However, in some cities, such as Amsterdam, gentrification of inner-city areas is squeezing immigrants into ever more restricted sectors of the housing market. It has taken immigrants some time to gain access to public housing: this has happened, for example, in France where the clearance of *bidonvilles* resulted in rehousing in peripheral, high-density housing projects (the *grands ensembles*), in the Netherlands where immigrants' access to social housing has been more carefully planned, and in Sweden where there has been a deliberate policy of integration. Outside of Irish, Asians, and some smaller groups (Cypriots, Italians) in Britain, there is very little evidence of international labour migrants moving into the owner-occupied sector. Of course, it must be remembered that in most European countries there is not the obsession with home ownership that there is in Britain.

Although the degree of ethnic segregation in European cities rarely matches the black and hispanic ghettoes of many US cities (Huttman *et al.* (eds.) 1991), immigrant residential patterns lend a distinct tone to many urban districts, reinforced by the clustering of ethnic shops and institutions such as mosques and social clubs. Now that most of the *bidonvilles* have been bulldozed away, only in English cities like Bradford and Leicester are there sizeable urban areas with approaching 100 per cent 'saturation' by immigrants—in these cases Asians. Although immigrants' spatial segregation in poor-quality housing is partly related to their low socio-economic status and recency of arrival, there is also an element of self-infliction: cheapness is of the essence (to maximize the rate of saving) and location near to kin and co-nationals is often desirable from the points of view of self-identity and security.

The immigrants' demographic impact is significant at both local and national levels. In many European cities the foreign arrivals have compensated for the decline in local population due to the flight to out-of-town locations. Thus, between 1967 and 1973 (the period of maximum influx), Stuttgart's foreign population grew from 50 000 to 100 000 but the city's total population growth was only 12 000; almost 40 000 Germans left the city during this period. Munich grew by 92 000 to 1.3 million but 80 000 of the additional people were foreign immigrants (Kirk 1981: 85). At a more specific spatial scale, immigrants give life to decaying, depopulating inner cities, their children enrolling in schools that would otherwise be closed down. However, with native children growing up and being educated in suburban schools, an educational polarization has developed which hardly bodes well for the social and economic integration of immigrant and second-generation pupils, most of whom leave school with few, if any, qualifications.

Immigrant fertility rates are usually considerably higher than those of native EC populations, partly because the immigrants come from countries where large families are the norm, and partly because they are concentrated in the reproductively active age groups. High immigrant fertility is not a permanent condition, however; various studies have shown that fertility decline amongst foreign-born women can be quite rapid.[6]

The position of migrant workers in the social structure of Europe has been subject to varying interpretations. The Marxist characterization of migrants as a marginal, inert *Lumpenproletariat* tends to ignore the fact that the migrants' social reference point may be their home society. It also ignores the social progress and political participation (e.g. in trade unions) that Europe's immigrants have achieved over the past 30–40 years (Miller 1982). Longer-term problems surround the future of the culturally ambivalent and

---

[6] In Britain, for instance, during the 1970s, total fertility (completed births per woman over the reproductive period) fell from 4 to 2 for West Indians and from 6 to 4 for Indian subcontinent women. It is predicted that the latter group will also approach 2 by the end of the century. For further details see Coleman (ed.) (1982).

poorly qualified second generation who are now entering a labour market that has little to offer them.

Return migration and regional development

Until the end of the 1970s, little was known of the scale and impact of intra-European return migration. As noted earlier, a 'productive return', with temporary labour migrants taking back money and skills to their home areas, was part of the pro-migration ideology of the 1960s, but nobody at that time thought actually to study the effects of return on the migrant areas. This defect has been rectified in the last 10–15 years (see e.g. King 1986).

First, it needs to be stressed that, in spite of the transformation of *Gastarbeiter* into settled immigrants, many labour migrants do return. It is impossible to say how many, and the proportion undoubtedly varies from country to country and from region to region. If a guess must be hazarded, perhaps a third return. Motives for return generally have less to do with unemployment and recession in the receiving countries, and more to do with a variety of social and psychological factors such as nostalgia, family obligations (for instance to ageing parents), and the desire to enjoy *nouveau riche* status back home. It is generally acknowledged that policies encouraging return—such as the repatriation bonus of 10 000 francs and a free ticket back to the country of origin offered by the French government during the late 1970s—have had little effect, since most of those who took the incentive were those who would have returned anyway (Poinard 1979).

The impacts of return migration on regional development in peripheral regions of the Community are hard to assess for they depend on many factors such as the scale of the return, the age profile of the returnees, the nature of their work experiences abroad, and the economic geography of the areas to which they return. For instance, rural upland districts where those migrants who return do so only on retirement will witness very little development stimulus. On the other hand, where migrants return at a relatively young age and with some capital and entrepreneurial ambitions, the results are more positive. The case of return migration from West Germany to Greece is briefly considered to identify some of these processes more clearly.

Mass emigration and return have been facets of Greek life for a century. Early waves of emigrants went to, and some returned from, the United States. Since the 1950s most migratory interchange has been with West Germany. Although the Greek data on migration are deficient in many respects, they are useful for determining the urban–rural balance of the flows. During the early 1970s 53 per cent of recorded emigrants left from rural areas, 11 per cent from semi-rural areas, and 36 per cent from urban areas. Most of the return flow (56 per cent) was directed to urban centres, with 8 per cent resettling in semi-rural areas, and 33 per cent in rural areas (Lianos 1975). Thus emigration and return act to reinforce the dominant internal rural–urban migration pattern of Greece. Like internal migrants, returnees from abroad are attracted by the better job opportunities, social infrastructure (notably education), and modern way of life of cities like Athens and Thessalonika. The urban orientation of the Greek return migration flow reflects a rejection of farming as a post-return form of employment. Even in rural areas, Greek returnees prefer to try to make a living from the tertiary sector by opening small shops or cafés, or operating taxi services. Only a small proportion of Greek emigrants have acquired significant skills or training whilst abroad. Since they only intended, at least initially, to stay temporarily in Germany any extended training or apprentice-ship was seen by them as unnecessary and an impediment to their aim of amassing savings and returning home quickly. In one survey only 15 per cent of returning migrants had acquired marketable skills in Germany, and less than half of these were able to find employment upon return which utilized such skills (Bernard and Comitas 1978). The significant amounts of capital brought back by returnees have tended to be invested in urban property or spent on consumer goods; relatively little is invested in employment-creating industrial enterprises and almost none in farming. Culturally many Greek returned emigrants remain ambivalent. In Germany their pay was good but they were second-class citizens with no political voice. In Greece everything is found to be shoddy, chaotic, and corrupt, yet they can at least be amongst fellow-Greeks and try to realize their private ambitions.

Economic restructuring and its impact on international migrants

We saw earlier that the oil crisis of 1973–4 led to a fundamental reshaping of European labour migration patterns: a reduction in their scale, at least for a time, and a switch to the migration of family reunion. The process of economic restructuring, more or less continuous throughout the 1980s, has further modified the character of international migration. Once again, the key mediating link has been the labour market. The structure of employment in Europe has been transformed. This change has favoured, most of all, growth in employment in services at the expense of agriculture and industry, especially manufacturing. Behind this simple sectoral shift, however, lie more complex changes.

Much has been written about the restructuring of the European (and world) economy in recent years. A whole new vocabulary has entered economic geography: post-Fordism, flexible specialization, advanced producer services, are some of the catchwords which are the shorthand for the fundamental economic and organizational transition that has taken place, from big 'smokestack' industries and mass-production factories concentrated by Weberian location factors in monocultural industrial conurbations, to a looser, more dynamic, more technological structure of smaller firms but also overlain by an increasingly powerful superstructure of multinational capital (Sayer and Walker 1992). Whilst this debate on economic restructuring has a strong labour-market content, in which the increasing segmentation of labour is often discussed, there has been little attempt to spell out the implications of restructuring for immigrant workers.

First, industrial restructuring has had profound effects on the immigrant workers already established in the Community. The history of their recruitment concentrated them precisely in those industries—mining, steel, chemicals, rubber, car manufacturing, etc.—which have suffered most from closure and lay-offs. The spatial impact of this deindustrialization has also been marked: industrial closures have left many immigrants trapped in old industrial regions and in inner cities with declining work opportunities.

Secondly, immigrants themselves have contributed to economic restructuring, especially to the tertiarization of European urban economies and to the rising number of small firms. Apart from some long-standing ethnic minority communities of seafaring and trading origin in ports and big cities like London and Mareseilles, 'ethnic entrepreneurship' is a relatively recent phenomenon and not as highly developed in Europe as it is in North America. Britain is an exception to this overall comparison. In this country, the Italian penetration of the catering industry started about a hundred years ago, and post-war immigrants have developed a number of specialisms: Chinese restaurants, Cypriot clothing firms, and Asian retailing are some examples. In Britain around a quarter of south-Asian men are self-employed, nearly twice the figure for the male population as a whole. Elsewhere in Europe, there are only limited data on ethnic entrepreneurship (Zegers de Beijl 1990). Although the majority of immigrants are in the same jobs, or the same kind of jobs, for which they were recruited, there has been a faster growth in small business formation amongst ethnic minorities than amongst native populations. In France, for instance, the number of self-employed foreigners rose by 50 per cent during 1983–9 to 5.6 per cent of the total immigrant labour-force. The figure for self-employed persons in Germany was 6.5 per cent in 1985 (cf. only 2 per cent in 1980); here there has been a strong growth of Turkish small-scale entrepreneurship as institutional barriers to non-EC immigrant settlement have slackened (Gordon 1991: 22–9).

Types of ethnic business obviously vary, but many serve only the ethnic community and are part of a parallel, enclave economy which functions according to different cultural and financial norms from the modern European economy of the Single Market. Typical examples include shops, small restaurants, import–export concerns, and travel agencies (to facilitate migrant travel to and from the homeland). Some small firms use ethnic recruitment networks, and especially family members, to provide the low-cost labour force that gives them both flexibility and a competitive edge.

In sum, the restructuring of the labour market through deindustrialization, the growth of high-level services, the expansion of the informal economy and the 'casualization' of whole sectors of employment has the effect of polarizing demand for immigrant labour into highly-skilled 'brain' migrants and low-skill 'brawn' migrants. The former represent both the hyper-mobile elite workers of Europe and elements of 'brain drain' from the Third World and, perhaps increasingly, from Eastern Europe. The latter, whose status in Europe is often illegal or semi-illegal, work less and less in factories and more and more in petty services and the informal economy.

Southern Europe: From emigration to immigration

In no part of Europe has the relationship between economic restructuring and immigration been more dramatically demonstrated than in the Mediterranean states of the Community: Italy, Spain, Portugal, and Greece. These countries, sources of mass emigration up to 20 years ago, are now countries of mass immigration. Informed observers estimate they contain around 2 million immigrants, including 1 million in Italy alone.[7] Yet Italy still has 6 million of its own nationals living and working abroad!

To be simultaneously a country of emigrants and immigrants is no longer illogical because of the international division of labour and the segmentation of the labour market within individual countries of new immigration. For the most part the jobs Italian emigrants do abroad, or those they would do if they remained at home, bear little relationship to the jobs done by immigrants in Italy. The international hierarchy of employment and wages thus allows Italians to migrate abroad and to get well-paid work in factories or in restaurants, as well as encouraging Third World migrants to come to Italy to take on jobs and levels of pay that Italians reject.

Italy has been the main target for this new wave of immigrants, and for

---

[7] For a detailed discussion of the Italian data, including geographical distribution within Italy, see Montanari and Cortese (1993).

several reasons. Italy's status as a major tourist destination makes entry easy. Most migrants have simply come in through the main airports, but some have entered by sea (e.g. from Tunisia to Sicily) or overland (e.g. via ex-Yugoslavia). Secondly, Italy's wealth and high standard of living have been powerful magnets. Third, the size of Italy's 'black economy' (reputedly the largest in the Western world) has been ready to absorb and 'hide' immigrant labour. A fourth facilitating factor, important in the case of some immigrant groups such as those from Cape Verde and the Philippines, has been the common bond of Roman Catholicism, and the role of religious agencies in arranging for immigrants to be smoothly transferred.

The case of immigration into Italy is a perfect example of two aspects of labour-market restructuring already mentioned: segmentation and casualization. The various immigrant groups have settled in niches in the Italian labour market which are characterized by precariousness, marginality, low status, and low pay. Moreover these niches have a distinct expression: specific nationalities perform specific jobs in specific geographic settings. Filipino and Cape Verde women work as housemaids in private residences; they are an urban, female and, at the individual level, widely dispersed and almost hidden group. Much more visible are Senegalese street hawkers, found in every big city and tourist resort selling bags, belts, shirts, sunglasses and wrist-watches. In western Sicily Tunisians work in the fishing industry and as casual workers in agriculture. As these examples show, immigrants reflect the growing informalization of the Italian economy. They are both post-industrial and, in a sense, pre-industrial workers. Unfortunately they are, as a whole, badly treated by their employers and by Italian society. Incidences of racism, violence, and even murder have been frequent (Andall 1990). Italy, like Spain and Greece, is still coming to terms with its new status as an immigration country.

Skilled international migration

As early as 1981 Salt wrote of the growing importance of the international migration of 'managerial, technical and related staff' and of the role of international organizations' internal labour markets in promoting this form of movement. At that stage, however, research on these issues had barely begun (Salt 1985: 155). The last ten years has seen a growing appreciation of the part played by skilled international migrants in the EC labour market, so much so that by the end of the 1980s the mobility of highly skilled manpower was regarded as the backbone of the European migratory system (Salt 1989: 450). Key mechanisms for this 'brain exchange' include: the internal labour markets of multinational companies, who shift their higher-status workers around Europe as part of corporate manpower planning; the increasing use of contract work systems for skilled labour; the key role of international recruitment agencies; and the function of international experience in individual career planning. Although most skilled international migration in Europe involves fairly balanced flows between highly developed regions, there is undoubtedly an element of periphery-to-core 'brain drain' which siphons highly educated people, such as young graduates, from areas of poor employment opportunity such as Ireland, Scotland, or Greece, and places them in metropolitan settings where their brain power is in demand.

Skilled international migration merges rather indistinctly with allied forms of mobility such as short-term contract work and extended business trips. Thus the upper end of the labour market is composed of a hyper-mobile elite, which contrasts with the largely immobile traditional working class. The migration of skilled people is now the main form of intra-EC international migration and is likely to remain so since the 'skilling of demand'—the increasing European need for scientists, technicians, managers, and other people with an international outlook—is a continuing process (Salt and Ford 1993). The role of the Single Market cannot be overlooked here: this is far more likely to increase the international mobility of highly educated, multi-lingual, career-minded professionals than it will the migration of poorly educated manual workers for whom linguistic and cultural barriers will remain as significant obstacles to movement. Although skilled migrants are invisible both statistically and because they do not form marked urban enclaves with a distinct cultural 'flavour', the geographical pattern of their movement undoubtedly has as its nodes the areas which have the greatest economic and decision-making power—Brussels, Paris, London, Frankfurt, plus newly-emergent industrial areas like Bavaria, Rhône-Alpes, and Milan. Key sectors are modern industry, finance, commerce, public institutions, and international bodies such as OECD, and of course the EC itself. The scale of this movement does not match the human tide of *Gastarbeiter* of earlier decades, but the skilled migrants' economic and strategic importance enhances their weight in the changing map of regional opportunity.

Refugees and asylum-seekers: Political or economic migrants?

High-status 'brainy' migrants and marginal, casual immigrants from the Third World represent the polarization of demand for immigrant workers which took place in the 1980s as a consequence of changes in the European labour market. However, far more prominent on the international political agenda have been refugees and asylum-seekers. Indeed, if the 1960s were the decade of the *Gastarbeiter* and the 1970s that of family reunion, the 1980s were the decade of the refugee. Asylum-seekers remain at the top of the European political agenda in the early 1990s.

In the first half of the 1970s an average of only 16 000 asylum-seekers arrived in Western Europe each year. By 1983 the figure had grown to 67 000. Since then, and especially since 1987, there has been a consistently high annual increase of about 33 per cent to reach 537 000 in 1991 (see Table 6.2). Germany took 42 per cent of the total inflow during 1983–91, followed at some distance by France, Sweden, Switzerland, the UK, and Austria. Hungary emerged as an important destination after 1989 reflecting its gateway function for refugees coming from the East. Taking the period 1983–9, the ten main origin countries for asylum-seekers were Turkey (13.3 per cent), Poland (11.6 per cent), Iran (10.1 per cent), Sri Lanka (7.4 per cent), Romania (6.4 per cent), Yugoslavia (5 per cent), Lebanon (3.9 per cent), Ghana (3.6 per cent), Zaïre (2.8 per cent), and Czechoslovakia (2.8 per cent).[8]

The figures in Table 6.2 on asylum requests cannot be easily matched by data on successful, settled entries because of differences between countries in their treatment of asylum-seekers. Some countries, like Germany, tend to

TABLE 6.2 *Distribution and growth in the numbers of asylum-seekers, 1983–1991* ('000s)

Receiving country	1983	1984	1985	1986	1987	1988	1989	1990	1991	Total	%
Germany	20	35	74	100	57	103	121	193	256	959	41.9
France	14	16	26	23	25	32	59	56	46	297	13.0
Sweden	3	12	14	15	18	20	30	29	27	168	7.3
Switzerland	8	7	10	9	11	17	24	36	42	164	7.2
UK	4	3	5	5	5	5	16	30	58	131	5.7
Austria	6	7	7	9	11	16	22	23	27	127	5.5
Netherlands	2	3	6	6	13	7	14	21	22	94	4.3
Belgium	3	4	5	8	6	5	8	13	15	67	2.9
ALL EUROPEAN STATES	67	102	168	201	182	234	346	453	537	2 289	100.0
of which EC	47	68	125	155	127	166	226	333	432	1 679	73.4

Note: Countries not included in the table, receiving less than 2% of the total for 1983–91, in decreasing order of importance: Italy, Denmark, Greece, Norway, Yugoslavia, Spain, Finland, Portugal, Ireland. No data available for Luxembourg. Hungary which reported no applicants up to 1988, received 5.6% of the total during 1989–90.

Source: Unpublished data from the United Nations High Commissioner for Refugees.

[8] Figures quoted here are asylum applications reported by European governments to the United Nations High Commissioner for Refugees; early figures from Ghosh (1991).

let aspiring refugees in whilst their cases are processed. The UK policy has been to turn them back at the airports, reflecting a growing belief that nowadays the majority of asylum-seekers are economic migrants in disguise (Salt 1989: 450). In many countries a large number of asylum-seekers have provisional status whilst the bureaucratic procedures grind on. Although such persons are temporarily safe from the pressures from which they are fleeing, they remain in a psychological limbo which is very unsettling.

Some degree of consensus has emerged in recent years on the need to curb the growing flows of asylum-seekers and the misuse of the asylum procedure as a pretext for economic migration. Measures adopted in 1991 rescind eligibility for refugee status in the case of migrants from the more advanced East European countries (Poland, Czechoslovakia, Hungary). An agreement signed in Dublin in June 1990 by all Community countries, except Denmark, harmonizes certain procedures for dealing with asylum requests; this makes the decision reached by the initial receiving country valid for other EC states. More controversial has been the Schengen Accord, also of June 1990, which imposes heavy fines for transport companies such as airlines for failing to ensure that their passengers have all the necessary documentation for entry into the country of destination; not all national parliaments within the EC have supported this.[9] However the failure of these various measures to contain the sharp increases in asylum claimants in the last few years indicates that new thinking is needed, both about the scale and mechanics of the problem, and about the whole concept of asylum. This is one of the major challenges for European migration policy in the 1990s (Salt and Kitching 1991).

Migration in the 1990s and beyond: Intra-EC, East–West or South–North?

Since 1989, as the latter part of this chapter has shown, migration has moved to the very forefront of European debate. Although the nature of labour-market demand in the EC has conditioned the new flows of the late 1980s and early 1990s somewhat, the real pressures now are the push forces. These come from two directions: from Eastern Europe since the collapse of the Iron Curtain; and from the South, where continuing poverty combined with an unremittingly high birth rate is fashioning a migration scenario that the West cannot ignore.

First, however, let us examine the prospects for increased labour migration within the EC after the establishment of the Single Market. Will the Single

---

[9] For details, see SOPEMI Annual Report for 1990: 31–2.

Market lead to inward investment in the economic and geographical periphery to stem outmigration by employment creation; or will it lead to further concentration of resources at the 'golden heart' of Europe, thereby continuing or even accelerating the drain of labour from the periphery? Unfortunately all that can be said in answer to this question is that there is considerable disagreement. The previous experience of Western Europe would indicate further accumulation at the core, but the doubling of Structural Funds, which was at the heart of the Delors package for the Single Market, might make some difference by building-up a stronger economy in peripheral regions. What can be said is that the removal of legal barriers to intra-EC migration in the 1960s did not produce a great increase of migration flows within the Community. Instead, as we have seen, the core economies of the EC increasingly looked to sources outside so that Italians, who made up half the foreign labour in the Community in 1960, constituted only 16 per cent in 1973. Rather perversely, free movement encouraged Italians to return home but non-Community immigrants to stay put. The one thing which will be different after 1992 is that the single market for labour will be complemented by a single market for other factors, notably capital. The earlier 'free movement' migrations were mainly relocations of low-skill labour; there was not a free movement of workers in banking, commerce, the public sector, and many professions. Although, for reasons of national security, the public sector will still be partially closed and the different qualification systems in the professions will also remain as barriers, the unification of the capital and commercial markets will stimulate further migration of highly qualified manpower (Molle and van Mourik 1988). However, most projections of the labour needs of Europe post-Single Market, at least to the year 2000, do not portend another massive wave of migration, either within the Community or from outside it. The growth effects of 1992 will be wealth-creating rather than employment-creating. At least in the short term, most labour needs will be satisfied by absorbing the existing unemployed (13 million), increasing female-labour participation rates, retraining, and labour-saving technology (Martin *et al.* 1990). Within the EC, probably only Ireland will witness high rates of net outmigration in the 1990s, continuing the Irish trend of the 1980s.

If the Single Market will not produce a boom in intra-European migration, what effect will events in Eastern Europe have? These events are not without irony, for the Iron Curtain, which prevented Eastern Europeans from migrating to the West, is being replaced by a 'welfare curtain' by which the West hopes to prevent the flood of immigrants from the East. Some East–West moves are already taking place. The unification of Germany incorporated

16.4 million East Germans into the EC, and 1989–90 saw an estimated 775 000 *Aussiedler*, or ethnic Germans, migrate to the 'mother country' from various parts of Eastern Europe and the Soviet Union. Whilst Italy succeeded in its much-publicized (but not widely condemned) efforts to repulse the Albanian 'boat people' in 1991, other steadier trickles of Eastern migrants entered via ex-Yugoslavia into northern Italy and via Hungary into Austria. The EC's toleration of East European 'tourist workers' who come on visitors' passports and work for a few weeks or months, mostly doing menial jobs, means that Stephen Castles' obituary for the European guestworker (Castles 1986) may have been premature. Perhaps the biggest unknown is the future scale of emigration from the former USSR. Several estimates have been made ranging from 3 million for the period 1991–3 all the way up to 20 million, including a high proportion of highly educated scientists and intellectuals. Reality will certainly see less Russians moving, perhaps between 500 000 and 1 million per year during the 1990s.

In the longer term, however, the real pressures will come from the South— from across the Mediterranean and from the wider realm of the developing (or not-developing) world. The strongest migration pressure will probably derive from population growth in the 'Islamic arc' around Europe: the Maghreb states, Egypt, Turkey, and Pakistan. Many of these states are also important sources of asylum-seekers and illegal immigrants who have been entering the EC in recent years. With a fertility rate of 5.1 children per woman, compared to 1.6 for Western Europe (1985–90 figures), North African countries will add 50 million people to their populations during 1990–2000. Projecting European demographic trends forward to the first part of the twenty-first century leads many experts to conclude that large influxes of immigrants will be needed to offset population decline and to rejuvenate an increasingly ageing population structure (see Lutz *et al.* 1991; Wattelar and Roumans 1991; Wils 1991). Once again, the labour market will be central to these projections. The excess of new entrants (mainly school-leavers) over departures (mainly retirements) in the EC labour market peaked at 1.2 million in 1981. Projections are for a deficit (excess of leavers over entrants) of about the same magnitude by 2025. With rising immigration already evident by 1985, populations resident in Europe will become more ethnically and racially mixed because of the widening variety of source countries and because immigrants bring with them higher fertilities and younger age structures.

How will Community policy respond to these pressures? Salt and Kitching (1991) foresee that European migration policy in the future will take place in a politicized, macro-regional forum with international conventions replacing the bilateral treaties of the *Gastarbeiter* era. However, an EC-wide immigration policy has yet to be achieved. The Schengen Agreement is not popular: amongst its initial five signatories (Benelux, France, Germany), France is worried about entry of immigrants from Poland and the former GDR, whilst Amnesty International and the ACP countries are concerned about refugee-determination, deportation procedures, sanctions against transporters, and other details (Matheson 1991). If a common immigration policy is not agreed upon, nation-specific policies will persist, perhaps with some attempt at harmonization or co-ordination. This messy *status-quo* situation will probably provoke a re-run of earlier migration scenarios in both Western Europe and the United States (Martin *et al.* 1990). Immigrants will arrive and work; vigorous debate on the economic and socio-cultural effects of immigration will ensue, leading to a loss-of-control feeling that promotes restrictive legislation; all parties will achieve something, but come off second-best. Thus employers will have access to cheap foreign labour at minimum risk; aliens can enter the Community, at least for a time; and European governments can assure their right-wing voters that they are doing something about the immigration issue. Surrounded as it is by complex questions of economics, culture, and ethics, the immigration of foreign workers can never be simple, and the Community still has much to learn.

Further reading

International migration has been widely researched by geographers and other social scientists. The literature on European migration is truly vast, encompassing thousands of studies in many languages. The major geographical study is J. Salt and H. Clout (eds.) (1976), *Migration in Postwar Europe: Geographical Essays* (London); regrettably a comparably thorough, more up-to-date survey has not been published. Another landmark study, by two Marxist sociologists, is S. Castles and G. Kosack (1973), *Immigrant Workers and Class Structure in Western Europe* (Oxford); disappointingly the second edition of this book (1985) differs from the first only by the addition of a brief Postscript. Other important studies include S. Castles, H. Booth, and T. Wallace (1984), *Here for Good: Western Europe's New Ethnic Minorities* (London); T. Hammer (ed.) (1985), *European Immigration Policy: A Comparative Study* (Cambridge); and R. Rogers (ed.) (1985) *Guests Come to Stay: The Effects of European Labour Migration on Sending and Receiving Countries* (Boulder, Colo.). For a recent survey of Europe's newest migrations see R. L. King (ed.) (1993), *Mass Migrations in Europe: The Legacy and the Future* (London). The journals *International Migration* and *International Migration Review* contain many articles on Europe as well as comprehensive book-review and literature sections.

7 Mobility and Illegal Labour in the EC

Solange Montagné-Villette

Working secretly, and usually illegally, is no novelty in the countries of the EC. This first began in the early years of the present century when modern administrative structures were being established in all the industrial states and grew steadily in parallel with social-security systems. Today, in some countries, such illegal work is part of a well-established tradition and is viewed by many as part of the national culture.[1] In contrast, illegal work at a 'community' level, such as is found in the EC and elsewhere, has a number of distinctive features that have so far received little attention, not least because the phenomenon is so recent. The increased mobility of the labour force, industry, and business has generated completely new and illegal employment practices, the forms of which are closely linked to the political, economic, and legal structure of the EC.

There are several manifestations of the growing prevalence of illegal employment practices: workers from poor countries in the EC seeking employment in other member states; the relocation and/or subcontracting of illegitimate industrial activities in the Mediterranean countries of Europe; immigrants from outside the Community working illegally within it. This chapter considers the phenomenon in detail, as well as examining its geopolitical consequences.

Illegal working, labour migration, and employment opportunities in the EC

For many years emigration from Spain, Greece, and Portugal has been the major source of illegal workers in the northern European industrial countries, but now that they are members of the EC the seeds of change are apparent. The standard of living in Spain is rapidly converging on the European average, although GDP per capita in Portugal and Greece remains at less than 60 per cent of the EC average, with generally very low wage

---

Chapter translated by Mark Blacksell.

[1] 'Illegal working in Europe', EC internal memorandum, 1989.

levels. In the circumstances it is not difficult to appreciate the continuing attraction of the rich countries in the EC for Greek and Portuguese workers, even if emigration levels are considerably reduced (see Chapter 6). Nor is it surprising that this source of cheap labour has come to the attention of European employers, constantly seeking means of reducing costs, increasing profits and facing up to international competition.

There is evidence that there are employers in the core nations of the EC who have devised highly flexible techniques for managing their labour forces by taking advantage of the variations in living standards and in the social security systems and employment legislation in member states (Montagné-Villette (ed.) 1991). Even if these people cannot strictly be categorized as illegal workers, they fulfil most of the necessary requirements, being involved in labour transfers and the technical avoidance of local employment legislation. A number of recent cases underline the high degree of organization, at a European level, behind this kind of manipulation of the labour market. They also illustrate its quantitative importance, especially in certain sectors of the economy.

TABLE 7.1 *Income per head in selected EC countries, 1990* (in $US)

Portugal	4 444
Greece	5 437
Spain	9 471
Italy	15 291
Germany (West)	21 231

Source: OECD (1991).

The international manipulation of labour resources in the Rush Portuguesa case

The Rush Portuguesa affair, which attracted media attention in 1989, clearly illustrates the 'shady' methods that are used to pay workers low wages in countries where wage levels are generally high, exploiting loopholes in the EC legislation. The case also exposes the limited effectiveness of the measures taken by France after 1974 to control immigration and illegal working in the absence of any coherent EC-wide policy. The facts of the case are briefly the following. In 1986 46 Portuguese workers employed by the construction and civil engineering firm Rush Portuguesa were discovered working on the construction of the new Atlantic TGV high-speed rail line to south-west France. The Portuguese registered company, whose headquarters are in Lisbon, was acting as a subcontractor for the main contractor, Bouygues. The French authorities took out an injunction against Rush Portuguesa, arguing that its workers were not authorized to work in France, because they had not paid any national insurance contributions to OMI (International Migration Office). Rush contested the case, arguing that they were involved in a public service project and that, as EC citizens, its employees were entitled to work there, since the Treaty of Rome conferred this right unconditionally. The French case was that Portugal (and Spain) could not bring workers into France without obtaining authorization from OMI during the transition period (to 1992), following their accession to the EC in 1986.

Notwithstanding the fierce legal battle, Rush Portuguesa continued its activities on French soil, but that is not to imply that the case was a trivial one. In 1987, the French authorities took out 34 separate injunctions for all the sites where Rush Portuguesa was acting as the subcontractor, alleging they were doing so illegally and also that they were employing illegal workers. What actually emerged was that the Portuguese workers were in effect working under the direct control of the main contractor. The case went to the European Court of Justice in The Hague, where France lost. As a direct result, there has been a sharp increase in the number of Portuguese companies involved, both legally and illegally, with this kind of construction work.

Over and above the legal arguments used to justify, or to ban, illegal working, there are important issues here for geographers. To what extent can the EC, theoretically a single, fully integrated entity where all of its citizens can move freely, tolerate socio-economic differences, and inequalities?

Ben Salah (1991) sees the institutional space as equivalent to the national territory and considers sovereignty to be absolute over the whole. He defines this space as 'the area over which a state claims to exercise competence in a more or less uniform fashion' (p. 151). He also makes it clear that the concept of legal space can be considerably more all-embracing '. . . notably when several states come together as they have done in the EC to form an international organization to promote political integration' (p. 151). In such a situation 'the legal space includes not only the physical territory, but also the communal laws which apply in the constituent territories' (p. 151). Bearing this in mind, what actually is the situation in the EC in the early 1990s?

Superficially, the arguments are straightforward; French firms seeking to reduce their costs subcontract to foreign firms to try, with varying degrees of success, to evade French law. This is nothing less than blatant and comprehensive exploitation of loopholes in European legislation, as well as a classic instance of the way in which illegal Portuguese workers are taken advantage of, with all the undesirable consequences that this entails.

Such misappropriation of legislation is nothing new. As early as 1926, the French government sought to limit the number of foreign workers entering France and, consequently, had passports stamped 'not eligible to work in France'. This had the immediate, perverse, result of increasing the number of illegal workers. In order to get around the new law people going through immigration claimed to be either 'self-employed, skilled, craftsmen, or businessmen', these categories being exempt from the new border controls. After 1935 the legal requirements were further extended and to work as a foreign skilled craftsman it became necessary to obtain a permit issued by the relevant professional body. The main result of the new law was to make illegal workers out of people who a few days previously had been pursuing their professions entirely legitimately.

Illegal working could be seen as a game of cat and mouse, but for the fact that real people are involved. On the other hand there are a number of new features of this system which simply cannot be ignored. Being an illegal worker is no longer an individual matter, but an integral part of working for certain firms that have decided to exploit this lucrative option so as to increase corporate profits. The EC provided the framework within which these labour movements occurred. It makes sense, therefore, to think in terms of a double change of scale, involving more people and a larger area.

The effect of these changes merits careful consideration, not only because of the rather sorry human consequences, but also because they threaten to undermine the fundamental basis of European integration. If the spirit of the Treaty of Rome is to create a huge and relatively homogeneous economic space, providing for free competition between different countries, then marked variations in levels of development must be ironed out as quickly as possible. Such homogenization of the economic conditions in the various countries began with the Common Agricultural Policy (Chapter 9) and the fight against regional disequilibria was then continued further through the European Regional Development Fund and the European Investment Bank (Chapter 1).

Arguably, Rush Portuguesa's legal victory demonstrates that the European Court of Justice accepts the principle of an unequal Europe. It is a Europe where certain Mediterranean countries form peripheral regions dominated economically by core regions made up of the richest member states. Using legal arguments that are probably well-founded (but which go beyond the present case), the European Court has, in effect, accepted that certain groups of EC citizens will not benefit fully from the social legislation, nor from the wage levels generally prevailing in the countries where they work. As a result, they have altogether more precarious existences. The traditional (and pragmatic) duality between rich and poor countries will have been replaced by a more abstract concept, based on a belief that the overwhelming priority in both economically strong and economically weak regions is to protect free enterprise, even at the expense of human rights.

The relocation of illegal working to the southern periphery: A Neapolitan example

Clothes and many luxury items, especially those whose manufacture involves a high level of manual labour, are expensive to produce because of the high labour costs. As a result, it is no longer economic to produce tailored clothes, luxury shoes, or hand-worked leather goods in France, or in the other higher-wage countries of the EC. Faced with this situation, EC firms and especially those in France, specializing in these kinds of goods, now routinely sub-contract the work to countries where wages are lower in Asia or North Africa (and sometimes Romania); alternatively, they may make use of the workers in the black economy in Italy. At the end of the 1960s such subcontracting was on a relatively limited scale and was confined mainly to northern Italy, but has now come to form a major part of the Neapolitan economy. Labour cost differentials (whether or not illegal workers were involved) between France and northern Italy were progressively reduced, as a result of the steady rise in the standard of living in the latter. This led French firms to be attracted instead to southern Italy, in particular Naples, where illegal working involving literally thousands of families enabled production costs to be reduced sharply.

Of course, the larger French firms producing luxury items have not turned, at least openly, to the illegal sector in Naples. But many small, semi-craft firms competing in the same corner of the market have based their entire production strategy on such illegal labour. Under the circumstances the choice of Naples is no accident. Although in theory they could have used illegal labour in France, or even in Morocco where it is still cheaper, Naples has become the centre of these activities, because it offers additional advantages. There is an established tradition of illegal working, prices are particularly competitive, and it is inside the EC, thus minimizing transport, border crossing, and tariff barrier problems. In every sense, therefore, there has been a real relocation of illegal working to a 'more suitable' region within the EC, just as if there had been a relocation of the labour-intensive industries themselves to countries where wage levels were lower.

Naples is being exploited as an underdeveloped economic region by European firms, which exploit its 'weaknesses'. Since the bulk of the illegal labour is concentrated in the city itself, this is where their activities are mainly concentrated.

The case of the luxury clothing firms on the Côte d'Azur is particularly interesting in this regard. The area is frequented by a wealthy clientele, partial to high living, so that industry there has specialized in the manufacture of up-market, sophisticated clothes. The way these products have to be made (up to 4 hours manual labour is spent on certain garments, costing between 300 and 400 francs for the labour alone) and the high cost of the materials used (silk, lace, embroidery, etc.), combine to raise the overall production costs to such a level that a strategy to reduce them has to be found for the goods to remain competitive. To illustrate how such reductions are achieved, we now consider the complex, and rather improbable, route by which tailored womens' suits come to be sold on the retail market at only 1500 francs each (Montagné-Villette 1987).

The suits are designed and cut by a ready-to-wear firm in Toulon and then transported to Naples in the personal baggage of the manufacturer. A Neapolitan subcontractor takes over responsibility for making-up the garments, but passes the actual work over to unregistered home-workers, who are paid about 70 francs per item. The suits are then sent back to Nice by way of Germany, again by plane. The choice of route may appear strange, but is explained by the fact that there is no direct air route between Naples and Nice. Initially the suits were taken via Rome, but this was abandoned after they were stolen by an organized gang.

The example illustrates, once again, the economic advantage to be gained from exploiting illegal working within the EC. However, in addition to showing how French firms profit from using subcontractors in Naples, another interesting issue raised by this traffic is that, by and large, it goes on openly. The French authorities seem to connive at it, even encourage it, and certainly know about what is going on. Illegal working is normally considered an undesirable practice. Why in this particular case is it not seen as a problem? Even if one takes the line that it is of no concern to the French authorities, it cannot be denied that in Toulon manufacturers are gaining an unfair advantage over those firms working legally. As in the earlier example, consideration ought to be given to stopping the traffic, if only to ensure that those firms working within the law are not damaged.

It must also not be forgotten that there are notional costs incurred by such illegal working. In contrast to legal work in France, illegal working in Italy yields no revenue to the public coffers, either in the form of fines or as taxes to the International Migration Office.

The potential economic dangers for the health of French firms, and the argument that condoning such illegal working in Naples may be morally reprehensible, are put on one side because of the counterweight of its considerable attractions. It enables retail prices in France to be reduced and a blind eye to be turned to the evasion of social security laws. In other words, although the French authorities seem to feel obliged to condemn non-compliance within the national territory, because of the weight of public opinion and a sense of high moral principle, they are quite prepared to accept the exploitation of workers in Italy.

Towards the 'apostasy' of legality?

This differential utilization of the EC space seems now to be 'normal' practice for many workers and firms, the case of the Winter Olympics in Savoie being just another example. An official inspection of the work going on in the Val d'Isère in 1989 revealed that nearly all the construction firms working on the Olympic site were employing Portuguese illegal workers. The firms argued in their defence that, in spite of exhaustive searches, they had not been able to find suitably qualified and available French workers. Therefore, they had no alternative but to call on Portuguese workers. Through the media, the politicians presented the case to the public as a stark choice: either employ Portuguese workers, or fail to meet the planned deadlines for these works, so important for both the region and for France. The appeal was certainly cleverly conceived, but it was also fallacious. Although no one ought to have been surprised by the fact that Portuguese immigrants were being employed generally within the EC, there was still an obligation to ensure that their terms and conditions of employment met the requisite standards. This was the real nub of the problem.

The above examples demonstrate that, in practice, the emergence of the unified EC space, far from reducing national and regional inequalities, has in certain instances actually increased them. The contradictions raised by a rich North and a less-developed South used as source of cheap labour are illustrated clearly here in the heart of the EC, mirroring in many respects the model of the North–South relationship between the industrialized and the developing countries. The problem would exist under any circumstances given the nature of the EC, but it is particularly prevalent in those areas where the conditions for moving goods and people are favourable.

The community space: A refuge for those left behind by economic growth

The attractions of illegal working in the EC by immigrants from outside the Community stem from the vast single market, with its unrestricted freedom of movement and high living standards. With a population of more than 320 million most of whom enjoy a good standard of living, the EC represents a ray of hope for the inhabitants of the Third World, as well as for those from the former planned economies of Eastern Europe. It offers the prospect not only of wealth, but also of a way of life that would never be attainable in their own countries. The rights granted by the EC to political refugees, the rights of entry offered by certain member states to citizens from their former colonies, as well as the opening up of all internal borders, have all contributed further to the inflow of illegal workers from outside the Community.

The EC: A 'haven' for refugees and illegal immigrants

It may seem paradoxical to claim that the political structure of the EC actually encourages illegal migration and illegal working when, since the global economic crisis, every member state has passed more and more restrictive immigration legislation, aimed at limiting the rights of entry for workers from outside the Community. However, the growing ease of movement within the Community, as well as inconsistencies between the legislation in the different member states, have encouraged immigration from outside and, in consequence, the extent of illegal working.

The relative ease of movement within the EC is a result, both of the ongoing Community policy to abolish frontier controls and the bilateral decisions of some member states to ease movement across their common borders. The Saarbrücken Accord, signed by Germany and France in 1983, reduced controls between these two countries. The Schengen Accord (1985) went much further, planning the gradual abolition of frontier controls between the Benelux countries, France and Germany. At the end of 1990, Italy and the five new German *Länder* which formerly constituted East Germany, also joined the Schengen group. Very shortly, these countries will form a unified area where people have virtually complete freedom of movement. Originally, the 1983 and 1985 accords were intended to facilitate the exchange and movement of workers from within the Community, but they have quickly shown themselves to be powerful instruments for importing immigration and illegal working from outside the Community.

To take one example, the Benelux countries and Germany want to restrict entry for certain categories of foreigners by obliging them to obtain short-term visas, but France does not require visas for these same people. As a result, they can enter through Paris and then without any difficulty, or control, move on to one of the other countries where immigration is more restricted.

Inconsistencies in the legislation of the different member states also help immigrants from outside the Community to gain entry to countries which are not actually signatories to the above accords. For example, the UK (which talks of ethnic minorities rather than immigrants) has admitted 2.2 million Indians, Pakistanis, and West Indians according to the 1981 Census. With British passports, they are entitled to move freely within the EC and to seek work in any member state. Many have done so. Even though the British government has been forced to limit severely the influx of immigrants and refugees from other Commonwealth countries, it is still the case that the UK is one of the main ports of entry for workers from outside the Community.

A law passed in 1983 introduced three categories of sovereignty for UK passport-holders ('full' citizen, citizen of territories administered from London, and citizen of an overseas territory) so as to limit the rights of abode in the UK. However, it did not resolve the problem referred to above (Documentation française 1986). Although only 'full' citizens have an automatic right to reside in the UK, people in the other two categories still have the right, as in the past, to hold a British passport and to enter the territory of the EC and move about there freely.

The exclusionary measures taken by the UK against immigrants from certain of its former colonies have also been the cause of the influx of Sri Lankans into France over the last few years. In May 1985 the UK government decided that all Sri Lankans wishing to enter the country would first have to obtain a visa. In June 1985, there was a reduction of 90 per cent in the number of Sri Lankans arriving at the UK's frontiers. At the same time, the other countries in the EC, in particular France, noticed a growing number of illegal workers from that same country.

These examples demonstrate the difficulties faced by the EC in pursuing a legislative programme aimed at economic harmonization, if it also wishes to control illegal immigration, which is another objective. As long as differences in immigration legislation persist, they will be used by the illegal immigrants themselves and by those trafficking in their labour.

Official encouragement for labour trafficking

Until 1989 the dictatorial regimes in Eastern Europe also took part, to varying degrees and from a variety of motives, in encouraging migration to the EC and illegal working. The lines of communication maintained by certain member states with the planned economies in the East often gave *de facto* encouragement to illegal immigration. Although not directly organized by the Eastern European governments, these movements benefited from their accommodating attitude and apparent support, as the following examples demonstrate.

The Polish network functioned, and still functions, in a way that is classic for North–South illegal working. The badly paid or generally wretched citizens of a poor country agree to work illegally in a high-wage country, notwithstanding the fact that the conditions of employment are deplorable. Even so, this particular network exhibited a number of peculiarities indicating the active connivance of the former Polish authorities. The system functioned in line with capitalist principles. European firms short of qualified manpower, or quite simply wanting to reduce wage costs, used Polish organizations to recruit skilled workers. They were paid in the currency and at the rates currently in force in the country where they were working and they soon found that they had substantial savings, which, even more importantly, could be changed on the black market in Poland.

It would appear that the ideological principles of the former Polish government were easily compromised by the prospect of economic gain. It is notable, for example, that Poles, who could normally only leave their country after undergoing a long and tedious administrative process, in these cases were easily able to obtain visas for these work contracts. The Polish authorities simply closed their eyes to this traffic in labour and foreign currency, because it offered a lifeline to their destitute people. They also extracted information about Polish communities living in the West or in the country where their citizens were working in return for the extension or renewal of visas.

The former East German authorities also seem without any doubt to have encouraged the traffic in manpower from Sri Lanka. The facts briefly are as follows. The Sri Lankans typically took a flight from Colombo to East Berlin via Moscow, alighting at Schönefeld airport and then travelling direct to West Berlin, using the Friedrichstraße metro station which the West Germans refused to police (Documentation française 1986). They then moved on to various different European countries, where they usually sought political asylum. It is inconceivable that the East German authorities, in all other respects kept so well-informed by a notoriously effective secret police, were unaware why Sri Lankans were landing in their hundreds in East Berlin without ever remaining there. It is also unlikely that this dictatorial regime, on the edge of bankruptcy, was not tempted to earn some much-needed hard currency from the traffic.

The decision taken by Germany (under pressure from the EC) in July 1985 to demand that all Sri Lankans should be issued with airport transit visas, which would only be granted if they already had a valid visa for entry into the country of final destination, made little or no difference to the situation. Germany remained a *de facto* Trojan horse for many illegal immigrants. For example, France recorded 1498 requests for political asylum in 1988, of which 1375 (91.7 per cent) had arrived illegally. 1078 of these requests were rejected and France, which had already accepted large numbers of Sri Lankans, thus also became a transit country for others who had asked for asylum in Switzerland, hoping to receive more favourable treatment there.

The opening of the Berlin Wall in 1989 and soon after the collapse of the Communist dictatorships basically did not change the position, on the contrary it may have exacerbated it.

The prospect of 'invading hordes'

The fears of tanks rolling in from the Warsaw Pact countries had barely disappeared before the full consequences of the free movement of people and ideas—something it had been promoting continuously for more than forty years—began to dawn on the EC. The spectre resurfaced of miserable hordes of starving people surging towards the West hoping to share in its wealth. With little exaggeration, it could be said that the Rome summit meeting of the EC in 1990 was dominated by the problem, or the myth, of the 'invading hordes'.

Even though it was impossible to plan for, let alone put exact numbers on the emigration from the countries of the East following their economic and ideological collapse, official experts suggested a figure of 20 million potential arrivals. The prediction caused considerable alarm amongst the ministers of the Community (*Le Monde* 1990). The French claimed that 'the possibility of this scale of emigration from the poor countries to the rich countries of Europe reopens the whole question of frontier controls'. The Greek representative stressed the changes that had already begun more than a year previously: 'Greece, a country traditionally with net emigration, is now having to cope with refugees from the parts of the Soviet Union bordering the Black Sea, from Bulgaria, and from Albania.'

It is certainly true that the picture, built-up from many different sources, was worrying. The annual influx of refugees from non-EC Europe stood at 100 000 a year throughout most of the 1980s, but in 1989 it jumped to 1 million (of which 700 000 were Germans it is true). The Soviet authorities indicated that between 500 000 and 600 000 of their citizens left the country in 1990, twice as many as in 1989. The foreign minister estimated that the figure would reach 1 million in 1991, once the Parliament had liberalized Soviet exit procedures from the country, but others put the figure for those who would like to emigrate as high as 45 million, 16 per cent of the Soviet population. Without doubt, these figures were maximized in order to persuade the EC to increase its financial aid, but even so they are not totally beyond the realms of possibility. The International Labour Office estimates

TABLE 7.2 *GNP per capita, 1988* (in $US)

Germany (West)	18 530
France	16 080
USSR (1986)	8 375
Hungary	2 460
Algeria	2 450
Poland	1 850
Tunisia	1 230
Morocco	750
Sri Lanka	420

Source: World Bank (1990).

that the transition to a market economy in the former USSR risks making 30 million people redundant in the near future. A report by the National Institute for Demographic Studies[2] foresees the possibility of between 1 and 1.5 million leaving the territory of the former Soviet Union every year for the next three or four years.

Such a massive wave of immigrants simply could not be easily absorbed into the EC, no matter whether they come from the South or the East. The current difficult economic climate (in particular unemployment), the social problems, and the need to integrate the immigrants already in the Community, as well as the xenophobia of a growing section of the population, are all likely to inhibit the legal acceptance of such numbers. In these circumstances, and with no other choices open to them, some of these potential immigrants will enter and work in the EC illegally in order to survive. What is more, they will be helped by the fact that there is no real European consensus on the whole question. As Hue[3] has said so forcefully:

Given the scale of the issues involved, the available micro- and macro-economic studies at all levels—national, European, and international—are both limited in scope and fragmented. The consideration given to the consequences of illegal working by Community institutions is almost nil, there has been almost no harmonization of regulations, and there are as yet no plans for co-ordination, a most serious omission as far as labour is concerned. (1991: 137).

Conclusion

In reality, the problems facing the EC as a result of the recent increase in mobility, especially as they affect poorer people, have only just begun to

---

[2] Unpublished study by the National Institute for Demographic Studies.
[3] G. Hue is a magistrate and head of the office set up by the French Ministry of Labour to control illegal working and the trafficking in labour.

emerge. They are very much larger and more worrying questions than those normally associated with the geography of inequality. The globalization of images, especially through television, now beams across all continents simplistic pictures of life-styles in the developed world offering prosperity and contentment. Not surprisingly, people everywhere are beginning to aspire to these models as they become aware of the glaring inequalities. The price of this new awareness must now be paid.

Whatever the area being considered, it is hard to underestimate the enduring effect of the new awareness. It is extremely difficult to stop or even to contain such migrations, and the illegal working that goes with them. No matter what scale is being looked at, the geography of inequality faces essentially similar questions. Is it realistic to assume that the disadvantaged inhabitants of impoverished urban areas will remain resigned to their mediocre lot, when wealth and security are constantly paraded before them? Is it any more realistic to assume that the Third World, where more than half of humanity lives in abject poverty, will not one day set out and march on the oasis eldorados that are the rich countries of the world?

Further reading

Clandestine working and illegal immigration are still subjects on which little research has been undertaken, because of difficulties in gaining access to the relevant information and the political sensitivity of the issues involved. However, some initial work on the legal and economic aspects can be found in Y. Moulier, J. P. Garson, and R. Silberman (1986), *Économie politique des migrations clandestins de main d'œuvre* (Paris). The sociological implications are discussed in S. Allen, and C. Wolkowitz (1988), *Home Working: Myths and Realities* (London); and in J. F. Lae, and A. M. Metaille (1988), *Travailler au noir* (Paris). An empirical study of the link between clandestine working and migration is S. Montagnée-Villette (1990), *Le Sentier, un espace ambigu* (Paris); a number of other relevant articles are to be found in *La Révue des Migrations Internationales* published by the Université de Poitiers.

PART V

Rural Adaptation

Rural adaptation

The one area of economic activity where the member states of the EC have acted in concert over a long period is agriculture and this section examines the agricultural policies of the past three decades and their consequences for the countryside and the people who live and work there.

Since the mid-1960s the Common Agricultural Policy (CAP), based on production subsidies and token structural reform, has been the dominant preoccupation of the Community and it has had a decisive impact on the development and present state of the rural landscape. However, the illogicality of a policy that produced highly priced food, much of which was not required to feed the population of the EC, and which was too expensive to be sold on the world market, was slowly recognized. Beginning in the 1980s, the CAP has begun to be totally rethought, but entrenched interests and disagreements about the direction that reform should take have meant that new policies have been slow to emerge and have often been less radical than the crisis facing agriculture required.

The main problem is that there are too many farmers in the EC working land that is agriculturally marginal, land which, with the help of the subsidies now used by the EC to sustain production, could well be used in other ways. There is a deep public affinity with the rural landscape in Western Europe and much sympathy for new policies, such as set-aside, which seek to emphasize nature and landscape conservation as part of an overall agricultural policy. Unfortunately, an important part of the rationale for the new direction is to reduce the level of EC expenditure on agriculture, so that there is no disguising the net reduction in public subsidy that the new policies herald.

The reality is that, despite the changes, the fundamentals of production subsidies still remain and, what is more, they are primarily directed towards northern Europe and the types of agriculture practised in the original six member states and those involved in the first expansion. Even if over-production had not created pressure for change, the markedly different crops and forms of agriculture in the Mediterranean countries that joined the EC in the course of the 1980s would have forced a fundamental rethink of the CAP.

It is abundantly clear that agriculture, in whatever form, cannot sustain the rural areas in the Community on its own; alternative forms of economic activity must also play their part. One obvious and dynamic possibility is tourism, which now employs 5 per cent of the total labour-force in the EC and can capitalize on the desire of Europe's largely urban population to become better acquainted with its rich rural and urban heritage. The price of reorientation is acceptance that the countryside and those who work it are not exclusively, or even primarily, engaged in food production. The reform of the CAP is going to involve a process of re-education that will take sometime to complete, but the new direction is inevitable and progress towards it will be inexorable whatever the strength of any rearguard action.

8 Set-aside and Landscape Preservation: The German Experience

Dietrich Denecke

Until well into the present century the general shortage of agricultural products and lack of foodstuffs have meant that rural land has been used and cultivated as intensively as possible. In the last twenty years, however, a radical change has occurred, occasioned not least by the agricultural policies of the EC. Overproduction has led to alternative crops being planted, the introduction of extensification, grazing, and set-aside programmes and, last but not least, widespread farm amalgamations. These changes and the policies which brought them about now largely dominate the nature of the agricultural industry in Europe. Farming is being rationalized and both livestock and arable production are becoming increasingly intensive with damaging environmental side-effects. Both processes are contributing to upset the delicate ecological balance in the agricultural landscape, the maintenance of which through traditional farming methods has become almost an article of faith. Assessing the scope for actually achieving an ecologically acceptable agriculture, which will further the aims of landscape conservation, has therefore become a crucial issue in the development of the EC, with important ramifications for the whole process of agreeing a common agricultural policy.

Fallow land and intensive farming: An historical perspective

Fallow and land not devoted to intensive agriculture were always a significant part of the traditional agricultural scene, accounting for an important part of the total area of farmland. Initially, fallow was part of the system of agricultural rotation and a means of sustaining the fertility of the soil, allowing depleted nutrient levels to recover so that grain and other crops could continue to be grown successfully. From the eighteenth century onwards, ploughed fallow was replaced in the three-year rotation by root crops, the so-called improved three-field rotation, which led to a significant

Chapter translated by Mark Blacksell.

intensification in the overall level of land use. The introduction of potatoes played a decisive role in this development. The subsequent change to the arable–grass system (Andreae 1955) heralded the introduction of a grass phase lasting between three and six years. The least intensive system was the field–forest rotation, which involved two years of cereal crops (rye and oats), followed by between four and six years of grass until scrub woodland had returned (birch forest). Only after between fifteen and twenty years could the woodland be cleared once again to allow the two years of arable crops to be grown. Until well into the nineteenth century this system was common in the Bavarian forest and other upland parts of central Germany.

Once arable farming was generally established, a process of reorganization which began in the eighteenth and nineteenth centuries, more than a third of the area of cultivated land at any one time was meadowland, grazing, or rough pasture. In addition there were large areas of unenclosed pasture and forest grazing, both of which were integral parts of the traditional rural economy. The eventual cultivation of this wasteland (for example, on the moorlands of north-west Germany) and the introduction of managed forestry effectively spelt the end of extensive grazing on unenclosed land.

In areas where the soils were particularly poor, there were large tracts of land, which could only ever be used for rough grazing. Waterlogging and changes brought about by activities such as forest clearance and turf cutting made anything other than the most extensive grazing impractical. Even as late as the seventeenth and eighteenth centuries fallow and wasteland used for grazing were still quite widespread in Germany. It was only in the second half of the eighteenth century that improvement gradually began to take hold, with intensively cultivated fields, seeded pastures (enclosed meadows and grassland for grazing animals), and managed forestry plantations (from the sowing of spruce seeds and beech nuts) all making an appearance.

There is, as yet, no comprehensive study of the development and distribution of fallow in central Europe at different periods, although preliminary research has been undertaken in some areas (see, for example, Diener 1928: 438–51). Nevertheless, it is clear that in the eighteenth and nineteenth centuries fallow and wasteland were to be found particularly in the drier areas; on chalky ground with thin soil (chalk grassland); in areas with sandy soils (heather moorland); and in the poorest parts of the central uplands of Germany. On a small-scale, marginal land in many locations was abandoned for cultivation (terraced slopes, narrow and waterlogged valley bottoms, areas on the forest edge) and allowed to remain fallow.

The present-day enforced abandonment of agricultural land gives renewed meaning to the above historical survey of the development of fallow and the way it was used. If land is once again to be made fallow, it is obviously relevant to know where such land existed in earlier times and how it was managed; forgotten land uses incorporating fallow can be revived. Models for the use and husbanding of fallow land may be derived from the study of traditional rotations incorporating fallow, leading to the development of rural conservation plans. Research on the development of vegetation on both grass and ploughed fallow is of particular relevance in this regard (see, for example, von Borstel 1974).

The emergence of social fallow (*Sozialbrache*) and the set-aside programme

The general growth in prosperity, and the associated development in commerce and services and opportunities for earning a living outside agriculture, as well the hugely increased scope for commuting into city centres from the surrounding rural periphery, all led to changes in the 1960s. They encouraged small farms, either to go out of business entirely, or to be reduced to the status of subsidiary activities. This trend was particularly noticeable in the western part of Germany where the economic hinterlands of the major cities were much enlarged. Uneconomic parcels of land, unwanted by the larger expanding farms as rented land, were either abandoned and left unused, or used less intensively. This phenomenon has been extensively studied by geographers (see, for example, Schulze von Hanxleden 1972; Walther 1984) and is now widely referred to as social fallow (*Sozialbrache*). The associated need for landscape conservation was recognized from the outset. Often with the help of government funds for agricultural restructuring, measures were taken, either to put land down to grass or forestry (Frankenberger 1960), or to combine extensive grazing with landscape conservation plans. Geographers, in particular, were quick to draw parallels between this modern process of reversion and the widespread abandonment of agricultural land that occurred in the late Middle Ages (Scharlau 1968).

It is important that present measures to reduce the amount of arable land are tied to the steps that were taken in the 1960s to promote landscape conservation. Green fallow takes arable land out of cereals or root crops and substitutes grass or legumes, and the scheme is part of the set-aside programmes of the EC and of the Federal Republic of Germany. It is a government programme, paid for from the public purse, to curb agricultural overproduction by means of taking land out of farming, either temporarily or more permanently depending on the situation. The programme has been

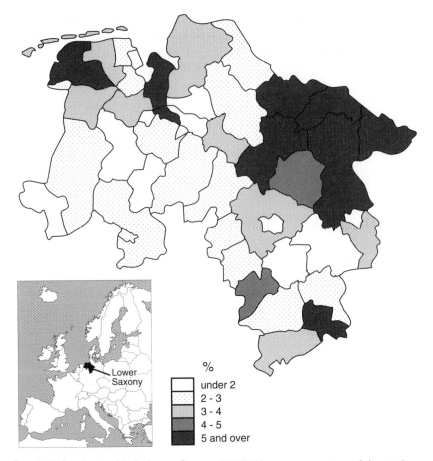

FIG. 8.1. Land set-aside in Lower Saxony, 1987/1988, as a percentage of the total area of arable land, by *Landkreise*

Source: Wilstacke and Plankl (1989).

discussed by the EC since 1981 and it is now gradually being put into practice. In 1986, the *Land* of Lower Saxony began a four year 'green fallow promotion campaign' and the data about this provide a means for evaluating the general efficacy of set-aside as a policy instrument (Arnold 1987; Wilstacke and Plankl 1989). The research undertaken so far on this programme has already enabled some preliminary conclusions to be drawn, illustrating clearly the areas in which the EC measures are most likely to be effective. A survey of the regional distribution of applicants for the years 1986–7 and 1987–8 (Table 8.1) shows that the land that is least well-suited to agriculture, the 30 per cent classified as moorland, has provided the highest proportion of applicants. The lowest percentages of area set-aside come from the coastal region and from south Oldenburg, areas where livestock farming is important and where there are pockets of very intensive production (5–8 per cent). If the two survey years are compared, it is only in the coastal region and in the south on the edge of the upland, that there is any marked increase (41 and 20 per cent respectively), clearly a delayed response to the programme (Fig. 8.1). It is also clear from the table that the larger farms of over 50 ha have participated most enthusiastically in the programme, although 44 per cent of the farms surveyed had more than 100 ha. It should also be noted that, on 80 per cent of farms, agriculture provided the main source of income for their owners or tenants. Altogether, in 1987–8, 7797 farmers took part in the programme, representing 13 per cent of the total and covering about 50 000 ha. There was a general increase of between 50 and 65 per cent in the number of farms going out of business between 1986 and 1988, the proportions being largest in the coast and moorland regions. The maximum amount of fallow on any single farm was 35 per cent.

The land not being kept as arable was sown once-off with either clover or a leguminous crop (known as pre-emptive planting) and then left for the required five-year period. Whether this land will subsequently remain unused agriculturally, or whether it will be used as pasture, or returned to arable, remains an open question.

The extent to which yields have been reduced varies considerably between the various crops, from 0.5 per cent for sugar beet to 8.3 per cent for peas and beans, but generally the reduction in yields is less than the reduction in arable area. In other words, the yields from the areas still being cultivated have generally risen. On the other hand, there would appear to have been no equivalent increase in livestock production. Farmers' reactions to the programme would seem, therefore, to have been to try to raise yields through more intensive cropping and increased fertilizer application on the remaining arable land. The bigger farms have increased in size and invested more in new machinery, but the smaller ones have reduced further their average size and their livestock holdings and, for the most part, have become part-time businesses.

The national figures for 1989–90 showed that in Germany as a whole, Lower Saxony has been the *Land* most actively involved in the set-aside programme (Table 8.1), followed by Bavaria and Baden-Württemberg (Golter 1986; Henze and Zeddies 1988; Wilstacke and Plankl 1989; König 1990). Overall in 1988, 25 289 farms covering 170 635 ha were involved with the set-aside programme. In 1989 the figures were 34 313 farms covering 222 384 ha, an increase of 35 per cent. In Germany as whole, 4.7 per cent

TABLE 8.1 *Set-aside in Germany (West), 1988*

Land	No. of contracts	Area (ha)	Areas set aside of which (%)					Percentage of area set-aside as		Average amount of land per contract holder in set-aside (ha)
			Rotation grass	Permanent grass	Forest	Rough grazing	Non-agric. uses	Arable land	Area in cereals	
Schleswig-Holstein	1 265	18 695	14.7	83.2	0.6	1.6	—	3.1	5.1	14.7
Hamburg	29	349	19.0	81.0	—	—	—	5.4	9.2	12.0
Lower Saxony	5 272	55 346	37.0	61.6	0.3	1.0	0.1	3.3	5.3	10.5
Bremen	2	12	42.0	58.0	—	—	—	0.6	1.0	6.0
North Rhine Westphalia	2 037	15 894	27.4	71.4	0.2	0.9	0.1	1.5	2.1	7.8
Hessen	2 996	13 243	36.8	60.2	0.5	2.1	0.4	2.6	3.6	4.4
Rhineland-Palatinate	1 864	11 085	34.1	61.0	0.7	1.5	2.7	2.6	3.5	5.9
Saarland	67	820	30.0	65.0		5.0		2.1	2.7	12.2
Baden-Württemberg	4 955	22 850	44.0	52.0	0.4		3.6	2.7	4.0	4.6
Bavaria	6 800	32 337		99.0	0.9		0.1	1.6	2.5	4.8
Berlin	2	4	25.0	—			75.0	0.5	0.7	2.0
GERMANY (WEST)	25 289	170 635	33.2	65.1	0.5	0.9	0.3	2.4	3.6	6.7

Source: König (1990).

TABLE 8.2 *Areas of land set-aside, number of holdings participating, and use of land by EC member states, 1988*

Member state	No. of applications	Area to be set-aside in (ha)	Percentage of area set-aside as:		Average area set-aside per applicant, (ha)
			Arable land	Area in cereals[a]	
Germany (West)	25 289	169 729	2.4	3.6	6.7
Italy	9 301[b]	155 606[b]	1.8	1	16.7
UK	1 750	54 779	0.9	1.3	31.6
Spain	518	34 229	0.3	0.4	66.1
France	1 002	15 707	—[c]	0.1	15.6
Ireland	77	1 310	0.1	0.3	17.0
Netherlands	195	2 621	0.3	1.3	13.4
Greece	n.a.	n.a.	n.a.	n.a.	n.a.
Belgium	32	329	—[c]	—[c]	10.2
TOTALS	38 164	434 310	0.9	1.3	11.3

[a] Calculations are on the basis of 1985 Eurostat data for land under cereals.
[b] Applications provisionally considered eligible. Actual area set-aside: 91 617 ha.
[c] Lower than 0.1 per cent.
n.a. = not available.

Source: Commission of the European Communities (1989a). The scheme was not applied in Denmark or Luxembourg in the 1988-9 agricultural season. Portugal is exempt.

of the land previously devoted to cereals was taken out of production, a figure which rose to between 10 and 17 per cent in a few of the most affected *Kreise* (counties). Of the various variants on set-aside, 67 per cent of the land was put down to green fallow, 31 per cent to rotational fallow, and only 1.8 per cent to permanent grass or woodland.

In the period 1986 to 1989 the effect of this subsidized fallow on the agricultural landscape has become clearly visible, but the impact is unlikely to be a permanent feature. The greening and the afforestation associated with the social fallow of the 1960s were far more effective in producing lasting extensification in some selected areas. The most obvious effect of the more recent, very lavish, government and Community measures is a reduction in cereal production (relief of downward market pressure), which in Germany in 1989 amounted to 100000 tonnes, mostly of summer wheat and winter barley.

In the other EC countries the take-up and implementation of the set-aside programme has varied widely (Table 8.2). In the UK it was seen as a realistic way of lowering price support and other agricultural subsidies (Baldock and Conder 1987). In France, on the other hand, the programme has hardly been taken up at all (Delorme 1987; Ilbery 1990). In Denmark and Ireland the institutions involved in the agricultural market have done everything they can to oppose adopting the programme in their respective countries. They have done nothing to advertise the programme, and it has not been widely taken up by farmers. The situation is similar in Belgium and the Netherlands, their excuses for not participating being the delays in introducing the programme, the unsatisfactory information and documentation, and the low level of subsidies on offer.

The relationship between the agricultural economy and nature and landscape conservation

Increasingly, nature and the rural landscape are in conflict with agriculture; in Germany agriculture poses the main threat, followed by forestry and tourism. The reasons for this are complex, but may be categorized broadly under three headings (see also Chapter 12):

(a) Direct conflicts engendered by changes in farming practices, that have led to the loss of a number of natural, or semi-natural, biotopes.

    (i) The removal of hedgerows, unwanted areas of waste ground, small woodlands, and minor water-courses.

    (ii) Coniferous plantations on open grassland, bogs and valley bottoms.

    (iii) The conversion of extensive meadowland into arable.

(iv) The abandoning of traditional extensive farming systems on areas of open grassland, moorland etc.

Natural and semi-natural biotopes are now only found on between 2 and 3 per cent of agricultural land in Germany.

(b) More intensive agricultural use being made of areas that previously were only farmed extensively.

(i) An increase in the use of fertilizers and pesticides.

(ii) Alterations in harvest times (invariably bringing forward).

(iii) Drainage schemes.

(iv) Simplified rotations, monocultures.

(v) More intensive grazing (effects on the summer alpine-pastures etc.).

(c) Negative effects on neighbouring ecosystems and the whole natural balance through the seepage into the ground- and surface-water of artificial fertilizers and pesticides, as well as more general changes to the water-balance through drainage schemes and irrigation etc.

Defence of the natural world and environmental protection must therefore be built into agricultural planning and policy, especially where the introduction of extensification measures provide a real opportunity for introducing forms of land use and farming techniques that favour landscape protection.

Set-aside and archaeological conservation areas

In Germany, the protection of archaeological sites is seen as a matter of public interest, the subject of legislation and the official responsibility of a government department, just like agriculture and the land registry. Despite this, however, there has so far been no attempt, either in principle or practice, at any meaningful co-ordination of extensification and set-aside measures and official plans for protecting archaeological sites. Many such sites, some of considerable size, are on agricultural land that is still being farmed. They are completely unprotected from modern cultivation techniques, which use sophisticated machinery to penetrate ever deeper into the soil profile, leaving it even more vulnerable to the ravages of soil erosion.

The new ancient monument protection legislation passed by the German *Länder* has resulted in official lists being drawn up of archaeological sites, including detailed site plans. These show very clearly where all kinds of archaeological sites are located—settlements, burial grounds, old field systems, etc. These are particularly valuable, because the detailed mapping of sherd finds enables the true areal extent of the sites, much of it hidden under ploughed land, to be properly defined. For example, fields containing hidden archaeological remains must now be properly surveyed.

From an archaeological point of view, therefore, there is an urgent need to identify relevant sites, not only on arable land, but on pasture and in woodland as well. To do this, extensive conservation and land-use plans need to be agreed, similar to those drawn up by archaeologists in England more than a decade ago (Pritchard 1978; Klindt-Jensen 1978; Shadla-Hall and Hinchcliffe (eds.) 1980). There is now a real opportunity to integrate the needs of archaeological conservation into extensification and set-aside programmes. The main problem to be overcome is that the relevant sites are rarely selected and reported by the farmers. The task is left to archaeological or farming officials and is an inevitable source of tension with the landowners.

Integrated agricultural and landscape preservation plans

In its 1985 'green paper' on agriculture the European Commission (1985) stated unequivocally, that in a modern industrial society the role of agriculture was not confined to strategic economic and social issues: it should also include the conservation of the rural environment. The green paper went on to emphasize the negative effects in the form of environmental damage, and of the growing technical approach to farming. It recognized the need to retain and nurture agricultural practices, which helped protect and conserve the rural environment and the cultural landscape as a whole. Every aspect of the EC's agricultural policy should be in harmony with the needs of environmental conservation and the paper expressly states that the set-aside programme should contribute to this goal. There has subsequently been discussion of the scope for protecting agricultural ecosystems and it is proposed that land made available as a result of the set-aside programme could be used for non-agricultural purposes in the framework of integrated countryside management programmes (Commission of the European Communities 1988b). As yet however, it has to be admitted that the EC has not succeeded in reconciling its agricultural and environmental policies (see Chapter 11) to any significant extent.

In Schleswig-Holstein, even before the EC's commitment stemming from its extensification goals, attempts had been made to combine set-aside with landscape and environmental conservation, a lead which the other German *Länder* followed. The foresight of Schleswig-Holstein is remarkable, for it was having to deal with agricultural land that was intensively farmed and encompassed a wide range of different natural conditions—marshland to moorland, coastal *Geest* to uplands. The main farming systems were dairying and grain production.

The extensification programme was by no means only aimed at controlling and reducing the level of agricultural output; from the outset it sought to provide protection for the environment and the landscape, to bring back natural flora and fauna and to develop new forms of land use. The programme was first set out in the Schleswig-Holstein Farmers' Journal (*Das Schleswig-Holsteinische Bauernblatt*) in 1985, under the headline 'Environmental protection is accorded the highest political priority'. What is proposed is a nine-category classification of ecological, or land-use types where environmentally friendly farming methods would seem to be appropriate (Table 8.3). The aim will be to evolve extensive, and more 'natural' forms of land use and farming, with any reductions in yield being compensated for by lower levels of expenditure. Farmers in the scheme have to adhere to an agreed and legally binding economic plan. For example, the wet-meadowland contract requires that water levels and the groundwater table may not be altered, that no fertilizers or sprays may be used, and that there are prescribed harvest times (Jones 1990).

A partial break from arable is operated, involving a 5 to 10 m wide border being left around cereal fields, so that natural plant communities can re-establish themselves. It represents a return to the same kind of small-scale

TABLE 8.3 *Numbers of contracts and areas of set-aside in Schleswig-Holstein*

Contract type	1985		1986		1987	
	No.	Areas (ha)	No.	Areas (ha)	No.	Areas (ha)
Wiesenvogelschutz	136	783	486	3 285	900	5 617
Brachvogelschutz	—	—	192	1 395	278	1 826
Birkwildschutz	—	—	14	48	15	52
Sumpfdotterblumenwiesen	—	—	53	200	213	873
Kleinseggenwiesen	—	—	11	40	46	146
Amphibiengrünland	—	—	129	930	1 296	12 188
Trockenes Magergrünland	—	—	9	39	40	334
Ackerwildkräuter	—	—	10	15	15	23
Ackerbrache	—	—	165	623	326	1 101
TOTAL	136	783	1 069	6 575	3 219	22 161

Notes: Wiesenvogelschutz = meadow bird-conservation area; Brachvogelschutz = fallow-land bird-conservation area; Birkwildschutz = black-grouse conservation area; Sumpfdotterblumenwiesen = marsh-marigold meadows; Kleinseggenwiesen = rush meadows; Amphibiengrünland = amphibian-rich wetlands; Trockenes Magergrünland = dry natural grassland; Ackerwildkräuter = farmland-game habitats; Ackerbrache = farmed-fallow land.
Source: A. Jones (1990: 13).

field pattern that existed before amalgamation and restructuring occurred, the main landscape features of which were grassland margins and hedgerows. The whole system is laid down and monitored by the *Land* Office for Green Spaces and the Office for Landscape and Nature Conservation.

In the first year, 1985, only 136 farms covering 783 ha took part, but this rose in 1986 to 1069 farms and 6575 ha, and in 1987 to 3129 farms and 2261 ha. There is clearly a steady increase and, so far, the programme may be deemed a success. It was given farther strong public and political support by the founding of the Schleswig-Holstein Farmers' Union, a body set up by the farmers themselves with the express intention of promoting landscape conservation and environmental protection. The main land-use types included so far are pasture (5617 ha) and wet-meadowland (12 188 ha), as well as wet, but heavily used land producing only small yields, where the cost of conservation measures will be low. Regionally, the marsh areas in the west and the areas covered by recent moraine deposits in the east are where most land has been designated, all land primarily devoted to dairying.

From a nature and landscape conservation point of view, the success of the programme will depend on whether the measures stabilize, or improve, the status of endangered animal and plant communities. Conservation plans concentrating on landscape and nature have so far been developed primarily for grassland that is now surplus to requirements, such as mountain meadows in the higher parts of the Central Uplands, water meadows in the wide valleys of eastern Bavaria, and unimproved limestone grasslands. If grazing or cropping for hay and silage are no longer practised there are immediate changes in the natural vegetation, bushy and woody vegetation reappears, and natural succession ensures that the land quickly begins to revert to forest.

Nature and landscape conservation plans must incorporate measures from the outset which limit the invasion of rank grasses and weeds, leading to a reduction in species variety. Open meadowlands are often especially attractive for recreation and are of importance as historic landscapes. The mountain meadows in the Harz Mountains, for example, originated as clearings caused by the over-use of the forest for mining and timber production. It was only in the eighteenth and nineteenth centuries that they began to be used as grazing for cattle from the Harz region. One of the proposals in present conservation plans for the Harz is subsidies for grazing sheep (Dierschke 1980).

Conclusion

Landscape conservation and a sustainable policy towards natural resources cannot be left solely to nature protection agencies and legislation. At the national end of the spectrum, they must be part of environmentally responsible agricultural and forestry policies. Locally, they must be put into practice with real commitment by those who actually work the land. Extensification and sustainable, ecologically sound farming methods are basically compatible with traditional practices and research should be undertaken into both their intrinsic importance and how they can best be applied in practice. Geography has a special contribution to make in this task, not least through initiating large-scale regional comparisons in Europe.

Further reading

The reduction in the land area devoted to agriculture is an issue that has so far been dealt with primarily in the planning literature. Geographical research has mainly involved applied studies, evaluation of developments, and the processes at work, as well as undertaking a limited amount of comparative work. Those interested in finding out more about the reduction in the amount of cultivated land, and the growing importance of landscape conservation, will find that the following provide a useful introduction to the main topics dealt with in this chapter.

T. Gunzelmann (1987) 'Die Erhaltung der historischen Kulturlandschaft. Angewandte historische Geographie des ländlichen Raumes und Beispiele aus Franken' (Preserving the historical cultural landscape: Examples of applied historical geography in Franconia), *Bamberger wirtschaftsgeographische Arbeiten* 4 (Bamberg) is a good example of research into historic and relict cultural landscapes. It is part of a long tradition of research into the evolution of the cultural landscape in historical geography and it uses examples from the south German region of Franconia to illustrate how historic rural landscapes are being conserved in the face of intensive land-consolidation programmes, through the preservation of historic sites, and the introduction of landscape protection measures.

The whole question of the contraction of the area under cultivation is considered in Schulze von Hanxleden (1972) 'Extensivierungserscheinungen in der Agrarlandschaft des Dillgebietes' (Extensification and the agricultural landscape of the Dill region), *Marburger geographische Schriften* 54 (Marburg). One of the main changes brought about by the industrialization that accompanied the economic upturn after World War II was rural depopulation. Small farmers were particularly badly affected, many farms being simply abandoned. Using the Dill region of Hesse as an example, Schulze von Hanxleden examines the problems associated with extensification, including the implications for rural social geography generally.

As far as the planned reductions in agricultural output, through set-aside and afforestation programmes, are concerned, the only available studies confine themselves to current problems and are based on the analysis of published official statistics. Two good examples are: A. Jones, (1990), 'New directions for West German agricultural policy', *Journal of Rural Studies* 6: 9–16; and L. Wilstacke and R. Plankl (1989), 'Freiwillige Produktionsminderung, empirische Analyse' (Voluntary reduction in production: An empirical analysis), *Schriftenreihe des Bundesministeriums für Ernährung, Landwirtschaft und Forsten*, Reihe A, Heft 366 (Münster). The ecological effects of set-aside programmes, as well as the whole issue of landscape protection in the areas affected, are considered by: B. Andreae (1984), 'Landbau oder Landschaftspflege? Räumliche Verteilung und Nutzmöglichkeiten brachgefallener Agrarstandorte in der BRD' (Farming or landscape conservation? The spatial distribution, and potential use, of set-aside land in the FRG), *Geographische Rundschau* 36: 187–94; and by U. Bremer (1988), 'Siedlungsstrukturelle, ökonomische und ökologische Wirkungen von Fläche- und Produktionsstillegungen in der Landwirtschaft' (The impact of reduced agricultural output and set-aside programmes on the settlement structure, economy, and ecology of the regions affected), *Forschungen des Bundesministeriums für Raumordnung, Bauwesen und Städtebau* 462 (Bonn).

There are very few comparative studies of the impact of European agricultural policy on the cultural landscape, but a good example is provided by V. Newcombe (1987), *Rural Schleswig-Holstein and Mid-Wales: A Comparative Study of Regional Development* (London).

9 The Common Agricultural Policy and the Development of Agriculture: Problems and Perspectives

Manuel Corbera

Introduction

At the present time the European Community is, undoubtedly, in general terms, the principal world agricultural power. It is the leading world producer of milk, butter, cheese, wine, and sugar; since the last enlargement it has also come to occupy the first place in terms of meat production and the second for wheat and barley (Table 9.1). Furthermore, it is self-sufficient in terms of most of the major products of its dominant climatic regimes, with only three exceptions of any importance: fresh fruit, maize, and sheep and goat meat (Table 9.2).

The position of the EC can be explained by reference to many factors. Amongst these are its natural resources: the dominant temperate climate, the disposition of relief, the excellent soils of its sedimentary basins and polders, and the complementarity of its Atlantic, continental, and Mediterranean agricultural production. However, the actual conditions of production are

TABLE 9.1 *Agricultural output in the EC and other major producers, 1989* (% of world production)

Product	EC12	USA	Canada	USSR
All meats*	18.6	16.9	1.8	11.7
Concentrated milk	28.2	20.0	1.6	13.2
Butter	22.5	7.6	1.3	22.9
Cheese	32.1	17.5	1.7	6.2
Wheat	14.7	10.3	4.5	16.8
Barley	27.7	5.2	6.9	30.8
Sugar	14.8	6.1	0.1	9.0

* Data for meat refer to 1988.
Sources: Comunidades Europeas (1991; 1992).

Chapter translated by Allan M. Williams.

TABLE 9.2 *Levels of agricultural self-sufficiency in the EC, 1987/1988* (%)

Product	%
Maize*	89.7
Rice*	95.1
All cereals	113.4
Potatoes	103.1
Sugar	123.5
All vegetables	105.6
Fresh fruit, non-citrus	84.5
Citrus fruits	70.3
Wine	103.4
All meat	101.7
Beef	107.3
Pigmeat	103.8
Sheep and goat meat, etc.	82.9
Chickens	105.1
Fresh milk	100.9
Condensed milk	175.0
Cheese*	105.9
Butter	105.0

* Data for maize and cheese are for 1986, and for rice are for 1988/9.
Source: Comunidades Europeas (1991).

also important. Amongst the latter, we can highlight intensive land utilization, good adaptation of production to natural conditions, the efficiency of agricultural structures, and the adoption of advanced production techniques which make it possible to sustain a highly intensive agriculture with high yields.

The situation of farming in the EC can also be explained—and perhaps this is the principal factor—as the outcome of the application of a common agricultural policy that has served to stimulate and direct the development of agriculture. The obvious conclusion is that in the absence of the Community framework none of the member states—not even France—would have achieved a global status amongst the producer countries similar to that held today by the EC. However, the privileged position of the EC in world agriculture has not only been the outcome of the aggregation of the agricultures of the twelve member states. It is also the outcome of the linked evolution of these countries over a period of time, while subject to the influence of common policy intervention measures. The aim of this paper is to evaluate the extent to which community policy can be considered to be responsible for the changes in agriculture, and also for the problems that encompass the sector.

The role of policy intervention in the agricultural sector

The peculiarities of capitalist agriculture: The requirement for agricultural policy

It has been clearly demonstrated that the development of agriculture does not follow in the footsteps of industry in the capitalist model. We can summarize the causes of these differences in terms of three features:

(a) *The ownership of land.* In effect, land constitutes a fixed and non-substitutable factor of production whose ownership calls for the immobilization of large quantities of capital. Clearly, the system of leasing allows for the substitution of the divided payment of a rent that the business person recovers in the commercialization of production. However, this system is not always possible and, in any case, detracts from investment in fixed capital (irrigation, business premises, etc.), while the suspension of leasing contracts means that such investments will remove the benefits of ownership.

(b) *Agriculture is subject to natural conditions and biological rhythms that are not always totally controllable.* Dependence on climatic conditions, for example, means that agriculture is subject to extremes. This signifies a lack of regularity in production which, from the point of view of a capitalist enterprise, is unacceptable. Another feature is that, in spite of biological advances, the cycles of agricultural production are rather long (usually annual frequencies but sometimes of several years, as in the cases of animal-rearing or forestry products). This requires the maintenance of circulating capital in the orbit of production during the period imposed by the productive cycle. It is clear that this last difficulty is also characteristic of some industrial production. In the latter the contradiction is resolved by investment in fixed capital which allows accelerated capital circulation. This solution is problematic in agriculture, not only owing to the biological or natural conditions which offer formidable and durable resistance to manipulation, but also as a result of non-utilization of machinery during prolonged annual periods of time, which contributes to its deterioration.

(c) *The rapid saturation of demand.* In effect, the demand for agricultural products is much more inelastic than for industrial ones. When a country arrives at the point at which its basic food needs are met, a further increase of production will give rise to an internal surplus. If there is also inability to export (perhaps as a result of the saturation of the international market), this leads to a fall in prices. To this is added the difficulty (mostly overcome today) of storing agricultural products, given their perishable character (Tamames 1988). The tendency of the agroprocessing industry—as with all industry—to reduce the proportion of raw materials that is used in the process of production (through a more intensive utilization of the former and the partial substitution of synthetic materials) only serves to accelerate the saturation of demand. There has been some diversification of the commodities produced and this has allowed for a small increase in demand, but this is insufficient to counteract the other effects.

These peculiarities of the agricultural sector have meant that capitalist enterprise is only partly implanted in it. Capital has been deterred by the difficulties of the agricultural sector and has been attracted by the returns that are possible in the industrial and service sectors. Only the agroprocessing industry has offered comparable returns and as a result of this—and, of course, of market mechanisms—has established a fuller connection of capital with the agrarian sector.

In contrast, family holdings predominate in Europe. As heirs of the peasantry of the *ancien régime*, these farms have tended to be excessively fragmented and have lacked sufficient capital to bring about a technical transformation that would permit an improvement in their incomes. In a system of absolutely free exchange, there would undoubtedly have developed an international division of labour; those countries with comparative advantages in certain respects, would have specialized in the production of raw materials and thereby would have come to monopolize the larger part of world production. Other countries, including some of the more industrialized ones, would have ended up as largely non-agricultural economies. Improvements to, and reductions in the costs of transport, together with the better resource and social conditions of the specialized agricultural countries, would have led to severe and unflagging competition for the small family farms of most European countries. Furthermore, as farmers came to see their incomes were lower than those in the other major economic sectors, there would have been massive abandonment of the sector and of rural areas in general.

However, the situation that would have been created under such conditions was foreseen by the European countries if only through some bitter experiences. In the first place, the failure of internal food supplies made them absolutely dependent on imports; the suspension of these imports—for whatever reason—would have exposed their populations to hunger, as indeed was experienced during World War II. In the second place, the disappearance of the agricultural sector would have led to a massive influx of workers into the manufacturing and service-sector labour markets. This would have lowered incomes in these sectors while also creating permanent social and political instability. Finally, abandonment of cultivation of the land potentially would have exposed large areas to erosion, thereby causing an ecological crisis.

For these reasons, for some years prior to the signing of the Treaty of Rome and the creation of the CAP, a large proportion of the European countries already considered farming to be a strategic sector that required political intervention in order to sustain agricultural improvements and, sometimes, even the conditions of production. France, for example, had established ONIC in 1936 (Office National Interprofessionel des Céréales) to control the market for cereals, fix prices, and to act as a credit agency which advanced funds to farmers against their harvest. After the war the Law of Leaseholding and Share-cropping offered farmers some protection *vis-à-vis* landowners. By 1960 the Law of Agricultural Guidance had already created SAFER (Sociétés D'Aménagement Foncier et d'Établissement Rural) and FASASA (Fond d'Action Sociale pour l'Amélioration des Structures Agricoles) whose respective objectives were the redistribution of agricultural land and demographic renewal in farm management. A policy of infrastructural improvement was also adopted by the German government during the 1950s. The 1953 *Strukturprogramm* and the 1955 *Plan Verde* had the concrete objectives of plot concentration and infrastructural improvement. In Italy, the correction of structural disequilibria, resulting from the persistence of the latifundia, was tackled from 1950 but its results can only be assessed as modest. The United Kingdom also introduced protectionism. Since the nineteenth century the UK had tended to abandon its own agriculture, instead relying on Commonwealth imports. However, it initiated a change in agricultural policy after World War II, via the 1947 Agriculture Act and subsequent legislation in 1957. This was, in some senses, a continuation of the emergency policies that had been introduced during World War II. The aim was to guarantee reasonable incomes for British farmers without unduly burdening consumers with the costs of this (Molinero 1990).

It is evident that the problem faced by all these diverse agricultural policies was how to reconcile the interests of farmers (that is, to maintain satisfactory levels of incomes), with those of the consumers (who demanded lower prices for basic food products). What has been said of consumers applies equally to businesses in the secondary and tertiary sectors; increases in the prices of agricultural products give rise, sooner or later, to increases in wages. Nevertheless, the result—perhaps inevitably—was that an important part of the burden of financing agricultural policy fell on the consumers (through prices which were higher than those on world markets, and taxation) and the other economic sectors. The only way of reducing the burden falling on governments, other than seeking out additional resources (such as the receipts received at frontiers from levies on imports), was to improve the conditions of agricultural production with a view to lowering the costs of production.

The advantages of a common agricultural policy

Naturally, the first six members of the Community were already fully aware of the problematic character of agriculture. The objectives of the future common agricultural policy, were already set out in the Treaty of Rome itself (Art 39): development of productivity, a fair standard of living for farmers, stabilization of markets, security of supply, and reasonable prices for consumers. However, this also underlined the common contradictions in this sector. Consequently it was a declared aim to seek out means which would allow for movement to an equilibrium.

One of the reasons why agriculture was the sector for which a common policy was first established, was that it was already clear at an early stage what the concrete aims of such a policy should be. In addition, there was realization of an unquestionably urgent need to reduce the problems that agriculture would face following the enlargement of the spatial and economic framework within which this sector operated. Georges Pompidou sought to convince the French—in his declaration to the National Assembly on 21 October 1964—that the CAP had been a French victory over Germany and was compensation for the competition which French industry would be likely to experience from the powerful German manufacturers (Teulon 1991). In practice, time has shown that the major benefits from the application of the CAP were not restricted to France. Germany, of course, also had the need for, and was eager for, a common agricultural policy. However, Pompidou's argument was far from being totally false; at that time, France did face a major economic burden in sustaining the agricultural sector. It was not only the fact that the CAP was in accord with the objectives set out in Rome that pushed along, with great urgency, the establishment of this policy. There was also the fact that the financing of the sector could be approached via the establishment of other resources, something which would be possible as a result of the new scale of the EC's operations.

Naturally, there were other reasons for the establishment of the CAP. Among these was the needs of the Community itself. Leaving aside the importance of the common market in agriculture, there were grave contradictions in this sector which could have mortgaged the future of the Community. Industrial competition within the Community could have developed within an unequal framework, differentiated by the distinctive wage requirements that would inevitably have followed from inequalities in agricultural prices (Tamames 1988). On the other hand, the establishment of a single market for agricultural products offered undoubted advantages beyond that of the simple enlargement of the market itself. It was not possible to rely on the incentives that competition offered farmers to bring about the objectives of raising incomes and adjusting production to regional potentials. At the time, the enlargement of geographical space would have allowed for compensation for frequent regional fluctuations. All this would give place to an increased, more stable and more diverse supply, but at comparatively more advantageous prices (Comunidades Europeas 1989*a*).

Forms of intervention and mechanisms

In principle, the only means of establishing an agricultural policy was to set up a protectionist regime within the Community space at the same time as internal barriers were eliminated. The earlier negative experience of the Benelux countries, in whose customs union (founded 1 January 1948) each state was given freedom to establish its own mechanisms for guaranteeing adequate levels of income for farmers (Tracy 1989), confirmed this argument. The question of exactly which policy to adopt was far from being simple because there were already important differences amongst the six members in their agricultural reference points. While France was clearly an exporter and benefited from external protection and the opening of the internal market, Germany was an importer of agricultural products, which therefore did not contemplate such measures with the same degree of enthusiasm. These differences became evident in the long negotiations over farm policy. Nevertheless, these obstacles were finally overcome.

The CAP was established from the beginning as a multi-dimensional policy. The first and the principal objective was and is guaranteeing the levels of farm income, through establishing protectionist mechanisms in the internal market or by compensating the producers of some products with little or no protection. This gave rise to four forms of market organization. The most general, and that which regulates more than 70 per cent of agricultural production, is at the same time the most protectionist and requires the greatest level of intervention. It assumes the establishment at the common frontier of a system of exclusions, a *prélèvement* that equalizes the prices (set on world markets) of imported products to the levels of community prices, and a 'restitution' payment which allows exports to the world market at competitive prices. At times, it also requires special intervention for many products (cereals, butter, processed milk powder, sugar, and beef) which, until recently, assumed excess production would be purchased at an intervention price which was considered the minimum that would guarantee farmers' incomes. For other products (pork, some fruit and vegetables, and table wine) which were also included in this form of market organization, the system of intervention constituted support for the private storage of excess output. Another type of market organization, one which effects approximately one-quarter of farm products (eggs, chickens, quality wines, flowers, and certain fruits and vegetables) is limited to establishing different intervention mechanisms against external producers, but without intervening in the internal market. For those products in which the EC has agreed with the GATT (General Agreement on Trade and Tariffs) not to establish protectionist barriers (rape, sunflower seeds, cotton, peas), the form of internal market guarantee has been to subsidize the processing industries that utilize Community products. Finally, some very specialized products (flax, hops, and silk for example) receive direct support (Comunidades Europeas 1989*d*).

Referring to the second dimension of the CAP, the objective has been to improve the conditions of agricultural production. In this respect, there were considerable structural divides amongst the six members. In some areas they maintained very different national policies which were not always oriented even to the same ends. Initially, the aim was to co-ordinate these national policies, and to finance some projects from a common fund. Only at the end of the 1960s (1968) was an integral structural reform plan presented; this became known as the Mansholt Plan. The principal objective of this plan was the modernization of farms, enlarging their size, rejuvenating their management, and raising their levels of professionalism and, more generally, that of those who worked in them. They proposed joint measures that should lead to a reduction in agricultural output and livestock numbers. But the cost of this plan was estimated at $US31000 million in 1970, a price that was considered to be far too high. This led to its adoption being delayed until 1972. Even then it was only partially implemented, being reduced to a bare minimum. The means of farm modernizing were limited to state guaranteed loans, subsidized rates of interest, and preferential acquisition of those lands that belonged to farmers who were leaving agriculture; assistance was available only to those farms that were able to survive economically. On the other hand, complementary measures were established for encouraging the cessation of agricultural activity by farmers whose activity was not economically viable and to facilitate the early retirement of those aged over 54. Finally, all farmers were offered opportunities for professional training and advancement.

The results: Successes, limitations, and problems

Positive results

The first positive result that needs to be highlighted is self-sufficiency, in large part, in the basic agricultural products. This objective, which is one of those recognized in Article 39 of the Treaty of Rome, was attained for some products from an early stage. But there has been considerable improvement even for those products that have not achieved this goal at the present time (Table 9.3).

TABLE 9.3 *Evolution of levels of EC self-sufficiency in the more important agricultural products (%)*

	Total cereals	Wheat	Sugar	Fruit and vegetables	Butter	Cheese	Beef	Sheep and goat meat
EC6	86	94	82	80	92	99	95	56
EC9	91	104	100	82	98	103	96	66
EC10	118	129	101	83	134	107	108	76
EC12	113	123	124	95	105	106	104	83

Sources: Comunidades Europeas (1989*c*; 1992).

Naturally, this advance has only been possible thanks to an increase in agricultural production that has taken place, to a greater or lesser extent, in each and every one of the member states. For the EC10 this averaged almost 26 per cent between 1973 and 1987 (Table 9.4).

This increase in production is in large part the result of Community intervention in the market through the mechanisms of protectionism and guaranteed prices. The guarantee of being able to sell all production, including any surplus, at a minimum (intervention) price that has generally been above that of the world market, has been a major incentive. Furthermore, this increase in production has been obtained despite a not unappreciable

TABLE 9.4 *Quantitative evolution of total EC agricultural production*

Countries	1967	1973	1981	1987
Belgium	78.7	100	101.5	114.8
Denmark	—	100	121.7	137.3
West Germany	89.0	100	110.8	115.4
Greece	—	100	121.3	123.4
France	83.6	100	103.4	129.1
Ireland	—	100	120.6	133.3
Italy	95.3	100	118.6	125.8
Luxembourg	98.0	100	96.9	104.0
Netherlands	74.8	100	108.6	158.0
United Kingdom	—	100	108.6	118.0
EC10	—	100	112.4	125.9

Source: Author's calculations based on information provided by Eurostat, Luxembourg.

TABLE 9.5 *Employment in agriculture 1960–1989* (% of total employed population); *and cultivated area, 1967 and 1988* (% of total area)

Year	EC6 %	EC6 Index	Denmark, Ireland, UK %	Denmark, Ireland, UK Index	Greece %	Greece Index	Spain and Portugal %	Spain and Portugal Index	EC12 %	EC12 Index
Population										
1960	20.8	100	10.8	100	57.1	100	42.7	100	21.1	100
1970	12.6	61	4.8	45	40.8	71	29.6	69	13.8	65
1980	8.5	41	3.7	34	30.3	53	21.6	51	9.6	46
1985	7.2	35	3.4	31	28.9	51	20.0	47	8.7	40
1989	5.9	28	3.0	28	27.5	48	14.6	34	7.0	33
Cultivated area										
1967	60.8	100	75.4	100	61.6	100	84.2	100	62.0	100
1988	54.7	90	75.6	100	43.5	71	53.0	63	566.9	92

Sources: Comunidades Europeas (1991; and 1992).

reduction in the quantity of agricultural land in use, as well as of a considerable part of the active agricultural population (Table 9.5). This highlights the strong advance in productivity.

This progress was most intense in the 1960s, that is to say in the early years of the Community's existence. Between 1968 and 1973 there was an annual average increase of 6.7 per cent, which later fell to 2.5 per cent (Comunidades Europeas 1985). In part, this was due to the economic crisis, which had a negative impact on the supply of employment in other sectors of the economy, and also the ageing of the rural population itself. This same dynamism, that is to say the strong decline in the active agricultural population during the 1960s and its later slowing down, was reproduced in a similar form in those current members of the Community which had not yet been integrated during the 1960s.

The increased productivity, which was seen as being favourable because of its effects in reducing the active agricultural population, has also been seen to be accompanied by an enlargement in the size of agricultural holdings (Table 9.6). At the same time, there has been modernization of these holdings, that is their mechanization and intensification through massive inputs of resources. During the 1960s alone, the stock of tractors in the Community increased twofold and that of harvesters fivefold, while the use of chemical fertilizers in the EC10 increased, during the 1970s, by more than 25 per cent.

All these changes occurred without substantially modifying the basic model of the agricultural enterprise. This continued to be family-based, as

TABLE 9.6 *Evolution by size of EC agricultural holdings, and of their cultivated areas (% of total)*

Size of holdings (ha) and area cultivated	1960		1970		1980		1987	
	EC10	EC12	EC10	EC12	EC10	EC12	EC10	EC12
1–5	51.0	—	46.9	—	47.1	50.2	46.2	49.2
% cultivated	11.3	—	8.3	—	7.3	7.8	6.4	7.1
6–10	21.6	—	18.9	—	17.0	17.0	16.2	16.8
% cultivated	13.4	—	9.6	—	7.7	7.8	6.6	7.1
11–20	16.8	—	16.9	—	14.9	13.9	14.4	13.5
% cultivated	20.5	—	17.2	—	13.6	12.9	12.9	11.6
21–50	10.4	—	12.9	—	14.9	13.1	15.8	13.7
% cultivated	26.9	—	27.9	—	29.5	26.5	28.5	25.8
> 50	0.2	—	4.4	—	6.0	5.7	7.5	6.8
% cultivated	27.9	—	37.1	—	42.0	45.0	46.8	48.9

Source: Author's calculations based on Comunidades Europeas (1989c).

is demonstrated by the fact that, in 1977, only 7.7 per cent of agricultural workers in the Community of Twelve were non-family employees. This proportion only rises to 19.5 per cent even if work-year data are employed for the statistical base (Comunidades Europeas 1992).

For many commentators, it seems that the objectives formulated in Article 39 of the Treaty of Rome were to blame for having been too generous. It is clear that consumers have had to pay prices above those of the world market. In any case, the approach does not seem reasonable if we consider that expenditure on food, drink, and tobacco constituted no more than 21.6 per cent of the final consumption of households in the EC12; this percentage is reduced further to 17.6 per cent if the analysis is limited just to expenditure on food (Comunidades Europeas 1991). That is to say, it is rather less than one-half of the proportion it occupied 30 years earlier. Since then, given these changes, agriculture has come to have little weight in the determination of wages in the industrial and tertiary sectors.

The problems of the CAP

The CAP is the outcome of a concrete situation and, in essence, was designed as a series of measures which served the interests of the first six members. It is directed principally to guaranteeing farmers' incomes, opting to intervene in agricultural product prices. This was a mechanism that rapidly showed symptoms of coming to a head as a grave Community crisis—surpluses and storage problems, and accentuated structural and spatial differences.

Surpluses

The guarantee of some minimum prices rapidly stimulated production. Initially, the intervention purchase of agricultural surpluses was conceived as a seasonal mechanism. However, the inelastic nature of demand transformed these surpluses into structural features. As early as 1968, that is to say, after only six years of the operation of the CAP, Mansholt was to refer to the principal surplus Atlantic products as the *enfants terribles*—milk, sugar, and white wheat. Despite this assessment, the direction of intervention was maintained, and surpluses began to increase precipitously which was further accelerated after the first enlargement (in 1972) and did not cease growing until after 1986 (Table 9.7).

TABLE 9.7 *Evolution of storage as a result of EC intervention* ('000s of tons at end of year)

	1979 EC9	1983 EC10	1986 EC10	1987 EC12	1988 EC12
Cereals	2 677	9 572	14 717	8 147	8 312
Olive oil	53	121	283	299	346
Milk powder	215	957	847	600	11
Butter	293	686	1 297	860	120
Beef carcasses	310	410	576	776	425
Alcohol ('000s hl)	—	—	4 026	9 000	10 556

Source: Comunidades Europeas (1989*d*).

In this way, the Community brought about a subsidization of agricultural production, a large part of which was in surplus. Furthermore, this was produced at costs of production substantially above those pertaining in world agricultural markets; therefore, it had to pay for the surpluses at a (intervention) price above world market levels. This type of policy proved to be enormously expensive.

The overall mechanism for financing the CAP, is the EAGGF (the European Agricultural Guidance and Guarantee Fund) which was established in 1962 in order to meet the differentiated requirements—guarantee and guidance—of the CAP. A part of its resources, if only a small part, came from the CAP itself via two sources: in the first place, from regulation levies applied to transactions with third countries (prior levies and restitutions), and secondly, the taxes raised as part of the common organization of the sugar market. But the largest part of the receipts of the EAGGF came from outside the agricultural sector (customs duties and some of the resources obtained by member states from their VAT levies). This can be seen as another direct blow against consumers and, in part, against the possibility of developing other policy options in other economic sectors, since EAGGF expenditure came to exceed 70 per cent of the EC budget (about 60 per cent in terms of net costs).

Given the dynamics that followed the increase in agricultural surpluses, there was no easing of the precipitous increase in expenditure on the Guarantee sector of the EAGGF. At the same time, the resources corresponding to this sector had been diminishing. This therefore required the extraction of a larger fraction of the VAT receipts collected by the member countries. (Table 9.8).

TABLE 9.8 *Resources and expenditures of EAGGF* (millions of ECUs)

	1975	1980	1985	1990
Gross expenditure	4 706.8	12 042.8	20 463.8	29 742.0
Evolution of total expenditure (1975 = 100)	100	256	435	632
% of EAGGF devoted to Guarantee expenditures	96.1	95.6	96.5	94.2
EAGGF income	534.0	1 719.2	1 121.7	1 152.4
Sugar quotas (income)	86.0	504.5	1 057.4	1 384.6
% of own resources in CAP income	13.2	18.5	10.6	8.5
Net expenditure	4 086.8	9 819.1	18 284.7	27 205.0
Evolution of net expenditure (1975 = 100)	100	240	447	666
% of all VAT receipts in EC devoted to CAP	—	0.72	1.00	1.30

Source: Comunidades Europeas (1981; 1989*d*; and 1991).

This situation has given rise to internal tensions amongst the member states, owing to the fact that financial solidarity is not viewed with the same enthusiasm by those countries with relatively reduced agricultural sectors, such as the UK. Even in the discussions that preceded the incorporation of the UK in the Community, the question of its contribution to the Community budget occupied a very important place. Given the essentially agricultural orientation of the EC budget, the UK considered it would be discriminated against in having to support those countries, such as France, which had strong agricultural sectors. Initially—but even then only after extensive discussions—the UK accepted limited contributions although only during a transitional period of seven years. However, in 1974, with the return of the Labour Party to power, it demanded the renegotiation of the conditions of entry. Failure to arrive at a compromise on this subject led to a crisis in 1980 when the UK blocked a proposed increase in agricultural prices until such time as its demand for a reduced budget contribution had

TABLE 9.9 *Imports and exports to and from the EC in 1988 by groups of countries* (millions of ECUs and % of the imports and exports extra-EC12)

		1979*	1983	1985	1990
Total World Trade of EC					
(millions of ECUs)	Imports	74 040	107 905	128 301	45 214
	Exports	49 454	82 288	100 920	23 716
	Balance	−24 586	−25 617	−27 381	−21 498
% Extra-EC12	Imports	54.2	49.4	47.3	38.4
	Exports	60.9	33.6	34.2	28.4
A % Industrialized	Imports	46.2	44.5	38.5	38.8
Countries, of which:	Exports	47.5	41.6	46.7	48.2
% USA	Imports	17.3	22.0	15.7	2.8
	Exports	12.5	15.2	18.4	13.4
% Japan	Imports	0.5	0.4	0.5	0.4
	Exports	—	3.8	4.5	6.6
% Western Europe	Imports	10.3	10.5	10.3	13.7
	Exports	—	17.0	17.3	21.5
% Commonwealth	Imports	10.9	9.7	9.9	9.5
(industrialized)	Exports	—	4.4	4.9	3.9
B % Less-Developed	Imports	46.2	48.0	53.5	51.4
Countries, of which:	Exports	43.7	45.5	42.6	41.2
% Mediterranean Basin	Imports	—	5.2	5.6	6.0
	Exports	—	14.8	14.3	12.5
% ACP (Lomé Treaty)	Imports	13.9	12.8	15.1	12.4
	Exports	—	9.0	8.2	6.7
C % Centrally Planned	Imports	7.2	7.2	7.8	9.8
Economies	Exports	8.7	12.4	10.1	0.6

*The 1979 data refer to the EC9; Western Europe includes Iceland, Norway, Sweden, Finland, Switzerland, Austria, and Yugoslavia; the industrialized Commonwealth includes Canada, Australia, New Zealand, and South Africa; the Mediterranean Basin includes Tunisia, Morocco, Algeria, Malta, Cyprus, Israel, Egypt, Syria, Jordan, Turkey, Lebanon, and Libya.

Source: Author's calculations based on Comunidades Europeas (1981; 1989*d*; and 1991).

been attended to. France responded to this obstruction with the threat of introducing protectionist measures for its own farmers. The result of this was agreement to limit the net contribution of the UK (Tracy 1989).

In a similar fashion, the continuing growth of surpluses, which made essential the conquest of foreign markets, has contributed to intensifying the criticisms made by third countries—principally the USA—against the Community, not only of strong autarky but also of 'dumping'. Such criticisms are not new and had already been highlighted in the Commission opinion of 1968. What is new is the insistence and the persistence with which they are now pursued. This is as much a product of intense pressures emanating from the storage costs of agricultural surpluses in the Community, as of the decrease in extra-Community exports as a consequence of growing self-sufficiency, and the high level of saturation that characterizes world markets. Such criticisms cannot simply be accepted at face value; they need to be specified more precisely.

The Community is not, of course, an 'autarkic fortress' in the agrarian realm, and neither does it seek to become one. After all, it is, with some variations, the first ranked world importer—very much ahead of the USA, Japan, and the USSR—and the second ranked exporter. In fact, despite its high degree of self-sufficiency, it still has a negative agricultural trade balance (Table 9.9), both in terms of food products (excepting cereals and beef), and more industrial products such as natural textile fibres, leathers, wood, and cork (Comunidades Europeas 1991).

However, it must be noted that one-half of the Community's imports were from the underdeveloped countries. In fact, the Community maintains an open market for a group of countries (66 in total) in Africa, the Caribbean and the Pacific Ocean, which are signatories of the 1975 Lomé Convention. In large part, these have colonial pasts linked to the member states: they are the old 'overseas countries and territories' and the less-developed 'Commonwealth'. To this should be added a series of favourable customs arrangements which have been conceded to the countries of the Mediterranean Basin and, to a lesser extent, to the countries of Latin America. In terms of imports from the industrialized countries, which constituted almost 40 per cent of the total in 1989, the larger part comes from non-Community Western Europe, EFTA, and Yugoslavia; these are all countries with which the Community maintains accords granting reduced customs duties for agricultural products. The main political problem centres on the USA which, in spite of accounting for a not unappreciable proportion of the agricultural imports of the Community, sees this market as being too highly protected.

Turning to extra-EC exports, the Community principally sells to the industrialized countries (48.2 per cent) and, in particular, to non-Community Western Europe (21.5 per cent) and the United States (13.4 per cent), although there are also good customers amongst the less-developed countries, especially in the Mediterranean Basin (12.5 per cent). With exports, the political problems also focus mostly on the USA; similarities in the composition of their excess production lead them into direct competition for the major customers in the world market. The USA considers that the EC adopts unfair practices such as reducing agricultural export prices (which are set at the level of the world market) through its system of Community restitutions.

The criticisms of the USA are clearly of interest. Its defence of absolute freedom in agricultural markets conceals a particular system of protectionism for its own agricultural sector, one that is based more on direct support for farmers. Despite this, and without invalidating completely what has been said earlier, it is clear that there is a tendency for extra-Community imports to account for a small and declining proportion of total imports. This is, in part, a consequence of the strong dynamism of intra-Community economic relationships and also of stagnation, including some instances of actual declines, experienced by some Community suppliers, such as the USA. This contrasts with the non-Community Western Europe (from where imports have increased in recent years), but also with some less-developed countries such as the group of ACP countries. With respect to exports, extra-Community countries have also seen their share decline in the last time period. Again this has principally affected the USA while exports have increased to non-Community Western Europe, to the centrally planned economies, to the Mediterranean Basin, and to the ACP. Finally, there is a general diminution of the proportion of the world market for agricultural products which the Community accounts for, which affects particularly the USA, but also the less-developed countries. The rest of Europe seems to have escaped this tendency and has actually seen an improvement in its level of economic exchanges with the EC.

The reason for these alterations in the distribution of economic interchanges is not only the reform of the CAP—which has reduced surpluses—but also the enlargement of the Community. Both issues, without doubt, have been influential, although more indirectly it seems than directly. The accession of Spain and Portugal has not yet had sufficient time to allow us to see its full effects, above all because it has been followed by a period of transition; in fact, there do not seem to have been major repercussions for the countries of the Mediterranean Basin. Nevertheless, the incorporation of the new members in the CAP has been viewed by the USA as a new limitation upon its share of the international market, just at the same time as the pressures generated by its own surpluses have attained dangerous heights. Since 1985, this has led it to launch a new export offensive (a special development programme to counteract the EC's restitution payments). This has been mainly targeted at the countries of the Mediterranean Basin. The Community responded by prohibiting the entry of American meat, accusing the USA of using hormones (the so-called 'hormone war'). In turn, the USA retaliated by imposing restrictions on imports from the Community. This 'war' has served to mar the Uruguay Round of GATT negotiations, begun in 1986, which seek to bring about, within the GATT framework, an equilibrium within the international market for agricultural products.

Consolidation and accentuation of internal differences

This has been another consequence of the orientation of the CAP. At the time when the EC6 was founded, there already existed important regional and social differences in agriculture. On the one hand there was what can be referred to as 'the first division', a relatively prosperous area comprised of the North European Plain and the Low Countries, where there was and is a high degree of specialization in either cereals and sugar beet (principally the Paris Basin and Lower Saxony), or in beef and dairying. On the other hand there were a series of areas, accounting for the larger part of the cultivated area of the EC, where specialization was less developed and agricultural conditions were comparatively poor. Naturally, within this large peripheral group there existed substantial differences, as much in terms of terrain and the inherent difficulties of the natural environment, as in terms of their structural inheritance. In this last respect, the Italian situation—the only Mediterranean country in the Community of Six—exemplified the special difficulties associated with land social structures.

The fact that the CAP was principally formed to serve the needs of more advanced producers was a response, amongst other things, to the needs of the weightier member states, which had already been developing strongly protectionist domestic and foreign policies. The search for a means of harmonizing national policies quickly and exclusively became channelled towards the homogenization of different protectionist methods. It seems that relatively little account was taken of Mansholt's preparatory studies for the CAP of the actual agricultural situation in the first six member states. In this he has already highlighted the existence of surpluses in certain products, amongst which were butter and sugar, and also the high degree of self-sufficiency of other products such as cereals. Similarly, little detailed attention at this time was given to regional differences, or to the different weight or distinctive features of agriculture in the member states. Italy, for example, was rather marginalized in the preparation of the CAP. Yet, compared to the other member states it had a far higher proportion of its active population employed in agriculture, a more highly polarized structure of farm sizes, and a larger proportion of its land was unfavourable for farming. Yet, it also had one of the richest agricultural areas in the Community, the Po valley.

The first enlargement of the Community consolidated this production model. However, over time the absence of effective means by which to correct the emerging disequilibrium came to appear more and more obvious. The structure of farm holdings evolved very much as a function of this model. Strong emigration in the 1960s allowed for enlargement of the area of the holdings, and this was complemented by an intensification of production. While these processes could be considered a success in the more-favoured areas, emigration depopulated other less-favoured areas without leading to any modification of the structure of farm holdings in the countries in question.

The economic consequences of the productive model predominated over the social and environmental ones. From 1968 the Second Mansholt Plan sought to initiate a structural policy (acceleration of the abandonment of agricultural employment, enlargement and intensification of holdings, withdrawal of land from agriculture, raising levels of qualification, etc.). However, steps were also taken to deepen the model of production itself: seeking out further increases of production, and reducing the costs of exploitation in order to increase competitiveness relative to world agriculture, thereby reducing the EAGGF's Guarantee expenditures. But only relatively insignificant aspects of the plan were applied, and their effects were minimal.

The same approach was followed, by and large, in most of the structural policies of the larger member states. Although these tended to be more efficient than the practically non-existent structural policies of the Community, they were also relatively ineffective. In the majority of cases, the objectives of national policies were little different from those of the Mansholt Plan; reduction in the number of farmers and in the units of production, and an increase in the size of the latter, while not compromising the family character of these holdings. The first interventions led to a more rigid land market. In France SAFER (Sociétés d'Aménagement Foncier et d'Établissement Rural) was established in 1960 with the aims of purchasing land to be resold to farmers on five year terms. In Ireland, the Land Commission acted along the same lines. In both cases the intervention of this mechanism, during the 1970s and the early 1980s, was limited and did not effect more than 15 per cent to 25 per cent of transactions. Denmark and the Netherlands placed the emphasis on avoiding speculation (controlling the purchase of land by companies and persons from outside the sector) and ensuring that farmland sold remained in economic production. In some cases, they tried—without too much success—also to favour leasing as a mechanism of structural adjustment (as in France through the Groupement Fonciers Agricoles). Only one country—Italy—seems to have followed a markedly different policy from the others; the persistence of the large latifundia in the south gave place, after the World War II, to a species of agrarian reform known as 'peasantization' (Arnalte *et al.* 1986). These direct national interventions, and the very limited measures adopted in 1972 by the Community, may or may not have had an effect. What is certain is that, except in the case of Italy, the dynamics of agrarian structures in the EC9 continued in much the same direction as previously, even if their rhythm declined during the mid-1970s. Community institutions did nothing to discourage this dynamic, declaring themselves in favour of greater concentration in agriculture in the future, following similar tendencies to those in industry. Ultimately, the Community backed the large farms that produced the larger part of Community output and which had benefited and could expect to benefit most from price policies. A glance at Table 9.6 shows what the results were. These policies clearly have produced a reduction in the number of farms and in the number of economically active persons in agriculture. However, the proportion of small farms (1–5 ha) in the total has not declined very much, but neither has the proportion of the largest farms (50 or more ha) increased dramatically. The most striking change is that a much larger percentage of the cultivated land is now concentrated in a greatly reduced number of large farms. That is to say, the adjustment of structures has given rise to a greater polarization and social differentiation amongst farmers.

This overall structural situation in the EC has, of course, also been affected by the incorporation of the Mediterranean countries (Greece, Spain, and Portugal) in the Community, at what was a relatively late date in terms of the evolution of its agrarian structures. The proportion of the active population in agriculture and of small farms is considerably higher in these countries than in the Community as a whole. Even so these accessions can not justify nor conceal the fact that Community price policy has served to promote a reduced, but powerful, group of large farms. It has also, to some extent, sustained a considerable number of small and badly remunerated holdings, which has contributed to maintaining the prevailing image of agriculture being based on the model of family farms. On the other hand, the effect of incorporating the Mediterranean dimension into the overall agricultural structures of the EC, ought to help to underline more clearly the considerable spatial differences in the Community and the need to correct such disequilibria.

It is clear that, even in respect of structural reform, the Community had already enacted some measures in 1975 through Directive 75/268 on Mountain Agriculture and other Less-Favoured Areas; this indicates that there was not total neglect. This directive foresaw the delimitation of these special zones in each member state and allowed for intervention through special support mechanisms. The objectives were the separation of the productionist line that inspired the CAP, from different objectives such as seeking to maintain minimum demographic densities or conservation of the landscape in the less-favoured regions. The means available ranged from subsidies to compensate for natural difficulties to subsidies for collective investments. Nevertheless, once delimited the areas affected by this directive could show the enormous extent of their difficulties (Fig. 9.1). This contrasted with the excessively reduced budget available to them within the Guidance sector. The expenditures of the EAGGF continue to be concentrated in the Guarantee section and these new areas did not even account for an important proportion of the expenditures of the Guidance Sector (Table 9.10).

TABLE 9.10 *Distribution of EAGGF expenditure*

	1983		1985		1987	
	ECUm	%	ECUm	%	ECUm	%
EAGGF Guarantee	15 811.6	94.6	19 744.2	95.6	22 960.5	96.2
EAGGF Guidance	904.6	5.4	919.7	4.4	917.7	3.8
Directive 75/268	135.8	0.8	118.1	0.6	220.0	0.9
Guidance sector		15.0		12.9		24.0
TOTAL, EAGG	16 716.2	100.0	20 662.9	100.0	23 878.5	100.0

Source: Comunidades Europeas (1989*e*).

Furthermore, a new obstacle had come to the surface earlier. The inequalities amongst member states, as much in terms of natural difficulties and agricultural structures as in terms of the weight of agriculture in their economies generally, are extensive. In fact, the rents obtained in some less-favoured zones in certain countries (Germany, France and, above all, the UK) are greater than those in the normal zones in the other, Mediterranean countries (Comunidades Europeas 1989*e*).

New members and the new orientation of the CAP

In 1986 the problem of the surpluses had reached a highly critical point. It was evident that it would not be possible to continue to maintain a policy which stimulated production at levels above the needs of the market and which absorbed the larger part of the Community's budget in order to maintain these. Furthermore the situation in the international market was equally serious and the trade 'war' with the USA made it clear that this situation was unsustainable.

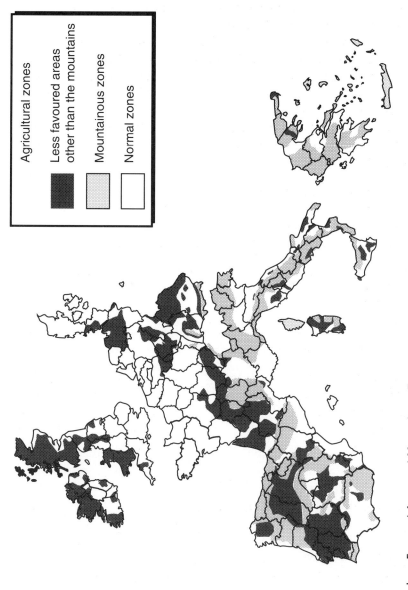

Fig. 9.1. Less-Favoured Areas and Mountainous Zones designated by the EC

Source: Comunidades Europeas (1989*e*).

On the other hand, the accession of the new Mediterranean members introduced a new agricultural dimension, above all in the area of structures. They added considerably to the active agricultural population and to the numbers of small holdings, which were rather underequipped and unprofessional in comparison to the Community's farms. They also extended the less-favoured areas, since practically all the agricultural areas of these new member states could be thus designated. In a sense, the accession of these new members was not problematic. Their production—essentially Mediterranean in character—did not contribute to further increases in the most critical areas of surplus. Given their positions as importers of milk and beef it could be expected that, even if slightly, they might ease difficulties in these sectors. However, these producers did offer strong competition to the Italian, Greek, and French Mediterranean regions.

Therefore, it was becoming clear that a reform of the CAP, as currently constituted, was likely to be totally inadequate with respect to the mounting problems in the agricultural sector. The policy redirection required would have to resolve, on the one hand, the problems of the surpluses, substituting a more market-orientated price policy in place of the earlier intervention mechanisms. On the other, it would have to take on board the problems of social and regional disequilibria, approaching these more decisively and with more resources. And all this had to be achieved without abandoning the objectives set out in the Treaty of Rome.

With respect to the first aspect, measures were necessary to limit production. In fact, since the 1970s some emergency measures had already been adopted in this respect (a co-responsibility levy on milk, and earlier restrictions on sugar production). As an emergency measure, a system of quotas had been introduced for milk in 1984 but, in fact, these had continued in existence because of the delicate nature of the market. Probably the key element in the reform of the CAP, was the introduction of the guarantee 'umbrella' or the system of guaranteed maximum quantities, which imposed automatic price reductions on all agricultural products that would otherwise have benefited from guarantee prices from the moment they exceeded a fixed quantity of production. In a complementary way, they have adopted other measures such as freezing or reducing intervention prices, or the system of compensation and incentives for withdrawing land from cultivation for a minimum period of five years.

In the area of structural policy, the earlier forms of intervention—modernization and rationalization—were continued, but at the same time the scale and the diversity of the problems faced had become even greater as a result of the accession of Spain and Portugal. As it was essential that structural measures did not give rise to any further increases in production, the support measures were directed at investments that sought to reduce costs, improved working and living conditions, and rationalized production. In other ways they reinforced the existing measures for early retirement, which had been handicapped by the low level of subsidies, and established a support plan for young farmers, subject to the viability of the holdings and to professional qualifications.

Other than these principal, and largely unmodifiable policies, there was also an attempt to direct greater attention to the needs of small farms, and in effect, therefore, to the less-favoured areas (see Chapter 12). In principle, a series of additional supports for small holdings were considered necessary in order to mitigate the negative effects on their economies that were likely to result from changes in the common organization of agricultural markets. That is to say, they considered income supports, such as direct grants for farms which did not otherwise achieve certain agreed minimum levels; these were accompanied by measures to encourage the establishment of complementary activities. Such measures give priority to the less-favoured regions, where the larger part of the small holdings are located.

Their references to these areas and, in general, to regional disparities, suggest that the Community is inclined to take such problems more seriously than before. Some concrete initiatives have materialized. Although the Integrated Mediterranean Programmes were introduced with the aim of mitigating the effects of integrating Spain and Portugal into the Community, this has not prevented them from being a positive experience in other respects. And in equal measure, the joint intervention of the structural funds (European Social Fund, ERDF, and EAGGF-Guidance) in promoting the development of the less-favoured areas, and of the rural zones, has had interesting results.

Results and perspectives

It is probably far too early to be able to assess the results of the new policy directions and also the effects of the last Mediterranean enlargement of the Community. Despite this, in some ways the results are already becoming evident while, on the other hand, there is no reason not to reflect on the embryonic problems that are emerging, which may threaten development in the not too distant future.

Of course, it is already possible to comment on the considerable success of the stabilizers that have been introduced into pricing policy. There has been an immediate reduction in the most critical surpluses, which has brought about in some cases (milk and butter) their virtual disappearance. Nevertheless, their success seems less certain in other respects, especially with regard to regional disparities. Judgement must also be reserved on the measures proposed in 1991 and 1992 in the shadow of the GATT negotiations (see Chapter 12).

The effects of the CAP reform seem to have had a considerable impact on those regions that have traditionally been more productive and which specialized in the products most in surplus. Nevertheless, similar forms of production have provided the agricultural base in other less-advantaged regions, including the Less-Favoured Areas, such as the larger part of Ireland and the north-east of Spain. However, although many of the less-favoured regions seem to have specific forms of production which are less directly affected by reforms of the common organization of agricultural markets, the very weakness of such areas makes them especially vulnerable to the new policy directions. Finally, the Community itself has calculated that the more negative effects will, by and large, have more impact on the less-favoured regions (Figs. 9.2, 9.3, and 9.4). If these are not remedied, they will be translated into a deepening of regional differences (Comunidades Europeas 1987).

Naturally, the Community is seeking to develop remedial action through the new directions of the structural policy and reform of the structural funds. Despite this, it has to be accepted that whatever action is taken, initially its impact will be limited, especially in contrast to the effects of the reforms of the organization of agricultural markets. Furthermore, the larger part of these structural measures are voluntary rather than obligatory for the member states, which also have to contribute to their costs. And anyway, the economic force that is destined to correct these disequilibria is already considerably reduced. There are already clear signs, however slight, of an increase in the rate of growth of finance for the Guidance Sector, in comparison to the experience of the Guarantee sector. Equally, it is impossible to deny that an important percentage of the Guidance fund (70 per cent in 1989) is directed to those states with the most severe structural problems and the most extensive less-favoured areas. However, it should not be forgotten that such funds continue to account for a very small part of the EAGGF's funds (only 5.4 per cent in 1989).

We therefore have to conclude this review with a measure of uneasiness. For the moment the Community has reversed the direction of changes in expenditure. From subsidizing an increase in production it has passed to subsidizing a reduction in the same, or, what is the same thing, from paying farmers to produce surpluses it has passed to paying them to produce less.

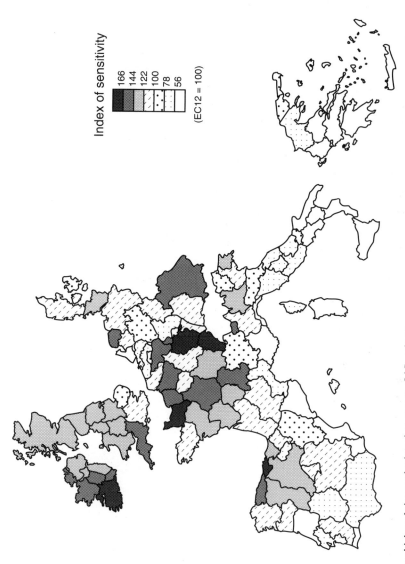

Index of sensitivity

166
144
122
100
78
56

(EC12 = 100)

Fig. 9.2. Sensitivity of the agricultural sector to CAP reform

Source: Comunidades Europeas (1987).

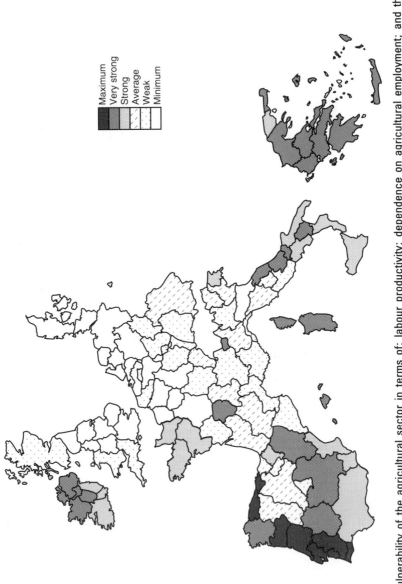

FIG. 9.3. Vulnerability of the agricultural sector in terms of: labour productivity; dependence on agricultural employment; and the regional economy

Source: Comunidades Europeas (1987).

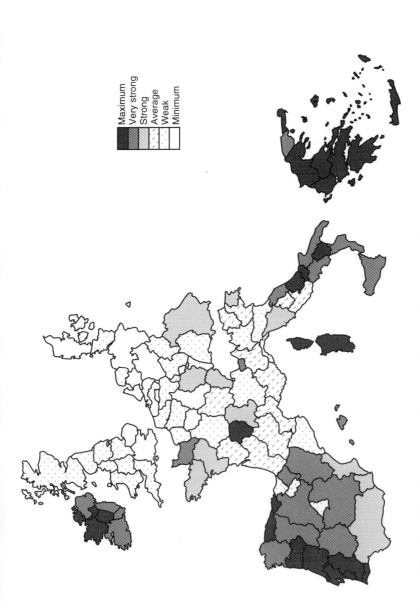

Fig. 9.4. Vulnerability of the EC regions in terms of: the overall economic strength of the agricultural sector; and sensitivity to reform of the CAP and enlargement of the Community

Source: Comunidades Europeas (1987).

Maximum
Very strong
Strong
Average
Weak
Minimum

But the guarantee policies still absorb the larger part of the Community's resources; intervention and restitution payments have not been suppressed only restricted. At the same time, the funds allocated to structural transformation and the correction of disequilibria still appear, at least in terms of resources, to be a symbolic course of action, generating more debate than concrete results. The outcome will depend on the fate of the McSharry proposals to reform the CAP, which is linked with the GATT negotiations.

Further reading

Leaving aside those publications on the CAP produced by the EC itself, the main contributions in Spanish have been written by agriculturalists and economists, rather than geographers. Nevertheless, there has been a spate of books and articles about the Spanish accession to the Community and the subsequent problems, and impact of, integration. Worthy of particular note are J. Moroto (1987), *El proceso de integración de la agricultura española en la Comunidad Europea* (Madrid), and Consellería d'Agricultura i Pesca de la Generalita Valenciana (1990), *Situación actuel y perspectivas* (Valencia). Recent additions to the literature are: F. Teulon 1991, *La politique agricole commun* (Paris); the special publication produced by the Ministerio de Agricultura, Pesca y Alimentación (1991), *Revista de Estudios Agrosociales*, no. 156, 2/1991; and L. V. Barceló, (1991), *Liberalización, ajuste y reestructuración de la agricultura española* (Madrid), which includes some useful general material on the Mediterranean region as a whole.

10 Tourism: Opportunities, Challenges and Contradictions in the EC

Allan M. Williams and Gareth Shaw

Tourism: A Community resource

Ever since the emergence of international mass tourism during the 1960s, tourism has been an essential thread in the socio-economic fabric of the EC. It is of major economic importance, employing more than one in twenty of the work-force, as well as accounting for a substantial proportion of GDP and of international trade. Tourism is also an instrument of social and cultural change, affecting the transfer of values and life-styles. Furthermore, it offers one of the few, major channels for potential mass international interactions between differing peoples and cultures within the Community (Williams 1991*b*). Finally, tourism is at the heart of cross-border international movements of people within the EC, a major focus of liberalization in the Single Market programme. One simple statistic summarizes the overall importance of tourism to the Community, which is that 64 per cent of all international tourism occurs within Europe, and the EC accounts for 75 per cent of all tourist income. In the EC, more than any other world region, the tourist industry is an essential component of both production and consumption.

The scale of tourism movements within the EC has been discussed in detail elsewhere (Williams and Shaw (eds.) 1991) and only the salient points need to be reiterated here. Firstly, there has been a sustained growth of international tourism to almost all EC member states. The greatest and earliest relative gains were in the Mediterranean states, with Italy, Spain, and Greece experiencing large absolute and percentage increases. Such increases have not always been sustained, certainly in the case of Spain, which recently witnessed a fall in British visitor arrivals. Portugal has had a more mixed experience, with rapid growth in the 1960s, being followed by stagnation in the 1970s. Certainly, the initial boost to these Mediterranean areas came from the development of inclusive, low-cost package holidays. Secondly, not all countries benefited equally from international tourism; there was, for example, only limited expansion in Belgium and the Netherlands, not surprising given their lack of any of the obvious socially constructed

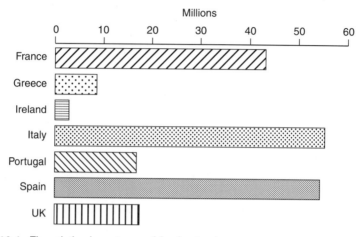

F IG. 10.1. The relative importance of foreign tourism
Source: Based on data from OECD (1990).

attractions of mass tourism—sea, sun, or skiing conditions. Even more remarkable is Ireland, which witnessed a decline in tourist arrivals in the 1970s and early 1980s. Indeed, it is worth stressing that four countries, namely Spain, Italy, France, and the UK accounted for 54 per cent of total European tourism revenue in 1989.

Some measure of the relative importance of foreign tourism is provided by Fig. 10.1 which, whilst not providing comprehensive coverage for the EC, indicates major international differences. In particular there is a group of Mediterranean countries where foreign tourists considerably outnumber domestic ones. The mainstay of these patterns of growth is still sea and sunshine, beach-orientated holidays. In this respect Mediterranean holiday packages have become the model of mass tourism, being based on low-cost charter air fares or self-drive locations. Spain is the most highly developed example of such tourism, leastways in terms of dependence on foreign visitors, whilst alpine locations form the other focus of international mass tourism.

A further dimension of growth is urban tourism, which contains two distinct strands: cultural and business or conference tourism. Every major European city experiences some form of tourism with London (59.5 million overnight stays in 1985) and Paris (15.8 million) (*Financial Times*, 8 June 1987) attracting most visitors. In some cases urban areas also attract new, large-scale tourist developments such as Euro-Disneyland near to Paris which is projected to have 10 million visitors per year. Cultural tourism tends to be more widely spread throughout the range of urban settlements given that it is based on diverse features ranging from archaeological remains, through to outstanding architecture, museums, art galleries, and special festivals. Urban tourism is also very strongly supported by business and conference travel, which together account for over 55 per cent of the demand for four and five star hotels, and almost 50 per cent of the revenue of scheduled air travel, hotel, and car hire in the Community. Such travel has also been growing at twice the rate of holiday travel. In contrast, rural tourism is another important segment of the EC market, accounting for 25 per cent of all holiday-makers in the Community (Commission of the European Community 1987c). This proportion varies from 8 per cent in Greece to 39 per cent in the Netherlands, reflecting not only environmental differences, but also socio-economic variations in the domestic market.

Given the undisputed importance of tourism to the economy and society of the EC, it is perhaps surprising that Community-wide policies have only slowly emerged. Indeed it was only in the 1980s, with the accession of Greece, Spain, and Portugal that there was some official recognition—however ineffective—of the importance of tourism to the Community. This chapter is concerned with the limited development of policy, together with an analysis of fledgling EC tourism measures. Before such a discussion we begin by examining the overall role of tourism within the Community. As we will show, tourism is an important economic generator, an agent of cultural change, a contributor to uneven regional development, and both threatens and conserves the environment. The last two dimensions, uneven development and the environment, are very much concerns of the Community in the 1990s, factors which have enhanced the profile of tourism within the EC. However, the fundamental importance of tourism lies in its economic role.

Tourism and the economy of the EC

It is estimated that tourism accounts for 7.5 million jobs in the EC, equivalent to about 6 per cent of the total. This is a more modest figure than the 15.5 per cent of jobs that are estimated to be directly or indirectly dependent on tourism according to the World Tourism Organization (1984). In truth there is a high level of error in all such estimates, given the paucity of detailed tourism statistics. Table 10.1 provides a summary of the available data on employment within hotels and restaurants, but even these must be treated cautiously, given differences in coverage. Not least, the official data fail to record the large numbers of casual workers in the industry and its links with the informal economy. Nevertheless, they give some measure of the importance of employment in tourism and also underline the dominance

TABLE 10.1 *Employment in hotels and restaurants, 1989*

	% Female	Total no.
Belgium	n.a.	119 131[a]
Germany	57.7	683 000[b]
Netherlands	42.5	126 000[b]
UK	58.0	556 300

[a] 1987 data
[b] 1988 data

Source: OECD (1990).

of female workers in most countries (the exception being France, the Netherlands, and Portugal). Employment in tourism is also important because, in the face of recession in the European economy, it has been one of the most consistent sources of job growth in recent years. Furthermore, tourism has been particularly important as a lead sector in many urban regeneration projects, a fact clearly identified by various government agencies in the UK (Department of the Environment 1990).

The tourism industry is also linked to the system of international migrant labour in the EC (see Chapter 6). It is one of the low-skilled, low-entry threshold sectors which habitually provides jobs for immigrants. According to OECD estimates, 24 per cent of workers in hotels and restaurants in West Germany in 1987 were international migrants. Similar patterns of employment are recorded in Paris, London, and other major cities and tourist areas. There is also a tendency for such immigrants to be employed casually and on the fringes of the black or grey economy (see Chapter 7). The typical intra-EC international migrant—leastways until the changes of the 1980s—was from one of the southern Mediterranean member states, and working in a northern member state.

Of course, not all tourism employment is casual or in the informal sector. Far from being peripheral to an economy or society, tourism can occupy a central niche. For example, there are many rural areas—in Denmark, Brittany, and south-west England amongst others—where tourism is an essential part of the rural economy. It may be a major source of full-time jobs or, as in farm tourism, provide additional income which is critical for the prosperity or even the survival of the household economy. This is increasingly recognized in EC agricultural policies, for tourism is often the main economic alternative promoted under farm-diversification policies.

Tourism is also important to national economic prosperity, one measure of this being the proportion of GDP accounted for by tourism. The EC's own estimates suggest that tourism accounts for 5.5 per cent of the

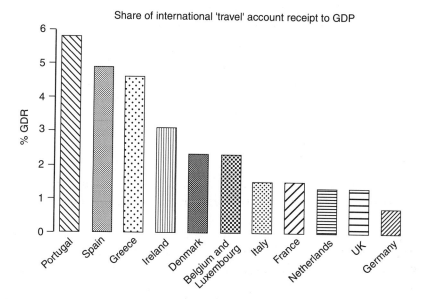

FIG. 10.2. International tourist receipts in Western Europe

Source: Based on data from OECD (1990).

Community's GDP and 8 per cent of its private consumption. Moreover, the strong income elasticity of demand and falling or static real costs have seen recent strong growth in the importance of tourism.

Measuring the contribution to GDP of tourism receipts is difficult because the major component of the latter—domestic tourism receipts—is not known for most countries. However, it has been estimated that, globally, domestic tourism expenditure is five to ten times greater than international tourism expenditure (World Tourism Organization 1984). The OECD provides a useful summary of the importance of international tourist receipts in Western Europe, based on estimates provided by national governments (Fig. 10.2). As would be expected, tourism makes its greatest contribution to GDP in the countries of mass tourism, that is, in the Mediterranean area.

Another economic dimension of tourism concerns its contribution to international trade and the current account. There are, of course, problems in measuring this contribution, particularly because of national multiplier and leakage effects (see Baretje 1982). Nevertheless, it is clear that in the 1970s (and most probably in the 1980s) international tourism income growth outstripped international trade growth.

Not surprisingly, tourism has been actively promoted by governments in a number of countries in order to increase foreign exchange earnings and improve the so-called 'invisibles' component of the balance of payments. International tourism flows in the EC have a clear North–South pattern: in 1986 tourism expenditure by nationals accounted for between 3 and 10 per cent of all imports of goods and services in most northern European states, compared with 4 per cent or less in the Mediterranean countries. In contrast, the pattern is almost completely reversed when considering tourist receipts relative to exports and services. Over 15 per cent of all exports derive from tourism in the Mediterranean countries (except Italy, which has important manufacturing exports), compared with less than 6 per cent in most northern European countries. The magnitude of the receipts and expenditure involved in international tourism is shown in Fig. 10.3. In absolute terms, the largest net earners are Italy and Spain, while Germany and the Netherlands have

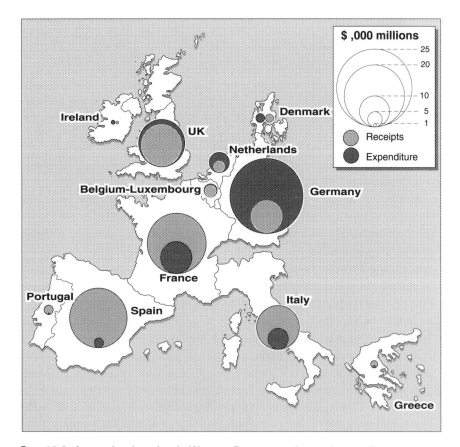

FIG. 10.3. International tourism in Western Europe: receipts and expenditure
Source: Based on data from OECD (1990).

the largest net deficits. Countries such as the UK and Denmark have relatively small net balances concealing very large inward and outward flows of receipts and expenditures. These data suggest that tourism generates a net distribution of wealth from the north to the south of Europe, and from the richer to the poorer states and regions.

Tourism and uneven regional development

While tourism does contribute to economic growth and development, its imprint is highly uneven between regions and localities. Even a crude index of regional concentration highlights two important features; the existence of strong polarization in the industry and significant variations between different segments of the tourism market. In this instance the differences are between domestic and foreign tourism (Table 10.2). While there is little argument about the existence of regional polarization in tourism, there is less consensus about whether this reinforces or modifies differences in income and employment.

TABLE 10.2 *A simple index of regional concentration*

	Index	No. of regions
Spain (1985/6)		
Domestic tourists	3.6	17
Foreign tourists	5.6	17
Hotels	5.6	17
Portugal (1984)		
Domestic tourists	4.2	20
Foreign tourists	7.2	20
All accommodation	4.2	20
UK (1985/7)		
Domestic tourists (nights)	3.2	15
Foreign tourists (Nights)	4.9	15
Hotels	3.5	15

Note: Index $= \Sigma \dfrac{\text{\% of all foreign visitors in } i}{\text{\% of all foreign visitors in } i \text{ if distributed equally among all regions}}$

Source: Valenzuela (1991); Lewis and Williams (1991); British Tourism Association (unpublished data).

The traditional—mainly periphery–centre view—is represented by Peters (1969: 11) who writes that '. . . tourism, by its nature, tends to distribute development away from the industrial centres towards those regions in a country which have not been developed'. It is argued that tourism is essentially a peripheral regional activity due to intrinsic demand and supply characteristics. Tourists are attracted to unspoilt coastal and rural areas and these, by definition, are to be found in underdeveloped and peripheral regions. The major constraint on this fundamental relationship is held to be accessibility, because some peripheral regions may be too remote to experience major tourism developments.

The hypothesis outlined above is, of course, highly simplistic. Not only does it confuse spatial and non-spatial concepts of peripherality and under-development, but it also adopts a narrow and passive view of the tourism product. Tourist attractions do not exist in any absolute sense. Instead they are socially constructed, in terms of both investments and marketing (Urry 1990). This is exemplified by the development of such tourist attractions as are to be found in the Languedoc–Rousillon region in France, at Euro-Disneyland outside Paris, and by the urban-industrial heritage of nineteenth century Britain. Furthermore, mass tourism resorts are not even necessarily localy located in peripheral regions. Many of Spain's premier resorts are located in Catalonia, one of the most prosperous regions in the country. The same applies to the numerous south-coast resorts in the UK. In both cases, early development was based on the conjunction of a socially valued natural resource (the coast) with the accessibility which came from their location in, or adjacent to, core economic regions. It would therefore be more accurate to argue that there are many different forms of tourism and that each has distinctive regional implications which do not necessarily conform to any simplistic periphery–centre or centre–periphery model (Williams and Shaw 1991).

Each of these tourism products has its own distinctive spatial forms. Moreover, they have different implications in terms of their contributions to centre–periphery patterns of regional development. Mass summer tourism is more likely than short-break winter tourism to favour peripheral regions, if only because of the accessibility constraints on the latter type of holiday. Many forms of urban tourism tend to focus on capital cities and therefore favour more developed regions but—at least in the UK—urban industrial tourism is mostly focused on the dominant industrial cities of the nineteenth century, such as Glasgow, which are mostly located in the now more peripheral economic regions. While there is no unequivocal evidence on the centre–periphery debate, it is evident that tourism has played a major role in the creation and remoulding of regional economic inequalities in the EC. But we should recognize that the patterns are far more complex than some commentators have suggested.

Tourism and European culture

While most attention has been focused on the economic importance of tourism, its actual and potential role in cultural formation is immense. Tourism plays a major role in the internationalization of values and tastes (Lanfant 1980). As such it is an important element of mass consumption. A growing awareness of this role provided one of the motives for the EC's designation of 1990 as the European Year of Tourism. The official report on the European Year of Tourism (Commission of the European Community 1991*b*, Section 1–2) stated that, 'The action programme adopted on 14 December 1988 stressed the integrating role of tourism to prepare for the establishment of the Single Market by the end of 1992 and for the creation of a genuine People's Europe.' It then goes on to stress that 'Intra-European tourism enables people, and in particular youth, to increase their knowledge of the culture and life-styles of member states of the Community and consequently to become more aware of European realities.'

The cultural objectives of the European Year of Tourism were highly idealistic. In practice, international tourism can often be a culturally barren experience, especially for the host population. Package holidays to popular resorts tend to be in cultural terms more akin to what Lenin saw of Germany during his famous return journey to Moscow in a sealed train, than they are to opportunities for greater cultural awareness. Package holiday tourists are rapidly transported by air and coach—often at night—to arrive in hotels, and sometimes entire resorts, which are dominated by their own national groups. In this respect, Pearce (1987*a*, *b*) has confirmed that there is a high degree of market segmentation between resorts and regions, particularly for UK and German tourists visiting the Mediterranean.

Not all package tourism, and certainly not all tourism, conforms to the model of cultural isolation posited above. In truth, the cultural experiences are enormously varied and, as Kariel and Kariel (1982) have argued, evolve over time. Initially, tourists visiting remote areas actively seek out cultural interchanges with the local populace. However, as tourist numbers grow, so the cultural exchanges are modified. External goods, services, and capital are brought in for the growing numbers of tourists who increasingly become integrated into tourism enclaves. However, few resorts are completely segregated. Rather, there is great variety amongst them. Even in Spain, with its archetypical 'costas', there are considerable differences between the various Mediterranean coastal tourism zones (Pearce and Grimmeau 1985).

Tourism and the environment

In the changing social and political climate of the late twentieth century, there is a growing awareness of the environmental impact of tourism (Krippendorf 1987). There is undeniably a tension between the requirements of conservation and of tourism, which acts in a number of ways (Shaw and Williams 1992). The relationship can be creative and positive, and tourism can contribute funds or appropriate functional uses which can help to conserve individual buildings or entire areas. On the other hand, tourism demands can scar landscapes and undermine ecologically precarious systems.

The pressures are usually greatest in areas of mass tourism, epitomized by Spain where there is the full gamut of environmental threats: polluted and overcrowded Mediterranean resorts, ski damage in the Pyrenees, second homes in the rural hinterland of Barcelona, and pressure of numbers on the Costa Doñana and Picos de Europa national parks. In the 1980s, the resorts had to contend with two particularly contradictory concerns: that the poor crime record and environmental image of the 'costas' was leading to stagnation in numbers and income, and that a further increase in numbers could lead to even more environmental crises. The concerns have now become sufficient to trigger some actions and, by 1991, Valenzuela (1991: 59–60) could write that:

Some progress has been made in the upgrading of coastal tourism in Spain. Preservation of unspoilt coastal landscapes and restoration of less seriously damaged ones are the major aims of the recently approved *Ley de Costas* (Law of the Coast) (1988). This established free public access to all the beaches, dunes, cliffs and marshes adjacent to the sea and prohibited any new construction within 100 metres of the shore.

The problems are not unique to coastal tourism. King (1991: 82–3) reports an equally depressing catalogue of environmental and artistic degradation in Italy's historic cities:

Florence receives, but no longer successfully absorbs, 7 million tourists per year, more than 20 times the city's population whilst in Rome over 18 000 visitors stream through the Sistine Chapel in a single day . . . High heels gouge out the tesserae of Roman pavements, frescoes deteriorate under the assault of the humid breath of a multitude of admirers, and fast-food restaurants proliferate in historic town centres to cater for the appetites of the tourist hordes.

Of course, the tourists occasionally have also contributed to environmental improvement, and there is an increasing trend toward a demand for green tourism from many of the Community's holiday-makers. Many derelict industrial landscapes and run-down areas have been rehabilitated to a large extent through adjusting to the needs of modern tourism. Alternatively, the income generated by farm tourism may be critical in the survival of small farms and, hence, of traditional rural landscapes. But whatever the precise impact of tourism on the environment it is evident that there is a strong and growing interrelationship between these issues. Some countries have been in advance of others and 'Among the Germans, seemingly sated by prosperity, ecological concerns have been seeping out from the Green movement for a decade and have become a key priority for all political parties' (*Financial Times*, 12 April 1989). The shift in public awareness was underlined by the 1989 European Parliament elections, in which Green parties attracted more than 5 per cent of the vote in Belgium, the UK, France, Germany, the Netherlands, and Italy. There was also a realization that the transnational nature of problems such as pollution of the Mediterranean required transnational action, an area in which the EC was apparently ideally suited to provide leadership. Finally, there was awareness that EC development policies sometimes encouraged developments which could increase environmental damage. For example, European Regional Development Fund (ERDF) projects for tourism could potentially threaten environmental standards through increased traffic or water pollution. The European Community has responded to these pressures with a series of medium-term Action Programmes initiated in 1972. The most important of these was the Fourth Community Action Programme, 1987, one of the principal objectives of which was to integrate environmental policies more fully with other EC sectoral policies, such as the ERDF and the Common Agricultural Policy (CAP). This has potential implications for the evolution of EC policies for tourism (see Chapter 11).

The EC policy framework: Challenges and constraints

The arguments for a 'Common Tourism Policy' are strong and have already been outlined in the first part of this chapter. Tourism is of substantial and growing economic importance, it contributes to uneven development, it is an instrument of cultural formation and internationalization, and has considerable potential to modify the environment. In addition, the market for tourism—since the 1960s at least—has been an international one in Europe, and the numbers of international tourists within the Community are likely to increase further in the short and long term. There is, therefore, a compelling logic for the EC to develop a coherent policy for tourism in the Community.

The pressures generated by the industry in the future are likely to intensify as participation increases. Although it has been estimated that 140 million persons in the EC had a holiday away from home in 1985, this only represented 56 per cent of the total population. Only 21 per cent habitually stay at home, while 23 per cent sometimes go away on holiday. Of those who went on holiday, 37 per cent went away once and 19 per cent took two holidays (Commission of the European Communities 1987b: 16). The ability to take holidays away from home is, of course, dependent on income. While most of northern Europe recorded tourism participation rates in excess of 57 per cent, Ireland, Spain, and Greece all had levels below 46 per cent, while in Portugal the rate was only 31 per cent (Commission of the European Communities 1987b: 7). The reasons for not taking holidays away from home are mainly economic; thus, only about one fifth preferred to stay at home, whilst almost half of those surveyed could not afford a holiday. Older people, those with larger families, and those living in rural areas are also less likely to take holidays away from home. The type of holiday taken is also influenced by occupation and income: for example, professionals are more likely than manual workers to take holidays abroad, to take longer holidays, and to use air travel. All of this points to a potentially massive increase in the level of international tourism within the EC in the 1990s, and beyond, as southern European tourism expands, and as social access to foreign holidays is widened in all the member states.

Added urgency has been given to the need for a Common Tourism Policy by the advent of the Single Market programme. One of the aims of this has been to extend single market conditions—the removal of trade and competition barriers—to the hitherto largely neglected service sector. This focuses on the need to deregulate air and road transport (see Chapter 5), to liberalize the conditions for the establishment and delivery of tourism services, and to eliminate national discriminatory practices. However, tourism is also affected by the wider goals of the Single Market programme, that is, to create a more politically and socially integrated Community as well as a genuine common market. However, tourism is influenced by this in two main ways (see Williams 1991a). First, the objective of creating a 'People's Europe' without internal borders will affect the movement of international tourists. Secondly, the idea of a Social Europe, with harmonized conditions of work, working hours, and entitlement to paid holidays is also important. It will impinge directly on labour costs in one of the most labour-intensive economic sectors in the Community, as well as affecting the total amount of paid leisure time available.

A common tourism policy or a policy vacuum?

Tourism policies in the EC have been most coherently formulated at the national level (see Williams and Shaw 1991, especially ch. 14); they encapsulate the promotion of tourism, state investment in tourism, labour market intervention, and environmental regulation. In recent years, there has been growing involvement of the local state with tourism. In the difficult economic climate of the 1980s, more and more local authorities came to see tourism as a vehicle for economic development or restructuring. These ranged from remoter rural areas (e.g. in Spain and Portugal) seeking to increase external income flows, to highly commercialized agricultural areas (as in southern England or northern France) seeking diversification in the face of cut-backs in the CAP (see Chapter 9), to areas of industrial decline (e.g. in Lancashire and Yorkshire, or the Ruhr) launching economic regeneration programmes. There is, therefore, no shortage of tourism policies in the EC, but there is as yet only the shadow of an EC policy for tourism.

In spite of the activity of national governments in the promotion of tourism policies, the EC has been slow to recognize the need for intervention at a Community-wide level. Much of the initial interest dates from the early 1980s, when the Commission of the European Communities (1982: 5) underlined the importance of tourism in a position paper and then later, in 1984, the Council issued a resolution on tourism policy. The growing awareness of the need for a Community policy on tourism was sharply increased by the growth in membership of southern European countries. Thus, in 1986 the EC proposed a tourism programme that would: facilitate tourism, improve its seasonal and geographical distribution, make better use of Community financial instruments, improve protection for tourists, improve working conditions within the tourism industry, and provide more information on this sector (see also Table 10.3).

The above proposals represent some progress, although it should be stressed that there are still considerable policy gaps. Indeed, it is significant that much of the action relies on other agencies or directorates, especially as tourism was not treated as a separate entity in the EC until recently.

Community policy for tourism may be broadly subdivided into five categories (Table 10.3). Some of these have already been mentioned in connection with the 1986 proposals, and most have made only minimal progress. The same is true of more recent attempts to develop a European Charter for Cultural Tourism for DG VII. The idea of the Charter is 'to establish principles and an action programme for the development of cultural tourism as an instrument of economic and social development of the regions of Europe'. In addition, an essential part of the Charter will be to ensure

TABLE 10.3 *The EC policy framework for tourism*

Freedom of movement and the protection of EC tourists
 (i)   easing customs checks
 (ii) reduction of police checks at frontiers
 (iii) social security provisions for tourists
 (iv) assistance for tourists and regulation of car insurance
 (v)   protection of tourists' interests, e.g. in complaints about the shortcomings of tourist services

Working conditions for those engaged in tourism
 (i)   right of establishment and freedom to provide tourist services
 (ii) vocational training grants and mutual recognition of qualifications
 (iii) aid from the European Social Fund
 (iv) promotion of staggered holidays
 (v)   harmonization of taxation
 (vi) promotion of energy efficiency

Common Transport Policy and tourism

Safeguarding the European heritage and tourism
 (i)   environmental protection
 (ii) art heritage

Regional development and tourism
 (i)   ERDF assistance
 (ii) EAGGF assistance

Source: Based on Commission of the European Communities (1985*b*).

that environmental factors are considered fully in the evaluation of tourist projects. The role of the charter is still largely symbolic, although increasingly environmental evaluations are being attached to projects in receipt of EC funds.

The most significant contribution of the EC to tourism has been through expenditure by two of its 'structural' funds, the ERDF and the European Agricultural Guidance and Guarantee Fund (EAGGF). ERDF expenditure is divided between quota (for individual countries) and non-quota funds. Under the quota scheme, the EC contributed some 69 million ECUs in 1975–81 to tourist projects jointly financed with member states, having a total value of 481 million ECUs. Under its operating rules, the EC provides up to 20 per cent of the costs of new or modernized accommodation (subject to not exceeding 50 per cent of the aid provided by the national government), and up to 30 per cent of the costs of infrastructure projects. In practice most (59 million ECUs) resources have been granted to infrastructural development. Non-quota funds have largely been channelled into a few select projects, especially in the frontier region between Ireland and Northern Ireland, in Aquitaine, Rousillon-Languedoc, Midi-Pyrénées, and the Mezzogiorno. Although ERDF grants have been important to particular projects and regions, tourism still has a very low priority within this fund. For example, Pearce (1988) estimates that tourism received only 1.4 per cent of all ERDF expenditures between 1975 and 1984. EAGGF funds have mainly been used to train farmers for tourist-related jobs, and to promote farm tourism and rural-craft industries. Compared with the funds provided for other EC expenditure, tourism still appears marginal to the interests of Community policy. It receives less than 1 per cent of total EC expenditure, compared to the 60–70 per cent traditionally directed towards agriculture.

Nevertheless, awareness of the importance of tourism in the EC continues to grow, a fact reflected in 1990 being declared the European Tourism Year, the objectives of which are outlined in Table 10.4.

TABLE 10.4 *Objectives of the European Tourism Year*

- To prepare for the establishment of a large area without frontiers, turning the integrating role of tourism to account in the creation of a People's Europe.
- To stress the economic and social importance of the tourism sector, *inter alia* in regional policy and job creation.

These broad objectives were in turn translated into three areas of new or supported co-ordinated actions by the Community, the member states, and private tourism organizations, aiming:

- To promote greater knowledge among the citizens of the member states, particularly young people, of the cultures and life-styles of the other states.
- To promote a better distribution of tourism over time and space while respecting the quality of the environment, particularly by encouraging the staggering of holidays and the development of alternatives to mass tourism, and of new destinations and new forms of tourism.
- To promote intra-Community tourism particularly by facilitating the movement of travellers and tourism from third countries to Europe.

Source: Commission of the European Communities (1991*b*) summary.

The objectives of the European Year of Tourism were clear and important. It is, however, a telling comment on the condition of EC tourism policy that the programme was considered to have been a gigantic flop. With a total expenditure of only 8 million ECUs—little more than the cost of a few days storage of surplus beef or butter mountains—the programme was condemned to mediocrity by the low priority accorded to tourism.

The ineffective tourism policy within the Community is at present implemented in three main ways. One is through actions proposed by the Tourism Task Force from the Directorate-General VII of the Commission, which is mainly concerned with tourists' protection. A second is through actions proposed by other sections of the Commission, for example through the use of structural funds. Finally, actions may be taken indirectly through the Commission's actions in other areas, such as improving access to medical treatment between the different member states.

The constraints on EC tourism

The international policy vacuum within which tourism operates within the EC is, to some extent, explained by the general neglect of the services sector, and of the Common Transport Policy (see Chapter 5). While there is provision in the Treaty of Rome for developments in both these areas, they received a far lower priority than trade, and especially agriculture, during the formative years of the Community. Consequently, as with all the attempts to develop new policy initiatives since the initial period of Community development, tourism policy has faced severe budgetary limitations and well-embedded interest groups (see Williams 1991a, ch. 6).

In addition, tourism policy has been constrained by several other considerations. In particular, the supply of tourism facilities rests mostly in private ownership. There are exceptions, such as the promotion of tourism, the ownership of the Spanish *paradores* and the Portuguese *pousadas* hotel chains, and tourist attractions such as museums and castles. But, by and large, tourism establishments such as restaurants, hotels, golf courses, and theme parks are in fragmented ownership. This is important in two ways. First, as in several other economic sectors, the potential role of the EC is severely circumscribed. It can offer grants (e.g. via the ERDF) to facilitate certain developments, and it can establish minimum controls or standards relating to the environment, health, or consumer standards. But it cannot directly control what investments occur, or where these will be located. Secondly, with a few exceptions such as air transport and tour companies, the small scale of tourism establishments is such as to approximate to near-perfect competition conditions. There is, therefore, not the same pressing logic for the Commission to intervene in this sector, as there is in manufacturing sub-sectors characterized by transnational companies and oligopolistic market conditions.

This analysis is, of course, somewhat simplistic, for there is a strong element of concentration in the package-holiday industry, an essential intermediary between the supply of and demand for tourism. The two principal points of origin are the UK and Germany (Fig. 10.4) which represent not only two of the three largest markets, but also the two countries where the package-holiday industry is most developed. In the third, France,

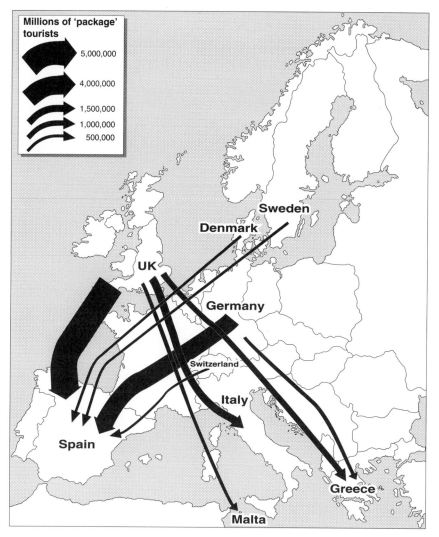

FIG. 10.4. Countries of origin of foreign package tourists
Source: Based on data from OECD (1990).

there is far greater emphasis on individual travel. Within these two countries there is also a very high level of concentration of ownership of the package-holiday industry. Thus, in 1987, the three largest tour operators in the UK—Thomson, International Leisure Group, and Horizon—had 52 per cent of the all-inclusive tour holiday market (Monopolies and Mergers Commission 1989). In practice, individual companies can dominate the flow of tourists to

TABLE 10.5 *Thomson market-shares for principal resorts, for summer 1987 and the profitability of holidays to these resorts*

Resort	Share of market (%)	Return on turnover (%)
Estoril	65.0	12.00
Costa Brava/Dorada	56.9	8.70
Tangier	56.6	8.50
Adriatic Riviera	55.8	−1.20
Tunisia	47.5	10.60
Neapolitan Riviera	46.5	10.50
Kefalonia	46.0	9.00
Costa Blanca	43.0	6.70
Sardinia	40.4	−13.20
Tenerife	39.9	6.50
Ibiza	38.7	6.40
Halkidiki	38.4	5.20
Majorca	36.5	8.70
Italian Lakes	36.0	4.60
Gran Canaria	35.6	8.30
Kos	35.5	6.20
Corfu	35.0	7.00
Venetian Riviera	34.6	−10.50
Crete	32.8	2.90
Mykonos	30.9	−20.00
Rhodes	30.8	10.00
Costa del Sol	30.0	5.20
Athens	26.7	3.90
Malta	25.7	6.10
Gibraltar	25.5	11.90
Minorca	23.1	1.40
Santorini	21.3	−0.80
Munich	20.6	2.60
Yugoslavia	20.1	11.90
Madeira	19.3	6.80
Skiathos	19.2	−1.50
Algarve	16.2	6.90
Costa Almeria	14.4	17.20
Lanzarote	13.8	−11.50
Switzerland	9.2	−21.90

Source: Monopolies and Mergers Commission (1989).

particular resorts. For example, in 1987 the Thomson Group alone (prior to its merger with Horizon) had more than 30 per cent of the UK market for 22 major resort areas; in four of these—Estoril, the Costa Brava/Dorada, Tangier, and the Adriatic Riviera—it had more than half the British market

(Table 10.5). There is no doubt that a few companies such as Thomson in the UK, and TUI in Germany, can, and do, exert a decisive influence on particular tourism markets. However, the fact that they exert their control *within* national markets means that, by and large, they have escaped the attention of the EC Directorate responsible for ensuring competition within the Community.

Even if the Commission does attempt to construct a more effective policy for tourism, its scope for action will remain constrained. There are two major areas for mass tourism in Europe, and neither of these is totally dominated by EC countries. The Mediterranean holiday experience is widely distributed amongst countries such as Turkey, Tunisia, and formerly Yugoslavia as well as member states such as Greece, Spain, Italy, and Portugal. Similarly, the Alpine holiday experience is offered by both non-EC countries such as Switzerland and Austria, and member states such as France, Italy, and Germany. Any attempt to impose higher (and more expensive) EC standards on the tourist industries of the Community will therefore affect their overall competitiveness. Given the volatile nature of tourism demand, any EC action in this arena is likely to encounter severe national opposition. On the other hand there is a growing demand for more environmental controls from conservationists, as well as from some, particularly middle-class, tourists. The rise of 'green tourism' has been noted in recent EC tourism policy documents, and such pressures are likely to increase in future.

Conclusion

International tourism policies have evolved gradually in the post-1945 period. In the late 1940s and early 1950s the emphasis was on the deregulation of international movements. Then, in the 1950s there was increased emphasis on tourism promotion as a means of generating international foreign exchange earnings (OECD 1974). By the 1980s broader social and environmental issues had begun to enter the dialogue, if not always the realities, of tourism policies. The EC has only recently become a player in the field of tourism policy and as yet, has been largely ineffective.

Yet, it is clear that a healthy and harmonious tourism industry will increasingly require an EC policy framework. The demands for new forms of European integration—such as a People's Europe—will make it more difficult to ignore tourism. Similarly, the proposed Social Charter will have major implications for tourists and the tourism industry. Further deregulation of transport will also be a major issue in the 1990s. There is also the continuing spectre of Europe's declining share of the world-tourism market, and potential new sources of competition in Eastern Europe (Hall 1991). In order to respond to this challenge, the EC will have to develop partnerships between institutions and amongst sectors and across national boundaries. In other words, there will have to be a Common Tourism Policy.

Further reading

Growth in the European tourism industry in recent years has been matched by the expansion of the literature on this subject—albeit from a low base. Two edited books provide overviews and case studies of national and regional developments in both Western and Eastern Europe: A. M. Williams, and G. Shaw (eds.) (1991), *Tourism and Economic Development: Western European Experiences* 2nd. edn. (London); and D. R. Hall (ed.), *Tourism and Economic Development in Eastern Europe and the Soviet Union* (London). EC policy is covered in a number of Community documents, including the influential Commission of the European Communities (1985), *Tourism and the European Community*, European File 11/85 (Brussels). The most powerful EC financial instrument for tourism is the ERDF, and there is an excellent review of this in E. Lowyck, and S. Wanhill (1992), 'Regional development and tourism within the European Community', in C. Cooper, and A. Lockwood (eds.), *Progress in Tourism, Recreation and Hospitality Management*, iv (London). The economics of the tourism industry are covered in M. T. Sinclair, and M. J. Stabler, (eds.) (1991), *The Tourism Industry: An International Analysis* (London). Urban tourism is discussed, with diverse European examples in C. Law (1993), *Urban Tourism* (London); and G. Ashworth, and J. E. Turnbridge (1990), *The Tourist Historic City* (London).

PART VI

Environmental Response

Environmental response

Politically the Community has found it difficult to establish itself as a force, independent of the governments of the individual member states, but in some areas the EC has been used to good effect to promote policies upon which the twelve separately would have found it difficult to agree. One such area is the environment and, since the early 1970s, an impressive body of legislation has been passed, which is now beginning to be implemented and enforced with considerable vigour. This section shows how, despite the fact that the environment was only included within its remit by the Single European Act in 1986, the EC has still had a decisive impact on policy. The need to comply with Community law has everywhere directed policy; in Ireland, for example, pollution control, forestry and nature conservation have all benefited substantially from EC legislation and initiatives.

The task of achieving minimum standards across the twelve member states is enormous, especially in view of the fact that national policies have so far failed to address satisfactorily the variations within individual countries. There are still, wide, and worrying, differences in living standards, community health, and quality of life, but these are now not only recognized, but are increasingly the subject of remedial action with EC standards providing the norm.

11 Environmental Policies and Resource Management

Mark Blacksell

The context

Policy development in the EC has always been hemmed in by the founding treaties, which establish those areas where it has competence, as opposed to those that are the preserve of the national governments of its member states (Charpentier 1988). The environment, as such, was ignored completely in the Treaties of Paris and Rome, making direct EC policy involvement in formulating solutions difficult to justify. This was despite growing public awareness and disquiet about environmental degradation and resource depletion throughout the 1960s and 1970s, as well as an emerging appreciation that it was unrealistic to view these issues in a purely national context. Not that the EC itself, growing as it did between 1958 and 1986 from six to twelve members and presenting an evermore fragmented and unwieldy geographical pattern in the process, was in any way a 'natural' spatial unit for developing solutions to an increasingly complex and varied range of environmental and resource management problems (Commission of the European Communities 1987*a*). The main attraction in the public's mind of the EC as an appropriate vehicle for environmental management was probably its explicit multi-nationalism, which underlined the apparent universality of a whole range of questions associated with the protection of the environment. Nothing illustrates the dilemmas more starkly than the pollution problems facing the shallow, semi-enclosed, seas that surround much of the Community. The Baltic, the Mediterranean, and the North Seas are all used as unregulated cesspits by the member states that adjoin them and the EC probably offers the best hope of brokering international agreement for controlling pollution and preserving their natural ecology. Not that the size of the problem should be underestimated. In the North Sea, for example (Fig. 11.1), huge amounts of nitrates, phosphates, and heavy metals are disgorged annually by the rivers of Belgium, Denmark, Germany, the Netherlands, Norway, Sweden, and the UK. In addition, there is pollution emanating from offshore oil and gas installations and from ships in one of the world's busiest shipping lanes in the English Channel.

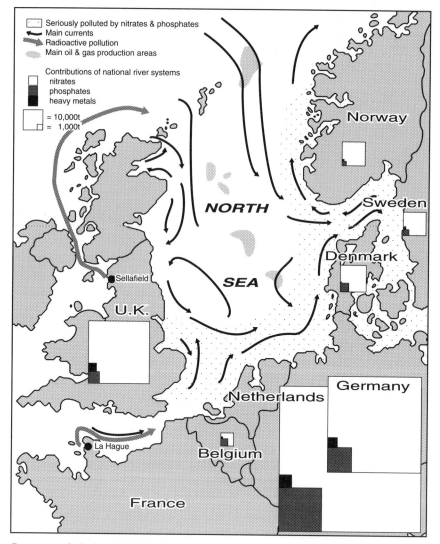

Fɪɢ. 11.1. Pollution of the North Sea
Source: Liersch (1990).

The perceived 'best' solutions to many of the most pressing environmental issues, such as the control of air and water pollution and waste management, vary markedly between the individual states in the EC, making it difficult to achieve any political consensus about how to tackle them (Commission of the European Communities 1990*b*). Wealthier societies are more easily persuaded of the advantages of long-term environmental gains over short-term economic advantages, so that there have been simmering tensions between the major industrial states at the core of the EC and some of the more recently admitted members on the northern and Mediterranean peripheries. Equally, island nations like Ireland and the UK, with short, fast-flowing rivers, tend to be less concerned about using them as sewers for waste disposal than are more continental states such as France and Germany, which are criss-crossed by major international waterways (Haigh 1987). In similar vein, air pollution that is conveniently blown away by the prevailing winds to descend on the territory of other states downwind tends to be viewed very differently by the polluter and the polluted. In general those member states on the western margins of the EC are prepared to accept emission levels into the atmosphere that are viewed as serious environmental threats by their partners further east, though such complacency is rapidly being challenged as more is understood about the subtle effects of long-term air pollution.

Over the four decades of its existence, the EC has had to tread a difficult path between the limitations imposed on it by treaty, the conflicting attitudes of its growing number of member states, and an increasingly independent body of European public opinion, aided and abetted since 1979 by the European Parliament. Initially its forays into the realm of environmental policy were explicitly linked to economic issues and measures to avoid distortions to free competition. However, after 1972, in the wake of the UN Conference on the Human Environment, they became progressively more distinct and separate. A series of Environmental Action Programmes (EAPs) culminated in the environment being incorporated as an area of EC policy competence in the 1986 Single European Act. When the Treaty on European Union (Maastricht Treaty), agreed in principle in 1992, was ratified by the member states, it further strengthened the role of the EC with respect to environmental legislation.

Since the Single European Act came into force the EC has assumed a stronger and more assertive role in the formulation and implementation of environmental policy. This chapter examines four key issues: first, the range of environmental questions addressed in the five EAPs; secondly, the meaning of the Single European Act and the proposed Treaty on European Union (Maastricht Treaty) and how they interact with the national legislation of member states; thirdly, areas of environmental policy-making, notably associated with the Common Agricultural Policy, which have evolved outside the strict confines of the environmental policy *per se*; and, finally, the difficulties associated with the implementation, monitoring and enforcement of more than 200 Directives and other types of legislative communication from the EC.

The Environmental Action Programmes (EAPs) and their implementation

Since 1973 five EAPs have been adopted, covering the years 1974–6, 1977–81, 1982–6, 1987–92, and 1993–2000 respectively. The first four have provided the overall context for the EC's environmental policy over the greater part of the past two decades (Commission of the European Communities 1987a; Koppen 1988), while the fifth carries the agenda forward to the end of the century (Commission of the European Communities 1992).

The first EAP was designed around two key concepts: 'the precautionary approach' and 'shared responsibility'. Together they encapsulated a determination to try and prevent damage to the environment, but where it did, to ensure that the costs did not only fall on those directly affected, but were spread across the community to include the perpetrators of the pollution, or other environmental damage, as well. The two principles set the tone of EC environmental policy throughout the 1970s and 1980s.

The nine general actions on which the first EAP were based are set out in Table 11.1, but the programmes also included specific measures designed to control toxic substances, known to have particularly deleterious effects on human health and the ecology of the environment, such as asbestos, cadmium, lead, mercury, nitrogen oxides, sulphur, and a range of pesticides. Also included were specific proposals for: controlling the water quality of international rivers, such as the Rhine and the Rhône; limiting the pollution caused by specific industries and certain methods of energy production; reducing marine pollution; and managing radioactive waste. In all cases firm proposals were to be presented to the Council of Ministers by the end of 1974.

TABLE 11.1 *The general principles enunciated in Part I of the EC's First Environmental Action Programme*

(i)   preventing pollution at source
(ii)   incorporating environmental considerations into all planning and decision-making
(iii)   adopting the polluter-pays principle
(iv)   assessing the impact of EC policies on developing countries
(v)   encouraging international co-operation
(vi)   promoting educational activities to increase environmental awareness
(vii)   ensuring action is taken at the most appropriate level (local, regional, national, EC, or international)
(viii)   co-ordinating and harmonizing the environmental programmes of individual member states
(ix)   improving the exchange of environmental information

Source: Commission of the European Communities (1984).

Not surprisingly, the timetable proved too optimistic, but nevertheless a stream of Directives was generated in the years that followed, covering air and surface-water quality, waste-disposal and contamination, and noise-levels. Quality standards were adopted with respect to surface water intended for abstraction for drinking, as well as for bathing waters. Maximum limits were placed on the sulphur content of various liquid fuels, while the controls on vehicle-exhaust emissions, first introduced in 1970, were tightened further. A framework directive, defining the concept of waste was adopted in 1975 and was followed by a whole series of measures dealing with specific substances, including oils, PCBs, and PCTs. Another Directive concerned the protection of the aquatic environment from pollution by dangerous substances (European Communities, Economic and Social Committee 1987).

The so-called 'dangerous substances' were contained in two lists, the first identifying particularly dangerous substances owing to their toxicity, persistence, and bio-accumulation; the second was a much broader spectrum of substances divided into seven categories according to the dangers they posed for the environment. For those in the first list, discharges must be prevented using the best technical methods available; for those in the second, either the EC or member states may define the standards, so long as these result in improvement in water quality.

The second EAP was very much a continuation and extension of the first. The requirements for water quality were further strengthened and extended, with controls over the sampling and measurement techniques to be used in monitoring, and minimum quality requirements for fresh waters to support fish and shellfish. A Directive was issued to prevent the pollution of groundwater by designated dangerous substances, and another concerned the disposal and treatment of certain very toxic wastes. The standardization of the notification, packaging, and labelling of dangerous substances had been the subject of an EC Directive since 1967, as part of a programme of harmonization, but an amendment to the original brought all new dangerous substances within its ambit in 1979. The need for EC-wide action on dangerous wastes is illustrated in Fig. 11.2, which shows the overall volume of waste generated in the Community and the large amounts of highly toxic materials that are moved across international borders. Of particular concern are the exports from Germany to the Netherlands, Belgium, and France, and the imports into the UK from virtually all the other member states.

In policy terms, an interesting addition to the remit during the latter part of the 1970s was nature conservation. A Directive was issued protecting the habitats of 142 endangered species of bird, restricting the numbers that can be hunted and traded commercially, and prohibiting certain methods of

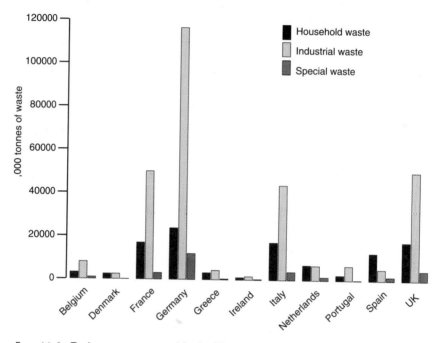

Fɪɢ. 11.2. Toxic waste generated in the EC
Source: Greenpeace Report (1991).

hunting and trapping. However, with member states responsible for enforcement, it has been honoured more in the breach than in implementation, as in many instances it was very unpopular with local communities. Birds in the Mediterranean are particularly at risk, with three times as many species endangered in most of southern France, Italy, and Greece as there are in the northern member states (Commission of the European Communities 1987*a*: 309).

A small, but significant, new development in the second EAP was the increased weight accorded to international co-operation by the EC in its own right, particularly with regard to joint initiatives and providing aid to developing countries in environmental matters. As a direct consequence, the EC became a signatory to a larger number, and wider range, of environmental accords: notably the Paris Convention (1974) on the prevention of marine pollution from land-based sources; the Barcelona Convention (1976) on the protection of the Mediterranean against pollution; the Bonn Convention (1976) on the pollution of the North Sea by oil; the Bonn Convention (1976) on the protection of the Rhine against pollution by chemicals; the Geneva

Convention (1979) on the prevention of long-distance transboundary air pollution in Europe; the Berne Convention (1979) on the conservation of European wildlife and habitats; and the Canberra Convention (1980) on the conservation of marine flora and fauna in the Antarctic.

The third EAP is materially different from the two that preceded it. Rather than dwelling on the specific measures to be taken, it concentrated more on general policy, in particular how best to integrate environmental considerations into other policy areas. The change of tone and emphasis was important, not so much because it was substantive in terms of new policy, but more because it was less defensive and no longer underlain by a sense of having to justify the inclusion of environmental legislation in the EC's remit. There was a distinct feeling of confidence that the environment was now *de facto* an accepted area of policy-making. This was reflected in a new and explicit determination to see that member states not only enacted the necessary legislation to implement Directives, but also that they were enforced. A striking example of this was the independent inspection by the Commission of Duich Moss on the island of Islay off the west coast of Scotland to ascertain whether the peat digging, prohibited in the interests of protecting the feeding grounds of rare wintering geese, had ceased. The intense suspicion that such external EC interventions can arouse in the member state affected is well illustrated in the very defensive UK House of Lords examination of the fourth EAP in 1987 (House of Lords 1987), even though the responsibility for ensuring compliance had always been, and remained, a national matter.

During the early 1980s the flow of new Directives continued steadily. Limits on the discharge of mercury, cadmium, and titanium dioxide were agreed, as well as air-quality standards for lead and nitrogen dioxide. There was a particularly significant development with respect to the damage caused by toxic waste, a new Directive, requiring that there be equal standards for civil liability throughout the EC, linked to a system of insurance. Rather than just protecting the environment, the EC was now trying to ensure that there was equal treatment for those adversely affected by pollution.

The fourth EAP, and the programme currently in force, reflects the new and unequivocal competence of the EC to legislate to protect the environment conferred by the Single European Act. In announcing the programme, the Commission also published a comprehensive survey of the state of the environment in the EC. This drew together a wide range of research into the factors affecting environmental change and attempted to provide some factual underpinning to justify its policies (Commission of the European Communities 1987a). In the EAP itself, the established areas where specific action has already been taken—air and water quality, the control of chemical substances, waste disposal, noise levels, and nature conservation—are supplemented by a series of additional ones (Krämer 1990).

There is a commitment to evaluate the potential uses, and abuses, of biotechnology, recognizing that it may be of great value in promoting environmental protection, while at the same time posing considerable risks. Of particular concern are the dangers to public heatlh and the environment posed by genetic engineering. For the first time, in the wake of the accident at the Chernobyl nuclear power-station in Belorussia, nuclear safety is included within the environmental remit. Previously this was dealt with exclusively under the terms of the 1958 Euratom Treaty, but it is now judged too important an area to be left to monitoring by the nuclear industry itself. There are 130 nuclear power-stations in the EC, generating nearly 40 per cent of all electricity requirements, but the distribution is very uneven (Table 11.2). Six member states have no nuclear power-stations at all, while France has 57 producing 75 per cent of its electricity. Under such circumstances, attitudes towards the nuclear industry and the threats it poses for the environment inevitably vary widely, with the EC caught uncomfortably in the middle as far as policy is concerned.

TABLE 11.2 *Nuclear energy in the EC*

	Number of nuclear power-stations	% of electricity derived from nuclear power
France	57	75
UK	34	20
Germany	21	33
Spain	9	36
Belgium	7	60
Netherlands	2	5

Source: Öko-Institut Freiburg (1991).

The importance of protecting the soil is recognized for the first time in the fourth EAP, as well as the need to co-ordinate environmental and agricultural policies, if effective progress is to be made to this end. Unfortunately, the programme gives no indication as to how such co-ordination is to be achieved. Although improving air quality has been a concern of all the EAPs, the fourth one is specifically committed to combating acid rain, in particular the damaging effects it is having on forests in many parts of the EC.

An important new departure in the fourth EAP is the recognition of the need to co-ordinate the management of environmental resources, if the health of fragile, and heavily polluted, environments is to be preserved. Mountain and coastal zones, in particular the Mediterranean, are singled out for special mention and the dangers facing urban areas, as well as the scale of the resources needed to combat them, are for the first time fully elaborated. In addition, there is a guarded acceptance that, although the polluter-pays principle must remain the cornerstone in the fight against pollution, central funds may be necessary for there to be effective remedial action in the economically less-favoured regions of the EC.

Perhaps the most significant new element in the fourth EAP, however, is the emphasis it places on the implementation and monitoring of EC Directives. It recognizes more clearly than ever before that, to be effective, policies have to be soundly based scientifically and implemented and enforced in such a way that member states do actually comply with them. Enforcement is an issue that has bedevilled the good intentions of the EC in environmental, as well as most other areas since its inception (see below).

The need for reliable environmental research and information across the whole of the EC is also recognized as vital and, spurred on by the new freedom to engage in research in its own right conferred by the Single European Act, the EC has taken a number of initiatives (Liberatore 1989). The CORINE project has been assembling a wide range of different environmental databases since 1985 and, within the context of successive Research and Development Framework Programmes, funds have been specifically earmarked for environmental research. However, as has been somewhat acerbically pointed out, this is relatively small in comparison with the funds allocated to the energy and industrial sectors and, in relative terms, is planned to decline rather than increase (House of Lords 1987).

The fifth EAP which comes into operation in 1993 will run up to the year 2000, subject to the outcome of a comprehensive review in 1995. It sets out unequivocally to chart a new direction for EC environmental policy, based on the concept of sustainability, spurred by the new obligations incorporated in the Treaty of European Union (Maastricht Treaty) and the manifest failure of previous programmes to initiate preventive actions commensurate with the scale of the environmental challenges facing member states. The overview of the state of the environment in the Community, published as part of the fifth EAP (Commission of the European Communities 1992, vol. 3), identifies six areas where further action is urgently required: atmospheric pollution, aquatic pollution, soil degradation, nature conservation, the urban environment, and waste management (Table 11.3).

Sustainability is a policy, the ultimate goal of which is to transform the global economic system so that it meets the needs of the present without

TABLE 11.3 *Environmental inventory at the start of the fifth Environmental Action Programme, 1993–2000*

Policy area	Progress to date	Future tasks
Atmospheric pollution	Reduced emissions of sulphur dioxide, particulates, lead and CFCs.	To control better greenhouse gases, such as carbon dioxide, nitrous methane; to improve the air quality in urban areas.
Aquatic pollution	Control of point sources of inland-water pollution; reductions in marine pollution from organic wastes, heavy metals, and radioactive discharges.	To control effectively agricultural pollution; to prevent entrophication of fresh and marine waters; to manage over-exploitation and pollution of groundwater; to combat pollution of the Mediterranean, the Baltic, the North, and other semi-enclosed seas.
Soil degradation	Improved waste management; control of sewage sludge and nitrates on land; 'Seveso' Directive on major industrial hazards.	To reduce excessive use of chemical fertilizers, pesticides and herbicides; continued soil deterioration due to contamination, acidification, desertification, and erosion.
Nature conservation	Protection for wild birds.	To combat threats from intensive agriculture; deterioration of coastal zones due to economic development; forest fires in the Mediterranean; tourist pressures in upland and mountain regions.
Urban environment		To reduce loss of amenity and cultural heritage due to urban growth and development
Waste management	Control of movement of toxic and hazardous wastes, especially across international frontiers.	To ensure better recycling and re-use of waste.

Source: Commission of the European Communities (1992), vol. 1.

compromising the ability of future generations to meet their own needs. The fifth EAP, entitled *Towards sustainability*, is seen as a step along the road and it certainly takes a much broader view of environmental policy than previous programmes. Six issues are singled out for particular attention: sustainable

management of natural resources, integrated pollution control and prevention of waste, reduction in the consumption of non-renewable energy,
improved mobility management, improved environmental quality in urban
areas, and the improvement of public health and safety. It is a huge remit
and, to target it more precisely within the period of the programme, five
sectors of the economy have been chosen for special attention: industry,
energy, transport, agriculture, and tourism. Each has been selected, because
it is undergoing rapid change in the 1990s and will, therefore, exert a decisive
influence on the EC environment to the end of the century.

The broader remit of the fifth EAP has also been heavily influenced by
the Treaty on European Union (Maastricht Treaty), which redefines and
extends the competence of the EC with respect to the environment, an issue
discussed in detail below.

The Single European Act and the Treaty on European Union (Maastricht Treaty)

The Single European Act, by inserting a new Title VII entitled 'Environment' into the Treaty establishing the European Economic Community, for
the first time provided a constitutional base for the Community's environmental policy and allowed the objectives of that policy to be clearly defined
(Vandermeersch 1987). The basic framework for the EC's environmental
policy is set out in the five paragraphs of Article 130r. Paragraph 1 identifies
three fundamental objectives: to preserve and protect the quality of the
environment; to contribute towards protecting human health; and to ensure
prudent and rational utilization of natural resources. These objectives are all-
embracing and in effect give the EC the scope, not only to incorporate
formally all those policies agreed within the context of the three EAPs that
preceded the Single European Act, but also almost any conceivable new
policy. The Commission's original draft of the Act included a list of much
more tightly defined objectives, but these were abandoned during the
preliminary negotiations in favour of the general goals described above
(Vandermeersch 1987).

Paragraph 2 sets out the ways in which the fundamental objectives are to
be realized. It requires that, where possible, policies be adopted which
prevent pollution and other forms of environmental damage ever occurring.
Failing this, the causes should be eliminated at source, rather than attempting
to ameliorate the impacts, and all costs should be borne by the polluter.
Through this latter provision, the Act gives retrospective formal recognition
to 'the polluter pays' principle that has been reiterated repeatedly in

environmental policy statements emanating from the EC, dating back to the first EAP in 1973. Finally, Paragraph 2 requires that environmental protection shall be a component of all EC policies, an issue that is elaborated elsewhere in the Act.

There is concern that environmental policies should be seen to be soundly based, both scientifically and socially. Paragraph 3 demands that full account be taken of: the available scientific and technical data; the environmental conditions in the various regions of the EC; the potential benefits and costs of action, or lack of it; and the economic and social development of the EC as a whole and the balanced development of the regions. In practice, these requirements allow for considerable discretion as between member states, in that specific attention is drawn to the need to take account of the conditions prevailing in any given region, and of the likely economic impacts.

There are always dangers in spelling out too categorically areas of competence between different levels of government, because it may serve to constrain, rather than liberate, action. In Paragraph 4, action by the EC in environmental matters is limited to those areas where the objectives set out in Paragraph 1 can be better achieved at EC, rather than at national level. The EC is subordinated to national governments and, somewhat perversely, therefore, enjoys potentially less freedom of action than before the Act came into force. Previously, the EC could only act strictly in pursuance of maintaining conditions for fair economic competition, but the latter were so difficult to define that in practice there was considerable scope for almost any environmental initiative. There were fears that, after the Single European Act, individual member states would move to limit this freedom, though there is little evidence so far of it actually happening (Vandermeersch 1987). Paragraph 4 also clearly limits the EC's financial liability in environmental matters; except in those cases where the measures are of an EC nature, the costs of any action fall on individual member states.

Finally, in Paragraph 5 both member states and the EC itself are required to co-operate with interested third states and with international organizations in the field of environmental protection. It is, however, stated explicitly that action by the EC shall in no way preclude individual member states from conducting their own negotiations and making separate agreements.

Article 130s lays down the legislative procedures that are to be followed in implementing proposals relating to the environment. One of the most radical features of the Single European Act is the introduction of qualified majority, as opposed to unanimous voting in some areas of policy-making, notably with respect to the completion of the internal market. In environmental matters, however, the principle of unanimity is retained, unless the

Council specifically decides with respect to a particular issue to proceed on the basis of a qualified majority vote. There are both advantages and disadvantages for environmental quality control in this decision. On the one hand, it ensures that the stringent standards of most environmentally aware member states are adopted, but, on the other, it allows recalcitrant member states with poor standards to block new initiatives.

Article 130t is ostensibly a catch-all provision, which explicitly permits any member state to introduce environmental protection standards within its own territory which are more stringent than the EC ones. It is, however, somewhat puzzling that this freedom is restricted to protective measures adopted in common. It is not clear whether the Article is only intended to apply to measures which are protective, and/or have not been adopted unanimously.

Other problems of interpretation arise from the Single European Act, because environmental provisions are also included elsewhere within Articles 100a and 100b, which deal with the harmonization of national laws, including environmental laws. Environmental impacts have to be considered in any new legislation and it is demanded that the EC 'take as a base a high level of protection', but nowhere is either the phrase 'take as a base', or 'a high level of protection' precisely defined. The intention seems to have been that the most stringent provisions pertaining in any member state should be taken as a starting point, but that the EC need not necessarily adopt these in its own legislation.

There are further possible conflicts between the different safeguard clauses in Articles 100a and 100b. Under the terms of Article 130t, member states have an absolute right to apply more stringent standards than the EC if they so decide. However, under 100a, Paragraph 4, they may do so only in so far as the standards do not restrict trade. As yet there is no evidence of any actual conflict arising from this apparent contradiction, but it does emphasize the inordinate complexity of both modifying the founding treaties and marrying them with twelve different bodies of national legislation.

The proposed Treaty on European Union (Maastricht Treaty) roots the environment even more firmly into the infrastructure of the Community. At a general level, Article 2 now requires that the pursuit of economic growth should always be sustainable, non-inflationary and not to the detriment of the environment, thus making it obligatory to include environmental considerations explicitly in all economic policies. The detail of the restated environment policy is contained in Title XVI, replacing Title VII in the Single European Act. For the most part, the thrust of the policy is unchanged, but there is an important new gloss in several places. Article

130r, Paragraph 2, reiterates the somewhat ambiguous aim of incorporating a high level of protection, but adds that this must be based on the precautionary principle and preventive action and that it must also take account of the diversity of situations in the different regions of the Community. Article 130, Paragraph 4, reaffirms that it is normally the responsibility of member states to pay for environmental policy initiatives, but in Paragraph 5 provision is made for EC financial support, where the costs are deemed to put a disproportionate burden on the budget of the public authority in a member state. The resources for this will come from ENVIREG, to be established under the new Cohesion Fund, part of the revised and unified Socio-Structural Funds to be put in place by the end of 1993.

Before leaving this discussion of the Single European Act and the Treaty on European Union (Maastricht Treaty), it must be emphasized that a treaty justification for environmental legislation, albeit a restricted one, existed prior to 1987. Under the terms of Articles 100 and 235 in the original Treaty of Rome establishing the European Economic Community, any legislative action was permitted, so long as it related to the smooth functioning of the common market, or to economic matters more generally. Using this rather vague umbrella, a large number of overtly environmental directives and regulations were issued by the Commission, both before and after the adoption of the EAPs.

The under-integration of environmental policies

The scope of environmental policy is never easy to define, in the sense that all forms of economic activity and development inevitably have environmental consequences. These difficulties have been apparent in the tortuous way in which environmental policy has been gradually embraced by the EC in the years since the Treaty of Rome was first signed. Prior to the Single European Act, EC actions to protect the environment, in theory at least, were constrained by the requirement that they promote the operation of the free market. To this extent they were an integral part of industrial, agricultural, energy, or some other policy, rather than an end in themselves.

With the growing complexity and extent of successive EAPs and environmental Directives, the explicit link with the creation of a free market has become less and less credible. In reality, notwithstanding the Treaty of Rome, environmental policy has to all intents and purposes been part of the remit of the EC since at least the mid-1960s. This was formally recognized in the Single European Act, but in a rather problematically pervasive and vague way. Not only was the EC required to develop a separate policy for the environment, it was also required to incorporate environmental considerations as part and parcel of all its other policies as well. As a result, the hoped for holistic approach has proved elusive and, in some crucial areas, environmental policies have been developed more or less independently of the core strategy as set out in the EAPs (Johnson and Corcelle 1989). The dilemma is now clearly recognized in both the Treaty on European Union (Maastricht Treaty) and the fifth EAP, but it remains to be seen whether true co-ordination will occur between environmental and all other areas of policy-making.

The problems of co-ordination are illustrated most clearly with respect to agriculture, both because of the close link that exists between the industry and the natural environment, and because it dominates EC policy in terms of expenditure, still consuming more than half the available resources. Within the EC bureaucracy, agriculture and environmental protection are dealt with by separate departments, DG VI and DG XI respectively, and each has evolved its policies more or less independently. A 1985 discussion paper, 'Perspectives for the Common Agricultural Policy' (Commission of the European Communities 1985c), reviewed a whole range of options for the future of agriculture and emerged from a working party that included members from both DG VI and DG XI. However, the fourth EAP makes little direct comment on agriculture, other than in its recommendations for protecting the soil. Passing reference is made to the environmental significance of changes in the nature of the farming industry and the proposed reforms of the Common Agricultural Policy, but the focus is on soil conservation, rather than addressing the wider impacts.

The dangers and limitations of this segmented approach are illustrated by the evolution of EC agricultural policy since the early 1970s (Lowe 1988). The overriding concern has been to limit excessive overproduction, and expensive storage of unwanted stocks of foodstuffs. Measures to reduce the levels of surpluses have been widely debated and have also been the subject of a string of Socio-Structural Regulations. Under the so-called 'extensification' measures, farmers may be paid premiums of up to twenty per cent to switch away from producing products deemed to be in surplus. It is envisaged that this might involve actually taking land out of agricultural production and leaving it fallow, or devoting it to some other use, such as forestry, or even non-agricultural activity. Another scheme is the designation of Environmentally Sensitive Areas, rural landscapes which because of their ecological or cultural value should be preserved in their traditional state. A number of member states, notably the UK, Germany, and the Netherlands have made such designations. However, like almost all the other measures included in the Socio-Structural Regulations, they are permissive rather than mandatory, so that their adoption has been patchy and variable across the EC (see also Chapters 8 and 12).

Most of the measures that have emerged from the Socio-Structural Regulations have so far had only limited effect in relation to their prime purpose of reducing surpluses, not least because they are only permissive. The implications for environmental policy are considerable, yet these Regulations are largely outside the control of the designated environmental policy-makers in the EC and most member states. Restrictions on the use of nitrogen fertilizers and less intensive grain production will fundamentally alter many arable landscapes and the mix of flora and fauna they support. In the Environmentally Sensitive Areas, rural islands are being created, immured from many of the changes affecting the countryside as a whole.

It may be unrealistic to expect a higher degree of coherence and co-ordination within the EC, given that environmental policy can, and should, touch virtually all other aspects of policy-making. Nevertheless, if the member states are serious about their commitment to the environment, they need to recognize more explicitly that the attitudes they adopt towards agricultural production, for example, are more important than most of the measures addressed by EC environmental policy *per se* for achieving their goals (see Chapter 12).

Policy implementation

The EC has only a limited range of legal instruments available to ensure that its policies are implemented and enforced; in environmental matters the most important are the Directive and the Regulation. Directives are binding on member states in terms of the results to be achieved and the time-scale for implementation, but permissive as far as the methods are concerned. Regulations, on the other hand, are binding in their entirety and have to be adopted forthwith.

For the most part the Commission has employed Directives and this has been dictated for two essentially practical reasons. On the one hand, the framework of national environmental legislation and legal systems vary to such an extent that the greater flexibility actually facilitates implementation. On the other hand, the EC itself has virtually no funds to support compliance and enforcement. Even if it had the direct powers conferred by Regulations, it would still be forced to rely largely on the goodwill and good offices of individual member states for effecting a Regulation, as opposed to a Directive (Haigh *et al.* 1986).

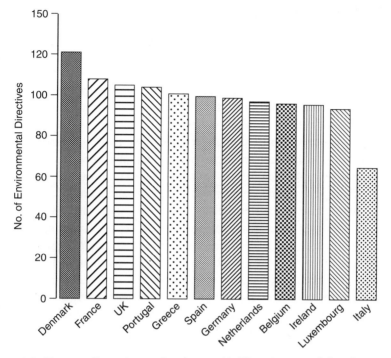

FIG. 11.3. The compliance by member states with EC environmental directives
Source: Hey (1991).

Member states are normally allowed between eighteen months and two years to comply with a Directive but, as is clear from Fig. 11.3, levels of compliance with the 136 Directives issued up to the end of 1991 vary widely. No member state has implemented them all, the most active being Denmark with 122 and the most laggardly Italy with 70 (Frühauf and Giesinger 1992). Naturally, the urgency does vary depending on the issues being addressed, but in some cases the failure to comply is very disturbing. For example, two years after the adoption of the Directive on the supervision and control of the transfrontier shipment of hazardous waste within the EC (inspired by the 1984 Seveso accident, when highly toxic dioxins were released into the atmosphere) only four member states—Denmark, France, Germany, and the UK had actually complied with its provisions. For the rest, varying degrees of progress had been achieved, but in the case of Luxembourg this was so paltry that proceedings had been instituted in the European Court of Justice to compel it to come into line.

Recourse to the European Court of Justice when faced with failure to abide by the three Treaties, or decisions stemming from them, is the ultimate weapon available to the EC against recalcitrant member states, although such a slow and unwieldy means of ensuring compliance is only invoked as a last resort. Even so, it is an option that has been used to good effect, so that the very threat of action in the European Court has become a spur to action. A notable success, in addition to Luxembourg and the 'Seveso' Directive, was the 1990 action which compelled the UK to accept that it must comply with the quality standards for drinking-water.

Regulations have been used sporadically to give the EC greater environmental clout, particularly in areas of international concern beyond its borders. For example, Regulations have established uniform EC rules for the international trade in endangered species of plants and animals, and banned imports of certain cetacean products, sealskins, and ivory from African elephants. However, internally, they have been deployed sparingly, partly because of a lack of central resources independent of national governments. Attempts in the early 1980s to establish an EC environmental fund were abortive and, since then, the emphasis has been on more limited objectives, such as data collection and dissemination and demonstration projects, aimed at creating a climate of opinion conducive to persuading member states to act. In 1984 a fund of 13 million ECUs was set up under Regulation 1872/84 to finance jointly with member states demonstration projects over a period of three years in the areas of habitat protection and clean technologies. In 1987, under Regulation 2247/87, this was extended for a further four years with funding of 24 million ECUs and, in addition to the original areas of competence, now includes the processing and recycling of wastes and effluents, the location and rehabilitation of landfill sites, measurement techniques for environmental monitoring, the protection of bird habitats, and soil conservation. Building on the success of the CORINE project, referred to above, Regulation 1210/90, adopted in 1990, has enabled the creation of a European Environmental Agency. Its function, once the haggling over where it is to be located is resolved, will be to collect, process, and distribute data on the environment, thus providing a scientific basis for EC environmental actions in the future.

However, Directives have always carried the bulk of EC environmental legislation and their central role was further strengthened by the Single European Act. Under the terms of Article 130r, Paragraph 4, the EC may only act centrally in environmental matters where it can be demonstrated that such action would be more effective than if it were undertaken by the member states individually. It goes on to establish that the responsibility for financing and implementing environmental legislation will lie with the member states, thus reinforcing the inbuilt preference for the use of Directives. The complex reality of attempting to merge twelve different national jurisdictions into a single body of environmental legislation is clearly recognized and it has been accepted that progress is more likely to result from co-operation and persuasion, rather than centralized, and probably unenforceable, dictates.

Conclusion

In drawing up a balance sheet of the successes and failures of EC environmental policy, the outstanding feature is that it exists at all (Krämer 1990). The environment was not mentioned in the Treaty of Rome and was only officially incorporated with the adoption of the Single European Act in 1986. Yet environmental legislation is now an important feature of the EC, while other areas, such as transport policy, energy policy, and social policy, which were explicitly included in the founding treaties, have seen little, if any, progress.

Nor have the achievements in the environmental field been mere tokens, despite the fact that much remains to be done. In a number of important areas, notably air and water quality, vehicle-emission control, waste management, the notification of new chemicals, and the protection of wild birds, EC Directives have set standards that are now being applied across the length and breadth of the twelve member states. It is a record of success that is only surpassed in North America, where federal political structures provide a much firmer basis for action at a continental scale.

Environmental legislation also performs a valuable service to the EC above and beyond its specific remit. The fact that all the member states accept and are implementing it, means that this is a powerful force behind the larger process of European integration. In some states, EC environmental legislation represents more or less the sum total of national legislation in this area. Even in those states where this is not the case, perspectives have been substantially altered by EC legislation, sometimes reinforced by decisions of the European Court of Justice.

Of course there is much that still needs to be done. As the 1992 survey of the state of the EC environment clearly demonstrated, pollution of all kinds still abounds, while not all member states accept that the EC is the appropriate body to legislate on environmental issues. There are genuine fears amongst the more enthusiastic members that further progress will be held back by the over-zealous implementation of existing Directives, with the more laggardly states combining to block new proposals. There is also considerable concern that the expansion of the EC to include more Mediterranean countries will produce a shift of emphasis towards the pressing problems of the South, while those in the more industrialized North are relatively neglected.

Such worries and uncertainties are well-founded but are part and parcel of policy-making in any democratic political grouping. New imperatives will continually jostle to find their way on to the agenda and, as far as the EC in 1992 is concerned, its environmental priorities are being fundamentally challenged from a different direction, even before it has begun to consider fully the issues in the Mediterranean countries. The closer association since 1990 of the countries of Eastern Europe, with their run-down industries and appalling environmental record, is already redefining the environmental agenda of the EC. There is a real danger that much of the progress achieved in the 1970s and 1980s might be jeopardized in the face of combating the infinitely more serious environmental problems of the eastern periphery. Careful political judgement will have to be exercised to ensure that the environmental progress achieved in Western Europe over the past forty years is not squandered, as the EC is restructured to allow for stronger ties with the emergent states in the East.

Further reading

The contribution of the EC to environmental protection in Europe has been extensively documented in most of the Community languages. The major policies are explained in Commission of the European Communities (1990), *Environmental Policy in the European Community* (Luxembourg), while two comprehensive summaries of the problems to be solved may be found in Commission of the European Communities (1985), *The State of the Environment in the European Community 1986* (Luxembourg); and Commission of the European Communities (1992), *A European Community Programme of Policy and Action in relation to Environment and Sustainable Development* COM(92) 23 final, 3 vol. (Luxembourg). A selection of good, and critical, reviews of EC policies for the environment are provided by: J. Charpentier (ed.) (1988), *La Protection de l'environnement par les communautés européens* (Paris); N. Haigh (1987), *EEC Environmental Policy and Britain*, 2nd edn. (London); and W. Frühauf, and T. Giesinger (1992), *Europa ohne Grenzen. Alarm für die Umwelt*, Spiegel Spezial (Hamburg).

12 The Effects of EC Policy on the Rural Landscape and Environment of Ireland

Michael B. Quigley

Introduction

Despite the fact that over 56 per cent of the population of the Republic of Ireland now live in towns there are relatively few large urban and industrial centres and the landscape retains a character that is essentially rural. Agricultural land use (including rough grazing) accounts for 80.8 per cent of the country's surface, by far the largest proportion in the EC (Commission of the European Communities 1989a). While mixed farming is in evidence in most areas, there is an overwhelming predominance of pastoral activity with approximately 80 per cent of agricultural output being derived from grass-based enterprises (Gillmor 1989). This situation arises from a combination of factors: in particular, the climate, soil suitability, and the existence of traditional markets for beef and dairy products, especially in the United Kingdom. The economy of Ireland is thus highly dependent upon agriculture which accounts for approximately 18 per cent of the gross domestic product, making it her single most important industry (Gillmor 1989). For this reason changes in EC agricultural policies are likely to be of greater significance for the economy and the environment of Ireland than for any other member state of the Community.

The rural landscape of Ireland is in a continual state of flux, being subject to a number of separate influences. First, subtle shifts occur in land-use patterns as the individual farmer's choice of enterprise mix and degree of specialization are influenced by changing market conditions. Such shifts have always been a natural response to the demands of the market place but, increasingly, they have become integrally linked with the common agricultural price policy, funded by the Guarantee Section of the European Agricultural Fund or EAGGF, which has also provided substantial improvement grants for processing and marketing produce. Although the farmers themselves are the principal agents of these land-use changes, they are responding in a rational manner to the available financial incentives and disincentives. Secondly, there exist a variety of horizontal policy measures aimed both at improving the internal efficiency and economic viability of farms and also the external rationalization of the rural economy by reducing the number of non-viable farms and encouraging diversification. These adjustment measures, which operate selectively, have a major impact on the rural landscape and the natural landscape. They are funded partly by the Guidance Section of EAGGF. Thirdly, substantial sums of money are being provided through the European Regional Development Fund and the European Social Fund as part of the Community Support Framework for Ireland. Although these funds are independent of the CAP they do, none the less, form part of the agricultural reform as they have a significant influence on farming activities and land-use practices. Thus, for example, the Operational Programmes for the Control of Farmyard Pollution, for Forestry, for Rural Development, and for Tourism will all have effects on the rural landscapes of Ireland. Finally, environmental policy and legislation impinge upon the operation of all the other policies already referred to. In this regard the role of the EC is particularly significant for Ireland. These legislative-policy instruments may operate variously to ameliorate some of the negative effects of other policies: by pollution control; providing environmental safeguards, especially with regard to structurally funded development projects; and acting positively to protect wildlife and habitats.

Joining the Community did not cause any sudden upheavals for Irish agriculture: it was already in a state of flux. The modernization and restructuring of agriculture, in addition to various rural infrastructural developments such as arterial drainage and land-clearance schemes, had already been set in train by national governments. But, although it is often difficult to attribute general changes in the landscape to specific causes, the twenty year period following the accession of the Republic of Ireland to the European Economic Community coincided closely with the most profound period of transformation in the structure of Irish farming, even if not unequivocally in terms of economic prosperity (Sheehy 1984). These changes have been wide-ranging in nature: from subtle visual alterations in the colour of intensively fertilized fields to manifest shifts in the geographical patterns of production and choice of farming enterprise; from the dramatic increase in the rate of afforestation to the environmental pressures brought about by changes in technology and land use.

This chapter will explore the degree to which policies emanating from Brussels now dictate the pace and direction of change in the rural landscape and the natural environment of Ireland. It is concerned with the effects on the environment, in the broadest sense, of policies relating to agricultural land use rather than with the economic state of agriculture itself. These policies are at once both composite, in that they deal with an array of diverse land-use concerns, and complex, operating variably in time and in space. They have continuously evolved by progressive fine-tuning, revision, and even reversal. Environmental effects have varied spatially because the policies themselves have had a regional dimension. Before examining the actual landscape modifications and environmental changes which have taken place in Ireland, it will be useful, initially, to outline the policy framework which has facilitated them. It will not be possible to explore in detail the impact on the rural landscape of all aspects of EC policy. Rather, it is intended to select some of the salient elements using specific examples. First among these will be the degree to which the market organizational aspects of the CAP have, via intensification, had a variety of environmental repercussions. Secondly, the consequences of agricultural restructuring, with the help of EAGGF funding, will be considered with regard to agricultural drainage schemes. The potential impact of structural funding under the Community Support Framework for Ireland will then be considered, using the case of forestry development as an example. Finally, some aspects of environmental policy and legislation which have a bearing on agricultural land use will be dealt with. The evolving relationship between the agricultural and environmental policies of the EC is particularly pertinent to Ireland because of its geographical peripherality and the marginal nature of much of its land for agricultural purposes.

Ireland and the policy framework of agriculture in the European Community

Since the foundation of the Irish state, agriculture, which was heavily export-oriented, enjoyed a protected domestic market and export subsidies. Ireland's accession to the European Community in 1973 meant that, although the most important decisions were now taken in Brussels rather than in Dublin, the market was equally distorted by the support-driven elements of the Common Agricultural Policy. At times, this accounted for more than 70 per cent of the Community budget and currently accounts for 62 per cent (Commission of the European Communities 1991e).

The objectives of the CAP, as enshrined in the Treaty of Rome, Article 39, are: to increase agricultural productivity; to ensure a fair standard of living for agricultural communities; to stabilize markets; and to ensure that consumers are adequately supplied with agricultural produce at reasonable prices. In addition, it asserts that account should be taken of 'the particular nature of agricultural activity which results from the social structure of agriculture and from structural and natural disparities between the various agricultural regions'. Although the stated objectives of the CAP have remained unchanged, the means of implementing the policy have been constantly shifting in response to changing economic, political, and environmental conditions within the Community. It is intended, here, to document the history of these policy shifts which have had significant effects on both the physical and human landscape in the Republic of Ireland.

Broadly, the CAP attempts to achieve its objectives by the dual mechanism of direct price support for farmers, on the one hand, and indirect funding to improve the infrastructure and economic viability of farmers with development potential on the other. In practice the support element of the policy has accounted for most of the financial provision, generally totalling over 90 per cent during the mid-1980s (see Chapter 9). The advantages to Irish farmers of higher prices and a large open market for agricultural products were immediately obvious. In the first five years of transition to full membership of the EC, Irish farmers benefited substantially not only in terms of real incomes (despite a considerable increase in the volume and price of farm inputs), but in terms of a 14 per cent increase in gross product (NESC 1989). In fact Irish agricultural prices were already rising in 1972, in anticipation of Community membership and so comparisons with 1970 are more appropriate; these show that real farming incomes rose by 70 per cent, while the volume of gross output rose by 35 per cent in the critical period 1970 to 1978 (Sheehy 1984). Overall, higher farm incomes were achieved through greater productivity, technological progress, and internal rationalization in the industry. The prosperity achieved in the early years of EC membership had a visible spin-off in that many farmers invested in improved farm infrastructure and dwellings, in addition to increasing their capacity (Convery 1989). However at the end of the transition period in 1978, the upward movement of Irish farm prices levelled-off. The following years saw a dramatic fall in real incomes, especially as the accumulation of food surpluses led to the introduction of measures to restrict production. In 1979 the setting-up of the European Monetary System, of which the Republic of Ireland became a member, meant a curtailment of the practice of adjusting Irish farm prices in line with the level of domestic inflation by means of green pound devaluations. The ensuing rise in Irish inflation thus caused a general deterioration in farm incomes (NESC 1989). The early 1980s saw a healthy recovery but, in the middle of that decade, further output restrictions, coupled with unfavourable weather conditions, caused another slump. A subsequent fall in the Irish rate of inflation led to yet a further recovery in the late 1980s. These particularly erratic fortunes of Irish agriculture over the past twenty years can be seen to have resulted from a combination of domestic economic difficulties and tightening of the EC price-support system.

On the whole, the price-support policy of the CAP has contributed to the production of a two-tier agricultural economy in Ireland because the greatest benefits have accrued mainly to farmers who had a strong resource-base with high levels of output and income (Conway 1986; the Commission of the European Communities 1991f). Although agricultural output for the country as a whole increased after accession to the Community, this increase was achieved by only 25–30 per cent of farms (Boyle 1982). One of the most enduring obstacles to economic prosperity in Irish agriculture has been the inherent structural problems of the rural economy (Cox 1985). Almost half the land area of the country is characterized by large proportions of small uneconomic holdings in areas that are, at best, marginal for agriculture. These farmers are predominantly owner-occupiers with age, marital, and educational profiles that are largely unfavourable to modern progressive approaches to the industry. Where there is leasing of land, it is mainly in the 'conacre' tradition involving an eleven-month arrangement which, in itself, is inimical to land improvement (Gillmor 1989). The original vision, embodied in the 'Mansholt Plan' of the 1960s, was to rationalize farming in the European Community by increasing the number of viable units through a process of technological upgrading of potentially productive farms, while at the same time, encouraging uneconomic operators to retire or transfer to off-farm employment, thus releasing more land for fewer farmers. Such aspirations for a streamlined agricultural industry proved to be politically unacceptable in Ireland as elsewhere. Moreover, their spirit was subsequently embodied, in somewhat diluted form, in three structural directives which had been introduced in 1972 and which were later implemented in Ireland, thereby replacing existing national development schemes. These were: the Farm Modernization Scheme (Directive 72/159/EEC); the directive to deal with retirement of older farmers and the redistribution of their land (Directive 72/160/EEC); and the scheme for socio-economic guidance and vocational training (Directive 72/161/EEC).

None of these schemes had any major effects on the overall structural problems in Irish agriculture. From 1975 to 1987 the number of farms decreased by only 4.8 per cent while average farm size changed very little (Morgan and O'Toole 1992). However, many individual farmers benefited from the modernization scheme, in particular, which was targeted mainly at farmers in the 'development' category. It provided a selective system of aids for farmers who had potential for bringing their incomes up to a level commensurate with those of non-farm workers. It thus discriminated against the lowest income group who were precluded from claiming the maximum assistance. One of the most significant aspects of these directives was that they began to establish that there were basically two types of farming: commercial, in which farmers would benefit directly from market policy, and non-commercial which would require infrastructural support to compensate for natural disadvantage.

This duality was given an important geographical dimension in September 1976 with the introduction of the Scheme for Farming in the Less-Favoured Areas, as embodied in Directive 75/268 (Gillmor 1977; O'Hara 1986). Under this scheme compensatory income supplements, in the form of headage payments, were paid to farmers in the designated areas which, in general, were represented by the western half of the country. Although, in reality, low income farmers benefited least from this scheme (Cox 1985), the principle of making livestock headage payments available indiscriminately to all farmers within the designated areas is incompatible with the notion of structural reform (Sheehy 1984; Sheehy and O'Connor 1985). Other area-specific measures aimed at improving the economic fortunes of farmers in disadvantaged areas were the Western Drainage Scheme, introduced in 1979 (Directive 78/628/EEC) and extended in 1981 (Council Reg. 2195/86), and a programme known as the 'Western Package' introduced in 1980 designed to stimulate agricultural development in the west of Ireland (Council Reg. 1820/80). This latter programme, which had as one of its stated aims 'the removal of infrastructural deficiencies,' was scheduled to run for ten years at a cost to the EC of £150 million (in addition to substantial exchequer funding). It provided grants for a wide variety of agricultural activities such as farm infrastructures, on-farm investment, land improvement, forestry, marketing, and the expansion of agricultural educational facilities. In 1985 this programme was revised and extended to include all disadvantaged areas in Ireland. Significantly, aid was made available under the revised programme for pollution control, basic animal housing, and fodder storage. The Farm Modernization Scheme was replaced in 1986 by the Farm Improvement Programme. This implemented the mandatory provisions of EC Council Regulation 797/85, for investment in farm structures where incomes were low but human potential was high, especially in the Less-Favoured Areas.

The CAP is a complex instrument and in some ways its objectives are ultimately incompatible. In theory it recognizes the importance of the social dimension of agriculture and yet, in practice, both the support mechanisms and even much of the structural funding have discriminated against low-income farmers of which there are many in the Republic of Ireland. For these farmers, alternative employment in the non-farm sector is not an available option in many cases. It has created a duality in Irish agriculture, both economically and regionally. On the whole Ireland has been a major net beneficiary of the CAP. Its application has, through both the price-support system and the structural schemes, facilitated the transfer of a considerable amount of funds into the Irish agricultural economy. The net value of CAP transfers to Ireland in 1986, for example, amounted to over £IR1100 million (NESC 1989). This level of input must have had a major impact, not only on the economic and social life of the country, but also on the physical landscape. Both the market policy and the structural policy have had negative effects on the environment, the former through intensification, the latter through the funding of development schemes in areas that are environmentally sensitive.

In recent years the CAP has come under increasing criticism from both within the EC and from external trading nations. The policy has certainly achieved its objective of self-sufficiency in food production in post-war Europe, as well as protecting the interests of producers through relatively high, albeit artificial, prices. And for consumers, prices are generally not out of line with inflation. But there is a growing awareness that the market imbalances caused by massive price-support systems must be addressed. By linking price-support to the volume of agricultural output, a positive feedback loop has been created which has led not only to an intensification spiral, with a variety of undesirable environmental side effects, but also to overproduction. Surpluses of food commodities within the EC are a patent reality. Between 1973 and 1988 the volume of agricultural production in the EC rose by 2 per cent per annum, while consumption within the Community rose by only 0.5 per cent per annum (Commission of the European Communities 1991e). The high cost of intervention storage, wasteful deterioration and export subsidies, have put enormous strains on the budget of the Community, as well as on international trading relations, especially in the context of GATT negotiations. The larger questions of the stability of world markets, and the ethics of 'dumping' surplus produce at rock-bottom prices on Third World economies, are hotly debated issues of global importance. For Ireland and elsewhere, the notion of bolstering the productivity of Less-Favoured Areas in order to produce more food is ultimately irreconcilable with attempts to reduce the level of food production in the Community at large.

In the light of a changing economic climate, there was an attempt, from the mid-1980s onwards, to make certain stabilizing adjustments to the CAP. An examination of a group of Commission documents produced in that period shows that the emphasis on high-productivity farming had already changed. In 1985 the Commission produced a Green Paper entitled 'Perspectives for the Common Agricultural Policy.' Several new and important guidelines for the future development of agricultural policy resulted from the debate which followed its publication. These guidelines related to three allied areas of concern: (1) market organization; (2) the incomes of small farmers and their role in the rural economy; and (3) the protection of the environment. The primary goal of reforming the market organization so as to reduce surpluses by means of a price policy that reflected the demand for food, was effected through financial disincentives such as the milk superlevy and co-responsibility levies. With regard to the incomes of small farmers, a new policy document published in the same year, entitled 'A future for Community Agriculture' (Document COM 85/750), drew attention to the need for effective action on income support for small family farms, as well as the maintenance of both the social and environmental fabric of the rural landscape. Following on from this, the Council Regulation on Improving the Efficiency of Agricultural Structures (Reg. 797/85) was introduced. This was effected through the Farm Improvement Programme, mentioned above, which assisted infrastructural developments, especially for young farmers in the Less-Developed Areas. It also provided grants for alternative rural land uses and activities. Significantly, there were over a dozen amendments to this regulation, introduced later in that year, dealing with the protection of the environment and proposed grants for reducing productivity (O'Farrell 1986). These provisions were given an even firmer footing two years later in the Agricultural Structures Directive 1760/87, which also deals with 'the adjustment of agriculture to the new market situation and the preservation of the countryside'. It supports the move towards extensification of agriculture and the provision of grant aid to maintain environmentally sensitive areas.

Despite the attempts at stabilizing agriculture during the late 1980s, there has been a need for a more radical rethink of the CAP as a whole in the 1990s. After 30 years of operation the policy has not succeeded in solving some of the most fundamental problems of EC farmers. Notwithstanding massively escalating expenditure, with the EAGGF guarantee budget increasing from 4.5 billion ECUs in 1975 to 31.0 billion ECUs in 1991, and despite the fact that 35 per cent of those active in agriculture have left the land in Europe, most farmers are not substantially better-off, in real terms, than they had been before. In addition, the inherent inequity of the support system has meant that 80 per cent of EAGGF funding has gone to 20 per cent of the Community's farmers. More significantly, the linking of support to the volume of production has led to a polarization of agriculture into two separate streams of development, each with attendant negative effects: on the one hand, intensification, with undesirable effects on the environment and, on the other, abandonment of agricultural lands with the catastrophic social effects of rural decay.

In February 1992 the European Commission produced a 'Reflections Paper,' (COM (91)100), on the state of the CAP; this formed the basis for the 1992 reform proposals which subsequently went before the European Parliament and the Council of Ministers later in the year. The 1992 CAP reforms aim at controlling production levels while, at the same time, guaranteeing farmers' incomes, not just by price guarantees but by direct compensatory aid measures, modulated by regional and other circumstances. They recognize the importance of preserving the rural character and family-farm structure of European agriculture. Furthermore, they see farmers as having a dual role: as producers of both food and, significantly, non-food commodities; and at the same time as environmental managers or guardians of the countryside. Incentives are to be offered to farmers for non-polluting and environmentally sound farming practices, for long-term set-aside, and farm afforestation.

Structural funding is now being seen more and more in the context of integrated rural and regional development with an added environmental dimension which was noticeably absent from earlier policy provisions. The new regime of EC funding was initiated at the beginning of 1989 following lengthy negotiations at the 1988 EC summit, at which it was agreed to increase the relative importance of such funds in the run-up to the establishment of the Single Market. The reform of the structural funds meant that they would account for over 30 per cent of the Community budget by 1993 and the emphasis would now be on the poorer regions of the Community. Funds are now to be applied for under the headings of the European Regional Development Fund, the European Social Fund, and the Guidance Section of the Community Agricultural Fund (EAGGF) which had previously dealt with agricultural structural funding. Some concern has been expressed about the inadequacy of environmental safeguards when large funds are available for development (IEEP 1990). The areas of the Community that are eligible for such grants are also very often the areas of greatest environmental sensitivity.

For the Republic of Ireland, one of the most striking consequences of EC agricultural policy has been the creation of a dichotomy in the rural economy between the more intensively capitalized and specialized enterprises on the one hand, and the more marginal and disadvantaged types of agricultural holding on the other. EC membership has thus conferred a more sharply defined geographical expression to a pattern of production that had merely been implicit heretofore. The overall effects of an evolving centralized policy fits quite well the Darwinian notion of 'the survival of the fittest', with the physical environment providing the inherent variation of resources, the changing climate of agricultural retrenchment, the selection pressure, and economic profitability, the principle of that selection. For those pre-adapted for survival, increasing capitalization, intensification, and specialization have been the order of the day. For the 'unfit' the only available survival mechanism is to diversify and adapt to new and sometimes alien niches, requiring considerable financial support such as extensification, set-aside, agritourism, and forestry.

Agricultural intensification and the effects

Intensification, involving an increase in output per unit of resource, is the hallmark of modern commercial farming. Inevitably, such farming depends to a large extent on the market mechanisms and price structures of the CAP as the level of that support is linked directly to the volume of agricultural output. The principal characteristics of agricultural intensification in Ireland include increases, first, in the levels of investment in mechanization and farm buildings; secondly, in livestock intensity, especially involving housed animals; and thirdly, in farm inputs, including inorganic fertilizers and concentrated feedstuffs. In addition, there has been the overall effect of gradually shifting patterns of land use with more regional specialization of farming enterprise. Receipts from the EAGGF Guarantee Fund in 1990 amounted to £IR1352 million. The effects of this EC funding have often been indirect in that relative price stability and profitability in the commercial farming sector, resulting from market policy, have an automatic feedback into farm improvement. At the same time various structural schemes such as the Farm Modernization Scheme and the Farm Improvement Programme have also benefited commercial farmers in particular. The pace of agricultural development has thus been accelerated over the past twenty years or so and, consequently, the rural landscape has undergone many changes. There have also been a number of undesirable environmental side effects although not all aspects of intensification necessarily involve a serious degree of environmental degradation.

The replacement of human and animal labour with mechanized means of production is one of the main features of modern agriculture. The 1970s was a period of considerable mechanization of Irish farming with, for example, tractor numbers showing a 72.4 per cent increase over the decade (Horner *et al.* 1984). One of the side effects of increasing mechanization has been the removal of hedgerows in order to increase field size, thus making for more efficient use of machinery (Webb 1985; Cabot (ed.) 1985). There is little documentation on the nature and precise timing of this phenomenon in Ireland but it has been estimated that 16 per cent of all hedges have been removed since 1938 (Webb 1988). This figure is relatively small by comparison with many Western European countries but hedgerows are one of the most important wildlife habitats in Ireland, especially for a large proportion of the bird fauna. This loss is all the more serious because Ireland has such a low percentage cover (0.5 per cent) of broad-leaved woodland (Temple Lang and Hickie 1992). In addition, hedgerows have become an integral part of the countryside and as such, provide an important visual amenity.

One of the most notable features of modern Irish agriculture has been the dramatic shift in recent years from hay-making to silage production as a source of winter fodder (Fig. 12.1). The greatest expansion in this techno-logical development took place during the mid-1980s and recent years have seen some levelling-off of the upward trend. Geographically, the greatest increases are to be found in the regions of the south-east and south-west, areas of intensive commercial farming (Morgan and O'Toole 1992). The use of forage harvesters allows for considerable labour-saving by comparison with traditional hay-making. The uncertainty of Irish summer weather also gives silage-making a distinct advantage. This significant trend in Irish agriculture

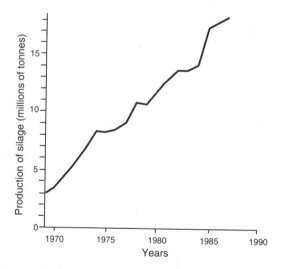

FIG. 12.1. Silage production in the Republic of Ireland, 1970–1990
Source: Gillmor (1991–2).

has been encouraged by a campaign of information dissemination and technical advice, in addition to a system of financial aids for the purchase of forage harvesters and storage facilities under the Farm Improvement Programme, the Operational Programme for the Control of Farmyard Pollution, and other policy measures.

The shift away from hay-making to silage production has affected the habitat of the corncrake (*Crex crex*) in Ireland. With an estimated 20 per cent of the European population resident in Ireland, the decline by 30 per cent since 1980 is a matter for concern (Mayes and Stowe 1989). Silage-making has also posed the most serious threat to aquatic environments in Ireland (Fitzmaurice 1983). Silage effluent has a very high polluting potential with BOD of 65 000 mg/l in addition to nitrates and phosphates (Morgan and O'Toole 1992). In recent years, leakages from silage clamps to groundwater has caused pollution in many springs and wells (Daly 1992). No less serious has been the effect of silage effluent on water-courses; this is often exacerbated by the fact that the period of silage-making usually coincides with that of lowest water levels in rivers, thus decreasing their dilution potential. Fish kills have resulted from a number of causes including nutrient enrichment which is undoubtedly due partly to leachate of agricultural origin (Fig. 12.2). But individual accidental point-discharges, particularly of silage effluent, is the most serious single threat to fish life. Salmonid species are particularly sensitive to deoxygenation and so the valuable game-fishing industry has been

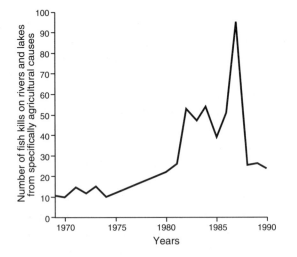

FIG. 12.2. Fish kills attributed to agriculture in the Republic of Ireland, 1970–1990
Source: Moriarty (1991).

adversely affected (Bracken and O'Grady 1992). Crisis point was reached in 1987 when the combination of an exceptionally dry summer and 122 fish-kill incidents (95 of them agricultural in origin) led to a campaign to increase awareness among farmers, in addition to introducing grants for pollution control and stricter enforcement of the Fisheries Acts. The situation has subsequently improved as evidenced by the fact that, despite a dry summer in 1990, only 23 fish kills were directly attributable to agricultural causes (Moriarty 1991). The prospects for further improvement are also good as there is likely to be more emphasis in the future on cereal-based feedstuffs rather than on silage (Harte 1992).

Although the size of the national cattle herd has remained relatively unchanged since EC membership, there has been considerable restructuring within both the beef-cattle and dairying sectors (Harte 1992). Between 1973 and 1989 the number of farms with cattle declined by 27.4 per cent while the average size of cattle herds increased by 24.3 per cent. This trend of increasing rationalization was even more marked in dairying: in the same period the number of farms with dairy cows decreased by 60.3 per cent while the average size of dairy herds increased by 147 per cent. The absolute number of dairy cows also declined steadily after 1985, a reflection of increasing EC restrictions on production at that time. But most remarkable of all was the extreme level of intensification and rationalization in the pig industry between 1975 and 1989, with the number of farms containing pigs declining from 35 700 to only 2500 and the average size of pig herds increasing from 29 to 400 (Harte 1992).

This kind of production has created an imbalance where, with the housing of animals and the importation of feedstuffs into the region, potential herd size is not governed by the size of the farm holding. This imbalance is manifest in the accumulation of large quantities of animal manure in such intensive livestock units; this has led to a very serious environmental hazard with regard to the storage, transport, and disposal of slurry. Between 1975 and 1990 there has been a 32 per cent increase in the volume of accumulated pig slurry (Morgan and O'Toole 1992). Land spreading is the usual method of disposal but, in the case of pig farming, the problem has been particularly acute: first, because of the extreme degree of regional specialization in this sector with a major concentration of production in the north midlands, especially Co. Cavan; and secondly, the fact that the poorly-drained drumlin soils of that part of the country are ill-suited to the absorption of this organic load.

The consequent level of pollution in the rivers and lakes of this important game- and coarse-fishing region has been alarming. Within the Cavan-Monaghan area 52.5 per cent of river sections have been classified as being

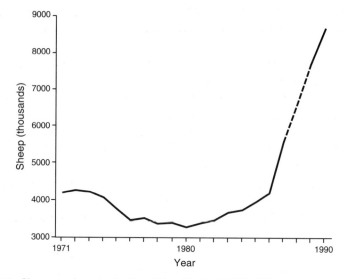

Fɪɢ. 12.3. Sheep numbers in the Republic of Ireland, 1971–1990

Source: Department of Agriculture and Food, Dublin.

polluted to some degree, with 30 per cent having moderate levels of pollution (McCumiskey 1992). The case of Lough Sheelin, where farming and fishing or tourism interests were in direct conflict, has been particularly well documented and publicized (An Foras Taluntais 1972, 1975; Champ 1990; Duggan and Champ 1992). The Lough Sheelin catchment has the heaviest concentration of pig-rearing in Co. Cavan but it was also one of the best-stocked natural trout-fishing lakes in Europe (Dodd and Champ 1983). Increasing nutrient levels, especially of phosphates, throughout the 1970s led to the growth of dense algal blooms, culminating in the virtual death of the lake so that by 1982 the fishing industry had collapsed with major loss to the local tourist economy. In the mid to late 1980s a combination of close monitoring, the banning of slurry spreading during winter months, and the development of an overall slurry-management strategy, involving its export to other areas, began to reverse the situation and to restore the health of the lake (Duggan and Champ 1992).

Recent trends in sheep-farming in Ireland demonstrate very clearly the importance of market developments at European level during the late 1980s (Fig. 12.3). Numbers of sheep had stood at just over 4 million during the early 1970s. From 1975 to 1984, the sheep population had decreased to an average of 3.5 million, which probably reflects the relative profitability of other farming enterprises during most of that period. From 1985 to 1990 the average annual increase in sheep numbers was 17 per cent, achieved mainly through the enlargement of flock size so that by the latter date the sheep population stood at 8.7 million (Department of Agriculture and Food 1990). During the 1980s sheep-farming was in fact the only farming enterprise that showed any growth (Walsh 1989).

An important factor affecting sheep numbers was the fact that in 1980, sheepmeat was incorporated into the CAP price-support system. More significant, at least in some regions, was the introduction of headage payments under Directive 75/268 within Less-Favoured Areas and also the introduction of the Ewe Premium Scheme in 1980 through Council Regulation 80/1837 (Harte 1992). The sudden expansion in sheep numbers can also be seen as a response by farmers to the restrictions placed on them by the introduction in 1984 of milk quotas which led to a decline in dairying activities. Thus the increase in sheep numbers was not so much a process of intensification as one of enterprise substitution, indicating the potency of EC policy in the decision-making of Irish farmers (Walsh 1989).

Much concern has been expressed about the environmental damage that can potentially result from overgrazing, especially in upland areas (Bleasdale and Sheehy Skeffington 1992) and in fragile coastal ecosystems (Quigley (ed.) 1991). Sheep grazing affects the vigour of plants through defoliation, trampling, and through alterations in the cycling of nutrients. Sheep, as selective grazers, have an effect on the species-composition of pastures, and on the competition between species in these ecosystems (Smillie and Morgan 1992). The degree to which grazing affects the vegetation is related not only to stocking rates but also to the period of the year when it is practised and the stage in the natural life-cycle of the heather (McAdam 1988). In extreme cases overgrazing may lead to the break-up of the ground cover and subsequent soil erosion which, itself, may have effects on the sedimentary discharge to streams and their associated fisheries (Bracken and O'Grady 1992). Recent research in Connemara has suggested that LFA headage payments and ewe premiums have encouraged farmers to overstock the hills which has led to major habitat loss, with little heather moorland remaining intact (Bleasdale and Sheehy Skeffington 1992).

The application of inorganic fertilizers to agricultural land has been another feature of the intensification of Irish agriculture. While artificial phosphorus and potassium applications have not increased significantly, nitrate fertilizer use has increased steadily since just before Ireland joined the EC (Fig. 12.4). The quantity of artificial nitrate applied in Ireland is approximately the same as that derived from animal manure. Despite their steady increase in use, however, the amounts applied are considerably lower

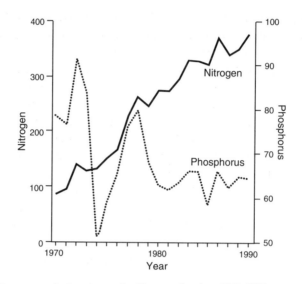

FIG. 12.4. Nitrogen and phosphorus fertilizer application, 1971–1990

Source: Department of Agriculture and Food, Dublin.

than in most EC countries and the risk of serious water pollution from this source is regarded as relatively slight (Morgan 1983; Morgan and O'Toole 1992). The relatively high rainfall in Ireland dilutes the leachate to safer levels (Daly 1992). Nitrate levels in the rivers of the south-east of the country have been shown to be related both to climatic conditions and to the percentage of the catchment that is ploughed (Neill 1989). The fact that Irish agriculture is predominantly grass-based means that leaching is less prevalent than it would be with tillage crops. In a recent study in the east of Ireland it has also been shown that the proportion of arable land appears to be a factor affecting nitrogen levels; 30 per cent of sample sites in a predominantly tillage area had levels exceeding the maximum admissible concentration set down in the European Council Directive concerning the protection of waters against pollution caused by nitrates from agricultural sources (91/676/EEC) (Thorn and Coxon 1992). However, point-sources of pollution such as slurry and silage pits may also contribute to these high levels.

The geographical patterns of agricultural enterprise in the Republic of Ireland have been well documented (Gillmor 1977, 1985; Horner *et al.* 1984; Walsh and Horner 1984). Irish agriculture was characterized by a certain degree of regional specialization which had evolved as a natural response to a variety of environmental constraints, such as climate and soil suitability, as well as market orientation and tradition. But although cereal production tended to be concentrated in the slightly drier and warmer south-east of the country, and dairying in the south and south-west, most farmers were, to some extent, engaged in a mixed form of agriculture.

This situation has been changing, however, with farmers beginning to concentrate on one or two enterprises on individual farms. Due to scale economies this has resulted in greater efficiency and higher productivity. The pig sector is an extreme example of this phenomenon where economies of scale have reduced the industry to a relatively small number of large specialized units, especially in Co. Cavan. The case of poultry production, which has become the regional specialization of neighbouring Co. Monaghan, has been equally remarkable. These core areas, ill-suited to both tillage and pasture, consolidated their position by intensifying production at the expense of areas where such enterprises were less central in the overall mix.

The state of the European market has also affected the production of arable crops in Ireland. While the 1970s was a period of concentration of tillage in the east and south-east of the country, and especially in the larger holdings (Horner et al. 1984), all regions of the country have experienced a decline in the area tilled in the period 1980 to 1990. Even in the south-east, 47 000 ha of tillage have been converted to pastoral use, and especially the production of silage (Morgan and O'Toole 1992). Farmers in Ireland have been quick to respond to the opportunities of the market. Even the casual observer of the countryside cannot have failed to notice the visual impact of newly introduced crops such as oilseed-rape and linseed. Approximately 5000 ha of rapeseed are now grown annually in the Republic of Ireland. In the last few years there has been a dramatic increase in linseed production, again in direct response to favourable market prices: in 1989 there were 30 ha sown by only 10 growers in the whole country; by 1992 approximately 4000 ha were produced by 350 growers (Department of Agriculture and Food, personal communication). With the current emphasis in the new CAP reforms on non-food crops, it seems likely that this crop will expand in future years. Hence the visual impact of these recent land-use changes has been quite striking, with the bright yellow of the rapeseed, the pale blue of the linseed, and the deep green of the well-fertilized fields all lending an unfamiliar appearance to the Irish rural landscape.

The EC and agricultural drainage in Ireland

Whether for reasons of a unique denudation chronology or tectonic history, the central area of Ireland is relatively flat and low-lying. Most of her major rivers originate in this area and flow sluggishly outwards to breach the upland rim of the country before attaining the sea. In addition, the scouring action of Pleistocene glaciers left a legacy of extensive poorly-drained lowland hollows in which fens and ultimately raised bogs have developed, especially in the vast central catchment of the River Shannon (Mitchell 1986). High rainfall, especially in the western fringes, and low evaporation rates further exacerbate the problem of water evacuation. Thus a combination of climatic, geological, geomorphic, and hydrological factors have conspired to produce large areas of wet mineral soils and peatlands which are ill-suited to agriculture on any intensive scale unless major remedial action is taken. The problem of a semi-permanent surplus of water on the land can be alleviated by means of arterial drainage, field drainage, or very often, a combination of the two. Arterial drainage involves the deepening and widening of existing drainage channels in order to evacuate the water from the catchment more efficiently and thus prevent periodic flooding. Field drainage involves the digging of drains and ditches in order to lower the water-table but this often requires that arterial works be completed first.

Such action has a high cost, both economically and environmentally. From the standpoint of land improvement and making a living from the land, such remedial works are unreservedly a good thing despite the high economic costs involved. From an environmental point of view land drainage is the cause of an alarming degree of environmental disruption and habitat loss throughout Europe (Baldock 1984). From the point of view of the EC policy-makers it is difficult to justify the destruction of the already diminished natural and semi-natural heritage of Europe in order to increase productivity in areas that are, at best, marginal for agricultural purposes at a time when food surpluses continue to mount.

While EC funds have made a significant contribution to the drainage of Irish wetlands, especially in the 1980s, Ireland already had a long history of land improvement through both arterial and field-drainage projects, stretching back to the 1840s when rural population pressure was often four times what it is today and cultivable land was at a premium. Such highly labour-intensive public works also helped to create employment in famine-ridden Ireland, and the notion of drainage as a public good was firmly ingrained in the minds of Irish rural populations thereafter (Kelly 1980). The 1945 Arterial Drainage Act established the principle that all such projects should be financed from the exchequer and that work should be undertaken only on the basis of whole river catchments. The Office of Public Works drew up a prioritized list of drainage catchments and applied themselves systematically to the task of draining them. Arterial drainage was at its zenith in the early 1960s with construction investment running as high as £IR14 million per annum (Baldock 1984). However, a decade later, when cost-benefit analysis was beginning to be applied, less than a third of that amount was being expended.

Once Ireland joined the European Community a new impetus was given to arterial-drainage works. The most substantial financial assistance for these works came in the form of the Western Drainage Scheme, which was instituted under EC Directive 78/628, and which affected three major river catchments in the west of Ireland only. Under this scheme 50 per cent of the cost of construction was reimbursed to the Irish government from EAGGF, up to a maximum of 18.1 million ECUs. The financial burden on the Irish government for the remaining 50 per cent of the costs was somewhat lightened by a relatively low interest loan from the European Investment Bank. Three years later an additional sum of 30 million ECUs was made available under EC Regulation 2195/81, although not all of this was for arterial drainage. In addition to these grants, smaller amounts of money were made available through special cross-border schemes involving 50 per cent EAGGF reimbursement, the remainder being shared by the governments of Northern Ireland and the Republic. The European Regional Development Fund also provided smaller grants for arterial work in three river catchments.

In Ireland grants for field drainage prior to EC membership were available through the Land Project which was set up in 1949. After Ireland became a member of the Community, this and other national schemes were replaced by the Farm Modernization Scheme, referred to above (Directive 72/159/EEC). However, the financial contribution of the EC to field drainage at that time was only about 5 per cent of costs. Even with the introduction of Directive 75/268 for the Less-Favoured Areas, most farmers in the west of the country did not benefit because many of them were not within the 'development farmer' category. In fact only 11 per cent of applications for grants came from within the Less-Favoured Areas. In 1979, with the introduction of the Western Drainage Scheme (Directive 78/628/EEC), the financial involvement of the European Community in field drainage in Ireland was considerably increased, at least in the western counties. Within these areas 70 per cent grants were available to farmers, half of which was met by the EC, the remainder by the Irish government with the help of the EIB loan referred to earlier. In addition, EAGGF offered 25 per cent grants to farming co-operatives for the purchase of drainage machinery. While the average contribution to field drainage by the EC has been calculated as approximately 20 per cent, this masks considerable regional variation. The fact that the decline in arterial-drainage activity in the early 1970s was arrested by a fresh input of funds following EC membership and that it has come to a virtual standstill since the ending of the Western Drainage Scheme in 1988, is a reasonable indication that EC monies helped to prolong the life of such works for longer than would otherwise have been the case in western areas. In its ten years of operation the Western Drainage Scheme was responsible for the field drainage of 150 000 ha. In addition, the Farm Modernization Scheme and the Farm Improvement Programme between them had facilitated the drainage of 370 000 ha of farmland (Department of Agriculture and Food, personal communication).

It now seems that major drainage projects are a thing of the past. Among the main reasons for this must be: (a) the feeling that the net financial gains of such schemes are doubtful, especially in the lower priority catchments; (b) the shift in agricultural policy away from high productivity towards extensification and alternative uses for agricultural lands that is implicit in the Agricultural Structures Directive and other aspects of CAP reform; and (c) the development of environmental legislation, the increasingly loud voice of lobbyists, and the general growth of environmental awareness. The Western Drainage Scheme has now been completed. It is unlikely that EC funds or European Investment Bank loans will be available for future schemes, and even exchequer funding has been curtailed significantly with only £IR3 million having been budgeted in 1992 (Temple Lang and Hickie 1992).

In the past 40 years or so the rural landscape of Ireland has been altered irrevocably by the implementation of drainage projects so that an estimated 20 per cent of farmland has been drained (Baldock 1984). The EC contribution to this has not only been substantial in financial terms but also critical in its timing and geographical focus. The revival of drainage activity in the late 1970s was facilitated by the injection of EC funds at a time when the economic climate favoured development and increased production. Most importantly the wet soils of western Ireland were improved for agriculture with the help of the Western Drainage Scheme. But such developments also had environmental costs which were hardly considered at that time when agricultural land use was seen as having a natural priority over other possible uses. These costs include the loss of wildlife habitats and reduction in biological diversity, the disruption of fisheries, and the alteration of landscape elements.

The destruction of wetland habitats through drainage activities has been a matter of serious concern throughout Europe (Baldock 1990). Ireland's wetlands are particularly important in the context of European bird migrations, as a temperate passage halt between the arctic and central Europe, and also as a wintering area for a wide variety of waders and wildfowl species

(Merne 1980). Very large numbers of these birds are dependent on the many Irish freshwater lakes, callows (flooded meadows), and turloughs (unique temporary lakes in karstic areas) which, due to water-table lowering, have been diminishing rapidly in extent and in number. Up to 70 per cent of the world's population of Greenland white-fronted geese (*Anser albifrons flavirostris*) winter on Irish wetlands (Baldock 1984) but their numbers have decreased in certain western areas due to drainage activities (Ruttledge and Ogilvie 1979). Of the 90 turloughs that have been identified in the west of Ireland 30 have already been destroyed (Coxon 1987) and with them the black-necked grebe (*Podiceps nigricollis*) has all but disappeared as a breeding bird in Ireland (Merne 1980). Similarly the drainage of callows and turloughs has affected the population of Bewick's swans (*Cygnus columbianus*) which represents over 20 per cent of the European population. A wide variety of other organisms, from mammals such as the otter (*Lutra lutra*) to a number of rare plant species has been affected to varying degrees.

There is also evidence that arterial drainage can cause serious damage to fisheries. Spawning beds are adversely affected by dredging and regrading of river profiles. The reduction of streambed diversity and bankside vegetation also has negative effects on fish habitats. In addition to the initial engineering works themselves, subsequent maintenance further damages the value of fisheries. In the Boyne, an important salmon-fishing river which was subject to major arterial drainage works, the re-establishment of wild salmon stocks in all its major tributaries has been very limited (McCarthy 1980).

Arterial-drainage works almost invariably involve a deterioration in landscape quality. The canalization of meandering rivers, the removal of vegetation, the construction of steeply graded riverbanks, and the deposition of spoil heaps all represent a potential loss to the aesthetic value and tourist potential of the countryside.

The role of the EC in Irish forestry

The modern Irish landscape is unusual in that, despite its particular suitability for the growing of trees, with growth yields of more than three times the EC average, the imprint of thousands of years of farming and woodland clearance has perhaps been more complete than elsewhere in Europe. Thus Ireland has the lowest percentage (6 per cent) of forested land of any European state, with the exception of Iceland. Without doubt then, one of the most conspicuous landscape changes that has taken place in recent years has resulted from the dramatic increase in the rate of afforestation, representing a fundamental change in land use in a country where there is no strong tradition of forestry and where it has usually been regarded, especially by farmers, as a land use of last resort (Hickie 1991*a*). The singularity of the case of Irish forestry is further adumbrated by the fact that, since independence in 1922 (when the percentage of forest cover was less than 1 per cent) the state has been, until recently, almost solely responsible for afforestation in the Republic; even now 85 per cent of forests are state-owned and managed. In addition the fact that 90 per cent of Irish forests are comprised of non-native conifer species, mainly Sitka spruce (*Picea sitchensis*) and lodgepole pine (*Pinus contorta*), adds to the peculiarity of the Irish situation.

Recent years have seen a major stimulus in forestry development which has resulted, to some extent, from the increasing unprofitability of farm enterprises in marginal lands but, more importantly, has been encouraged by shifts in government forestry policy. Both the National Development Plan 1989–93 and the Operational Programme for Forestry signalled the government's intention to develop the forestry industry in the Republic of Ireland with a doubling of annual planting targets from 15 000 to 30 000 ha, thus giving Ireland the highest annual planting rate relative to area. At the same time there have also been significant institutional changes in the industry; first, with the setting-up of a semi-state company 'Coillte Teoranta' to take over and manage all state forests on a purely commercial basis; and secondly, the encouragement of private-sector planting with generous grant schemes administered, first under the EC Programme for Western Development (the Western Package) introduced in 1981 and later under the Operational Programme in 1989. The total projected cost of the latter programme, over its five-year operation was set at over £IR163 million with 70 per cent of the cost being provided by the EC. Before the implementation of the Western Package there was no grant aid for forestry from the EC; even then, farmers were slow to avail themselves of it until the scheme was about half-way through (Mulloy 1992). Almost £IR15 million had been provided by the EC for forestry under this scheme. In the decade between 1980 and 1990 the area of grant-aided private planting increased from a mere 268 to over 9000 ha per year. Under the Operational Programme farmers are entitled to recoup up to 85 per cent of the approved costs of afforestation as well as for woodland improvement and reconstitution.

With more and more marginal land being taken out of agricultural production, and such generous planting grants being made available to farmers, the relative proportions of private and public sector planting are being radically altered; rates of private planting already surpassed those of Coillte by 1990. In addition to the Forestry Operational Programme, further

EC and exchequer funds for forestry are being provided under the Rural Development Operational Programme as well as a Forest Premium Scheme, the Farm Improvement Programme, the Interreg Programme (affecting cross-border developments with Northern Ireland) and smaller research (STRIDE) and educational programmes (Eurofortech) (Mulloy 1992). Consequently, although the major landscape and environmental changes that are currently taking place can be said to result directly from national forestry policy, there is little doubt that without EC funding such policies could not be put into effect. There is scope for expansion in the Irish forestry industry but once again normal market forces have been distorted and national land-use traditions suppressed by an artificial grant-driven system supported largely by EC monies. This is not necessarily a bad thing provided such developments are benign and not in conflict with the interests of fishing, tourism, and the conservation of landscapes and wildlife.

For conservationists perhaps the greatest concern about forestry has been the planting of blanket bogs especially in the lowland areas of the west of Ireland. These bogs are regarded as being of global importance, representing a diminishing and unique biotope (An Foras Forbartha 1981; Foss 1991; Doyle 1992). In addition, they constitute an extensive wild landscape of immense natural beauty. Such areas have been utilized for forestry since the 1950s when the technology for their development became available. So far, 18 per cent of these blanket bogs have been drained and planted with conifers, and some sites of prime conservation value have already been destroyed (Hickie 1991a).

There has been considerable debate about the effects of coniferization on surface-water acidification and on fish and other aquatic life (Hickie 1991a). Studies in both Scotland and Wales have shown the deleterious effects on coniferous plantations on fish life in certain catchments (Egglishaw et al. 1986; Stoner et al. 1984). Relatively little detailed research has yet been done on the effects of afforestation on surface water acidification in Ireland. One study in Connemara and south Mayo has demonstrated that in poorly buffered, acid-sensitive catchments, there is a direct relationship between the area under plantation forest within such catchments and the acidity and aluminium levels of the water. Most of the catchments studied showed pH values below the minimum laid down for salmonid species by the EC Directive on Freshwater Fish (Allott et al. 1990). While extrinsic factors such as sea-spray effects, air-borne pollution, and acidic lithologies play a contributory role in acidification within these prized fishing catchments, afforestation with coniferous trees is the prime culprit. Preliminary results from more recent ongoing experiments in Connemara have shown that soil water is more acid under Sitka spruce forest cover than on open peatland sites (Farrell and Kelly-Quinn 1992).

However, one of the most serious problems stems from the ground-preparation stages prior to planting on peaty water-logged soils, whereby drainage channels are dug and the surface ploughed. The hydrology of whole catchments is altered and the increased runoff leads to the silting of salmonid nursery beds. The lowering of the water-table then leads to the decomposition of the peat and the release of organic acids to the streams. Coniferous needle fall may also add to this problem. Due to the low level of nutrients in these soils, fertilizers are usually applied which, through runoff from the drains, can change the nutrient status and vegetation communities of the rivers and lakes in these areas.

Nowadays investment in forestry, whether it be by Coillte or by private individuals, must be based on a sound financial return. Afforestation on peatlands, with their comparatively low levels of productivity, is a less attractive option than on marginal mineral soils such as, for example, the drumlin soils of the north midlands and there has, in recent years, been some move away from the blanket bogs. Grant aid has been the leaven for the current expansionary trend in Irish forestry. It has made it more attractive as an investment both for private speculators and for farmers, especially those in marginal lands who, in a climate of agricultural retrenchment, have had to consider alternatives to traditional food production. Many such farmers had previously found forestry unattractive, not only for reasons of tradition, but also because of the relatively long-term nature of the investment and the risks of wind-throw and other types of damage. But generous grant aid can help to cushion the effects of even the most uneconomic enterprises. Moreover, the planting targets set out in the Operational Programme for Forestry, in addition to the openness and availability of the western bogs, may mean that these areas will continue to come under pressure from forestry development. Unfortunately, legislative safeguards in this area are exiguous.

In addition to the negative effects on forestry on the natural environment, there is also evidence that the cultural heritage of the country is being adversely affected. In a recent preliminary report, attention was drawn to the damage or destruction of 132 archaeological sites through forestry development (Stout et al. 1991). This damage is being inflicted at all stages of the forestry process from ground preparation, which destroys the stratigraphic context of the site, to the clear-felling of trees which often destroys the monuments themselves. Drainage of wetland areas prior to afforestation also destroys well-preserved archaeological remains.

Agricultural development and environmental protection

After twenty years of membership, the benefits to Ireland of EC-sponsored social, economic, and infrastructural developments are unquestionable and are often clearly reflected in the landscape. As a predominantly agricultural country the greatest impact of increasing European integration has been the implementation of the all-pervasive CAP; rural land use has been greatly affected by both its market management and its structural adjustment aspects. And as we have seen, both aspects of the policy have also had negative environmental effects, despite the fact that environmental considerations have often been part of its stated objectives. However, EC policy aimed at direct environmental control has been slower to evolve and has been piecemeal in nature. Moreover there has been an absence of an integrative approach to developmental and environmental policies. The environment has been at the mercy of the vicissitudes of all development policies including the CAP and of a variety of projects supported by EC structural funds. Particularly in the late 1970s and early 1980s this support often reinforced, financially, certain ill-conceived national policies, leading at times to a deterioration in the quality of the environment. Natural and semi-natural ecosystems and a variety of wildlife habitats have thus been modified or destroyed and landscapes of great natural beauty have been altered.

An example of this has been the damage caused to the fragile coastal ecosystems of the north and west of the country where, as in their Scottish counterparts, traditional management practices have been carried out for centuries (Quigley 1991). These coastal sand plains or *machair* areas, which also represent a unique and diminishing Gaelic cultural landscape, are of great conservation importance internationally; they are included in the CORINE database as sites of European significance. With the help of EC financial aid they have been severely threatened and, in some cases, irreparably damaged by intensive farming practices including overstocking, fertilizer application and the subdivision of extensive commonage into small parcels of land. These practices not only alter the ecology of the machair plains but also disrupt their geomorphic development and destroy their unique landscape quality.

In the late 1980s and particularly since the European Commission's 1985 Green Paper, there has been an attempt to reduce output and stem the creation of food surpluses, not only by price control but also through the encouragement of extensification, set-aside, and the conversion of production. The move away from intensive forms of agriculture cannot but benefit the environment in general. The current CAP reforms include an Agri-Environmental Action Programme to help farmers, with generous financial support, to manage their farms in environmentally friendly ways including long-term set-aside (Sheehy 1992). However, land removed from intensive production must not simply be abandoned; many important wildlife habitats are essentially part of managed systems such as the grazed machair grasslands mentioned above (Hayden 1992). In general, the recent evolution of agricultural policy has had positive effects on the rural landscape and the environment has thus benefited even if by default.

A variety of EC directives concerned with the quality of water, for salmonid species, for human consumption, and other pollution matters have had an indirect bearing on farming practices and have helped to raise awareness of the dangers of environmental deterioration of natural watercourses. More significantly, the CAP began to assume a proactive role in environmental protection with the designation of Environmentally Sensitive Areas (ESAs) in pursuance of Regulation 797/85. Under this scheme farmers are grant-aided to farm their land in traditional, extensive ways in order to protect fragile environments. However it is doubtful whether such indirect and discretionary mechanisms, which come under the auspices of the Agricultural Directorate, can afford sufficient protection to areas of particular ecological vulnerability or conservation importance. In any event, this mechanism has found very limited application in the Republic of Ireland so far, with only two pilot sites having been designated (one a machair area) and these with limited financial resources (Temple Lang and Hickie 1992). It is too early to tell whether there have been any real environmental benefits in these areas.

Statutory environmental protection in Ireland is still in a relatively primitive state. Planning controls do not extend to most aspects of agricultural or forestry developments, which are some of the most environmentally damaging (UPTCS 1987). Under national legislation, the Wildlife Act 1976 offers protection to animal species and endangered floral species (Temple Lang 1983). It also authorizes the establishment of Nature Reserves and Refuges for Fauna. Areas of Scientific Interest (ASIs), which account for about 5 per cent of the land surface, have no statutory protection unless they are within National Parks or are additionally designated as Refuges for Fauna or Nature Reserves (Wright 1992). Several ASIs have been seriously damaged or destroyed, often with the aid of EC grants or loans from the European Investment Bank (Temple Lang and Hickie 1992). The Wildlife Service has listed 243 ASIs of international importance but only 36 of these are legally protected. The only other protection afforded to Irish species is the Flora Protection Order covering 68 species of plants.

By far the most important advances in the area of conservation and environmental protection have resulted from EC legislation. Three significant milestones which potentially impinge on land use are the Directive on the Conservation of Wild Birds (79/409/EEC), the Environmental Impact Assessment Directive (85/337/EEC), and the Directive on the Conservation of Natural and Semi-natural Habitats and Wild Flora and Fauna (43/1992/EEC) (Wright 1992). The EC Bird Directive is a potentially powerful legal instrument in that it deals with the protection, not only of bird species but also of their habitats. In particular, Special Protection Areas (SPAs) are required to be established for certain endangered and migratory species. Of the 20 SPAs currently designated, 10 are outside Nature Reserves and unfortunately are therefore not protected from development, but only from pollution and litter (Temple Lang and Hickie 1992).

The Environmental Impact Assessment Directive (EIA) has great potential as a measure for conservation and environmental protection from both private and public development projects. Unfortunately its implementation in Ireland, which was delayed until 1990, has been fraught with problems: first, its application has been minimalist in the areas that are discretionary for member states; seondly, the threshold size for given developments requiring environmental impact assessment, such as forestry (200 ha), are too large and there is no safeguard against the cumulative effects of adjacent sub-threshold developments (Farrell and Kelly-Quinn 1992); and thirdly various difficulties of interpretation have arisen (Meldon 1992). Moreover, environmental assessment procedures are not required for a number of rural-based developments seeking EC structural funding such as the construction of interpretive centres, golf courses, and other tourism projects. These have proved very controversial in recent years. Many forms of agricultural development such as rural restructuring, although they may have significant environmental impacts, are not subject to EIA. However it is now mandatory for all intensive pig and poultry units to submit environmental impact statements with their planning applications (Dodd 1992).

Probably the most significant piece of EC environmental legislation which will have a bearing on the future land use of rural areas is the Habitats Directive. It is designed to protect certain natural habitats including, in the case of Ireland, sand-dunes, raised and blanket bogs, turloughs, and limestone pavements (Wright 1992). EC grant aid for these *Annexe I* habitats has been set at 75 per cent and 50 million ECUs are being made available for the purchase and management of important sites in the Community as a whole under the ACNAT Regulation (COM 90/125) for the period 1992–3. In addition, it will offer legal protection for endangered species and their habitats even outside the protected areas.

It is probably true to say that the worst environmental effects of the CAP are now over. Many of the structural schemes funded by the Guidance Section of EAGGF have now run their course and even intensification of the commercial farming sector is slowing down. Although silage and slurry spillages still occur, even these problems are being contained as the level of farmer awareness and know-how increases. But despite moves toward more environmentally friendly farming practices, the need for strengthening environmental legislation is greater now than ever before. The potential threats to the environment posed by increased structural funding under the various Operational Programmes are probably more serious than all the consequences of the CAP. Because large sums of money are being made available over a limited time-span there is a danger that plans, prepared in haste in order to secure the funds, may not take sufficient precautions for the protection of the environment. As Europe draws towards closer union, regional policy is likely to present the landscape of Ireland with its greatest challenge.

Further reading

There is a wide range of materials relating to the geography of agricultural activity and rural development, to policy formulation, and to environmental issues in Ireland. However, these materials are fragmentary and have widely varying emphases. As yet, there is a relative paucity of literature which attempts to synthesize these areas. A recent publication, R. L. King (ed.) (1993), *Ireland, Europe and 1992*, Geographical Society of Ireland (Dublin), contains several papers which examine, on a sectoral basis, the impacts of EC membership on Ireland, including agriculture and the environment. Likewise, an earlier publication, P. Breathnach, and M. E. Cawley (eds.) (1986), *Change and Development in Rural Ireland*, Geographical Society of Ireland (Dublin), examines some of the same themes at an earlier stage.

The geographical aspects of Irish agriculture are treated comprehensively in the work of D. A. Gillmor. For example, his 1977 book, *Agriculture in the Republic of Ireland* (Budapest), while now somewhat out of date, still provides an invaluable background to Irish agriculture up to the early 1970s. Also, chs. 6 and 8 in D. A. Gillmor (ed.) (1989), *The Irish Countryside* (Dublin) review the current situation with regard to land-use changes, forestry, recreation, integrated rural development, and the environment in Ireland.

A useful overview of the evolution and implementation of Irish agricultural policy during the 1980s, especially in the context of developments at EC level, is provided by the proceedings of the annual conferences of the Economic and Rural Welfare Centre of *An Foras Taluntais* (The Agricultural Institute), now replaced by *Teagasc* (The Agriculture and Food Development Authority).

The most up-to-date and comprehensive review of virtually all aspects of the environment in Ireland is to be found in J. Feehan (ed.) (1992), *Environment and Development in Ireland*, The Environmental Institute, University College Dublin (Dublin). Some of the papers contained in this volume have already been cited in the above chapter, but the current state of affairs with regard to a very wide range of environmental issues in Ireland is dealt with in this book.

13 Environment, Health, and Health Care: European Comparisons and an Italian Case-Study

Cosimo Palagiano

Introduction

The environment is one of the keys to the health conditions of communities. This provides the basis for much of the research in ecological medical geography although, as Joseph and Phillips (1984) remind us, medical geography can also contribute to the study of health-care delivery. While it is well-established that there are significant social and spatial variations in the incidence of diseases and ill-health, as there is in access to health care, most studies to date have been global (for example, Howe 1986) or at the level of the nation state (for example, Cliff and Haggett 1988). The EC, in contrast, is a relatively neglected level of analysis, even though the Community is increasingly becoming involved in health-related issues via, for example, its environmental policies, the proposed Social Charter, and policies to intensify or extensify agriculture.

The aims of this chapter are threefold. First, to review health conditions in the EC, using a variety of indicators of service provision and of health conditions. This emphasizes that there continue to be differences in life expectancy and the incidence of diseases even within this relatively homogeneous group of prosperous states. Secondly, to illustrate the continuing existence of variations in health conditions within countries. Italy is chosen as a case-study for two reasons: because of the persistently deep regional cleavages which exist in this country and the fact that there is relatively little material in English on its health conditions, compared to say northern European states (see Joseph and Phillips 1984). Finally, we address the question of the actual and potential importance of health issues to the European Community.

Health conditions in the European Community

Methodological issues

There is a fundamental link between health conditions and the environment, and the European Community provides a useful framework within which to examine this relationship. There are, for example, major differences in terms of natural features which vary according to latitude, altitude, distance from the sea, and exposure, as well as in social, cultural, and economic structures. In particular, economic development levels range from some of the world's more prosperous countries to those that have experienced profound economic and political transformations in the course of the last three decades. All of these features have links with health conditions, although not in any deterministic manner. Furthermore, this is not to say that there are 'natural' areas which can be distinguished at ground level, and which can be related in any simple way to variations in health care. Instead, the relationship between health and the environment is influenced by factors which are partly very localized and partly very extensive. In addition, there are numerous difficulties involved in evaluating health conditions; these are highly subjective and complex features which are difficult to disentangle from many other economic and cultural features in individual countries, regions, and localities.

It is, of course, true that the essential focus of our investigations should be the relationships between the various factors which influence the health conditions of a population rather than of a region. However, a spatial focus provides a useful analytical dimension. We can define dynamic areas which vary according to the influence and intensity of the relationships which determine health conditions in any given time period. These dynamic areas can be called health areas. In practice it is difficult to define the precise boundaries of health areas. In part this is precisely because the relationships are so dynamic and, in part, because of the large spatial scale of the available statistics; these conceal considerable local variations within large regional aggregates.

Data sources

The European Community does not collect and publish health condition statistics on any comparable and systematic basis, not even in its EUROSTAT series. However, some of the relevant indicators, such as mortality and the causes of death are reported in the EC bulletin *Population and Social Conditions*. More detailed data are provided by the World Health Organization in its *World Health Statistical Annual* and in UNICEF's *The State of the World's Children*. For individual countries, it is necessary to rely on Statistical Yearbooks. As noted earlier, this means that there are difficulties in using such statistics for comparative purposes. These problems are aggravated in the case of the EC where there are considerable inconsistencies between the data sets for different countries. As ever, therefore, with secondary data, there are important limitations to the interpretation of relationships from secondary data sets.

Health conditions: Some indicators

One of the basic indicators of the health of a nation is life expectancy at birth. In recent decades this has increased consistently throughout the member states of the EC. This is due principally to a decrease in infant mortality and, to a lesser extent, to changes in those factors which permit the prolonging of life. An important feature is the process of catching up which has occurred in the 1970s and 1980s. Between 1960 and 1988 there were sharp increases in life expectancy in southern Europe and Ireland, and especially in Portugal. These improvements mirrored those realized in economic development, standards of living, and in health care. By 1988 there was a high degree of consistency across Europe and average life expectancy varied only between 73 and 77 years. However, there still exist a number of important social differences—by gender, class, etc.—in terms of life expectancy.

Although there has been some convergence of life expectancy, infant-mortality rates remain sensitive indicators of the health of a country. Between 1960 and 1988 there was a very marked decrease in this indicator right across the EC. Differences persisted in 1988, and in Portugal were almost twice as high as in the Netherlands. However, the most striking feature of Fig. 13.1

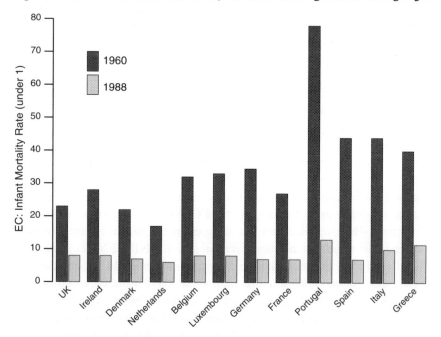

FIG. 13.1. Infant mortality in the EC, 1960 and 1988

Source: Based on data from *Statesman's Year-Book* (1990).

TABLE 13.1 *Some causes of death in the countries of the EC, age-standardized* (per 10 000 people)

	Infectious and parastic diseases	Mental disorders	Endocrine, nutritional, and metabolic diseases	Diseases of the circulatory system	Neoplasms
UK	0.5	2.4	1.3	49.9	9.6
Ireland	0.06	0.5	2.0	58.4	9.7
Denmark	0.5	1.3	2.1	49.2	10.5
Netherlands	0.5	0.6	3.5	40.7	10.4
Luxembourg	0.3	2.4	2.1	53.8	9.8
Germany	0.3	1.0	3.2	49.3	9.2
France	1.1	2.2	2.4	31.0	10.2
Portugal	0.9	0.4	3.2	46.8	9.0
Spain	0.9	0.9	3.1	42.7	9.1
Italy	0.4	0.5	3.6	42.8	11.0
Greece	0.7	0.2	1.1	49.8	7.1

Source: WHO (1990).

is the massive reduction in such variations, with the Mediterranean countries and Ireland rapidly catching up with northern Europe. This is most marked in the case of Portugal where the ratio with the Netherlands decreased from approximately 4:1 to 2:1 during the three decades.

While there is aggregate convergence in the EC, there are significant differences in terms of the causes of death. The sharpest indicator of health is the prevalence or incidence of various causes of ill-health. However, in practice the only comparative data available is on the causes of death. Furthermore, these have to be standardized by age so as to control for international differences in the demographic profiles of the member states. Meade *et al.* (1988) provide a formula for the calculation of specific death rates for given diseases, and these are applied to the eleven countries (that is, excluding Belgium) that we have usable data for in 1988 or 1989 (Table 13.1). At the time of writing, data were only available for Belgium for 1985–6 and, moreover, did not include mental diseases as one of the causes of death.

The first point to note is the strong incidence of deaths from diseases of the circulatory system. To some extent, these data distort the real picture of the underlying cause of death, for a heart attack or other circulatory failing may only have been the final cause of death, and may have been brought on by other health problems. Secondly, there are some systematic variations in the relative importance of the causes of death in the EC, and these merit consideration in some detail. They can be summarized thus:

(a) Infectious diseases are relatively more important in France, Spain, and Portugal and least important in Luxembourg, Italy, and Ireland. This pattern does not coincide with the traditional divide drawn between northern and southern Europe. There is no easy explanation for this, and the causes have to be sought in terms of detailed analyses of individual infectious and parasitic diseases in particular countries and their relationships to various ecosystems. There is neither the space nor the data available here for such a detailed analysis. In addition, it should be borne in mind that the level of variation is limited and can be partly explained by data-quality inconsistencies.

(b) There is a stronger, but again less than perfect, association of death from mental diseases with the North–South divide. This is relatively most important in Luxembourg, the UK, and France and least important in Greece, Portugal, Italy, and Spain. We can only speculate about the possible causes and these must include climate, living and working conditions, and diet, although there is no adequate single theory which accounts for the variations.

(c) Southern Europe tends to have higher rates of death from endocrinal, nutritional, and metabolic diseases. Again, however, the pattern is far from simple for Greece has the lowest rate in Europe while the Netherlands has the second highest. Diet is the most likely cause although it is difficult to be precise about this. One interesting consequence is that the growing convergence across Europe in tastes and eating habits, and in the availability of international foods, may lead to greater uniformity in the incidence of this cause of death in future.

(d) The distribution of diseases of the circulatory system is broadly similar to, although the inverse of that for, infectious and parasitic ones. This is by far the largest single source of deaths in all the EC countries, but it is particularly significant in the UK, Ireland, Denmark, Luxembourg, and Germany. Interestingly, the Netherlands and, especially, France have low rates. There are hypotheses that this is related to diet or to stress but none are conclusive.

(e) Neoplasms have a distribution which is similar to circulatory diseases, that is, it reveals the same basic North-west–South-east divide. The main exception is Greece which, at 7.1, is significantly below the rate found in all other countries.

Health service provision

Health service provision in the EC follows a number of different models. These reflect differences in philosophy concerning the balance between, for example, primary and secondary health care, public and private provision,

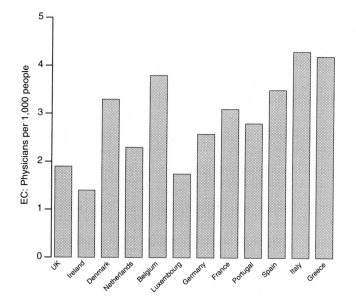

FIG. 13.2. Physicians per 1000 people in the EC, 1990

Source: Based on data from *Statesman's Year-Book* (1990).

and institutional versus community care. There are also differences stemming from the forms and functions of government, and the resources
available. As this is an area of only minimalist EC interventionism—such
as facilitating the mutual recognition of medical qualifications, and the
standardization of pharmaceutical testing—it is still very much dominated
by national structures. Given these qualifications, it is difficult to make
meaningful international comparisons of health-care provision. Only the
most general of indices can be used and even these must be interpreted
cautiously.

One index of health care is the relationship between the number of
physicians and population numbers. In simple aggregate terms, the southern
European states have the highest level of provision (Fig. 13.2). There are
more than 3.5 doctors per thousand in Greece, Italy, and Spain. This is
significantly higher than in northern Europe with the exception of Belgium.
In much of northern Europe, including the UK and the Netherlands,
provision is less than 2.5 per thousand. The position is more or less reversed
if hospital-bed provision is considered (Fig. 13.3). Northern Europe—with
the anomalous exception of the Netherlands—has more than 8 beds per
thousand. In contrast, there are 6.2 beds per thousand or less in Portugal,

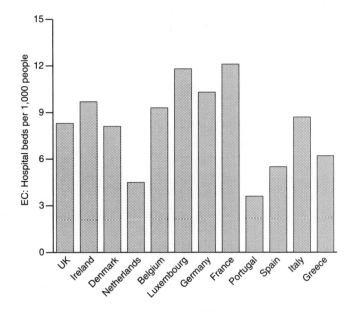

FiG. 13.3. Hospital beds per 1000 people in the EC, 1987

Source: Based on data from *Statesman's Year-Book* (1990).

Greece, and Spain. Italy, with a ratio of 8.6 ranks alongside the northern European states.

While these data identify some systematic variations within the EC, further information about the health facilities in the various countries is necessary before conclusions can be drawn with any confidence. Most obviously, there are differences even in the definitions of physicians and hospital beds. Moreover, the quality of health facilities varies according to a number of variables, including: the relationship between the public and the private sectors; the costs and efficiency of the various national systems; the emphasis on preventive versus responsive care and precocious diagnoses; the quality of the medical labour-force and of the available equipment; and the effectiveness of the service. One of the most obvious indices of the existence of serious quality differences is the large-scale international migration of patients within the Community. For example, in 1988 1940 of the 12 077 patients in the Institute Gustave Roussy of Paris Villejuif were Italians (Geddes 1991).

It is arguable that, in a sense, the 'seriousness' of a disease depends to a significant degree on the quality of treatment available, and that this varies considerably amongst the member states. While international comparisons are important, data limitations currently restrict this to simplistic generalizations. Not least, this is because there are enormous regional and social variations within particular countries, each of which has its own distinctive health-care system. The next section of this paper provides a detailed case-study of one country.

Health and health care in Italy

There has recently been considerable press and popular attention to the contention that Italy has one of the highest qualities of life in Europe. However, this paper argues that it is not possible to use terms such as 'best' in this context while Italy has low-quality health provision. There are difficulties in obtaining a bed in a hospital and in obtaining access to the most recent health technology. This is stressful not only for those who are ill but for healthy persons who fear the consequences of becoming ill. In addition, there is fierce competition for resources between public and private health institutions. Private clinics are very expensive but generally offer more immediate and higher-quality services.

In part the problems of health care in Italy stem from the low level of resources which it attracts. Between 1975 and 1989 the real expenditure on public-sector health care, expressed as a proportion of GDP, increased very little (Fig. 13.4). However, expenditure on the private sector increased from 0.8 per cent to 2.0 per cent of GDP during the same period. This means that total expenditure did increase and surpassed 7 per cent of GDP by the late 1980s. Nevertheless, health-care expenditure in Italy lags significantly behind that in the other more developed economies, whether comparisons are made with the OECD, the G7, or the EC (Fig. 13.5). This is particularly noteworthy for total expenditure.

There is a theoretical argument that competition between public and private facilities could be constructive and mutually reinforcing, but in practice this is rarely the case. One of the key criteria is whether the coexistence of the public and private sectors contributes to balancing geographical and social differences in provision. In Italy, because there has been no programmed or planned joint development of the two sectors, many groups and individuals not only have no choice of diagnosis and treatment but also cannot be admitted to the best health facilities. In practice, admittance to private facilities depends on payment while influential friends help secure admission to a public one. Alternatively, the chances of obtaining good quality care depend on living in the 'right' location; that is, not in

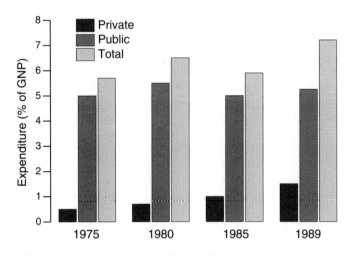

FIG. 13.4. Expenditure on private and public health care in Italy, 1975–1989
Source: Geddes (1991: 28).

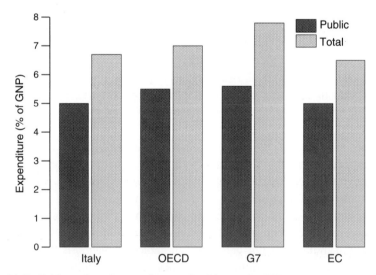

FIG. 13.5. Public and total expenditure on health care in 1987 as a percentage of GNP in Italy, the OECD, the G7 countries, and the EC
Source: Geddes (1991: 29).

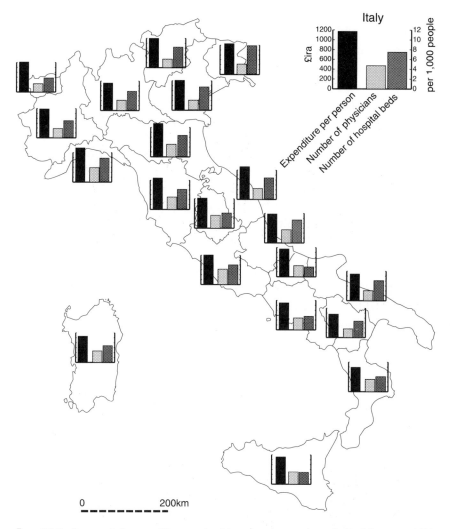

FIG. 13.6. Per capital expenditure on health care; the number of physicians per 1000 people; and the number of beds per 1000 people in the Italian regions, 1989

Source: Geddes (1991: 32).

southern Italy but in the large urban areas where good contacts are essential keys to the gateway of access.

Health facilities in Italy

There is a highly uneven regional distribution of health care facilities in Italy (see Fig. 13.6). Expenditure levels are consistently higher in the north and the centre, peaking at 1382 lira per capita in Liguria. In contrast, they reach a nadir of 953 lira per capita in Basilicata in the south. There is also an uneven distribution of hospital beds, and this serves to underline the limitations of national-level data. Although Italy has a high ratio of beds per 1000 people in the EC context (Fig. 13.3), some southern regions—namely, Molise, Campania, and Sicilia—fall below the minimum threshold of 6 beds per 1000. Italy also has the largest number of doctors per capita in the EC (Fig. 13.2), although there is no clear regional pattern in this case. To some extent these statistics are deceptive and reveal more about the oversupply of doctors matriculating from medical schools than about health care. While the ratio of those graduating to those who matriculated in medical studies was only about 10 per cent in 1970, it had risen to 35 per cent in 1980, and was 30 per cent in 1989. As a result there has been a much larger supply of trained doctors emerging from university courses than had been planned for.

The uneven distribution of facilities contributes to the interregional and international migration of Italians seeking health care. Within Italy this can be measured in terms of a health-service immigration, emigration, and attraction ratios. The percentage of 'emigrants' is calculated as the ratio between the number of residents from each region hospitalized in another region and the total number of hospitalized residents for that region. The percentage of 'immigrants' is estimated as the ratio between the number of admissions of non-residents relative to the total number of admissions in each region. Finally, the immigrant and emigrant ratios can be weighted by the distance between the region of residence and the region of hospitalization so as to calculate the health-service attraction ratio. Coefficients of weighting ranging from 2 to 5 are attached respectively to whether admissions are to bordering regions, to non-bordering regions in the same macro-region (northern, southern, or central Italy), to a region in a bordering macro-region, or to a region in a non-bordering macro-region. These various ratios are shown in Table 13.2 for general and specialized hospitals.

The most attractive regions for both levels of facilities are the regions of northern Italy (Liguria, Lombardia, Emilia Romagna, Friuli-Venezia Giulia, and Veneto), and Lazio which is the region of the capital, Rome. The least attractive regions for middle-assistance facilities are to be found in the south (Molise, Campania, Basilicata, Sicilia, Sardegna, and Calabria). For high-assistance facilities the least attractive regions are again to be found in southern Italy, together with Valle d'Aosta and Trentino Alto Adige, two northern mountainous regions. Liguria is the most attractive region for both levels of facilities and has two important hospitals in Genoa, the Istituto Giannina Gaslini and the Istituto Scientifico. Ironically, it also has one of

TABLE 13.2 *Attraction ratios for general and specialized hospitals in Italy in terms of immigration/emigration for health treatment, 1989*

Regions	Attraction ratio, general hospitals	Attraction ratio, specialized hospitals
Piemonte	0.31	0.38
Valle d'Aosta	0.56	0.07
Lombardia	17.62	8.63
Trentino A.A.	0.45	0.05
Veneto	1.52	9.81
Friuli V.G.	5.85	5.15
Liguria	19.19	16.25
Emilia R.	6.71	4.36
Toscana	1.46	1.08
Umbria	0.78	0.49
Marche	1.20	1.56
Lazio	6.51	4.14
Abruzzo	0.35	1.26
Molise	0.18	0.08
Campania	0.13	0.09
Puglia	0.24	0.16
Basilicata	0.02	0.13
Calabria	0.003	0.005
Sicilia	0.02	0.01
Sardegna	0.01	0.008

Source: After Crotti (1991): 137–63.

the highest levels of international health migration to seek care outside of Italy.

A measure of the importance of international health migration is provided by comparing expenditure on the National Health System and on foreign health care. Although they are measured according to different absolute scales in Fig. 13.7, this does serve to highlight the ratio between them. Despite the well-publicized rapid increase in the costs of the National Health System, expenditure on foreign health care has risen even more rapidly. Italians are particularly attracted to use French health-care provision, especially for treatment of neoplasms, and they are widely used by both public and private institutions. For example, at the Institute Gustave Roussy in Paris in 1988, 36 per cent of the Italian patients were there on the recommendation of a private institute, 18 per cent had been recommended by a public institution, and 46 per cent had personally elected to be treated there. In a sense, all such foreign treatment can be seen as a leakage of resources from the Italian system as well as a comment on its efficacy.

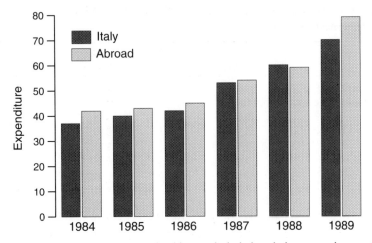

FIG. 13.7. Domestic expenditure on health care in Italy in relation to total expenditure on health care, both domestic and foreign, by Italians

Source: Based on data from Istat (1991).

Health conditions in Italy

The state of health of a nation depends primarily on the efficacy of its health system. This is the case in Italy despite the importance of a small but significant international migration to health care. Other elements, such as physical and biological factors are normally of lesser importance. One indication of the state of health of a country is the morbidity–mortality ratio. In general, the higher the level of a country's economic development, then the lower the mortality rate is in comparison to the morbidity rate. This reflects the efficiency of their health systems. It was for this reason that we first considered the system of health care in Italy. The state of health in Italy is conditioned by its relatively poor health-care system; this is poorly organized for the treatment of ill-health and especially for preventive care and precocious diagnosis.

Unfortunately, current statistics on morbidity are not available for Italy. However, there are available the results of some sample questionnaire surveys, although these give evidence of the perception of disease rather than of the disease itself. The Istituto Centrale de Statistica (Istat) undertook inquiries into health conditions in 1980 and 1983; the sample consisted of 25 000 families distributed between 1500 communes. It covered a wide range of diseases, accidents, and states of incapacity. There is of course a considerable difference between personal perception of being ill from particular diseases and the actual incidence of these. For example, the low

TABLE 13.3 *Perceptions of illness: Regional differences per 1000 people in the levels of reporting selected complaints*

	Northern and central Italy	Southern Italy
Respiratory diseases	83.7	67.4
Osteomuscular diseases	25.2	18.2
Digestive diseases	16.9	12.3
Symptoms not defined	14.4	38.7

Source: Istat (1991).

proportion who considered that they suffered from tumours partly reflects the fact that doctors do not always reveal the true causes of illnesses to their patients. Some of the results are summarized, by region, in Table 13.3. The results are striking. There is a higher perception in the north and centre of being ill from respiratory, osteomuscular, and digestive diseases, and this may possibly be due to climatic and dietary conditions. However, while the south has lower rates for these named diseases, it also has a much larger proportion with non-defined symptoms and this must reflect the poorer levels of health care in the region.

Mortality statistics probably provide a more accurate picture of health conditions in Italy, not least because they are more reliable than morbidity statistics. Italy has one of the highest life-expectancy ratios in the world. Currently, this is 71.05 years for men and 77.78 years for women. This compares to 42.6 and 43.0 years, respectively, at the beginning of the century, and to 67.24 and 72.27 years in 1960–2. There are, however, regional differences within Italy. As might perhaps be expected life expectancy in parts of the south—notably Campania and Sicily—is two or three years less than the average. Surprisingly, this is also the case in some of the northern regions. Furthermore, these differences cannot be explained by demographic differences as the rates have been standardized to take into account variations in age profiles.

One of the principal influences on life expectancy is infant mortality. At the beginning of the century infant mortality in Italy was 170 per thousand; by 1965 it had fallen to 32.6 per thousand and, by the present, to 10.3 per thousand. This is above the level in northern Europe but that gap has been closing in recent decades (Fig. 13.1). Infant mortality varies from 10.1 per thousand in northern regions to 14.7 per thousand in southern ones. The differences at province level are even more marked and the maximum (23.6 per thousand in Enna) is four times greater than the minimum which is to be found in Trieste.

Turning to general mortality, the pattern of causes in Italy is similar to that in other industrialized countries, with a prevalence of cardiovascular diseases (253 421 in 1991) and tumours (152 734). Infectious diseases which were once very widespread were of little importance (1556) in 1991. The significance of infectious diseases may increase with the diagnosis of Aids but there were still only 4074 deaths from this cause between 1982 and 1990; 20 per cent were recorded as being heterosexual.

There are regional differences in the distribution of these causes of death in Italy, but at present it is not possible to isolate particular geographical causes of death. We can only note that the incidence of death from cardiovascular diseases is increasing in the south and decreasing in the north, while deaths from tumours are increasing in the north. Infectious diseases as a cause of death are more widespread in the southern regions. Climate, hygiene, diet, and the efficiency of the health-care system are all important factors which vary regionally, but their precise contribution cannot be assessed.

Another cause of death is accidents at work. In 1988 there were 1 103 652 recorded accidents at work, 1568 of which resulted in deaths and 35 799 in permanent disabilities. Over time this has been declining, although at varying rates in different sectors. Taking 1983 as a base-line figure of 100, by 1988 the mortality rate from accidents had fallen to 72 in agriculture and to 73 in industry. In contrast, road accidents increased from 271 894 in 1980 to 286 790 by 1990. However, the number of resulting deaths fell from 8537 to 6621. Accidents, whether at work or on the road, may in future be more affected by increasing EC intervention in health and safety laws and in transport planning.

The European Community and health issues: Concluding remarks

This paper has demonstrated the continued existence of health disparities in the EC despite some convergence in standards of health care and in health conditions over recent decades. The question arises as to whether this is an important issue for the EC as an institution, or whether this is a clear case of subsidiarity pointing to the need for national or even local decision-making. Health care has certainly not been a priority for the Community in the past, leastways not as a direct object of initiatives. However, a case can be made for greater EC involvement with health issues on several accounts:

- health is a key element of the quality of life and, therefore, is an important component of social and economic inequalities, which the EC is committed to ameliorating;

- the delivery of health care raises issues of mutual recognition of qualifications as a barrier to the free movement of labour;
- in future, the rights of establishment for the delivery of health services could become an important issue;
- health conditions contribute to the effectiveness of the labour-force and the competitiveness of the EC;
- it is arguable that health issues will become of greater concern to the EC if the Social Charter is to have more than token importance;
- the EC is concerned with environmental standards—such as air and water purity—and as such has a direct bearing on health conditions, where diseases or ill-health have environmental causes;
- uneven development, which is influenced by the EC, will contribute to regional and local demographic imbalances (large proportions of very young or elderly persons) and this will lead to additional pressures on health and other care services in these areas.

At first sight, the EC's involvement in health care and conditions seems very limited. An example of direct involvement is the campaign launched in the late 1980s by the Community, entitled *Europe Against Cancer*. This sounds impressive but, with the exception of some decrees regulating maximum tar content in, and health warnings about cigarettes, this amounts to little more than a series of declarations and minor expenditures. For example, a European Code has been published, and grants have been made available to facilitate international exchanges for training and research purposes. However, while the direct involvement of the EC is limited, consideration of the broader aspects of health outlined above emphasizes that its indirect role is highly significant.

Probably the most significant area of EC intervention in terms of health, currently, is the environment (see Chapter 11). The relationship between the two has been established by research in ecological medical geography. There are serious problems of both air and water pollution in the EC, and these impinge on health conditions. The main forms of air pollution are: particulates which can irritate or even be toxic to the respiratory system; sulphur oxides which have a pathological effect on the respiratory system; nitrous oxide and nitrogen dioxide which can damage the macrophagic leading to pulmonary oedema; carbon monoxide which can cause vertigo, headaches, and numbness; hydrocarbons which can irritate the respiratory system or lead to tumour growth; and lead which can attack the brain and the nervous system.

In terms of air pollution, the Community is responsible for producing an estimated 750 million tonnes a year of carbon dioxide; this erodes the ozone layer and makes possible a higher incidence of skin cancer. The Community

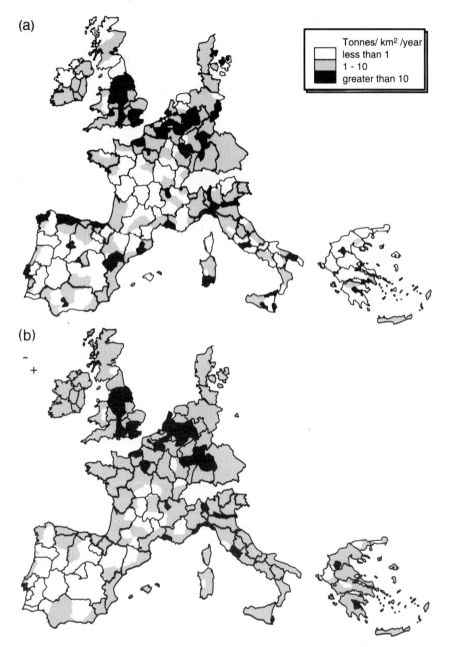

(a)

(b)

FIG. 13.8. (a) Sulphur dioxide (SO^2), and (b) Nitrogen dioxide (NO$_x$) emissions in the EC, 1985

Source: Commission of the European Communities (1991*a*).

also produces more than 14 million tonnes annually of sulphur dioxide as well as large quantities of nitrogen oxides, hydrocarbons, and carbon monoxide; all of these are potentially harmful to health, especially via cardiovascular and respiratory diseases. As Fig. 13.8 shows these pollutants have a distinctive geographical pattern; the highest levels of emissions in both sulphur dioxide and nitrogen oxides are to be found in the more developed regions of the European Community. These have tended to stabilize in recent years, suggesting that the hazard to health is being gradually brought under control. Unfortunately, this is not the case for emission levels are continuing to grow in the less-developed regions of the Community as they experience industrialization and the growth of car ownership. The EC is gradually becoming involved in regulating emissions via the agreement of targets to reduce power-station output and car-exhaust standards.

Water pollution is another potential source of ill-health. There are a number of carcinogenic compounds present in water, and the cumulative consequences of these over the long term can be increased risk of tumours and damage to certain tissues. Industries, mining, and households all contribute to contamination of water sources but the major source of groundwater pollution is high levels of nitrate concentrations. These are closely related to the use of agricultural fertilizers and the disposal of manure from intensive livestock farming areas. In the early 1990s it was estimated that '. . . 800 000 people in France, 850 000 in the UK, and 2.5 million in the former Federal Republic are drinking water with nitrate concentrations above the EC standard' (Commission of the European Communities 1990a: 121). The EC has issued directives bearing on water-quality standards and is now imposing these on the member states. However, progress will be relatively slow as many of the contaminants in the soil are still being leached into the water-source areas. There are estimates that it could take at least 25 years for Germany to reach acceptable standards of drinking-water because of this problem. To some extent the Community has aggravated these problems because of the encouragement provided by the Common Agricultural Policy for the intensification of agriculture. As groundwater provides some 75 per cent of drinking-water in the Community this is a critical issue, but there are also serious pollution problems in rivers and lakes, as well as in coastal bathing waters.

When the Treaty of Rome was signed it was little envisaged that health would or should become a focus of EC interest. However, over time the logic of such involvement has become ever clearer. The development of the CAP, and its ecological consequences, was and is the first major reason for this. Subsequently, the EC's technology programmes, which include biotechnology research, and the Single Market, which includes removal of health and other checks at borders and the standardization of pharmaceutical and other products, have added to this. Furthermore, many health issues have strong international dimensions—pollution clearly knows no borders— and the EC is a more appropriate level than the state to tackle these. However, there is in reality no coherent Community policy for health and, given the importance of this to economic and social life in the Community, this must be considered a policy vacuum.

Further reading

There is a wide range of literature available on the geography of health and health services in Europe. A classic general study is still A. E. Joseph, and D. R. Phillips, (1984), *Accessibility and Utilization: Geographical Perspectives on Health Care Delivery* (New York), while N. D. McGlashen, and J. R. Blunden (1983), *Geographical Aspects of Health Care: Essays in Honour of Andrew Learmonth* (London) contains a number of interesting papers on health care and health-care delivery in various European countries. Two works specifically on the situation in Italy, C. Palagiano (ed.) (1991), *Geografia della salute in Italia* (Milan), and M. Geddes (ed.) (1991), *Las salute degli Italiani* (Rome), give a very good indication of the geographical differences within a single country, as does J. Labasse (1980), *L'Hôpital et la ville: géographie hôpitalière* (Paris).

PART VII

Conclusion

Conclusion

The final section looks to the future. If the first forty years of the EC have revealed anything, it is the danger of making over-prescriptive plans in a rapidly changing world. That is not to say that planning ahead—as in the EC's 'Europe 2000' project—is a futile exercise, but any vision must be formulated in a way that enables it to accommodate new opportunities and new threats.

In the early 1990s three challenges stand out. (1) The need to strengthen the political cohesion of Europe, both within the EC and more widely, so that irreconcilable splits do not develop between the North and West, and the South and East. (2) The need for urgent, positive, action at Community level to improve the competitiveness of EC industry, so that it can withstand pressures from elsewhere in the world, particularly North America and Asia. (3) The need to take further concerted action to protect the European environment, a task which transcends national boundaries and must be the subject of international efforts. All are formidable tasks, but one lesson of the first forty years of the EC is that, despite unavoidable pitfalls and temporary setbacks, progress on big issues at a European level is possible and rewarding.

14 Development, Distribution, and the Environment: Future Challenges for Europe

Allan M. Williams and Mark Blacksell

Introduction

Since its establishment the Community has faced a number of critical decisions and has stood at a number of crossroads in its evolution. The French 'empty chair' policy and the initial establishment of the CAP framework in the 1960s, the first enlargement of the Community in the 1970s, and the Single Market programme and the Single European Act in the 1980s were all examples of these critical junctures. In December 1991 it seemed that the Community had reached just such a watershed at the Maastricht summit when it embarked on the seemingly inevitable pathway to economic and political union. Subsequently, the Danish referendum and the Exchange Rate Mechanism crises in 1992 and 1993 threatened to postpone and perhaps even cancel some, if not all, of the Maastricht agreements on integration in the Treaty on European Union (Maastricht Treaty). At the time of writing we are simply too close to events to assess in detail the long-term effects of either the Maastricht agreement or any renegotiation which may occur. However, it is clear that the EC is likely to face an increasing number of critical turning points in the decade ahead.

A fundamental issue for the Community is the articulation of the relationship between development and distribution. The original free-trade emphasis of the Community has over time been replaced by increased attention to what are fundamentally distributional issues. For example, reform of the CAP is essentially a reshaping of the redistribution of resources between consumers and producers and amongst different sub-groups of these. The Regional and Social Funds are, of course, even more overtly concerned with redistributional matters. Many other areas of Community interest, including small firms, tourism, transport, and labour migration are also characterized by such issues. The dilemmas faced by the Community are especially acutely exposed in the environmental arena. The environment is essential to both consumption and production and there are complex trade-offs between these, not least because the consumption of the environment by recreation and tourism is itself an important element of production. This is also an area of competition between different levels of decision-making: the EC, the national governments, and sub-state bodies can all claim competence and subsidiarity (most appropriate level) with respect to environmental policy. This chapter therefore examines the twin issues of development and the environment both because they are critical to the future of the Community and because they illustrate some of the broader distributional issues that it faces. The context for understanding the role of the Community in such areas is provided by the larger global economic and political setting, and this is the subject of the following section.

A changing Community in a changing world

One of the greatest challenges facing the EC is maintaining competitiveness relative to the other leading global economic powers. In common with the rest of the world economy, the EC experienced strong growth in the 1960s, faltering growth in the 1970s and early 1980s, followed by a burst of growth in the late 1980s before plunging into economic crisis in the early 1990s. Thereafter, the outlook is uncertain. An optimistic view is that the Single Market programme will realize a number of what economists refer to as static and dynamic economic gains for the Community; while these may not equal the 4 per cent boost to GDP, and the creation of 1.8 million jobs predicted by the Cecchini report (1988), the benefits could still be substantial. In the longer term there is also the possibility that economic and monetary union (EMU) will boost growth via reductions in the costs of intra-Community transfers and greater international monetary stability. A more pessimistic view is that the conditions required for entry into the final stage of the EMU are so severe that, even though offering increased stability, the move to the single currency will be deflationary.

There are a number of uncertainties that could adversely effect the economic outlook. These include the rising but still not fully quantified costs of German unification, potential and actual political instability in Eastern and Central Europe and the former Soviet Union, and the future of the troubled American economy. The USA economy certainly has structural problems, as is evident from its budget and trade deficits, with the former alone amounting to an accumulated total of $US2.3 trillion by the end of the 1990s. It is not surprising then that domestic economic issues dominated the 1992 presidential election. Potentially this could lead to greater American protectionism, especially if the Uruguay Round of the GATT talks is not successful. Protectionism is a more realistic scenario for the USA than for its rivals given that the size of its domestic market insulates it to some extent from foreign trade. Another possibility is that the USA may seek to tackle its double-deficit problems by reducing public- and private-sector consumption. The effects of this, at least in the medium term, could be to reduce imports and therefore the level of demand for exports originating from the EC; this is no mean threat given that the USA accounts for about 23 per cent of world production. There is also doubt as to how rapidly the USA economy can recover from slump in the early 1990s. The answer to this and many other related questions is made even more difficult because ultimately they depend on whether the USA has the political will-power to solve them.

Japan is the EC's other major competitor and its economic growth and internationalization are well-documented (see Dicken 1992). This is based on a complex of factors including its impressive 18 per cent savings rate. However, the stock-market crash in Japan in the early 1990s could weaken the long-term investment capacity of the major Japanese corporations, but there is no reason to expect that Japan will lose its overall competitiveness, especially in the leading-edge new-technology sectors. The organizational and entrepreneurial culture of Japan, combined with its accumulated foreign investment and R and D strength, give it a massive competitive advantage, even in the face of strong appreciation of the yen.

The EC is also likely to face increased competition from other countries. The strength of the Asian 'tigers' (Hong Kong, South Korea, Singapore, and Taiwan) is already well known. These countries have moved from import substitution, to export-led growth to, in recent years, establishing branch plants in their major markets, including the EC. In addition, a number of other newly industrializing countries, especially in Asia and Latin America, are seeking to increase their share of world trade (Dicken 1992). This also applies to countries nearer at hand, including the Eastern and Central European economies, which are embarking on transformation programmes and are rebuilding their trade links with Western Europe. These programmes are premissed on increased international trade, the most obvious destination of which is the EC. The extent of competition that will emanate from Eastern and Central Europe is difficult to gauge because of uncertainties over the speed of market reforms, the ability to balance public and private initiatives, and the need to establish effective accounting procedures, regulatory frameworks, etc. Turkey—whose economy grew at an average rate of 7 per cent throughout the 1980s—also poses a growing industrial challenge to the Community (Balkir 1993). The challenge is concentrated in particular industries, such as textiles and footwear, in which the EC is most vulnerable.

Turkish and Eastern European membership of the Community also remains on the agenda, and could signify further changes in the EC's trade, competitiveness, and global position.

In summary, therefore, the most that can be said about the economic future is that it is clouded with greater uncertainties than at any other time since the inception of the Community. This uncertainty is compounded by the fact that, in effect there is no central guidance or management of the world economy, which was vividly illustrated by the international currency crises during 1992 and 1993. Moreover, it is a tenet of economic life that uncertainty tends to undermine confidence, investment, and growth. What is surprising is how quickly confidence in the future of Europe can change. In the early 1990s, with the approach of the Single Market and the prospect of EMU, there was remarkable confidence in the future strength of Europe; this was certainly sufficient to concern the Americans who became alarmed at the prospect of a strong 'Fortress Europe'. Yet, by 1992, with signs of recession, the growing national and EC costs of German unification, and the faltering progress of EMU, confidence was ebbing. Redistributional decision-making is therefore likely to have to take place in an increasingly difficult economic climate in the future.

The second major challenge which faces the Community is one such redistributional issue, namely the inherently uneven nature of development. There are differences between countries and, as emphasized in Chapter 1, between regions. Such inequalities have been persistent over time and have been markedly greater than those in Japan or the USA. The Commission of the European Community (1991d: 28) writes that '. . . the ten least developed regions, located mainly in Greece and Portugal, have average incomes per head which are less than one third of the average for the ten most advanced regions'. The precise pattern of regional inequality is of course changing and, for example, some of the core areas of the UK have declined relative to northern Italy and eastern Spain. In addition, flexible accumulation has lead to the growth of new industrial areas outside of the traditional metropolitan concentration (see Garofoli 1992).

Regional inequalities are a symptom of a deeper structural feature of the Community; as a capitalist organization it is necessarily characterized by class and income inequalities. Regional inequalities are only one, if an important, manifestation of these deeper structural cleavages. This is illustrated by estimates of the numbers in the Community living in relative poverty (i.e. numbers in each country receiving 50 per cent or less of the national average income) in 1985: 14.4 per cent of households, 19.4 per cent of children, and 19.6 per cent of the elderly (Commission of the European Communities

1985*a*). These aggregate figures conceal considerable variations; whereas more than 20 per cent of households in Spain and the UK were in relative poverty, the figure was less than 5 per cent in Belgium, the Netherlands, Denmark, Ireland, and Greece. The incidence of poverty is closely allied to that of unemployment, and again this is highly uneven. In May 1992 the seasonally adjusted unemployment statistics showed rates of more than 15 per cent in Spain and Ireland but 5 per cent or less in Germany, Portugal, and Luxembourg (Eurostat data). The neoclassical view that growth would serve to reduce social inequalities has long since been discredited. Indeed, we have little reason to believe that there will be any major amelioration of relative inequalities and poverty. Yet, the tensions that this can generate have been evident in social conflicts and sporadic outbursts of violence in many parts of Europe. While these may be focused on inner-city or race and immigration issues, it is difficult to discount the argument that one of the underlying factors is deep-rooted social disadvantage. Moreover, the experience of the USA emphasizes that economic growth does not necessarily lead to either social harmony or to a narrowing of structural inequality.

One of the lessons for the Community is that social inequalities are not just the product of market forces. Instead, EC policies can have a direct effect on the levels and forms of inequality. Thus plans to reorientate the Common Agricultural Policy, to channel funds into certain kinds of technology programmes, to increase or decrease trade protection, or to create the Single Market all influence unemployment and poverty. The Social Charter agreed at Maastricht, except by the UK, was in part a recognition of the interest and responsibility of the Community in this direction as, indeed, were the creation of the Social Fund and the European Regional Development Fund in, respectively, the 1960s and the 1970s. But what cannot be ignored is that the resource redistribution required to bring about a greater degree of equality between and within countries is enormous. For example, under the 'Delors package' to compensate the poorer member states for the negative effects of the Single Market, Portugal and Greece were both scheduled to receive EC structural assistance equivalent to more than 3 per cent of their GDPs by 1992. There have also been demands for a massive compensation fund to counterbalance the effects of EMU; outline agreement on this was reached at the 1992 Edinburgh summit. Furthermore, there are large inequalities within countries. Whether the political will-power exists to allow more than tokenism in EC interventionism in such issues is questionable. This challenge will increase if the Community agrees to further enlargements so as to encompass Turkey or some of the countries of Central and Eastern Europe.

Another important element in the long-term evolution of the Community is demographic trends, which will also impinge on development and distributional issues. In the 1970s and 1980s there was a fall in the birth rate and a relatively stable death rate, so that natural population growth was virtually zero. This is predicted to decline after the year 2000 (Commission of the European Communities 1991a: 40). As a result, the proportion of the Community population aged over 65 by the year 2015 is likely to exceed 18 per cent. There will, therefore, be increasing demands in many regions for Community resources for social infrastructure. The general ageing of the demographic profile of the EC could, however, to some extent be offset by increased migration from outside the Community. The labour requirements of the EC in the 1990s are considerably different from those of the 1980s, so there is unlikely to be pressure from within the Community to encourage labour immigration. However, there will continue to exist strong pressures from outside the Community from both economic and political immigrants (see Chapters 6 and 7). This will come from Central and Eastern Europe, leastways until these economies experience significant growth, and the crisis in Yugoslavia is resolved. Germany has been the principal focus of such migration in recent years, but the proposed greater freedom of movement within the Community means that the implications are wider. In the coming decades there is also likely to continue to be pressure from the poor and unemployed of the Third World. This gives rise to the grim prospect of 'Fortress Europe' assuming a more militaristic form as the Community seeks to close its frontiers to legal and illegal immigration.

Only the most obvious of socio-economic trends have been touched upon here. Many other trends will also impinge on life in the European Community. These include changes in tastes and life-styles, greater residential and labour mobility within the Community, continuing tertiarization of the economy, and the impact of agricultural policy changes. The impact of all these trends will vary across Europe, according to national and regional economic and cultural differences. However, the expanded role of the EC will mean that Community-level policies will play a significant role in reshaping how its peoples live and work. One of the greatest challenges facing the Community will be to find the most effective balance between market forces and public actions at different levels of the state. These dilemmas are brought into focus in the following discussion on cohesion, competitiveness, and the environment.

Cohesion, competitiveness, and the environment

A number of developmental and distributional trends have been identified in the previous section. One of the key areas is the relationships between competitiveness, cohesion, and the environment. The contradictions and complementarities in these relationships are likely to become increasingly exposed by events in Europe and on the world stage.

Competitiveness is a major concern for the Community. The challenge posed by Japan, the USA, and increasingly the 'Asian tigers' (the Newly Industrializing Countries of Asia), and China has already been discussed (but see also Williams 1991a; Dicken 1992). Indeed, the Single Market Programme can be interpreted primarily as an attempt to make the Community more competitive in the face of such competition rather than as an integrationist programme *per se*. Nevertheless, there are two major environmental implications of the Single Market programme that should be noted. First, the Community, in the name of standardization, harmonization, and the creation of a level playing-field, is developing a number of EC-wide programmes and standards which have implications for the environment; these include car-exhaust emissions and water purity. Secondly, despite its enormous economic power, the EC is still condemned—as are all capitalist economies—to competing in the global marketplace. There may, therefore, at least in the short run, be an environmental price to be paid for remaining globally competitive. Quite simply there is a limit on the short-term costs that can be imposed on any industrial sector if it is to remain competitive. This is why the Commission has placed such stress in recent years on reciprocal relationships with third countries. The Community has already demanded reciprocal access to product, labour, and capital markets in those countries which seek to export to the EC. This was evident in the negotiations leading to the establishment of the European Economic Space (the combined EC and EFTA trading areas). It is not inconceivable that, in future, environmental and social conditions will be included in these reciprocal demands to ensure that there is levelling of all dimensions of the field of competition. The importance of international trade is underscored by the simple fact that between 1950 and 1990 world trade grew at twice the rate of the expansion of world GDP.

There is also a question concerning whether there is a trade-off between the promotion of growth and decreasing/increasing levels of regional and social inequalities in the Community. Development of the poorer regions can be interpreted variously as increasing the productive capacity of the Community or diluting the strength of the core regions and hence of the EC as a whole. The Treaty of Rome stressed that one of the objectives of the Community should be to promote economic and social harmony throughout the Community. It was assumed that market forces would ensure the achievement of such a balance in the longer term. In reality, of course, social and economic inequalities have persisted, sometimes increasing in scale, throughout the Community's existence (see Chapter 1). The EC's policy response has been the Social Fund, the European Regional Development Fund, European Investment Bank loans, agricultural guidance expenditure, the Integrated Mediterranean Programme, and a number of other specific programmes such as those to assist the transition to full membership of Portugal and Greece. In the 1980s and the 1990s there was concern that economic and social imbalances could derail the moves to greater integration. This was converted into demands by the poorer member states for increased structural assistance to offset the costs of increased competition in the Single Market and for a 'cohesion' fund to assist the convergence necessary for economic and monetary union (discussed in Williams 1993). While the debate on cohesion has heretofore concentrated almost exclusively on economic indicators, it is likely that the terms of reference could be enlarged to encompass the much wider concepts of the quality of life and social well-being (see e.g. Coates et al. 1977), which necessarily include environmental concerns. The prospects of enlargement of the EC to include some or all of the countries of Central and Eastern Europe—where there is an immense inheritance of environmental degradation—will reinforce this trend. The social agreement attached to the Maastricht agreement is also concerned about such distributional issues. It can be presented as an attempt to ensure that the benefits of improved working conditions are shared throughout the Community; there is however a price to pay for it in the removal of some of the advantages of more flexible and lower labour costs from some of the poorer member states and hence reducing their growth potential.

Finally, it must be emphasized that environmental issues will neither merely be passively drawn along by the course of events in the cohesion debate nor simply be reactive to the demands of economic development. Instead, there is a large and proactive environmentalist lobby. It has strong roots in northern Europe as is evident in the growth of conservationist bodies in these countries where it is also claimed that the middle class is in danger of 'loving the countryside to death'. There is also evidence that the environmentalist movement is putting down roots in the poorer member states such as Ireland (see Chapter 12) and Spain (see e.g. Bangs 1991). Accession to the Community of the Alpine and Scandinavian countries, which have well-organized environmentalist interests, would reinforce this tendency. In the last decade environmentalist movements have recorded a number of notable successes: in the 1989 European Parliament elections Green parties obtained more than 10 per cent of the vote in France, the UK, and Belgium; plans to build more nuclear power-stations have been aborted in several countries; environmental issues now have to be taken into account routinely in all new major development proposals in the Community (see Chapter 11); and there are serious moves, including set-aside and diversification, to make farming more ecologically sensitive.

It is likely that the pressures emanating from environmentalist bodies will increase in future, as knowledge increases about the environment, leisure time expands, and life-styles become more segmented. However, it would be wrong to see this as a new societal trend. There is long-standing concern about the environment, even if this has only been effectively articulated in recent years. In 1986 an EC survey (Commission of the European Communities 1986) showed that 72 per cent of the population considered the environment to be an urgent problem and only 3 per cent did not consider it to be a problem at all. What was really significant was how widespread they considered the sources of possible damage to the environment (p. 29). Substantial proportions considered that the following constituted threats:

59% factories that discharge dangerous chemicals into the air or water;
37% rubbish on the streets, open spaces etc;
35% over use of insecticides, fertilizers, etc. in agriculture;
33% industrial water abandoned wherever it is convenient;
33% oil pollution in the sea and on the shore;
23% vehicles;
20% acid rain;
12% illegal building which spoils the countryside;
11% waste of rare natural resources such as minerals;
 9% industrial and traffic noise;
 6% erosion of farmland.

There is then a ground swell of public opinion in the Community in favour of environmental protection and improvement, and this transcends many areas of Community interest and policy. Given also the logic that many environmental problems are international in origin and diffusion, and therefore require international intervention, there is potentially a major role for the Community in this area. What is surprising is that, at face value, EC environmental policy is very limited (see Chapter 11). For example, there appears to be little policy *per se* with respect to the urban environment. However, it is '. . . important to recognize that the majority of Community policies have, directly or indirectly, an influence on urban areas' (Commission of the European Communities 1990a). This includes projects financed under the Social and Regional Funds, as well as sectoral, industrial, and research policies. In future the scope of such policies may increase. The EC Green Paper on the Urban Environment sets out a number of potential lines of action including: encouragement of transport innovations; measures to protect the heritage of European cities; promotion of small firms with sound environmental practices; and the management of urban energy and urban waste.

The list of measures proposed for the urban environment, and other environments, appears impressive but, in reality, the powers of the Community are circumscribed. It is worth considering these constraints in some detail as they illustrate limitations which exist in other areas of Community interest. First, the role of the state is circumscribed by the capitalist nature of the economy. This means that in most areas the Community has little direct power to bring about developments. Instead, its role is that of restricting certain activities and of encouraging others via financial incentives or investments that will facilitate private-sector initiatives. Second, many issues—whether acid rain or industrial growth—are global rather than macro-regional in nature. The EC may be able to represent European interests more effectively than could individual governments, but ultimately it does not have sufficient power to bring about desired end goals without wider international assistance. Third, decision-making in the EC is characterized by inter-governmentalism, and, since the Luxembourg compromise, by the principle of unanimity in voting within the Council of Ministers. The Single European Act and Maastricht have increased the amount of majority voting and the powers of the Parliament. However, unanimous voting is still the order of the day in respect of most significant issues. This applies particularly to the environment which is considered to be an area of national interests. The first two of these constraints are fixed, leastways in the foreseeable future. This is why the debate about the third constraint—that is about political union—is of such importance for the future of Europe. It should be added that there is also a fourth constraint which is the ability of the EC to implement effectively its legislation. For example, in the field of environmental laws the average rate of transposing EC directives into national laws by December 1991 was only 86 per cent with Italy only achieving a rate of 59 per cent.

While there is clear logic to increased EC involvement in environmental policy, there is no guarantee that this will come about. For example, in October 1992 the EC's environmental commissioner, Karel van Miert, expressed the fear that Community environment policy could be made a sacrificial lamb in the power struggle between Brussels and the member states over subsidiarity. The principle of subsidiarity is that political decisions should be taken as close to the people they are going to effect as is practically possible. In practice, this would mean continuing diversity in

Diff. in meaning of subsidiarity

decision-making structures given the major differences which exist within the EC in terms of the devolution of power from the central to the local state or to the regions. Subsidiarity in the UK means reinforcing the powers of Whitehall whereas in Germany it means increasing the powers of the *Länder*. Environmental policy therefore runs the risks of fragmentation as one of the prices to be paid for securing the ratification of the Maastricht agreement.

As a final note it is appropriate to reiterate that issues such as development, distribution, and the environment will be addressed within a wider framework than the EC. The Community is not commensurate with Western Europe, let alone with Europe. However, it has advanced rapidly from the position in the 1960s, when it was little more than a free-trade area of six nation states which were also formulating a common agricultural policy. There is now at least the prospect that, within two decades, virtually all European countries could be member states. In addition, the Community has become involved in an ever-widening array of activities; as well as influencing the production of agricultural and industrial goods and services, Community law impinges on such diverse areas as equal pay for men and women, preservation of the landscape, airline competition, and the ways in which food is stored and served in restaurants. We would argue therefore that 'the European challenge' has, in effect, become 'the EC challenge', and this applies to the member states, the other European countries, and indeed the rest of the world.

Further reading

A review of the relationship between the external environment of the EC and its internal development is provided by A. M. Williams (1991), *The European Community: The Contradictions of Integration* (Oxford). The specific challenges of pan-European integration are examined in A. H. Dawson (1993), *A Geography of European Integration* (London), while the challenges of Maastricht and the idea of a 'Social Europe' are addressed in M. Wise, and R. Gibb (1993), *Single Market to Social Europe: The European Community in the 1990s* (London). A very useful empirical summary of the 'state' of the EC in the 1990s and of likely trends is provided by the EC's Directorate-General for Regional Policy (1991), *Europe 2000: Outlook for the Development of the Community's Territory* (Brussels). The future of the Community—to the year 2020—is also addressed in I. Masser, O. Sviden, and M. Wegener (eds.) (1992), *The Geography of Europe's Futures* (London).

References

Abbati, C. D. (1986), *Transport and European Integration* (Brussels).

Abrahamson, M. and Johnson, P. (1974), 'The social ecology of Madrid: Stratification in comparative perspective', *Demography*, 11: 521–32.

Allen, S. and Wolkowitz, C. (1988), *Homeworking, Myths and Realities* (London).

Allott, N. A., Mills, W. R. P., Dick, J. R. W., Eacnett, A. M., Brennan, M. T., Clandillot, S., Phillips, W. E. A., Critchley, M., and Mullins, T. E. (1990), *Acidification of Surface Waters in Connemara and South Mayo*, report by duQuesne Ltd. (Dublin).

Allum, P. (1973), *Politics and Society in Post-war Naples* (Cambridge).

An Foras Forbartha (1981), *National Heritage Inventory, Areas of Scientific Interest in Ireland* (Dublin).

An Foras Taluntais (1972), *The Management of Animal Manures in the Catchment Area of Lough Sheelin*, Report No. 1 (Dublin).

—— (1975), *The Management of Animal Manures in the Catchment Area of Lough Sheelin*, Report No. 2 (Dublin).

Andall, J. (1990), 'New migrants, old conflicts: The recent immigration into Italy', *Italianist*, 10: 151–74.

Andreae, B. (1955), 'Die Feldgraswirtschaft in Westeuropa: Standortfragen, Formen, Probleme und Entwicklungstendenzen', *Berichte über Landwirtschaft*, Sonderheft 163 (Hamburg).

Arnalte, E., Avella, L., and Roca, A. (1986), 'Mercado de la tierra y dinamica de las estructuras agrariasen los paises de la CEE', *Agricultura y Sociedad*, 41: 255–83.

Arnold, A. (1987), 'Das niedersächsische Grünbracheprogramm', *Zeitschrift für Agrargeogreaphie*, 5.

Augustin, J.-P. and Pailhé, J. (1989), 'Mérignac, ville majeure de banlieue', *Révue géographique des Pyrénées et du Sud-Ouest*, 49–64.

Balabanian, O., Bouet, G., Deslondes, O., and Lerat, S., *Les états mediterranéens de la CEE* (Paris).

Baldock, D. (1984), *Wetland Drainage in Europe: The Effects of Agricultural Policy in Four EEC Countries*, Institute for European Environmental Policy International and Institute for Environment and Development (London).

—— (1990), *Agriculture and Habitat Loss in Europe* (London).

—— and Condor, D. (eds.) (1987), *Removing Land from Agriculture* (London).

Ballesteros, A. G. (1977), 'Notes sobre el crecimiento natural y real de los distritos de Madrid', *Revista Internacional de Sociologia* 23: 429–40.

Balkir, C. (1993), 'Turkey and the EC: Foreign trade and direct foreign investment in the 1980s', in C. Balkir and A. M. Williams (eds.), *Turkey and Europe* (London).

Bamford, C. G. and Robinson, H. (1983), *Geography of the EEC* (Plymouth).

Bangs, P. (1991), 'Nature Conservation in Spain', unpublished Ph.D. thesis, University of Keele.

Baretje, R., (1982), 'Tourism's external account and the balance of payments', *Annals of Tourism Research*, 9: 57–67.

Barker, M. L. (1982), 'Traditional landscape and mass tourism in the Alps', *Geographical Review*, 72: 345–95.

Barrere, P. and Cassou-Mounet, M. (1980), *Les villes françaises* (Paris).

Barrett, S. (1982), *Transport Policy in Ireland* (Dublin).

—— (1987), *Flying High: Airline Prices and European Regulation* (Aldershot).

—— (1990), 'Regulation to deregulation', *Transport*, May, 114–15.

Begg, I. (1989), 'The regional dimension of the "1992" proposals', *Regional Studies*, 23: 368–76.

Ben Salah, T. (1991), 'L'applicabilité des normes internationales aux travailleurs étrangers clandestins', in S. Montagné-Villette (ed.) *Espaces et travails clandestins* (Paris), 151–6.

Berlinguer, G. and Della Seta, P. (1976), *Borgate di Roma* (Rome).

Bernard, H. R. and Comitas, L. (1978), 'Greek return migration', *Current Anthropology*, 19: 658–9.

Berry, B. J. L. (ed.) (1976), *Urbanization and Counter-Urbanization* (Beverly Hills, Calif.).

Berthaux, C. (1988), 'Le tournant de la PAC', *Ecoflash*, INSEE-CNDP, 34.

Binet, N. (1986), 'Péri-urbanisation et politiques de l'habitat dans l'agglomération rennaise', in Instituto de Estudios de Administración Local, *Études sur les espaces urbains* (Madrid), 361–74.

Blacksell, A. M. Y. (1977), *Post-War Europe: A Political Geography* (Folkestone).

Blackwell, J. and Convery, F. J. (eds.) *Promise and Performance: Irish Environmental Policies Analysed*, The Resource and Environmental Policy Centre, University College Dublin (Dublin).

Bleasdale, A. and Sheehy Skeffington, M. (1992), 'The influence of agricultural practices on plant communities in Connemara', in Feehan (ed.), *Environment and Development in Ireland*.

Böhning, W. R. (1974), 'The economic effects of the employment of foreign workers, with special reference to the labour markets of Western Europe's post-industrial countries', in *The Effects of the Employment of Foreign Workers* (Paris), 43–123.

Borstel, U. O. von (1974), 'Untersuchungen zur Vegetationsentwicklung auf ökologisch Grünland und Ackerbrachen hessischer Mittelgebirge', doctoral thesis, Universität Gottingen.

Boyle, G. E. (1982), 'The total factor productivity of Irish agriculture 1960 to 1980: A preliminary examination', paper read to the Agricultural Economics Society of Ireland (Dublin).

—— and Kearney, B. (1983), 'Intensification in agriculture: Trends and prospects', in Blackwell and Convery (eds.), *Promise and Performance*.

Bracken, J. J. and O'Grady, M. F. (1992), 'A review of freshwater fisheries research in Ireland', in Feehan (ed.), *Environment and Development in Ireland*.

Braudel, F. (1966), *The Mediterranean and the Mediterranean World in the Age of Philip II* (London).

Briggs, A. (1968), *Victorian Cities* (Harmondsworth).

British Tourism Association (1991), *UK Tourism Statistics* (London).

Broek, J. O. M. and Webb, J. W. (1973), *A Geography of Mankind* (New York), 2nd edn. (1978).

Brown, R. G. and Sorenson, F. (1989), 'New Developments in European Air Transport', *Proceedings, PTRC 17th Annual Summer Meeting, Seminar A* (London).

Brucker, G. (ed.) (1979), *People and Communities in the Western World*, ii. (Homewood, Ill.).

Brunet, J. (1990), *Montpellier Europole* (Montpellier).

Bruton, R. and Convery, F. J. (1982), *Land Drainage Policy in Ireland*, Economic and Social Research Institute (Dublin).

Cabot, D. (ed.) (1985), *The State of the Environment* (Dublin).

Calmes, R. and Mykolenko, L. (1985), *L'Europe agricole* (Paris).

Carfantan, J.-Y. (1985), *L'Europe verte sous influence* (Paris).

Carriere, J.-P. (1990), *Les transformations agraires en Portugal* (Paris).

Carter, H. (1981), *The Study of Urban Geography* (London), 3rd edn.

Castells, M. (1983), *The City and the Grassroots* (London).

Castles, S. (1986), 'The guest-worker in Western Europe: An obituary', *International Migration Review* 20: 761–78.

—— and Kosack, G. (1973), *Immigrant Workers and Class Structure in Western Europe* (London).

Cazes, G., Domingo, J., and Gauthier, A. (1985), *L'Espagne et le Portugal aux portes du marché commun* (Montreuil).

Cecchini, P. (1988), *The European Challenge: 1992, the Benefits of the Single Market* (London).

Central Statistics Office (1962), *Statistical Abstract of Ireland* (Dublin), Tables 327, 309, and Table XXXVI, 365.

—— (1991), *Ireland Statistical Abstract* (Dublin), Tables 12.4, 310, and Table XXX, 393.

Champ, W. S. T. (1990) 'Lough Sheelin: A Study in Conservation', *Business and Finance*, 19 July.

Charpentier, J. (ed.) (1988), *La protection de l'environnement par les communautés européennes* (Paris).

Charrié, J.-P., Genty, M., and Laborde, P. (1992), *Les petites villes en Aquitaine 1962–1990* (Bordeaux).

Chartered Institute of Transport in Ireland (1987), *The Irish International Road Freight Industry: A Study of its Competitiveness* (Dublin).

Cliff, A. D. and Haggett, P. (1988), *Atlas of Disease Distribution: Analytical Approaches to Epidemiological Data* (Oxford).

Coates, B. E., Johnston, R. J., Knox, P. L. (1977), *Geography and Inequality* (Oxford).

Coleman, D. A. (ed.) (1982), *Demography of Minority Groups in the United Kingdom* (London).

Commission des Communautés Européennes, Direction Environment (1990), *Green Book for the Urban Environment* (Luxembourg).

—— Direction Générale des Politiques Régionales (1991), *Europe 2000: Les perspectives de developpement du territoire communautaire* (Luxembourg).

Commission of the European Communities (1982), *A Community Policy on Tourism* (London and Brussels).

—— (1984), *Ten Years of Community Environment Policy*, (Brussels and Luxembourg).

—— (1985*a*), Poverty in Figures, Eurostat (Brussels).

—— (1985*b*), *Tourism and the European Community*, European File 11/85 (Brussels).

—— (1985*c*), *Perspectives for the Common Agricultural Policy* 8480/85, COM(85) 333 final (Brussels).

—— (1985*d*), *A Future for Community Agriculture* (Brussels).

—— (1986), *The Europeans and their Environment in 1986* (Brussels).

—— (1987*a*), *The State of the Environment in the European Community 1986* (Luxembourg).

—— (1987*b*), *Europeans and their Holidays*, VII/165/87–EN (Brussels).

—— (1987*c*), *Rural Tourism* (Brussels).

—— (1988*a*), *Urban Problems and Regional Policy in the European Community* (Luxembourg).

—— (1988*b*), *Research Programme on Competitiveness of Agriculture and Management of Agricultural Resources*, COM 457 (Brussels).

—— (1989*a*), *The Agricultural Situation in the Community* (Brussels).

—— (1989*b*), *A Community Transport Market: Background Report* (Brussels).

—— (1990*a*), *Green Paper on the Urban Environment* (Brussels).

—— (1990*b*), *Environmental Policy in the European Community*, European Documentation, Periodical 5/1990 (Brussels and Luxembourg).

—— (1990*c*), *The European Regional Development Fund* (Brussels).

—— (1990*d*), *Annual Report on the Reform of the Structural Funds* (Brussels).

—— (1991*a*), *Europe 2000: Outlook for the Development of the Community's Territory* (Brussels).

—— (1991*b*), *Report by the Commission to the Council and the European Parliament on the European Year of Tourism* (Brussels).

—— (1991*c*), *Proposal for a Council Decision Concerning the Establishment of a Network of High-Speed Trains* (Brussels).

—— (1991*d*), *The Regions of the 1990s* (Brussels).

—— (1991*e*), *The Development and Future of the Common Agricultural Policy*, Supplement 5/91 (Brussels).

—— (1991*f*), *The Development and Future of the Common Agricultural Policy* (COM 91/258) (Brussels).

—— (1992), *A European Community Programme of Policy and Action in Relation to the Environment and Sustainable Development* COM(92) 23 final, 3 vols.

Community of European Railways (1989), *Proposals for a European High-Speed Network* (no publication details given).

Comunidades Europeas: Comite Economico y Social (1981), *Aspectos agricolas de la adhesion de España a la Comunidad: Dictamen de iniciativas* (Brussels).

—— (1982), *La política agrícola de la Comunidad Europea, Documentacion Europea*.

—— (1985), *La política agrícola común* (Madrid).

—— (1987), *Situación y evolución de las regiones de la Comunidad ampliada en el dominio agrícola* (Brussels and Luxembourg).

—— (1989*a*), *Una política agraria común para los años noventa, Documentacion Europea*.

—— (1989*b*), *Una política agraria común para los años noventa* (Luxembourg).

—— (1989*c*), *Anuario estadístico agricultura 1988* (Luxembourg).

Comunidades Europeas: Comite Economico y Social (1989*d*), *La situación de la agricultura en la Comunidad: Informe 1988* (Brussels).

—— (1989*e*), *Las explotaciónes agrarias de las zonas desfavorecidas y de montaña de la Comunidad* (Brussels).

—— (1991), *Anuario estadistíco agricultura 1990* (Luxembourg).

—— (1992), *La situación de agricultura en la Comunidad. Informe anual* (Brussels and Luxembourg).

—— (various years), *La situación de agricultura en la Comunidad. Informe anual* (Brussels and Luxembourg).

Confederation of Irish Industry (1985), *Irish Road Statistics, 1985* (Dublin).

Convery, F. J. (1989), 'European economic policies and Ireland', in R. W. G. Carter and A. J. Parker, *Ireland: A Contemporary Geographical Perspective* (Dublin).

Conway, A. G. (1986), Prospects for the CAP and its modification, in An Foras Taluntais, *The Changing CAP and its Implications*, Economics and Rural Welfare Resource centre, 13th Annual Conference (Dublin).

Corbera, M. (1987), 'El papel de la politica agraria comun en la evolucion de la agricultura familiar', *Anales de Geografia de la Universidad Computense*, 7: 241–51.

Costa, P., Lando, F., and Zanetto, G. (1980), 'Rinnovo urbano e transformazioni sociali nel centro storico di Venezia', *Sistemi Urbani*, 2: 385–410.

Costa-Lascoux, J. (1989), *De l'immigré au citoyen* (Paris).

Council of the European Communities (1972*a*), 'Council Directive (72/159/EEC) of 17 April 1972 on the modernization of farms', *Official Journal of the European Communities*, L 96/1.

—— (1972*b*), 'Council Directive (72/160/EEC) of 17 April 1972 concerning measures to encourage the cessation of farming and the reallocation of utilised agricultural area for the purpose of structural improvement', *Official Journal of the European Communities*, L 96/9.

—— (1972*c*), 'Council Directive (72/161/EEC) of 17 April 1972 concerning the provision of socio-economic guidance for and the acquisition of occupational skills by persons engaged in agriculture', *Official Journal of the European Communities*, L 96/15.

—— (1975), 'Council Directive (75/268/EEC) of 28 April 1975 on mountain- and hill-farming and farming in less-favoured areas', *Official Journal of the European Communities*, L 128/1.

—— (1980), 'Council Regulation (80/1820/EC) of 24 June 1980 for the stimulation of agricultural development in the less-favoured areas of the west of Ireland', *Official Journal of the European Communities*, L 180/1.

—— (1985), 'Council Regulation (85/797/EC) of 12 March 1985 on improving the efficiency of agricultural structures', *Official Journal of the European Communities*, L 93/1.

—— (1989), *Background Report: A Community Transport Market* (London).

—— (1991) '(91/676/EC) of 12 December 1991 concerning the protection of waters against pollution caused by nitrates from agricultural sources', *Official Journal of the European Communities*, L 93/1.

Cox, P. G. (1985), 'The impact of EC structural policy in Ireland', in An Foras Taluntais, *The Challenge Facing Agriculture in Difficult Times*, Economics and Rural Welfare Research Centre, 12th Annual Conference (Dublin).

Coxon, C. E. (1987), 'The spatial distribution of turloughs', *Irish Geography*, 20: 11–23.

Crotti, N. (1991), 'La migrazione sanitaria. Valutazione ed interpretazione del fenomeno: problemi organizzativi e assistenziali', in Geddes (ed.) *La salute degli Italiani*.

Daly, D. (1992), 'Groundwater resources: A review of development, quality and pollution issues', in Feehan (ed.), *Environment and Development in Ireland*.

Della Seta, P. (1978), 'Notes on urban struggles in Italy', *International Journal of Urban and Regional Research*, 2: 303–29.

Delorme, H. (1987), 'An outline of French views on French conversion programmes', in Baldock and Condor (eds.), *Removing Land from Agriculture*, 40–3.

Department of Agriculture and Food (1990), *Annual Report of the Minister* (Dublin).

—— (1992), *1991 Annual Review and Outlook for Agriculture and the Food Industry* (Dublin).

Department of the Environment, Northern Ireland (1989), *Transportation Programme: Northern Ireland, 1989–1993* (Belfast).

Department of the Environment (1990), *Tourism and the Inner City* (London).

Dicken, P. (1992), *Global Shift* (London).

Diener, H. O. (1928), 'Zur Geschichte der Brache in Bayern', *Landwirtschafliches Jahrbuch für Bayern*, 19: 438–51.

Dierschke, H. (1980, 'Estellung eines Pflegeplanes für Wiesenbrachen des Westharzes auf pflanzensoziologischer Grundlage', *Verhandlungen der Gesellschaft für Ökologie*, 8: 205–12.

Documentation française (1985), 'L'Agriculture mediterranéene et l'elargissement de la CEE: Problèmes politiques et sociaux', *Documentation française*, 505.

—— (1986), *The Struggle to Control the Trafficking in Labour, 1984–1985* (Paris).

Dodd, V. A. (1992), 'Planning for intensive livestock production units', in Feehan (ed.), *Environment and Development in Ireland*.

—— and Champ, W. S. T. (1983), 'Environmental problems associated with intensive animal production units, with reference to the catchment area of Lough Sheelin', Blackwell and Convery (eds.), *Promise and Performance*.

Donges, J. B. (1984), 'La politica agraria de la CEE: Relaciones con paises no miembros', *Informacion Comerical Española*, 609: 143–51.

Doyle, G. J. (1992), 'Progress and problems in the conservation of Irish peatlands, 1983–1991', in Feehan (ed.), *Environment and development in Ireland*.

Dublin Chamber of Commerce (1990), *Corridor to Competitiveness: Developing Ireland's Primary Sea Route to the Internal Market* (Dublin).

Duggan, P. and Champ, T. (1992), 'Lough Sheelin reviewed', in Feehan (ed.), *Environment and Development in Ireland*.

Dumas, J. (1990, 'Métropole cherche technopôle désespérement: Réflexion géographique sur quelques non-décisions bordelaises', in CESURB, Recherches urbaines no. 2 (Bordeaux), 61–9.

Economie européene (1988), '1992: The new European economy', no. 35, March.

—— (1989), 'Horizontal integration, takeovers and competition policy in the European Community', no. 40, May.

—— (1990a, 'Annual economic report 1990–1991: The Community in the 1990s— towards economic and monetary union', no. 46, Dec.

Economie européene (1990*b*), 'The sectoral impact of the single market on industry: The challenge facing member states', special issue.

Egglishaw, H., Gardiner, R., and Foster, J. (1986), 'Salmon catch decline and forestry in Scotland', *Scottish Geographical Mazagine*, 102: 57–61.

Erdmenger, J. (1983), *The European Community Transport Policy* (Aldershot).

Estibanez-Alvarez, J. (1988), *Las ciudades* (Madrid).

L'État du Monde (1990), *L'État du Monde*, edn. la Découverte (Paris).

European Communities, Economic and Social Committee (1987), *European Environment Policy, Air, Water, Waste Management* (Brussels and Luxembourg).

European Conference of Ministers of Transport (1988), *Investment in Transport Infrastructure in ECMT Countries* (Paris).

Eurostat (1990), *Basic Statistics on the Community* (Brussels).

Evers, H.-D. (1975), 'Urban expansion and landownership in underdeveloped countries', *Urban Affairs Quarterly*, 11/1: 117–29.

FAO (1981), *Agricultura: Horizonte 2000* (Rome).

Farrell, E. P. and Kelly-Quinn, M. (1992), 'Forestry and the environment in 1992. Groundwater resources: A review of development quality and pollution issues', in Feehan (ed.), *Environment and Development in Ireland*.

Feehan, J. (ed.) (1992), *Environment and Development in Ireland*, The Environmental Institute, University College Dublin (Dublin).

Fennell, R. (1979), *The Common Agricultural Policy of the European Community* (London).

Ferras, R. (1977*a*), *Barcelone: Croissance d'une metropole* (Paris).

—— (1977*b*), 'Les autres catalanes: Le proletariat urbain à Barcelone', *Revue géographique des Pyrénées et du Sud-Ouest*, 48: 191–8.

Fitzmaurice, P. (1983), 'Farming and the enforcement of water pollution control', in Blackwell and Convery (eds.), *Promise and Performance*.

Foss, P.J. (1991), *Irish Peatlands: The Critical Decade* (Dublin).

Frankenberger, R. (1960), Die Aufforstung landwirtschaftlich genutzter Grundstücke als Index für sozialgeographische Strukturwandlungen in Oberfranken, *Münchener Geographischer Hefte*, 18 (Munich).

Fried, R. C. (1973), *Planning the Eternal City: Roman Politics and Planning since World War II* (New Haven, Conn.).

Frühauf, W. and Giesinger, T. (1992), *Europa ohne Grenzen: Alarm für die Umwelt*, Spiegel Spezial (Hamburg).

Garcia, T. (1985), *Consecuencia Sobre las Agriculturas Regionales de la Adhesion de España a las Comunidades Europeas* (Madrid).

—— (1986, 'Reflexiones sobre el libro verde y la crisis de la política agrícola común', *Revista de Estudios Agrocsociales*, 136: 756–60.

Garofoli, G. (1992), *Endogenous Development and Southern Europe* (Aldershot).

Gaspar, J. (1976), 'A dinamica funcional do centro de Lisboa', *Finisterra* 11: 37–150.

—— (1984), 'Urbanisation: Growth, problems and policies', in A. M. Williams (ed.), *Southern Europe Transformed* (London).

Geddes, M. (ed.) (1991), *La Salute degli Italiani* (Rome).

—— (1992) *La Salute degli Italiani*, Rapporto 1992 (Rome).

General Consumer Council for Northern Ireland (1991), *Going Places: Transport Links between Northern Ireland and Europe* (Belfast).

Genty, M. (1986), 'Les actions d'urbanisme opérationnel dans le centre historique d'une ville moyenne: L'exemple de Périgueux', in Instituto de Estudios de Administración Local, *Études sur les espaces urbains* (Madrid).

George, P. (1986), 'Les étrangers en France: Étude géographique', *Annales de Géographie*, 95/539: 273–300.

Ghosh, B. (1991), 'Trends in world migration: The European perspective', *Courier*, 129: 46–51.

Gillmor, D. A. (1977), 'The EEC scheme for farming in the Less-developed Areas', *Irish Geography*, 10: 101–8.

—— (1985), *Economic Activities in the Republic of Ireland: A Geographical Perspective* (Dublin).

—— (1989), 'Agricultural development', in R. W. G. Carter and A. J. Parker (eds.), *Ireland: A Contemporary Geographical Perspective on a Land and its People* (London).

—— (1991–2), 'Agricultural impacts and the Irish environment', *Geographical Viewpoint*, 20: 5–22.

Golter, F. (1986), Möglichkeiten und Grenzen von Flächenstillegungen, *Neues Archiv für Niedersachsen*, 35: 219–28.

Gomez, C. (1987), *Politica Socioestructural en Zonas de Agricultura de Montaña en España y en la CEE* (Madrid).

Gordon, I. (1991), *The Impact of Economic Change on Minorities and Migrants in Western Europe*, University of Reading Geography Department, Discussion Paper no. 2 (Reading).

Government of Ireland and Commission of the European Communities (1990), *Operational Programme on Peripherality: Roads and Other Transport Infrastructure 1989 to 1993* (Dublin).

Graham, B. J. (1990), 'Deregulation of Domestic Passenger Air Transport Services in the United Kingdom, 1980–89: A Case Study of Northern Ireland', *Environment and Planning C: Government and Policy*, 8: 327–46.

Greenpeace Report (1991), *The Single European Dump: Free Trade in Hazardous and Nuclear Waste in the New Europe* (Brussels).

Grenon, M. and Batisse, M. (eds.) (1989), *Futures for the Mediterranean Basin* (Brussels).

Gwilliam, K. M. (1989), 'EEC Transport Policy Issues', *Proceedings, PTRC 17th Annual Summer Meeting, Seminar A* (London).

Haigh, N. (1987), *EEC Environmental Policy and Britain*, 2nd edn. (London).

—— Bennett, G., Kromarek, G., and Lavoux, T. (1986), *European Community Environmental Policy in Practice. Comparative Report: Water and Waste in Four Countries. A Study of the Implementation of the EEC Directives in France, Germany, Netherlands and United Kingdom* (London).

Hall, D. R. (1991), 'Introduction', in D. R. Hall (ed.), *Tourism and Economic Development in Eastern Europe and the Soviet Union*, (London).

Hall, P. and Hay, D. (1980), *Growth Centres in the European Urban System* (London).

Hamilton, K. (1990), *Transport Policy* (London).

Hampson, B. (1988), 'Airports After Deregulation', *Proceedings, Chartered Institute of Transport in Ireland (Southern Section) Conference*, 89–102.

Harte, L. N. (1992), 'Farm adjustment in Ireland under the CAP', in Feehan (ed.), *Environment and Development in Ireland*.

Hayden, T. J. (1992), 'Current status and future prospects for conservational wildlife in Ireland', in Feehan (ed.), *Environment and Development in Ireland*.

Henze, A. and Zeddies, J. (1988), 'Vergleichende Nutzen-Kosten Bewertung von Betriebsstillegungen und Teilflächenstillegungen', *Schriftenreihe des Bundesministers für Ernährung, Landwirtschaft und Forsten*, A 355 (Münster).

Hey, C. (1991), 'Weißbuch der Europäischen Umweltverbände: Konzepte für eine Umweltgemeinschaft', *Zeitschrift für Politische Ökologie*, Sonderheft 3.

Hickie, D. A. (1991*a*), *Forestry in Ireland: Policy and Practice* (Dublin).

—— (1991*b*), 'Acid test', *Living Heritage*, 8: 6–7.

Horner, A. (1991), 'Geographical aspects of airport and air-route developments in Ireland', *Irish Geography* 24: 35–47.

Horner, A. A., Walsh, J. A., and Williams, J. A. (1984), *Agriculture in Ireland: A Census Atlas* (Dublin).

House of Lords (1987), *Fourth Environmental Action Programme with evidence*, Select Committee on the European Communities, Session 1986/7, report 08(III) (London).

Howe, G. (1986), *Global Geocancerology: A World Geography of Human Cancers* (Edinburgh).

Hudson, R. and Lewis, J. (1985), 'Introduction', in R. Hudson and J. Lewis (eds.), *Uneven Development in Southern Europe: Studies of Accumulation, Class, Migration and the State* (London).

Hue, G. (1991), 'Légalité, efficacité et travail clandestin', in S. Montagné-Villette (ed.) *Espace et travails clandestins* (Paris), 133–8.

Hull, A., Jones, T., and Kenny, S. (1988), *Geographical Issues in Western Europe* (Harlow).

Hundt, R. (1964), 'Die Bergwiesen des Harzes, Thüringer Waldes und Erzgebirges', *Pflanzenökologie*, 14.

Huttman, E., Blauw, W., and Saltman, J. (eds.) (1991), *Urban Housing: Segregation of Minorities in Western Europe and the United States* (Durham, NC).

IEEP (Institute of European Environmental Policy) (1990), *The EC Structural Funds: An Environmental Briefing*, 2, World Wide Fund for Nature (Godalming).

Ilbery, B. W. (1986), *Western Europe: A Systematic Human Geography* (Oxford).

—— (1990), 'Adoption of the arable set-aside scheme in England', *Geography*, 76: 69–73.

Istat (1991) *Annuario Statistico Italiano, 1990* (Rome).

Jalabert, G. (1989), *The Urban System and Territorial Management in Medium-sized Towns: Castres* (Toulouse).

Johnson, S. P. and Corcelle, G. (1989), *The Environmental Policy of the European Communities* (London).

Jones, A. (1990), 'New directions for West German agricultural policy: The example of Schleswig-Holstein', *Journal of Rural Studies* 6: 9–16.

Jones, E. (1990), *Metropolis: The World's Great Cities* (Oxford).

Joseph, A. E. and Phillips, D. R. (1984), *Accessibility and Utilization: Geographical Perspectives on Health Care Delivery* (New York).

Journal of International Migration, URA CNRS 165, University of Poitiers.

Kain, R. (1981), *Planning for Conservation, an International Perspective* (London).

Kariel, H. G. and Kariel, P. E. (1982), 'Socio-cultural impacts of tourism: An example from the Austrian Alps', *Geografiska Annaler*, Ser. B, 64:1–16.

Kayser, B. (1972), *Cyclically-determined Homeward Flows of Migrant Workers* (Paris).

Keeble, D. (1976), *Industrial Location and Planning in the United Kingdom* (London).

—— (1989) 'Core-periphery disparities, recession and new regional dynamisms in the European Community', *Geography*, 74: 1–11.

Keles, R. and Payne, G. (1984), 'Turkey' in M. Wynn (ed.), *Planning and Urban Growth in Southern Europe* (London).

Kelly, P. (1980), *Time to Reconsider Arterial Drainage* (Dublin).

Killen, J. and Smyth, A. (1989), 'Transportation', in R. W. G. Carter and A. J. Parker (eds.), *Ireland: A Contemporary Geographical Perspective* (London).

Kindleberger, C. P. (1967), *Europe's Postwar Growth: The Role of Labour Supply* (Cambridge, Mass.).

King, R. L. (1976), 'The evolution of international labour migration movements concerning the EEC', *Tijdschrift voor Economische en Sociale Geografie*, 67: 66–82.

—— (ed.) (1986), *Return Migration and Regional Economic Problems* (London).

—— (1990), 'The social and economic geography of labour migration: from guest-workers to immigrants', in D. Pinder (ed.), *Western Europe: Challenge and Change* (London).

—— (1991), 'Italy: Multi-faceted tourism', in A. M. Williams and G. Shaw (eds.), *Tourism and Economic Development: Western European Experiences* (London) 2nd edn.

Kirk, M. (1981), *Demographic and Social Change in Europe 1975–2000* (Liverpool).

Klassen, J., Nebel, J. and Pletsh, A. (1988), 'Der städtische Raum in Frankreich und in der Bundesrepublik Deutschland', in G. Di Mio, *Les democraties industrielles, crises et mutations de l'espace* (Paris).

Klatman, J. (1972), *Les politiques agricoles: Idees fausses et illusions* (Paris).

Klindt-Jensen, O. (1978), 'Archäologische Denkmale und Umweltgestaltung', *Veröffentlichungen des Zentralinstituts für Alte Geschichte und Archäologie des Akademie der Wissenschaften der DDR*, 9: 103–6.

König, M. (1990), 'Flächenstillegungen: Ergebnisse 1989/90', *AID Informationen*, 28 and 39.

Koppen, I. J. (1988), *The European Community's Environment Policy: From the Summit in Paris, 1972, to the Single European Act, 1987*, Working Paper no. 88/328, European University Institute (Florence).

Krämer, L. (1990), *EEC Treaty and Environmental Protection* (London).

Krippendorf, J. (1987), *The Holiday Makers* (London).

Kroll, J.-C. (1987), *Politique agricole et relations internationales: Les enjeux en France et dans la CEE* (Paris).

Laborde, P. (1986), 'Logement et différenciations sociales dans les villes européennes', *Espaces, Population, Sociétés*, no. 1.

—— (1989), *Les espaces urbains dans le monde* (Paris).

—— (1991), 'Identité urbaine et publicité', in Centre d'Études Nord du Portugal-Aquitaine, *L'identité régionale* (Paris), 121–9.

Lae, J. F. (1988), *Illegal workers* (Paris).

Lagana, G., Pianto, M., and Segre, A. (1982), 'Urban social movements and urban restructuring in Turin, 1969–76', *International Journal of Urban and Regional Research*, 6: 223–45.

Lanfant, M. F. (1980), 'Introduction: Tourism in the process of internationalisation', *International Social Science Journal*, 23: 14–43.

Le Monde (1990), 'The EC attempts to stem an influx of emigrants from Eastern Europe'.

Leigh, M. (1977), 'Mediterranean agriculture and the enlargement of the EEC', *World Today*, 33: 207–14.

Leontidou, L. (1985), 'Urban land rights and working-class consciousness in peripheral societies', *International Journal of Urban and Regional Research*, 9: 533–56.

—— (1990), *The Mediterranean City in Transition: Social Change and Urban Development* (Cambridge).

—— (1993a), 'Informal strategies of unemployment relief in Greek cities: The relevance of family, locality and housing', *European Planning Studies*, 1: 43–68.

—— (1993b), 'Postmodernism and the city: Mediterranean versions', *Urban Studies*, 30: 949–65.

Lewis, J. R. and Williams, A. (1984), 'Portugal', in M. Wynn (ed.), *Housing in Europe* (London).

—— —— (1987), 'Productive decentralization or indigenous growth? Small manufacturing enterprises and regional development in Central Portugal', *Regional Studies*, 21: 343–61.

—— —— (1991), 'Portugal: Market segmentation and regional specialisation', in A. M. Williams and G. Shaw (eds.), *Tourism and Economic Development: Western European Experiences* (London).

Lianos, T. P. (1975), 'Flows of Greek out-migration and return migration', *International Migration* 13: 119–33.

Liberatore, A. (1989), *EC Environmental Research and EC Environmental Policy*, Working Paper no. 89/407, European University Institute (Florence).

Lichtenberger, E. (1976), 'The changing nature of European urbanization', in Berry (ed.), *Urbanization and Counter-Urbanization*.

Liersch, K. M. (1990), 'Der Zustand der Nordsee', *Geographische Rundschau*, 42: 351–3.

Logan, J. R. (1978), 'Rural-urban migration and working-class consciousness: The Spanish case', *Social Forces*, 56: 1159–78.

Lowe, P. (1988), 'Environmental concern and rural conservation politics', in M. Whitby and J. Ollerenshaw (eds.), *Land Use and the European Environment* (London).

Lutz, W., Prinz, C., Wils, A. B., Buttner, T., and Heilig, G. (1991), 'Alternative demographic scenarios for Europe and North America', in W. Lutz (ed.), *Future Demographic Trends in Europe and North America* (London).

Lyttleton, A. (1979), 'Milan 1990–1992: The city of industrial capitalism', in G. Brucker (ed.), *People and Communities in the Western World*, ii (Homewood, Ill.).

McAdam, J. H. (1988), 'The impact of sheep and cattle grazing on upland pasture', in W. I. Montgomery, J. H. McAdam, and B. J. Smith (eds.), *The High Country: Land Use and Land-Use Change in Northern Irish Uplands*, Institute of Biology (Northern Ireland Branch) and the Geographical Society of Ireland (Belfast).

McCarthy, D. (1980), 'Impact of drainage on fisheries', in National Board for Science and Technology, *Impacts of Drainage in Ireland* (Dublin).

McCumiskey, L. M. (1992), 'A review of surface water resources', in Feehan (ed.), *Environment and Development in Ireland*.

McElrath, D. C. (1962), 'The social areas of Rome: A comparative analysis', *American Sociological Review*, 27: 376–91.

MAPA (1986*a*), *Adhesion de España a la CEE-Agricultura* (Madrid).

—— (1986*b*), *El sector lacteo en España y en la CEE* (Madrid).

—— (1986*c*), *Ayundas de la CEE al sector agrario* (Madrid).

—— (1988), *Principales disposiciones de la CEE en el sector agroalimentario* (Madrid).

—— (1989), *El futuro del mundo rural* (Madrid).

—— (1990*a*), *Aplicacion de la P.A.C. en España (Campana 89–90)* (Madrid).

—— (1990*b*), *Plan de desarrollo en zonas rurales de España (1989–1993)* (Madrid).

Marcelloni, M. (1979), 'Urban movements and political struggles in Italy', *International Journal of Urban and Regional Research*, 3: 251–68.

Martin, P., Hönekopp, E., and Ullman, H. (1990), 'Europe 1992: Effects on labour migration', *International Migration Review*, 24: 591–603.

Massot, A. (1985), 'Las ayudas estatales a la agricultura en la CEE', *Agricultura y Sociedad*, 34: 89–121.

Matheson, J. H. E. (1991), 'The immigration issue in the Community: An ACP view', *Courier*, 129: 56–9.

Mayes, E. and Stowe, T. (1989), 'The status and distribution of corncrakes in Ireland', *Irish Birds*, 4: 1–12.

Meade, M. S., Florin, J. W. and Gesler, M. W. (1988), *Medical Geography* (New York).

Meldon, J. (1992), *Structural Funds and the Environment: Problems and Prospects*, An Tasce, The National Trust for Ireland (Dublin).

Merenne-Schoumaker, B. (1983), 'Self-service and retail complexes in Europe: Recent developments', *Société géographique de Liège*, Oct.: 63–78.

Merne, O. J. (1980), 'Impact of drainage on wildlife', in National Board for Science and Technology, *Impacts of Drainage in Ireland* (Dublin).

Miller, M. J. (1982), 'The political impact of foreign labour: A re-evaluation of the Western European experience', *International Migration Review* 16: 27–60.

Mitchell, F. (1986), *The Shell Guide to Reading the Irish Landscape* (Dublin).

Molinero, F. (1990), *Los espacios rurales: Agricultura y sociedad en el mundo* (Barcelona).

Molle, W. and van Mourik, A. (1988), 'International movements of labour under conditions of economic integration: The case of Western Europe', *Journal of Common Market Studies*, 26/3: 317–42.

Monopolies and Mergers Commission (1989), *Thomson Travel Group and Horizon Travel Ltd.* (London).

Montagné-Villette, S. (1987), L'industrie du prêt-à-porter en France', doctoral thesis, Sorbonne, Paris.

—— (1990), *Le sentier, un espace ambigu* (Paris).

—— (ed.) (1991), *Espaces et travails clandestins* (Paris).

Montanari, A. and Cortese, A. (1993), 'Third World immigrants in Italy', in R. L. King (ed.), *Mass Migrations in Europe: The Legacy and the Future* (London).

Morgan, M. A. (1983), 'Fertilizers and environmental quality', in Blackwell and Convery (eds.), *Promise and Performance*.

Morgan, M. A. and O'Toole, P. (1992), 'Recent changes in farming in Ireland: Implications for the environmental impact of current and posible future agricultural developments on hill land ecosystems', in Feehan (ed.), *Environment and Development in Ireland.*

Moriarty, D. (1991), *Fish Kills in Ireland 1990*, Fishery Leaflet no. 149, (Dublin).

Moroto, J. (1987), *El proceso de integracion de la agricultura española en la Comunidad Europea: Situacion actual y perspectivas*, Conselleria d'Agricultura i Pesca de la Generalita Valenciana (Valencia).

Moulier, Y., Garson, J. P., Silberman, R. (1988), *The Political Economy of the Illegal Trafficking in Labour* (Paris).

Moyano, M. (1989), *Sindicalismo y politica agraria en Europea: Las organizaciones profesionales agrarias en Francia, Italia y Portugal* (Madrid).

Mullan, C. (1988), 'Deregulation: The Aer Lingus Competitive Response', *Proceedings, Chartered Institute of Transport in Ireland (Southern Section) Conference*, 9–28.

Mulloy, F. (1992), 'Forestry development: Review of existing and prospective EC policies and implementation', in Feehan (ed.), *Environment and Development in Ireland.*

Murphy, P. F. (1988), 'Building a Sea Bridge Between Ireland and the Continent', *Proceedings, Chartered Institute of Transport in Ireland (Southern Section) Conference*, 46–62.

Naylon, J. (1981), 'Barcelona', in M. Pacione (ed.), *Urban Problems and Planning in the Developed World* (London).

Neill, M. (1989), 'Nitrate concentrations in river waters in the south-east of Ireland and their relationship with agricultural practice', *Water Research*, 23: 1339–55.

NESC (National Economic and Social Council) (1989), *Ireland in the European Community: Performance, Prospects and Strategy*, Report 88 (Dublin).

Nonn, H. (1986), 'A "model" example of how to replan an old urban centre: Colmar (Haut Rhin)', *Essays in honour of Madame Beaujeu-Garnier* (Paris).

OECD (1969), *Agricultural Development in Southern Europe* (Paris).

—— (1974), *Government Policy in the Development of Tourism* (Paris).

—— (1979), *The Agricultural Policy of Greece* (Paris).

—— (1989), *Politiques, marchés et échanges agricoles* (Paris).

—— (1990), *Tourism Policy and Intenrational Tourism in OECD Countries* (Paris).

—— (1991), *National Economic Surveys* (Paris).

O'Farrell, F. (1986), 'CAP and the environment', in An Foras Taluntais, *The Changing CAP and its Implications*, Economics and Rural Welfare Research Centre
(Dublin).

O'Flanagan, T. P. (1980), 'Agrarian structures in north-western Iberia: Responses and their implications for development', *Geoforum*, 11: 158–69.

—— (1982), 'Land reform and rural modernisation in Spain: A Galician perspective', *Erdkunde*, 36: 48–53.

Ogden, O. E. (1991), 'Immigration to France since 1945: Myths and reality', *Ethnic and Racial Studies* 14: 294–318.

O'Hara, P. (1986), 'CAP structural policy: A new approach to an old problem?', in An Foras Taluntais, *The Changing CAP and its Implications*, Economics and Rural Welfare Resource Centre (Dublin).

Öko-Institut Freiburg (ed.) (1991), *Energie Report Europa* (Frankfurt am Main).

Ostrowski, H. (1976), *Les ensembles historiques et l'urbanisme*, Centre de Recherche d'Urbanisme (Paris).

Pearce, D. G. (1987*a*), 'Spatial patterns of package tourism in Europe', *Annals of Tourism Research*, 14: 183–201.

—— (1987*b*), 'Mediterranean charters: A comparative geographic perspective', *Tourism Management*, 8: 291–305.

—— (1988), 'Tourism and regional development in the European Community', *Tourism Management*, 9: 13–22.

—— and Grimmeau, J.-P. (1985), 'The spatial structure of tourist accommodation and hotel demand in Spain', *Geoforum*, 16: 37–50.

Pearce, J. (1981), *The Common Agricultural Policy* (London).

Peters, M. (1969), *International Tourism: the Economics and Development of the International Tourist Trade (London)*.

Pickvance, C. G. (1985), 'The rise and fall of urban social movements and the role of comparative analysis', *Environment and Planning D: Society and Space*, 3: 31–53.

Piore, M. J. (1979), *Birds of Passage: Migrant Labour and Industrial Societies* (Cambridge).

Podbielski, G. (1981), 'The Common Agricultural Policy and the Mezzogiorno', *Journal of Common Market Studies*, 19: 333–50.

Poinard, M. (1979), 'Le million des immigrés', *Révue Géographique des Pyrénées et du Sud-Oest*, 50: 511–39.

Pritchard, G. (1978), 'Farming on archaeological sites in Norfolk', in P. Brandon and R. Millman, *Historic Landscapes: Identification, Recording and Management*, occasional paper, Department of Geography, Polytechnic of North London, 88–90.

Quigley, M. B. (ed.) (1991), *A Guide to the Sand Dunes of Ireland*, European Union for Dune Conservation and Coastal Management (Dublin).

Regni, B. and Sennato, M. (1973), 'Appunti sulle transformazioni morfologiche della citta di Rome dai programmi napoleonici al 1930', *L'Universo*, 53: 897–924.

Reig, E. (1986), *La política agraria de la Communidad Economica Europea: Repercusiones internacionales* (Valencia).

Remica (participants in CNRS Recherches Régionales sur le Midi de la France et la Catalogne) (1977), 'Effets spatiaux de la croissance économique a Barcelone', *Révue géographique des Pyrénées et du Sud-Oest*, 49: 171–90.

Road Freight Transport Survey (1988) (Dublin).

Robson, B. (1988), *Those Inner Cities: Reconciling the Social and Economic Aims of Urban Policy* (Oxford).

Rodrigues, M. J. (1990), *The Challenge of the European Single Market for Industrial Employment*, Internal report, EC Commission.

Roelants, F. (1988), *Agricultura europea y medio ambiente: Un porvenir fertil* (Barcelona).

Ruttledge, R. F. and Ogilvie, M. A. (1979), 'The past and current status of the Greenland White-fronted Goose in Ireland and Britain', *Irish Birds*, 1: 293–363.

Saenz, J. L. (1986), *El Fondo Europeo de Orientacion y Garantia Agricola (FEOGA): Estructura y funcionamiento* (Madrid).

Salt, J. (1976), 'International labor migration in Western Europe: A geographical review', in M. M. Kritz, C. B. Keely, and S. M. Tomasi (eds.), *Global Trends in Migration*, Center for Migration Studies (New York).

—— (1985), 'Europe's foreign labour migrants in transition', *Geography*, 70/2: 151–8.

—— (1987), 'The SOPEMI experience: Genesis, aims and achievements', *International Migration Review*, 21: 1067–73.

—— (1989), 'A comparative overview of international migration trends and types', *International Migration Review*, 23: 431–56.

—— and Clout, H. (eds.) (1976), *Migration in Post-War Europe: Geographical Essays* (London).

—— and Ford, R. (1993), 'Skilled international migration in Europe: The shape of things to come', in R. L. King (ed.), *Mass Migrations in Europe: The Legacy and the Future* (London).

—— and Kitching, R. (1991), 'Movimenti migratori: Analisi delle tendenze storiche', *Politica Internazionale*, 19: 5–19.

Santos, J. A. (1987), *A politica agricola commun e a agricultura portuguesa: A politica de preços e de mercados* (Lisbon).

Sayer, A. and Walker, R. (1992), *The New Social Economy: Reworking the Division of Labor* (Cambridge, Mass.).

Scharlau, K. (1958), 'Sozialbrache und Wüstungserscheinungen', *Erdkunde*, 12: 289–94.

Schulze von Hanxleden, P. (1972), 'Extensivierungserscheinungen in der Agrarlandschaft des Dillgebietes', *Marburger Geographische Schriften*, 54 (Marburg).

Servolin, C. (1988), *Las politicas agrarias* (Madrid).

Shadla-Hall, T. and Hinchcliffe, J. (eds.) (1990), *The Past Under the Plough* (London).

Sharp, M. (1989), 'The Community and new technologies', in J. Lodge (ed.), *The European Community and the Challenge of the Future* (London).

Shaw, G. and Williams, A. M. (1990) 'Tourism and development', in D. Pinder (ed.), *Western Europe: Challenge and Change* (London).

—— —— (1992), 'Tourism, development and the environment: The eternal triangle', in C. P. Cooper and A. Lockwood (eds.), *Progress in Tourism, Recreation and Hospitality Management*, 4 (London).

Sheehy, S. J. (1984), 'The Common Agricultural Policy and Ireland', in P. J. Drudy and D. McAleese (eds.), *Ireland and the European Community* (Cambridge).

—— (1992), 'Evaluation of the current proposals to reform the Common Agricultural Policy', in Feehan (ed.), *Environment and Development in Ireland*.

—— and O'Connor, R. (1985), *Economics of Irish Agriculture*, Institute of Public Administration (Dublin).

Smillie, G. W. and Morgan, M. A. (1992), 'Assessment of environmental impact of current and possible future agricultural developments on hill-land ecosystems' in Feehan (ed.), *Environment and Development in Ireland*.

Smyth, A. W. (1989), 'EC Transport Policy for 1992: Problem or Opportunity', *Proceedings, Joint Conference Organized by Northern Ireland/Irish Council of the European Movement*, The Queen's University, Belfast.

—— (1991), 'Transport: 1992—Can and will EC regional policy overcome the problems of transport peripherality?', Paper, April 1991 UK Consumer Congress (Belfast).

Statesman's Year-Book (1990) (London).

Stoner, J. H., Gee, A. S., and Wad, K. R. (1984), 'The effect of acidification on the ecology of streams in the Upper Tywi catchment in West Wales', *Environment Pollution*, Ser. A, 35: 125–57.

Stout, G., Gibbons, M., and Foley, C. (1991), *Forestry and Archaeology*, Irish Association of Professional Archaeologists (Dublin).

Sutherland, P. (1988), 'Creating a Single European Market: The role of a competitive transport system', *Proceedings, Chartered Institute of Transport in Ireland (Southern Section) Conference*, 103–17.

Tamames, R. (1988), *La Comunidad Europea* (Madrid).

Temple Lang, J. (1983), 'The Wildlife Act and the EEC bird conservation measures', in Blackwell and Convery (eds.), *Promise and Performance*.

—— and Hickie, D. (1992), 'The Wildlife Act and European Community conservation measures: An up-to-date review', in Feehan (ed.), *Environment and Development in Ireland*.

Teulon, F. (1991), *La politique agricole commun* (Paris).

Thomas Cook European Timetable (1992) (Peterborough).

Thorn, R. and Coxon, C. (1992), 'Nitrates, groundwater and the Nitrate Directive', in Feehan (ed.), *Environment and Development in Ireland*.

Topalov, C. (1976), 'La politique du logement dans le processus revolutionnaire Portugais (25 Avril–11 Mars 1975)', *Espaces et Sociétés*, 17–18: 109–36.

Tracy, M. (1989), 'Politica agraria e integracion europea', *Agricultura y Sociedad*, 51: 21–52.

Tsoucalas, C. (1986) (in Greek), *State, Society, Work in Post-War Greece* (Athens).

Tsoulouvis, L. (1985), 'Perceptions of Urban Development and Planning Policies in Thessaloniki (Greece)', Ph.D. thesis, LSE (London).

UPTCS (Union of Professional and Technical Civil Servants) (1987), *Our Natural Heritage: A Policy for Nature Conservation in Ireland* (Dublin).

Urry, J. (1990), *The Tourist Gaze: Leisure and Travel in Contemporary Societies* (London).

L'Usine nouvelle (1990), *L'Usine nouvelle*, no. 2251 (Paris).

Valenzuela, M. (1991), 'Spain: The phenomenon of mass tourism', in A. M. Williams and G. Shaw (eds.), *Tourism and Economic Development: Western European Experiences* (London), 2nd edn.

Van den Berg, L. (1982), *Urban Europe: A Study of Growth and Decline* (Oxford).

Vandermeersch, D. (1987), 'The Single European Act and the environmental policy of the European Economic Community', *European Law Review*, 12/06: 407–29.

Walsh, J. A. (1989), 'Enterprise substitution in Irish agriculture: Sheep production in the 1980s', *Irish Geography*, 22: 106–9.

—— and Horner, A. A. (1984), 'Regional aspects of agricultural production in Ireland 1979–1980', *Irish Geography*, 17: 95–101.

Walther, P. (1984), *Die Brachlandentwicklung im Schweizer Alpenraum 1950–1980 als geographischer Process*, diss. Univ. of Zurich.

Wattelar, C. and Roumans, G. (1991), 'Simulations of demographic objectives and migration', in OECD, *Migration: The Demographic Aspects* (Paris).

Webb, R. (1985), 'Farming and the landscape', in F. H. A. Aalen, *The Future of the Irish Rural Landscape*, Trinity College (Dublin).

—— (1988), 'The status of hedgerow field margins in Ireland', in J. R. Park (ed.), *Environmental Management in Agriculture: European Perspectives* (London).

Weg, H. van der (1982), 'Revitalization of traditional resorts', *Tourism Management*, 3: 303–7.

White, P. E. (1984), *The West European City: A Social Geography* (London).

—— (1986), 'International migration in the 1970s: Revolution or evolution?' in A. M. Findlay and P. E. White (eds.), *West European Population Change* (London).

—— (1993), 'Immigrants and the social geography of European cities', in R. L. King (ed.), *Mass Migrations in Europe: The Legacy and the Future* (London).

Whitelegg, J. (1988), *Transport in the EEC* (London).

Williams, A. M. (ed.) (1984), *Southern Europe Transformed* (London).

—— (1991*a*), *The European Community: The Contradictions of Integration* (Oxford).

—— (1991*b*), 'Globality and community in culture and development', *World Futures*, 33–3: 1–24.

—— (1993), 'Turkey: The Mediterranean context', in C. Balkir and A. M. Williams (eds.), *Turkey and Europe* (London).

—— and Shaw, G. (1990), 'Tourism and regional economic development: Perspectives on Western Europe', in S. Hardy, T. Hart, and T. Shaw (eds.), *The Role of Tourism in the Urban and Regional Economy*, Regional Studies Association (London).

—— —— (eds.) (1991) *Tourism and Economic Development: Western European Experiences* (London). 2nd edn.

Wils, A. B. (1991), 'Survey of immigration trends and assumptions about future migration', in W. Lutz (ed.), *Future Demographic Trends in Europe and North America* (London).

Wilstacke, L. and Plankl, R. (1989), 'Freiwillige Produktionsminderung: Empirische Analyse', *Schriftenreihe des Bundesminsters für Ernährung, Landwirtschaft und Forsten*, A 366 (Münster).

—— —— (1989), 'Erprobung der Flächenstillegung in Niedersachsen: Inanspruchnahme und Wirkungen des niedersächsischen Grünbracheprogramms 1987/88', *Schriftenreihe des Bundesministers für Ernährung, Landwirtschaft und Forsten*, A 369 (Münster).

World Bank (1990) World Development Report (New York).

World Health Organization (1990) *Annual Statistics* (Geneva).

World Tourism Organization (1984), *Economic Review of World Tourism* (Madrid).

Wright, T. (1992), 'Future direction in conservation', in Feehan (ed.), *Environment and Development in Ireland*.

Wynn, M. (ed.), (1984*a*), *Planning and Urban Growth in Southern Europe* (London).

—— (ed.) (1984*b*), *Housing in Europe* (London).

Zegers de Beijl, R. (1990), *Discrimination of Migration Workers in Western Europe*, ILO International Migration for Employment Working Paper no. 49 (Geneva).

Index